The Textual Effects of David Walker's *Appeal*

MATERIAL TEXTS

Series Editors
Roger Chartier
Leah Price
Joseph Farrell
Peter Stallybrass
Anthony Grafton
Michael F. Suarez, S.J.

A complete list of books in the series is available from the publisher.

The Textual Effects of David Walker's *Appeal*

Print-Based Activism Against Slavery,
Racism, and Discrimination, 1829–1851

Marcy J. Dinius

PENN

UNIVERSITY OF PENNSYLVANIA PRESS

PHILADELPHIA

NATIONAL
ENDOWMENT
FOR THE
HUMANITIES

This book has been made possible in part by a major grant from the National Endowment for the Humanities: Democracy demands wisdom.

Copyright © 2022 University of Pennsylvania Press

All rights reserved. Except for brief quotations used for purposes of review or scholarly citation, none of this book may be reproduced in any form by any means without written permission from the publisher.

Published by
University of Pennsylvania Press
Philadelphia, Pennsylvania 19104-4112
www.upenn.edu/pennpress

Printed in the United States of America on acid-free paper
10 9 8 7 6 5 4 3 2 1

Library of Congress Cataloging-in-Publication Data
Names: Dinius, Marcy J., author.
Title: The textual effects of David Walker's Appeal : print-based activism against slavery, racism, and discrimination, 1829–1851 / Marcy J. Dinius.
Other titles: Material texts.
Description: 1st edition. | Philadelphia : University of Pennsylvania Press, [2022] | Series: Material texts | Includes bibliographical references and index.
Identifiers: LCCN 2021042877 | ISBN 9780812253788 (hardcover) | ISBN 9780812298390 (eBook)
Subjects: LCSH: Walker, David, 1785–1830. Walker's appeal, in four articles. | Walker, David, 1785–1830. Walker's appeal, in four articles—Influence. | Stewart, Maria W., 1803–1879. | Apess, William, 1798–1839. | Quinn, William Paul, 1788–1873. | Garnet, Henry Highland, 1815–1882. | Brown, Paola, active 1828–1852. | American literature—19th century—History and criticism. | Canadian literature—19th century—History and criticism. | American literature—African American authors—History and criticism. | American literature—Indian authors—History and criticism. | Canadian literature—Black authors—History and criticism. | Antislavery movements—North America—History—19th century. | Slavery in literature. | Antislavery movements in literature.
Classification: LCC PS217.S55 D56 2022 | DDC 326—dc23
LC record available at https://lccn.loc.gov/2021042877

CONTENTS

Introduction   1

Chapter 1. "Look!! look!!! at this!!!!": Reading Walker's *Appeal*   29

Chapter 2. Immediate Effects: William Lloyd Garrison's *Liberator* and Maria W. Stewart's *Religion and the Pure Principles of Morality*   80

Chapter 3. Taking the Texts: William Apes's "An Indian's Looking-Glass for the White Man"   109

Chapter 4. Taking Walker's *Appeal* West: Reverend William Paul Quinn's *The Origin, Horrors, and Results of Slavery*   137

Chapter 5. "As Being Bound with You": Henry Highland Garnet's 1848 Edition of Walker's *Appeal*   165

Chapter 6. The Northern Exposure of Walker's *Appeal*: Producing and Reproducing African American Antislavery Literature and Authorship in Canada   198

Conclusion. Walker's Ideal Reader: W. E. B. Du Bois   231

Notes   241

Index   285

Acknowledgments   297

INTRODUCTION

David Walker's *Appeal to the Coloured Citizens of the World* likely effected the abrupt end of Frederick Douglass's early literacy lessons. David W. Blight, in his 2018 biography of Douglass, estimates that "Frederick was about eleven years old" when "Hugh Auld suddenly forbade with stern anger any further instruction in reading for the young slave."[1] The year, then, was 1829 or early 1830, when Walker published the first and second editions of his powerful indictment of slavery and racism and was circulating them throughout the South. While the young and barely literate Douglass likely was not aware of the existence of Walker's pamphlet, Hugh Auld almost certainly was. In his declaration to his wife, Sophia, that "it was unlawful, as well as unsafe, to teach a slave to read," as Douglass put it in his 1845 *Narrative of the Life of Frederick Douglass, An American Slave*, Auld was drawing on newspaper reports about White southerners' reactions to Walker's *Appeal* circulating in the South.[2]

Copies of the first edition of the pamphlet had reached Baltimore before January 15, 1830, when William Lloyd Garrison noted that he and the early abolitionist Benjamin Lundy had had a copy "for some time past" in the office of their Baltimore-based newspaper *Genius of Universal Emancipation*.[3] By then and throughout 1830, both southern and northern newspapers regularly carried sensational stories about the *Appeal*'s appearance in numerous southern cities, arrests of Black and White people found in possession of copies of the pamphlet, and heated legislative debates and strict laws passed to forbid slave literacy, limit free and enslaved Black people's mobility, and punish anyone possessing "incendiary" or "seditious" print.[4] While Maryland was among the few slaveholding states that did not legally prohibit teaching enslaved people to read and write—despite what Auld told his wife—his sudden, vehement, and perhaps physically violent reaction to Sophia Auld's educational efforts stands as an important but overlooked record of the fear that Walker's *Appeal* provoked in White slaveholding households, and of the practical and legal effects of this fear on individual Black lives.[5] But as

Douglass consistently foregrounds in each of his tellings of this story, Auld's efforts to thwart Douglass's education and teach his wife proper slave management resulted in an unintentional, yet even more profound and lasting lesson for the young Douglass: that reading and writing were directly connected to power and, eventually, freedom from slavery.

What we should infer from Douglass's story of his frustrated introduction to literacy thus has significance beyond Douglass himself. Certainly, the story demonstrates the tie between Douglass's literacy and his self-liberation and his development as a prolific and accomplished writer against the long odds of both. But it also evinces how David Walker's publication and circulation of his *Appeal* in 1829 and 1830 dramatically impacted multiple forms, and generations, of Black literacy and textual production.[6] If Walker's pamphlet and the controversy surrounding it motivated Auld's interdiction of Douglass's education, and that interdiction also powerfully motivated Douglass to gain an education by any means necessary and eventuated in his autobiographies and all his other writings, then our sense of Walker and his pamphlet must change as well. Rather than seeing Walker's *Appeal* as a discrete event, we should recognize its publication, distribution, and responses to it as giving rise to Douglass becoming not only "a man of words," as Blight designates him, but also the most canonical nineteenth-century African American writer (xvii).

* * *

I begin with this new contextual reading of one of the most emblematic scenes in Douglass's autobiographies to shine a high-wattage light on what I call the *textual effects* of Walker's *Appeal*—that is, its most productive and powerful, but still underrecognized and underexamined consequences for American literary history. These, I argue, far exceed the standard account of what Walker has meant both to U.S. literature and lives, particularly Black and Indigenous lives. By now, Walker's *Appeal* has been firmly canonized, if not to the extent as Douglass's *Narrative*. In history textbooks and anthologies of American literature and African American literature alike, Walker's *Appeal* is commonly cited and reproduced as representative of the turn to radical antislavery and an exemplar of Black militancy and nationalism. In representing it as such, both historical and literary historical introductions to the text tend to foreground the *Appeal*'s position on violent resistance to slavery. In this reading, the ultimate gauge of its political, historical, and literary significance is Walker's militancy and, further, the *Appeal*'s primary historical and cultural effect is measured by its possible link to actual violent resistance to slavery, most frequently by associating it with the 1831 rebellion in Southampton, Virginia, led by Nat Turner.[7]

Certainly, Walker's justifications of violent self-defense and resistance were momentous and remain significant. But continuing to foreground violence over the text's other arguments, features, and resonances effectively limits Walker's *Appeal* to understanding it on the same terms by which it was suppressed in the nineteenth century by slavery's most anxious defenders and its equally anxious nonviolent opponents. Nearly twenty years ago, Elizabeth McHenry argued that "these angles of analysis have been overemphasized."[8] Her placement of Walker's *Appeal* at the head of her groundbreaking study of "the various ways black Americans acquired and used literacy" and the "literary activities of free blacks and the legacy of the antebellum institutions that they built to promote reading and share texts" opened up new and important possibilities for more complex considerations of Walker's pamphlet and its possible effects (3). Numerous scholars in different disciplines have seized on the opportunity, producing a significant body of scholarship recognizing the *Appeal* and the impacts of Walker's arguments on slavery, racism, Black Americans' struggle for freedom and equality, and literature.[9] Yet while our thinking about how Walker's *Appeal* powerfully moved its readers and what it moved them to do thus has grown more complex, literature scholars have not read either Walker's very complex text, or the texts that were written by readers who were most affected by it, as closely and comparatively as we could and should. By doing so, we see that the activism that Walker models in his *Appeal* is primarily, extensively, and deeply textual, and that his *Appeal*'s most immediate, concrete, and significant impact was to move Black, Indigenous, and White Americans to write and publish what became a significant body of literature.[10]

The Textual Effects of David Walker's "Appeal" is the first book-length study dedicated to print as Walker's primary mode of activism, and as the primary effect of his pamphlet's three editions. I examine at length how Walker specifically crafted his *Appeal* in ways that incited four of its Black readers, and one of its Indigenous readers, to political and social activism in print, moving them to write, publish, and circulate their own works arguing against slavery, racial discrimination, and White supremacy and advocating racial uplift and specific strategies for elevation. This body of literature—what we might think of as a canon of some of the most important essays in American literature and history with Walker's *Appeal* as the source text, and with consequences for the rest of American literary history—has not received extensive study as such. Here, I focus on five pamphlets written and published by Maria W. Stewart, William Apes, William Paul Quinn, Henry Highland Garnet, and Paola Brown between 1831 and 1851. When considered together, this set of publications makes unmistakably clear that each of these Black and Indigenous activist writers had carefully read and studied Walker's words, arguments, and evidence in relation to their own situations and responded accordingly. To understand why and how these readers responded as they did, I dedicate Chapter 1 to examining Walker's multifaceted, and primarily text-based, strategies for reaching and inciting his readers to take specific actions.

This book foregrounds Walker's and these writers' significant efforts as part of our ongoing scholarly revisions of literary and print history in North America, the hemisphere, and the Atlantic World. Literary history still has much to understand about the major contributions of African diasporic and Indigenous peoples to these histories. Walker's work and legacy are a major part of this story, with much more to be discovered about their significance. When some of its most obvious effects are foregrounded and examined at length—as Stewart's, Apes's, Quinn's, Garnet's, and Brown's pamphlets are here—we are better able to see both the interrelation and the international scope not only of literary and print history but also of intellectual history, political theory, scientific inquiry, and social activism in the eighteenth and nineteenth centuries. As we will see in Chapter 1, Walker closely studied, absorbed, and challenged the lessons of several major works of Enlightenment history, political theory, scientific inquiry, and pedagogy, as he displays throughout the text of the *Appeal*. I examine how Walker, based on these readings, took a specifically encyclopedic and pedagogical approach to contending with the problems of slavery and racism in his *Appeal*. In Chapter 1, I focus on how he adopted and adapted influential late-eighteenth-century encyclopedic and pedagogical sources and their logic and argumentation to work for Black Americans. To understand how he did so, I closely read the complex text of the *Appeal* structurally—that is, by recognizing the organizational structure that Walker gave it based on his reading of Lindley Murray's *English Grammar, Adapted to Different Classes of Readers* (1795), and by dividing the *Appeal* up and organizing my readings by the "different classes" of readers that Walker distinctly addresses within his main audience—Black Americans—and also White Americans, who Walker knew were reading as well. I dedicate the chapters that follow to understanding how some of Walker's most sympathetic readers responded to his example by adopting and adapting his *Appeal* and its logic and argumentation to work for them and people like them.

More specifically, Chapter 2 focuses on Maria Stewart's *Religion and the Pure Principles of Morality: The Sure Foundation on Which We Must Build* (1831), which Stewart addressed to free Black women, an audience that Walker's masculinist and patriarchal *Appeal* had neglected. Chapter 3 takes up William Apes's "An Indian's Looking-Glass for the White Man," a scathing political polemic published as part of his 1833 religious pamphlet *The Experiences of Five Christian Indians of the Pequod Tribe*. In Chapter 4, I concentrate on William Paul Quinn's hybrid religious tract and political pamphlet *The Origin, Horrors, and Results of Slavery*, published and circulated in the American near West in 1834. Chapter 5 presents a new reading of Henry Highland Garnet's 1848 edition of Walker's *Appeal* as Garnet bound and issued it together with his own "Address to the Slaves of the United States." And I conclude with Paola Brown's *Address on the Subject of Slavery*, which extended and adapted Walker's *Appeal* to post–Fugitive Slave Law Canada in 1851. As these brief summaries begin to suggest, I examine how these five authors individually and specifically revised, renewed, and extended Walker's original *Appeal* so that it would include, represent, and reach additional people affected by U.S. racial slavery and discrimination in new times and places through their pamphlets. I closely read each of these pamphlets in relation to Walker's and on its own terms, and as both a written and material text. My aim is to recover as much as possible about the argumentative and textual complexities of these direct and different responses to the powerful incitements of Walker's lessons and arguments and the forms he gave them in print. In doing so, I also consider their important contributions to U.S. and hemispheric literary and print history and political theory.[11]

As we will see more fully in the chapters that follow, this group of writers theorized and practiced authorship in ways that both embraced and challenged literary and print conventions, with Walker setting the example and the others both following and evolving it. While each of them was rhetorically self-deprecating as an author—in performing adherence to the traditional modesty trope that had been deployed by White writers for centuries—they were also boldly self-assertive in several more important respects. All six authors wrote in the first person. They each insist in their texts that their acknowledged limitations as authors are the result of racist restrictions put by White people on their educational opportunities. And they all share the powerful personal feelings and experiences that moved them to study on their own and write, doing so to move others like—and unlike—them to take similarly powerful actions, for themselves and/or on behalf of their racial groups. Numerous important aspects of their texts also demonstrate that these intellectual activist authors understood and practiced writing and publishing as fundamentally collective, more than individual, enterprises. Their common goal in writing was advancing the greater good, more than gaining individual glory or profit. When read together, their works represent a sustained, multiracial literary effort to realize a United States in which Black and Indigenous women and men are not just self-evidently, but actually equal citizens with the power to exercise all the rights and freedoms on which the nation was founded.

As pamphlets, all of these essays were relatively cheaply and easily printed, circulated, and read. Their authors thus harnessed the combined power of print format and several literary genres—including the polemical essay, the didactic reform essay, the spiritual autobiography, the printed sermon, and literary biography—to extend their physical and argumentative reach far and wide—north into Canada, deep into the South, west to at least Ohio, and likely farther. Yet their textual brevity and physical vulnerability as pamphlets in comparison to heftier bound books also made them less likely to survive beyond their moment and, consequently, less subject to the attention of literature scholars, who have focused on more readily available and traditionally literary texts. As Joanna Brooks and Joseph Rezek have emphasized, the materiality of Black texts has factored significantly in both historical and scholarly determinations of whether, how much, and which Black texts matter. And as Cheryl A. Wall has rightly observed with respect to their shared genre, "the status of the essay in literary studies in general and African American literary studies in particular" has been marginal at best, "seem[ing] to exist alongside literature's major genres."[12] Even so, copies of all of these pamphlets have been preserved, with the exception of Quinn's, which now seems only to exist in a photocopy facsimile at Howard University's Moorland-Spingarn Research Center.[13] Their material survival alone is evidence that essays they contain were understood as important publications in the nineteenth century and continued to be recognized as such into the twentieth. As Leon Jackson explains, "African American bibliophiles and their white supporters . . . collected texts," including the ones in this study, "because of the ideas they contained."[14]

When we consider these pamphlet-essays together in our time as an archive of significant solidarity and collective political action in theory and practice among authors of color in the United States and Canada, they expand our understanding not just of American political protest and reform literature but also of American literature. These essays all powerfully assert and attest that their authors and others like them are full-fledged human beings, Christians, and American and Canadian citizens, equally deserving of the natural rights that they understood God to have given all people. They also all recognize that conceptions of the human and of natural rights necessarily will evolve as people of color come to be included, and their pamphlet-essays begin to imagine and to realize—collectively, in print—the fruits of making good on this great potential.

Very recently, Zakiyyah Iman Jackson has brought significant attention to important, underrecognized African diasporic critiques of and alternatives to Western scientific and philosophical conceptions of the human that are contemporary with Walker's, Stewart's, Apes's, Quinn's, Garnet's, and Brown's essays in her book *Becoming Human*. Her archive for doing so focuses on "African diasporic cultural production that does not coalesce into a unified tradition that merely seeks inclusion into liberal humanist conceptions of 'the human' but, rather, frequently alters the meaning and significance of being (human) and engages in imaginative practices of worlding from the perspective of a history of blackness's bestialization and thingification: the process of imagining black people as an empty vessel, a nonbeing, a nothing, an ontological zero, coupled with the violent imposition of colonial myths and racial hierarchy."[15] Whereas Jackson emphasizes that her project is not "an effort justifying or trying to convince anyone that black thought has something to say about European Continental thought and [that] it is valuable to do so" and rather "just gets on with the work of reading black arts and letters philosophically," I am interested in how the writers that I focus on definitely have something to say about European Continental thought and find significant value in doing so (35–36). My thinking in this respect is indebted to Carla L. Peterson's important articulation of how this dialectic shapes African American writing and thought: "African-American writers constructed a productive discourse generated from within the community that borrows the vocabulary and categories of the dominant discourse only to dislocate them from their privileged position of authority and adapt them to the local place."[16]

By attending to these six writers' sincere interests in both Enlightenment and Christian values, ideas, and ways of thinking and writing, I do not propose this set of texts as a counterarchive and counterargument to Jackson's and other posthuman scholarship but rather as another strain of Black and Indigenous writing and thought that is as significant to ongoing revisions of histories of literature, science, philosophy, and, most broadly the Enlightenment, including Jackson's. As she rightly notes, "We often isolate African diasporic literary studies from the fields of science and philosophy," but when we widen our view, African diasporic literature "introduce[s] dissidence into philosophical and scientific frameworks that dominate definitions of the human: evolution, rights, property, and legal personhood" (2). All the essays in this book introduce just such dissidence—and dissonance.

This project originated with my attention to the unusual, visually and aurally striking typography and punctuation of Walker's *Appeal* and their inextricability from his arguments—what I refer to here as the textual effects within Walker's text.[17] I borrow this meaning of *effects* from modern amplified music: that is, something (be it a pedal or software) that a musician uses to modify the signal from their electric instrument to alter its amplified sound.[18] Such musical effects offer a helpful analogy for thinking about how Walker strategically manipulated visual elements of his printed argument. Through these textual effects, it sounded (and still sounds) emphatic, infuriated, sarcastic, exasperated, proud, and defiant, both to silent readers imagining Walker's voice speaking to them from the text, and to audiences having the pamphlet read to them by someone in different contexts—from gatherings of enslaved people to closed-door legislative sessions held upon the pamphlet's arrival in slaveholding states. In Chapter 1, I briefly revisit how Walker used these typographical and punctuational effects as part of my now broader analysis of a range of several specifically textual elements and strategies that Walker deployed in his *Appeal* to reach different audiences within his main audience of Black Americans as well as White Americans. As we will see, in addition to conveying Walker's own affect, the *Appeal* works in multiple and complex ways as a text to evoke specific thoughts and feelings in its readers individually and as groups, and to provoke specific actions from them—be they Black or White; free or enslaved; literate or illiterate; northern or southern; antislavery, proslavery, or ambivalent. Bringing these two kinds of effects together, this book as a whole argues that Walker's textual strategies worked to reach many different kinds of readers and move them to take specific actions based on what they learned and how they came to think from reading his *Appeal*.

Revision is also a central concept, if not consistently a key word, in this study, linking all of these texts and their literary, intellectual, historical, social, and political effects together. As with effects, I mean revision here in a double sense: (1) the act of correcting, amending, and/or improving a text (including its language, grammar, punctuation, and arguments); and (2) etymologically, as re-viewing/reexamining anything—in this project, topics, ideas, and fields of study—to understand it differently or better, and to adapt it to different and, ideally, better uses. Though Walker does not use the word *revision* when he insists, "See your Declaration Americans!!! Do you understand your own language?"—then reproduces its declarations of humans' natural equality and rights by adding his own emphatic typography so that they literally see and figuratively hear not just its words, but their meaning—the etymological sense is clearly in effect here at the culmination of his appeal (85).

Walker intended his *Appeal* as a critical revision of both the Declaration of Independence and the Constitution, as his organization of the text into a preamble and four articles, his arguments about rights and duties, and his exegesis of the Declaration make explicit. More subtly, he also wrote his pedagogical and encyclopedic essay as an adaptation of two other key late eighteenth-century texts: Lindley Murray's *English Grammar*, as I have begun to suggest, and, more surprisingly, Thomas Jefferson's *Notes on the State of Virginia*. Numerous scholars have noted Walker's critical engagement with Jefferson's influential natural philosophical claims about racial difference in *Notes*; what has gone unrecognized is how Walker critically revises both Jefferson's Enlightenment reasoning and encyclopedic writing style in his *Appeal*, which I detail along with his adaptation and application of Murray's *Grammar*, as part of Chapter 1. In engaging with his contemporary foes, Walker also saw each of his pamphlet's subsequent editions as an opportunity to revise his own text, in the interest of realizing it and its arguments—no less than the founding documents and their principles—to their fullest potential, as I also examine in Chapter 1.

Similarly, Stewart's, Apes's, Quinn's, Garnet's, and Brown's pamphlets affectively, argumentatively, temporally, and geographically broadened and deepened the political and cultural effects of Walker's original *Appeal* by revising it in different ways to suit different audiences and times, and evolving social, political, and legal conditions. While they all echo Walker's rhetorical style, none of them followed his example of giving it typographic and punctuational force to the degree that Walker did. The chapters that follow closely examine how Stewart, Apes, Quinn, Garnet, and Brown—like Walker—all approached other aspects of writing, print, and the materiality of printed texts both conventionally and unconventionally, in ways that significantly complement their messages and that were meant, ideally and powerfully, to move others like them to act effectually for change.

In considering all of these texts together as an ongoing, collaborative project of revision, it is well worth returning to Henry Louis Gates Jr.'s seminal study *The Signifying Monkey* for foregrounding how "black writers read, repeated, imitated, and revised each other's texts to a remarkable extent" as a defining feature of the African American literary tradition.[19] In concentrating on this set of texts written by a more diverse group of authors, published within a narrower time frame, and directly derived from Walker's *Appeal*, several ideas from John Bryant's concept of the fluid text are helpful to thinking about their dynamic interrelationship. As Bryant most simply defines it, "a fluid text is any literary work that exists in more than one version. It is 'fluid' because the versions flow from one to another."[20] We see this dynamism across not just Walker's three editions of his pamphlet but also in Stewart's, Apes's, Quinn's, Garnet's, and Brown's pamphlets, as they adopt and adapt versions of Walker's rhetoric and arguments, and sometimes his words, in revising his original case for the equality and rights of Black Americans to suit specific groups of people in changing social, legal, and political circumstances.

Bryant affirms the importance of taking such a broadened analytical and contextual view of textual transmission, arguing that when we do, "we begin to envision a fuller phenomenon, tied to historical moments but always changing and always manifesting one set of interests or another. The very nature of writing, the creative process, and shifting intentionality, as well as the powerful social forces that occasion translation, adaptation, and censorship among readers—in short, the facts of revision, publication, and reception—urge us to recognize that the only 'definitive text' is a multiplicity of texts, or rather, the fluid text (2)." As we see suggested here, Bryant primarily introduced this concept of the fluid text at the turn of our century to challenge the *definitive text* as the dominant term and concept in scholarly editing since the mid-twentieth century. Even so, his insistence on the inevitable dynamism of texts is particularly relevant to understanding Walker's *Appeal* as a source text for these five pamphlets—or eight, when we factor in all three of Walker's editions—and considering their complex interrelationship. It is all the more relevant in attempting to take into account not only these reader-authors' individual creativity, shifting intentionality, and engagements with other texts but also the changing social issues and conditions of their immediate contexts. Moreover, Bryant's observation about the relationship between material and immaterial dimensions of textual fluidity applies directly to the two kinds of textual effects around which I have organized this book: "The irony is that the more one perceives the variable materiality of a text"—here, from the typographic and argumentative changes in emphasis across Walker's three editions, to Garnet binding Walker's *Appeal* with his "Address to the Slaves" in 1848—"the more one begins to focus on the immaterial processes of change that create the variances, the flow of texts"—thus, the changing social, political, and legal conditions of racial slavery and related forms of oppression and resistance to them, and these author-activists' revisions of Walker's *Appeal* in their specific and timely pamphlets (4).

Whereas Bryant's idea of fluidity focuses more on the text than on the author, given the influence of poststructuralism on his intervention in editorial theory, I foreground both the individual and the collective agency of the authors of these pamphlets. Through close consideration of their written and material texts, we can recover—to a degree—how they read Walker's *Appeal*, some of the most important choices they made as thinkers and writers in adopting and adapting its rhetoric and arguments and making their own, and some of the actions they took to publish and circulate their pamphlets. Specific historical circumstances shaped all aspects of Walker's, Stewart's, Apes's, Quinn's, Garnet's, and Brown's agency and the forms it took, including those I have just listed. Their power to act was in every way constrained to different degrees by discriminatory laws and customs; in their texts, they all emphasize the actions they were taking in their individual lives as intellectuals, writers, and activists and specific actions they wanted their readers to take to gain true equality and freedom. Yet the range of specific, collective, and coordinated actions these reader-writers took have gone underrecognized as meaningful texts and events in both literary history and history more broadly.

Both poststructuralist theories of authorship and the historian Walter Johnson's important challenge to scholars' interest in restoring agency to enslaved and dispossessed people should give us pause here.[21] Johnson rightly cautions that "by continuing to frame their works as 'discoveries' of Black humanity, indeed, historians unwittingly reproduce the incised terms and analytical limits of a field of contest (black humanity: for or against) framed by the white-supremacist assumptions which made it possible to ask such a question in the first place" (114). In foregrounding Walker's, Stewart's, Apes's, Quinn's, Garnet's, and Brown's resistant, creative, and collective actions as readers, writers, editors, and publishers (in all cases except Stewart's) and their texts' insistence on Black and Indigenous Americans' humanity, I ultimately am less interested in discovering and/or restoring these writers' agency than in attending carefully to their own theorizations of what counts as a meaningful form of agency—and as full-fledged humanity—and to the material forms that some of these actions took in practice, that is, to their effects in print.

By doing so, this project joins with literary scholarship that emphasizes reading and writing as powerful forms of agency and activism—especially for people for whom different forms of literacy are proscribed or denied—and that recognizes historical writers as literary and political theorists in their own times and on their own terms. With respect to the former, I am particularly indebted to the field-changing interventions and contributions of Carla Peterson and Elizabeth McHenry. Peterson's *"Doers of the Word": African-American Women Speakers and Writers in the North (1830–1880)* is a pathbreaking book dedicated to the idea that "speaking and writing constituted a form of doing, of social action continuous with [Black women writer-activists'] social, political, and cultural work" (3). And McHenry's *Forgotten Readers* both calls for and accomplishes "a more complex vision of what constitutes resistance" by African Americans to different forms of oppression by focusing on nineteenth-century Black literary societies in the North, arguing that they "were formed not only as places of refuge" but also "as acts of resistance to the hostile racial climate" of the United States (17). Peterson's and McHenry's field-changing work motivates my argument that historians' persistent focus on violent resistance as the most significant effect of Walker's *Appeal* has overshadowed reading, learning, writing, revising, publishing, and circulating more print as its most verifiable and consequential effects. Their work inspires and informs my extended literary and book historical readings of Walker's, Stewart's, Apes's, Quinn's, Garnet's, and Brown's pamphlet-essays.

With respect to foregrounding historical writer-activists as theorists in their own right, some of the most relevant recent such scholarship has focused on citizenship—also a key word and concept for Walker—and I build on this work here. Carrie Hyde, in *Civic Longing: The Speculative Origins of U.S. Citizenship*, focuses on how "early political commentators redirected their interpretive energies away from the letter of the law and became authorial participants in the cultural fabrication of 'citizenship'" (6). With respect to Black Americans' significant contributions to this effort, Derrick R. Spires argues that "black writers theorized and practiced citizenship in the early United States through a robust print culture" and examines how this "theorizing developed over time as a collaborative, multimedia, polygeneric cultural and intellectual process for sustaining life in a fundamentally unjust society" in his *Practice of Citizenship: Black Politics and Print Culture in the Early United States* (2, 3). Most specifically, Melvin L. Rogers's incisive close reading of the key terms *appeal, colored,* and *citizens* in Walker's title and throughout his text also underwrites much of my study of print cultural effects of Walker's pamphlet. As Rogers succinctly and compellingly puts it: "To use 'citizen' to address 'colored' folks at a time when those two terms were increasingly seen as incompatible calls out a form of political activity that is not itself dependent on the juridical framework from which blacks were excluded." Walker's "use of key terms—citizen and appeal—exemplify the ways blacks constituted themselves as political actors at the very moment their ability to do so was called into question or denied" (209). On Hyde's, Spires's, and Rogers's models, *The Textual Effects of David Walker's "Appeal"* contributes an important case study constellated around Walker's pamphlet, considering these reader-writer-activists' theories and practices of citizenship in not just the United States and Canada but also and most specifically in the republic of letters. As their pamphlets make argumentatively and materially clear, Walker, Stewart, Apes, Quinn, Garnet, and Brown all considered print cultural citizenship to be a vital dimension of civic citizenship and participation in print culture as a powerful form of resistant agency.

In expanding our scholarly focus on the effects of Walker's *Appeal* so that we recognize these writers' contributions to theories and practices of citizenship—particularly to print-centered forms of citizenship and agency—I emphatically do not mean to suggest that violence is an illegitimate, unnecessary, or less important form of resistance or of bringing about greater social and political liberation from oppression. As Judith Butler has recently asserted, "One of the strongest arguments for the use of violence on the left is that it is tactically necessary in order to defeat structural or systemic violence, or to dismantle a violent regime."[22] David Walker devotes part of his *Appeal* to making just such a strong argument for exactly these reasons. Nor by observing that historians and literary historians have tended to foreground these militant aspects and effects of Walker's text at the expense of others do I mean to suggest that violent resistance has been the primary concern of scholarship on the U.S. antislavery movement, or that we have adequately understood the place and meaning of violence in Walker's arguments. As Kellie Carter Jackson has recently observed, "In the history of the movement to abolish slavery, the shift toward violence among African Americans remains largely unaddressed." This project both heeds her call that "the ways in which black abolitionists utilized violence deserves a more sustained and nuanced analysis," and shares her recognition that "Black resistance was central to abolitionism" by emphasizing the specifically textual and verbal forms of resistant action that Black abolitionists took.[23]

This centrality of Black resistance makes a similarly sustained and nuanced analysis of Walker's *Appeal* most necessary, so that we can better understand the range of actions Walker meant to incite with his pamphlet and its arguments, and how his most attentive readers responded. As Lori Leavell has rightly observed, "Though Walker and Garnet are routinely referred to as 'militant' and identified as forerunners of the Black Power movement, black militancy in the antebellum period has not been adequately theorized. In fact, scholarship tends to collapse distinctions between antebellum black militancy in print and its other forms."[24] Leavell is careful to use the term *militancy* more precisely, "to indicate justifications of and/or calls for collective physical resistance in print" (152), and she compellingly argues that "a book history approach" to Walker's *Appeal*—specifically focusing on Garnet's edition—"complicates conventional wisdom about the place of black militancy in the period's anti-slavery print culture" (166). I build on her important conclusion that, from such careful study, "black militancy emerges less as the sensational phenomenon preserved in our historical accounts and more as cultural capital harnessed to revitalize specific political projects," by shifting our analysis from physical to other forms of resistance that Walker and the writers featured here, including Garnet, theorized and advocated in and through their pamphlets (177).

As we will see in Chapter 1, Walker aimed primarily to motivate his literate Black readers to read his pamphlet aloud to those who could not read so that they would receive his message of their basic humanity and rights—including their right and duty to defend both against the exceptional violence of U.S. racial slavery by whatever means were necessary—and to impress upon his most educated Black readers the need to study on their own, engage in detailed textual critiques, and make learned public arguments on behalf of the entire race for their equality and advancement in U.S. society. Justifying violence as a no less available and legitimate form of self-defense for Black Americans than it had been for White Americans during the American Revolution—and urging it as enslaved people's duty to throw off such tyranny—were only some of the radical lessons of Walker's *Appeal*, not the sum of it. Despite historians' consistent association of the 1831 uprising led by Nat Turner with Walker's pamphlet, we still have no hard evidence that it was directly inspired by Walker. But literary scholars do have clear textual and material evidence that Walker's broader pedagogical aims were realized in the pamphlets written, published, and circulated by Stewart, Apes, Quinn, Garnet, and Brown between 1831 and 1851 as well as in numerous newspaper accounts of different audiences' reactions to the pamphlet.

By collecting and considering at length these print responses to Walker's *Appeal* together for the first time, I mean neither to propose them as a subprint culture, a counterarchive, or constitutive of a counterpublic, nor to invite suggestions that they represent little more than five idiosyncratic responses to Walker's also idiosyncratic political pamphlet in the same format and genre(s).[25] Rather, as I have begun to suggest with the concept of revision, by thinking about Walker's *Appeal* and Stewart's, Apes's, Quinn's, Garnet's, and Brown's pamphlets together, we can more clearly recognize the vitality of the *Appeal*, both in the three editions Walker published before his death and beyond Walker as its individual author, as these writers both individually and collectively revised and expanded his lessons and arguments with their own to meet changing political, legal, technological, and geographical contexts. In addition to Bryant's concept of the fluid text, then, we might also think of Walker's *Appeal* in this light as a living text, as the Constitution was considered to be by some early American political and textual theorists.[26]

Walker not only used the structure of the Constitution as a model for his pamphlet, with its preamble and four articles, but also specifically sought to revise and renew it with his text's rearticulations and fuller realizations of the nation's founding ideals. Over time and space, as politics evolved and the nation expanded, Stewart, Apes, Quinn, Garnet, and Brown each breathed new life into Walker's original and revised *Appeal*s by adapting his arguments' logic and rhetoric in their own pamphlets to advocate for specific groups—women, Native Americans, Black emigrants to the American West and Canada, and enslaved Black Americans in the context of global revolutions from below—within "the coloured citizens of the world" to whom

Walker dedicated his *Appeal*. That is, by both explicitly and implicitly positioning their own writings in conversation with Walker's, these writers not only revived but also revised and evolved the three editions of Walker's original *Appeal*. They did this in ways that allowed them to address rapid changes in the legal, political, geographic, and cultural conditions of slavery and racism between 1831 and 1851, with the idea that their pamphlets and their lessons and arguments would be just as urgent, relevant, and consequential as the *Appeal* had been in Walker's time.

More specifically, with respect to Walker's revising and evolving his own text over the three editions that he published, I focus in Chapter 1 on specific aspects of how he actively edited and significantly expanded its second and third editions, both published in quick succession in 1830. We will see Walker in direct conversation with his Black and White readers at the time as well as with his printer(s), responding to both through new in-text additions, discursive footnotes, and corrections to ensure that his carefully crafted printed text matched the affective, pedagogical, and argumentative force of his equally carefully crafted written text.[27]

Responses to the pamphlet were swift in law, letters, and Black communities, and Walker kept up with them all by reading in newspapers about his pamphlet's effects, as he made clear in important additions to its final edition. In Chapter 1, I show how he took advantage of specifically textual features—including asterisked discursive footnotes, additions to the body text that were signaled as such both typographically and verbally, and consistent punctuation and typographical emphasis—to respond to these print responses through significant revisions to his text. As we will see, these changes allowed him to call attention to new southern laws written to prohibit Black people from reading his pamphlet in apparent violation of the Bill of Rights, to White abolitionists' condemnations of his pamphlet's "bad spirit," and to his indictments of relatively well-educated and prosperous free Black men for selfishly continuing to tend to their own interests instead of further spreading the good news of his *Appeal* to their less-fortunate brethren.[28]

Again, the chapters that follow are dedicated to how Stewart, Apes, Quinn, Garnet, and Brown each took notice of this call to duty and responded with their own pamphlets. Specifically, in Chapter 2, I examine Maria Stewart's *Religion and the Pure Principles of Morality* as almost immediately extending Walker's *Appeal* to Black women in Boston and beyond. As Stewart noticed, Walker had largely neglected his sisters in favor of addressing his "brethren" and appealing to them to resist specifically as men. I analyze Stewart's use of bold language to address sensitive aspects of Black women's gendered and embodied experiences of slavery and racism and, ultimately, to argue that Black women, not Black men, would be the agents of Black liberation. In discussing how this powerful feminist argument came to be published, I consider what Stewart and her pamphlet offered to her publisher William Lloyd Garrison. As part of doing so, I spend some time examining how Garrison distinctly imitated the characteristic graphic appearance of the *Appeal* in his antislavery newspaper, the *Liberator*. Garrison deemed Walker's *Appeal* "one of the most remarkable productions of the age" even as he "deprecated its spirit"; as we will see, the two-mindedness of this response is visible in the pages of the *Liberator* and his promotion of Stewart.[29] I also closely read his advertisements for Stewart's pamphlet in the *Liberator* for how he effectively positioned her as his discovery of a nineteenth-century Phillis Wheatley, who similarly advocated Black women's collective resistance through faith and feminine propriety in her White-sponsored writings. By examining this intertextual network in detail, this chapter establishes the inextricability of Walker's *Appeal*, Garrison's *Liberator*, and Stewart's *Religion and the Pure Principles of Morality*—texts that scholars frequently have associated with each other but have tended to isolate when analyzing them closely. By doing so, I recover a complex and productive cycle of influence and differentiation in early radical antislavery and antiracist print in Boston. More specifically, I consider how different kinds of strategic imitation underwrite these two important initial revisions of Walker's *Appeal*, examining how Garrison and Stewart differently emulated and contradicted Walker's example for their different ends.

Chapter 3 focuses on another Bostonian and contemporary of Walker's, the Indigenous American writer and activist William Apes, and his essay "An Indian's Looking-Glass for the White Man." Apes placed this political and highly polemical essay at the end of *The Experiences of Five Christian Indians*, an otherwise conventional religious tract of conversion stories that he published in 1833. I argue that Apes arranged his pamphlet in this order as part of a covert publication strategy for a text that would have been not just controversial but also obvious as an adaptation of Walker's confrontational *Appeal*. His strategic placement of his polemic allowed him to surprise potential White Christian allies with his bold, ministerial confrontation of their moral and political hypocrisy in the Age of Jackson and under the policies of Indian Removal Act. I also consider how Apes heeded Walker's specific advice to read Thomas Jefferson's *Notes on the State of Virginia* for its influential—and as Walker reasoned, irrational—claims about racial difference. I focus on how Apes significantly added force to Jefferson's assertions of Indians' (his designation) equality with, if not superiority to, White people by borrowing the racial hierarchy he established in *Notes*—an argumentative move that significantly distanced Apes from Walker even as he rhetorically stayed close to Walker's model.

Chapter 4 follows Walker's *Appeal* west with the itinerant African Methodist Episcopal minister and later bishop William Paul Quinn via his 1834 pamphlet, *The Origin, Horrors, and Results of Slavery*—a significant portion of which Quinn reproduced directly from Walker's text. While Quinn's borrowing has been noted by scholars, it has not been analyzed at length. Quinn's later appointment as a bishop in the African Methodist Episcopal Church, following his incredibly successful missionary work in the American near West, makes him an important part of the AME Church's print history and his relation to Walker that much more significant. I read Quinn's text as the first significant instance of unattributed borrowing from the *Appeal*—and, thus, as one of the more surprising effects of Walker's specific prioritization of his arguments' circulation over his property right as an author. I also situate Quinn's borrowings in relation to Methodist textual traditions of unattributed borrowing, revising, and repurposing that began with church founder John Wesley, and that I first introduce in Chapter 3 as part of considering Apes's adaptations of both Walker and Jefferson for his ministerial message to White Americans. For Quinn, reaching free Black settlers in the near West and converting them to the early AME Church and antislavery activism were of the utmost importance. I argue that borrowing from Walker's text (as well as from a text by White antislavery author Thomas Branagan), blending others' words with his own, and thus revising Walker's *Appeal* into a hybrid political pamphlet and religious tract were Quinn's chosen means for most effectively reaching and converting his western flock.

In contrast to Stewart, Apes, and Quinn, Henry Highland Garnet chose to reissue Walker's *Appeal* just as Walker had written it, with express permission from Walker's widow. In Chapter 5, I focus on how Garnet's reissuing of Walker's *Appeal* in 1848—the year of global revolutions—bound with his own controversial "Address to the Slaves of the United States of America" allowed him to update Walker's text without revising a single word, and to renew Walker's appeal to enslaved Black Americans in an incredibly important world historical moment. I emphasize how Garnet's binding of his and

Walker's texts together in one pamphlet allowed him to realize the central rhetorical conceit of his "Address to the Slaves," in which he declares, "We therefore write to you as being bound with you."[30] For Garnet, materially substantiating the sympathetic connection that he sought to forge between Black Americans was crucial to restoring Walker's direct communication with the enslaved, renewing his justification of violent resistance as a revolutionary right, linking Black Americans' resistance to rights-based revolutions underway around the world, and theorizing Walker as not just a major American author but also the author of the antislavery movement itself.

In contrast to Garnet, and more like the example of William Paul Quinn, Paola Brown extended Walker's *Appeal* to fellow emigrants to Canada in the wake of the Fugitive Slave Act by republishing most of it under his own name and with the revised title *An Address on the Subject of Slavery* in 1851. For doing so, Brown—who is thought to have emigrated to Canada soon after Walker published his *Appeal*, and who became an activist in the Black settlements there—was exposed as a fraud by a more recent arrival, Thomas Smallwood. Smallwood exposed and pointedly condemned Brown's appropriation in the preface to his own slave narrative, which he also published in Canada in 1851. In Chapter 6, I situate both Brown's pamphlet and Smallwood's charge at the intersection of the Fugitive Slave Law and ongoing debates about international copyright law. Whereas Walker prioritized his *Appeal* reaching as many "coloured citizens of the world" as possible in 1830, Brown and Smallwood published their works under much different laws and customs. In 1851 both texts and people were circulating in ways that occasioned vigorous debate and controversial new laws with international implications. Considering the complicated political and legal circumstances of fugitive people and print, I make a case for Brown following the spirit of Walker's wishes—even as he personally profited from the unattributed appropriation—and for Smallwood enforcing the letter of the *droit d'auteur* in the republic of letters of which he considered himself and Walker to be proper citizens.

I conclude with a look at W. E. B. Du Bois's copy of Walker's *Appeal*, recently acquired by Emory University, and the manuscript traces that it bears of how Walker prompted Du Bois to respond as a reader-activist. I focus on the penciled long brackets in its margins that show how Du Bois—who was in many ways Walker's ideal reader—was intellectually, affectively, and physically moved by the *Appeal*'s boldest claims about equal rights, including the right to resist oppression. And I read Du Bois's manual corrections to the text for how they register his realizing Walker's wishes for print to represent him, his voice, and his arguments unerringly. I conclude with some thoughts about the significance of Walker's pamphlet—which was aggressively confiscated and destroyed in Georgia in the 1830s—now being preserved as a treasured cultural text in Atlanta, and made more accessible than ever via digital facsimiles on the internet, at a time when White supremacy has been reasserted with both lethal and subtle force.

* * *

As I hope these brief chapter summaries begin to suggest, all of these texts both challenge and conform to dominant uses of and expectations for authorship, literature, publishing, printedness, personhood, citizenship, and agency, in their times as well as in ours. Put most broadly, Walker, Stewart, Apes, Quinn, Garnet, and Brown each made strategic, complicated, and sometimes contradictory choices as readers, writers, editors, reprinters, revisers, and appropriators who all turned to print as their weapon of choice in their fights against slavery and discrimination and their struggles to realize a truly egalitarian and democratic society. They made these choices in the interest of reaching very different audiences, prompting these readers to respond according to their different circumstances and abilities, and effecting radical changes for peoples' rights and lives. What is more, these writers' decisions and their political and legal positions structured both their messages and the material forms that they took.

While I present these writers' pamphlets as textual effects of Walker's *Appeal*, they are by no means its only effects in print. As a range of scholars have importantly emphasized, any archive is necessarily subjective and incomplete, and archives of materials related to historically marginalized and oppressed populations have been most vulnerable.[31] Therefore, all who work on such materials must always make conscious and difficult choices. I have chosen to narrow my focus—for the reasons explained above and elaborated in what follows—to examples that share a specific print format (the pamphlet) and genre (the essay, and several of its subgenres) that were written by African American and Indigenous American activists.

As the example of Douglass with which I began suggests, Walker's *Appeal* provoked many more readers than these five to respond in print. What follows necessarily devotes some attention to some of these responses in the interest of understanding the broader print context of Walker's *Appeal* and the five pamphlets featured here. Throughout, I cite several of the countless newspaper articles printed in the South and North about the circulation of Walker's pamphlet, and refer to some of the numerous laws written to restrict both the circulation of other so-called seditious and incendiary texts and Black people's literacy and mobility. As part of considering Maria Stewart's pamphlet and the circumstances of its publication, I also devote some necessarily extended attention to William Lloyd Garrison—Stewart's publisher—and his *Liberator*, which Garrison decided to establish in Boston instead of Washington, D.C. Walker had attracted the South's attention to Boston as the source of sensational antislavery print, and Garrison capitalized on it as a site of likely support for his newspaper from its established Black activist community, of which Walker, Stewart, and possibly Apes were a part. I consider as well a series of White abolitionists' addresses to the enslaved people that were written and delivered in the early 1840s as part of my reading of Henry Highland Garnet's 1843 "Address to the Slaves" that he first published in his 1848 edition of the *Appeal*. But I have specifically chosen to foreground works by Black writers and an Indigenous American writer who responded in kind to Walker's *Appeal*—that is, by specifically writing and publishing pamphlets—to concentrate on the set of productive responses that most closely followed, argumentatively and materially, Walker's model of the *Appeal* and its proven impact in forcing inequality to the front of the American conversation.[32]

By focusing on these substantial and positive print effects, however, I do not mean to obscure the significant and primarily negative lived consequences of Walker's *Appeal* for millions of Black Americans—that is, the very real, mentally and physically painful, and sometimes fatal experiences of oppression that resulted from laws that White Americans passed and customs they enforced in the wake of Walker's publication and circulation of his pamphlet. Frederick Douglass's experience of having his reading lessons cut short by the fearful Hugh Auld is just one prominent example of oppressive White responses to Walker's pamphlet and their outsized effects on individual Black lives. Other enslaved people were individually and collectively treated much more harshly, with their living quarters sacked by White people on the pretense of searching for prohibited reading materials, and enslaved and free Black people throughout the South were jailed and/or beaten and/or killed for possessing or being rumored to possess "seditious" print. Potential White allies to whom Walker mailed copies of his pamphlet were persecuted, prosecuted, and chased out of the South as well.[33]

Nor do I mean to devalue actual violence or the threat of violence by Black people as responses to Walker's appeals to freedom and equality; as Kellie Carter Jackson importantly asserts, "the politics of violence helped prepare the nation to view black people as equal Americans with inalienable rights" (2). Again, while Walker's *Appeal* has achieved canonical status, its violent reputation and the harm done to Black lives by Whites' responses to it continue to overshadow the productive, beneficial, and enduring effects that are most substantially recoverable in the consequential pamphlets that I foreground here.[34] And while these pamphlets and their arguments' positive contributions to the lived experiences of African and Native Americans in the slaveholding and racist United States do not, and never could, compensate for the oppression and violence that White people used Walker's pamphlet as an occasion to inflict on Black (and White) bodies, I hope that shifting our attention to these pamphlets and their enduringly powerful and meaningful lessons and arguments helps us do greater justice to vitally important, if less sensational, forms of agency and resistance to such injustice.

While it is important to try to understand Walker's, Stewart's, Apes's, Quinn's, Garnet's, and Brown's motivations, choices, and circumstances and their consequences at the time—through close reading, using methodological approaches borrowed from descriptive bibliography and book history, and historical contextualization—it is no less significant to understand that these pamphlets also have consequences for us in our time.[35] These writers' appeals take on renewed relevance and urgency in our current social, political, and environmental situation, as discrimination, violence, and forced migration dominate the lives of many Black and Indigenous people and people of color in the United States and the world. And most of these essays are now more readily accessible throughout the world than ever, but that availability is still significantly limited by the structural discrimination of the digital divide. We are also in the midst of a surge in activism and scholarship on communities of color, with tremendous activity in research and publishing and unprecedented financial support for research and hiring in these fields—at least until the global pandemic that began in 2019 and institutionally unequal austerity measures and attacks on critical race theory set in. This dissonance of our moment resonates with the simultaneous increase in legal and cultural discrimination against Black and Indigenous people, and people of color, and in means to combat it—particularly through relatively cheaply produced and easily circulated print—that these writers experienced in the nineteenth century.

If this resonance is unsettling, it can be productively so. For scholars at work on historicizing forces of oppression and effectual responses to them—particularly literary scholars working in the vibrant fields of early Black and Indigenous print—these pamphlets have much to contribute to our understanding of historical and contemporary theories and practices of authorship and personhood; literature and its genres; generative imagination and imitation; intellectual inquiry, property rights, and the greater public good; and legal and imagined communities and citizenship. These texts and topics are crucial not just to the humanities, but to humanity—specifically, the idea of humanity that Walker, Stewart, Apes, Quinn, Garnet, and Brown saw as yet to be fulfilled. As Jesse McCarthy has recently put it in recognizing the Movement for Black Lives as an effect of Walker's *Appeal*, "It is no coincidence that today it is Black Americans who are once again trying to save the country, to invest in finishing the work of making this place a home that we can live in. In what is a long-standing pattern, the 'coloured citizens' of this country are at the forefront of practicing civics. Indeed, what could be more republican than risking one's health to restore the health of the body politic?"[36]

* * *

In offering the book that you have in hand (or on-screen) as part of this ongoing collective work, I shift here into a more essayistic mode to acknowledge my tremendous debt to the community of scholars with whom this work is in conversation—particularly Erskine Peters, Dorothy Porter, Marilyn Richardson, Carla Peterson, Peter P. Hinks, Elizabeth McHenry, Frances Smith Foster, Hillary Wyss, Ian Finseth, Maureen Konkle, Phillip H. Round, Lori Leavell, Gene Andrew Jarrett, Benjamin Shearer Beck, Eric Gardner, Leon Jackson, Lara Langer Cohen, Christopher Hager, Benjamin Fagan, Tara Bynum, Cheryl Wall, and Derrick Spires—and to articulate my motivations.[37] Their work spans from early recoveries and initial analyses of Walker's, Stewart's, Apes's, Quinn's, and Garnet's pamphlets and countless other important and understudied texts by African American and Indigenous American authors, through the recent book historical turn to these and an even greater number and variety of texts by writers of color in the Americas. I join them in "read[ing] both the outsides as well as the insides and theoriz[ing] the mediatory connections between the two," as Leon Jackson encourages us to do in his 2010 essay on the state of the field of African American cultures of print (293).

More specifically, with respect to recovery and initial analysis, I am grateful for the early recovery work of Dorothy Porter and her 1971 anthology *Early Negro Writing, 1760–1837.* Porter painstakingly assembled this landmark collection during her years as a librarian and scholar at Howard University. Drawing upon her work, Peter P. Hinks first noted that William Paul Quinn derived much of his pamphlet's text from Walker's. This is just one of the many rich connections he makes in his 1997 monograph *To Awaken My Afflicted Brethren: David Walker and the Problem of Antebellum Slave Resistance.* This first major study of Walker's writing, publication, and circulation of his *Appeal* and its political and cultural impact remains a feat of archival research and an invaluable resource for any scholar interested in David Walker as it continues to inspire scholars to learn and discover more about the *Appeal* and its effects.

Erskine Peters introduced me to Walker and Maria Stewart in a graduate-level African American literature course that I took as an undergraduate at the University of Notre Dame. I began my work on Walker with a copy of a then-new edition of the *Appeal*, edited by Sean Wilentz, that Peters ordered for the course, and my work on Stewart's pamphlet comes from Marilyn Richardson's important 1987 collection *Maria W. Stewart, America's First Black Woman Political Writer: Essays and Speeches* that Peters guided us in reading both in relation to Walker's *Appeal* and on Stewart's own important terms.[38] That I have held on to those books for over twenty years is a material indication of how much Peters's thoughts and provocations have stayed with me and fostered my own. I am very grateful for his and Richardson's scholarly and pedagogical examples.

Porter, Hinks, Richardson, and many of the scholars whose works I have drawn on in this project conducted their research by spending countless hours in physical, rather than digital, archives, meticulously collecting these texts and recovering the circumstances of their writing, publication, and receptions. The rise of digital databases and archives has made an unprecedented number of texts available and unexpected connections among them more readily visible, as the University of North Carolina's online archive *Documenting the American South* allowed me to see with Paola Brown's *Address on the Subject of Slavery*, Thomas Smallwood's *Narrative of Thomas Smallwood*, and Walker's *Appeal* through a quick search.[39] Yet, as many scholars have emphasized, such technologically enabled possibilities do not replace actual archives or material texts but rather complement them.⁴⁰ My own and others' research in a number of both kinds of archives and with archivists—in my case, particularly Philip Lapsansky, James N. Green, and Cornelia King at the Library Company of Philadelphia—has enabled us to fill in some of the inevitable gaps in the scholarship that brought us to these texts in the first place and to continue building on that foundational work. The painstaking recovery work of these history and literature scholars stands as the foundation upon which we build the digitally enhanced archival work of today. Both kinds of archival recovery make clear that this work is not only never done but it is also always ongoing. As Walker's, Stewart's, Apes's, Quinn's, Garnet's, and Brown's pamphlets all attest, we contribute our best—and never the last word—to intellectual pursuits and conversations that will extend well beyond our lives and times, as technologies of publishing, accessing, and archiving continue to change and as our ways of using and thinking about them will, too.

My thinking about African Americans' engagements with print, both as individuals and as part of collectives, has been and continues to be shaped by Gates's, Peterson's, and McHenry's foundational books as well as Frances Smith Foster's 2005 essay "A Narrative of the Interesting Origins and (Somewhat) Surprising Developments of African-American Print Culture." Peterson's and McHenry's feminist attention to the pivotal role and significant labors of Black women and faith communities in producing and consuming print has guided me in considering the distinct masculinism of Walker's *Appeal*, Stewart's powerful appeal on behalf of Black women in the opening that Walker created, and the fact that all the pamphlets in this study were religious as well as political texts, with three authored by ministers and all six intended for readers who belonged to faith communities. More recently, Eric Gardner's *Black Print Unbound: The "Christian Recorder," African American Literature, and Periodical Culture* (2015) and Benjamin Fagan's *The Black Newspaper and the Chosen Nation* (2016) present important case studies of Black communities of faith and print as they engaged with many different kinds of print and value systems at once. All of these books model vital methodologies of reading that attend to the multiple voices in conversation, both within and in relation to newspapers, and to the inextricable relationship of print and orality. The readings that follow are greatly enriched by their examples.

Gardner's *Unexpected Places: Relocating Nineteenth-Century African American Literature* (2009) specifically encouraged me to look and think beyond the northeast United States in tracing the textual effects of Walker's *Appeal* and offered indispensable guidance in reading Quinn's and Brown's pamphlets from the American near West and post–Fugitive Slave Law Canada. With respect to complex engagements with print in nineteenth-century Indian Country and communities within these Indigenous communities, Hillary Wyss's *Writing Indians: Literacy, Christianity, and Native Community in Early America* (2000), Maureen Konkle's *Writing Indian Nations: Native Intellectuals and the Politics of Historiography, 1827–1863* (2004), and Phillip H. Round's *Removable Type: Histories of the Book in Indian Country, 1663–1880* (2010) have richly developed my thinking about both the individual and communal stakes of Apes's confrontation of White Americans via Walker, Jefferson, and the Bible.

During my extended study of Walker's *Appeal*, struggling (in the best and most privileged sense of the word) to understand the many strange (also in the best sense) things about it as a text and its effects on other texts, I am very glad to have been in ongoing conversations with Christopher Hager and Derrick Spires as our books were in progress, and to read theirs while writing this one. Hager's *Word by Word: Emancipation and the Act of Writing* (2013) offers invaluable guidance in how to read texts that are "strange" (both to us and to their authors) by challenging traditional understandings of literacy. He focuses on writers and readers who wrote and read as best they could, and he reads their work as best he can on their own terms. His careful work offers a valuable model for how to attend as justly as possible to works by writers who were simultaneously and inevitably writing on the dominant culture's terms as well. While Hager focuses mostly on manuscripts, I situate the writers and readers of printed texts in this project within the broader idea of literacies (plural) that he recognizes in his—a breadth that Walker also recognized and engaged with at the time. I also attempt the kinds of reading and writing that Hager models as a scholar who is mindful of one's own educational privileges and different racial identity and experiences, and the limits these necessarily place on even the most earnest, imaginative, and deeply felt efforts to understand different abilities and experiences.

Lara Cohen and Jordan Stein have contributed meaningfully as well to expanding my thinking about what kinds of imagination and labor count as authorship. Here, I have in mind Cohen's theoretically inflected readings of examples of generatively unoriginal practices of particular African American authors in *The Fabrication of American Literature* (2012), and the introduction and essays in the Cohen- and Stein-edited collection *Early African*

American Print Culture (also 2012). I draw on this work as part of an ongoing scholarly effort to broaden our understanding of authorship and literature beyond romantic originality—a concept that was integral to, not just concurrent with, Enlightenment scientific racialism. And with respect to thinking about Walker's extended engagements with Jefferson's scientific racialism and racism, and Enlightenment intellectual inquiry and textual discourse more broadly in several of the chapters that follow, I am indebted to Ian Finseth's and Gene Andrew Jarrett's important readings of Walker's *Appeal* in light of, and argument with, Jefferson.

As I was thinking about all the authors in this study and what it meant to be a "good" or "bad" citizen in the republic of letters, in these six authors' specific terms, times, and communities, Spires's *The Practice of Citizenship* was published. It could not have come at a better time, nor offered a more insightful study of the exceptionally high stakes of these concepts and practices for African Americans, who both theorized and practiced citizenship even as it was denied to them otherwise. And as I have begun to suggest, Cheryl Wall's important call to "move consideration of the African American essay from the margins to the center" has made it clear to me that the genre in which Stewart, Apes, Quinn, Garnet, and Brown most broadly wrote has factored significantly in their neglect (1). With this in mind, I read their works not just as pamphlets but also and specifically as essays, guided by Wall's attention to the genre's complexities and its innovation by Black writers. As she notes, "A hallmark of the form is the window it opens into the writer's mind. Readers watch writers think their way through a topic" (7). I appreciate her etymological understanding of the genre and have written this section of my introduction in this spirit. I am also very grateful for Wall's nuanced close readings of some of the knottiest aspects of Walker's essay and logic, which have helped me tremendously in thinking through and distinguishing Walker's textual aims, strategies, and pedagogical, literary, and political theories, and their effects on readers, including Stewart and Garnet.

As each of these scholars attests in their contributions to an already substantial body of work, much more remains to be done: not just on "African American cultures of print and the media—spoken, written, and digital—that enmesh them" (as Leon Jackson broadly frames the corpus), but also on specific print formats and genres, in our theoretically and historically informed efforts to decenter the individual in the history of authorship and the novel in the histories of literature and print.[41] Thus, I offer this book, its reconstruction of a specific community of readers, writers, ministers, and activists centered on Walker's *Appeal*, and my close and contextual readings of their political and religious pamphlets that follow, as my contributions to this vital scholarly work. I look forward to this dynamic conversation expanding and continuing as we broaden and deepen—that is, continue to revise—our understanding of both the past and the present to make them ever more inclusive, equitable, and humane.

CHAPTER 1

"Look!! look!!! at this!!!!"
Reading Walker's *Appeal*

This chapter grows out of my previous work on the radical punctuation and typography of Walker's *Appeal*, in which I focused on Walker's unusual and deliberate integration of the text's visual form, its informational and argumentative content, and its performance.[1] That essay did not do as much as it might have to differentiate among the different audiences that Walker sought to address with his *Appeal*, or to recognize how Walker carefully crafted his text to reach these different audiences in their particular circumstances. Here, I offer a more sustained analysis of the complex ways in which the *Appeal*'s organizational structure and its punctuation, typography, and other textual features—specifically, the third edition's notice to readers, the preamble, the many footnotes and in-text additions to the third edition—work to engage, instruct, and activate very different audiences.

To do so, I build on Elizabeth McHenry's pathbreaking scholarship on the *Appeal* that initially pushed scholars to read it for more than its contributions to Black nationalist ideology and its defenses of violent resistance.[2] In her attention to how "Walker's *Appeal* was able to address not only his principal audience, the public constituted by the black community, free or slave," but also the "national public" (30), McHenry emphasizes Walker's accomplishment with respect to the former, given that the majority of Walker's principal audience "could not read" (34). "Walker knew this," she affirms, and therefore "design[ed] a document and imagin[ed] a system of distribution for it that would reach and benefit even the semiliterate and illiterate black population," thereby strengthening racial solidarity. Of these strategies, McHenry focuses on Walker's "insist[ence] that those who could must read the text aloud to those who could not" (34). My previous work on the *Appeal* also takes up this question of voicing, specifically examining how the radical punctuation and typography of text worked—and still works—like dynamic markings in printed music, directing readers who were reading and performing it aloud to those who could not read, or reading silently, to speak, or imaginatively hear, and share in Walker's powerful emotions. Of his anger and its typographical expression in particular—that is, what I analogize with effects, in the sense of amplified music, in the introduction to this book—Tara Bynum compellingly argues that this "acting [of] itself out in [a] public way" is "designed to take all of us somewhere." "What Walker's anger begins—a new way of being—ends with the feel-good fellowship of building a new kind of collective humanity," Bynum concludes.[3] While I share her optimism about Walker's ultimate ends, I focus in this chapter on the *Appeal*'s various means, reading it as a demanding text that expects a lot from its readers, often in ways that make them feel various negative emotions—not just angry but also frustrated, ashamed, betrayed, distanced, fearful, among others—to spur them to do specific acts of good toward realizing that ultimate feel-good end of collective humanity that Bynum foregrounds.

In analyzing how Walker's text directs its different readers in how to read, think, and variously respond—that is, in how its effects work to affect readers and effect their actions—I both draw from and build on recent scholarly readings of the *Appeal* that also focus on Walker's textual strategies for addressing and activating his Black and White audiences. What follows offers the first fine-grained close readings of the subaudiences within these main audiences, and of the parts of the text in which Walker directly instructs and advises them. To inform these readings, I build on groundbreaking and revelatory ongoing archival research by scholars dedicated to learning how Walker and others circulated the *Appeal* in the world as a material text.[4] Walker's strategies for reaching his readers within the text and with copies of his text must be considered together; thus, I am especially grateful for other scholars' laborious archival work and mean for my work here within the text to complement their fieldwork. One of the ways that I do so is by recognizing the text of Walker's *Appeal* as itself also an archive. Walker frequently tells us within it precisely what and how he read, in passages that model textual exegesis for his intended audiences, and in in-text and detailed footnote citations.

Among the numerous works that Walker cites are two influential late eighteenth-century texts that, I argue, Walker both adopted and adapted to write his *Appeal*. One is Lindley Murray's bestselling textbook *English Grammar*,

Adapted to Different Classes of Readers, first published in England in 1795 and republished throughout the United States in the early nineteenth century as a foundational text in early American education. In the first section below, I read Murray's introduction to his *Grammar* and recover how Walker found in it an important and useful strategy for organizing his text for his different classes of readers, and a model for explaining this organization to them so that they would know how to make the best use of his text. More broadly, reading Walker's *Appeal* in light of Murray's *English Grammar* foregrounds how the *Appeal* is not just a polemical, oratorically minded essay on, but also a didactic grammar of, U.S. racial slavery. This chapter is dedicated to showing how it works as such, through close readings that attend more fully to the ways in which it reaches its quite different classes of readers, what it wants to teach them, and what it specifically instructs them to do with that knowledge.

In the sections that follow, I also foreground Walker's deep and extended engagement with Thomas Jefferson's *Notes on the State of Virginia*, the other highly influential and foundational eighteenth-century work, in the realms of political and natural philosophy, that Walker most prominently cites and repeatedly contradicts in the *Appeal*. Several scholars have examined Walker's powerful critiques of Jefferson's and other Enlightenment thinkers' influential scientific theories of the sub-humanity, intellectual inferiority, limited literary achievements, and political unfitness of people of African descent. As Gene Andrew Jarrett notes, Walker "is arguably the first black author to critique *Notes* in Jefferson's own terms."[5] Jarrett has examined at length how Walker does so in the *Appeal*. Similarly, Ian Finseth has presented an important reading of Walker's engagement with Enlightenment natural and political philosophies that focuses on his powerful, if at times contradictory, counterarguments in the *Appeal*.[6] Here, I shift our focus to consider how Walker found a productive example in Jefferson's freely discursive, highly intertextual, encyclopedic, and critical *Notes*—specifically, what I have identified as the eighth American edition, printed in Boston in 1801, using Walker's detailed citations—admiring it as a specimen of Enlightenment inquiry and writing, even as he rigorously critiqued Jefferson's reasoning with respect to race and absolutely rejected his conclusions.[7]

Both Jefferson's *Notes* and Walker's *Appeal* confound multiple genres of writing in their encyclopedic approach to their overlapping topics.[8] Among those that we can discern more prominently is the polemical essay. According to Stephen W. Brown, the polemical essay's "emphasis on the values of the written word and upon subjectively contextualizing its topics" occasioned "a style of encyclopedia-making" during the Enlightenment that was "more critical, more aggressive, and more literary"—a shift most prominently marked by Denis Diderot's *Encyclopédie* (1751–1772). Brown also importantly notes that Diderot's "editorial choice . . . to embrace the more important and controversial entries with an individualistic and even polemical tone" brought about a major shift in the function of encyclopedias as well—"challeng[ing] the reader to reflection rather than simply providing information."[9] As Daniel Brewer summarizes its accomplishment, Diderot's *Encyclopédie* is "the text most representative of the French Enlightenment, providing massive testimony to the Enlightenment belief in the value of unfettered inquiry into all sectors of human knowledge."[10] Jefferson read the *Encyclopédie*, circulated it to his peers, and imitated the style of its essays as a writer.[11] Thus, it is in this broad intellectual and literary context of the Enlightenment that I understand not just Walker's specific arguments with Jefferson and, through him, Enlightenment theories of race but also how Walker, throughout his *Appeal*, models reasoning, close reading, and the Enlightenment thinking and learning through writing that he sees in Jefferson's encyclopedic *Notes* and challenges his Black readers who are most like him to practice.

Taking this broad view, I argue that Walker both adopted and reformed the culturally and personally influential examples of late eighteenth-century philosophical inquiry, discourse, and writing that he found in both Murray's *Grammar* and Jefferson's *Notes on the State of Virginia* to suit his and all Black Americans' ends. By doing so, Walker not only extended but also significantly transformed Enlightenment Age philosophical inquiry, instruction, writing, and understanding—into the nineteenth century, and also into African American political, scientific, literary, and pedagogical theory and practices— in ways that made sure that these powerful modes of thinking, learning, writing, and understanding were both available to, and further transformable by, all people of African descent.

Walker's intellectual inquiries and didactic lessons for all of his readers are at once highly rational, affective, and affecting. His emotions consistently rise as he dilates on its main points, and he arranges and presents the text visually to evoke and amplify his readers' emotions as well. In the most heated moments of the more freely discursive portions of the text, he also often switches which audience he is addressing (typically, from free, educated Black readers to all White Americans), and/or addresses multiple audiences at once. Therefore, to isolate specific passages and analyze them for Walker's strategies for engaging different readers is to risk both overemphasizing structure and order in what is a freely discursive and highly expressive text, and oversimplifying the complicated polyvocality, intertextuality, and multiple modes of address in the *Appeal*. With these concerns in mind, I foreground Walker's engagements with and transformations of his sources (primarily Murray's *Grammar* and Jefferson's *Notes*) over those source texts themselves. I also aim to strike a balance between mostly discrete readings of passages aimed at mostly distinct audiences and considering the text and pamphlet as a whole, to get at both the immediate and broad social, legal, political, and intellectual effects of Walker's *Appeal* as not just a radical political pamphlet and an impassioned jeremiad, but also a grammar and encyclopedia of U.S. racial slavery.

Appealing to "Different Classes" of Readers

In article 2—which Walker dedicates to exploring "Our Wretchedness in Consequence of Ignorance"—he specifically notes that he has "examined school-boys and young men of colour in different parts of the country, in the most simple parts of Murray's English Grammar" to assess the level and quality of their educations (38). His most educated Black and White readers equally and immediately would have understood why Walker was invoking this textbook as authoritative in relation to his inquiries. As Charles Monaghan and E. Jennifer Monaghan explain of Lindley Murray's *English Grammar, Adapted to the Different Classes of Learners* (1795) and *English Reader* (1799), "Murray's works gained instant acceptance in the new republic" and his "books were reprinted by printers all over America," becoming "steady sellers for four decades, surpassing even Noah Webster's totals," with Murray selling sixteen million copies of his works in the United States in the first half of the nineteenth century as "the largest-selling author in the world."[12]

Among these many American reprintings, an 1825 edition of *English Grammar* printed by Thomas Bedlington in Boston would have been readily available to Walker at the time; it is even more available to many of us now thanks to digitization.[13] It includes Murray's 1795 introduction to the text, which explains both his textual strategies for reaching the different classes of learners indicated in its full title as well as his philosophies of language, thought, and understanding that inform his *Grammar*. In explaining the latter, Murray declares most basically that "words are the signs of our ideas, and the medium by which we perceive the sentiments of others, and communicate our own." Because language is, therefore, the means "with which we transfuse our sentiments into the minds of one another," a "competent knowledge" of words, their relation to each other, and ideas is essential. Without it, Murray cautions, "we shall frequently be in hazard of misunderstanding others, and being misunderstood ourselves" (6).

This hazard of misunderstanding is not only person to person, but ultimately social, and with great consequences, Murray underscores: "many of the differences in opinion amongst men, with the disputes, contentions, and alienations of heart, which have too often proceeded from such differences" are attributable to the "want of proper skill in the connexion and meaning of words" and "a tenacious misapplication of language" (6). Raising the stakes of this branch of learning even higher, Murray concludes this line of Enlightenment Age thought by invoking his fellow eighteenth-century Scottish rhetorician and philosopher Hugh Blair: "All that regards the study of composition, merits the higher attention upon this account, that it is intimately connected with the improvement of our intellectual powers. For I must be allowed to say, that when we are employed, after a proper manner, in the study of composition, we are cultivating the understanding itself."[14]

That Walker took these lessons from Murray's introductions to heart is apparent throughout his *Appeal*, and most clearly in article 2, which, again, focuses on the importance of education for all Black Americans. Within the article, he specifically instructs his free Black and more liberally educated readers, "Let the aim of your labours among your brethren, and particularly the youths, be the dissemination of education and religion." He also emphasizes to both his liberally and partially educated free Black readers that reading "well, as trifling as it may appear to some, (to the ignorant in particular) is a great part of learning," and distinguishes this more advanced form of literacy from merely "scribbl[ing] tolerably well" (35). And he closes article 2 by citing the testimony of an eight-year-old Black boy from his adopted home state of Massachusetts about how the local school committee has strictly limited instruction in grammar to White students only. As these passages begin to suggest, Walker, like Murray (and Blair) considered the in-depth study of grammar—including words, syntax, pronunciation, punctuation, and "perspicuity and accuracy" in spoken and written communication, as Murray breaks it down—as essential to the full development of all human minds and to understanding between all human beings. For Walker, the stakes could not be higher: "There is a great work for you to do, as trifling as some of you may think of it," he affirms to all of his Black readers. "You have to prove to the Americans and the world, that we are MEN, and not *brutes*, as we have been represented, and by millions treated" (35).

I read Walker's emphasis here on the importance of studying grammar as an invitation to linger on Murray's introduction to his *Grammar* and suggest that Walker also took to heart its lessons about how to structure an intricate text on a highly complex subject so that it would be both legible and useful in different ways to people with different degrees of education. In the second paragraph of his introduction, Murray notes, "In books designed for the instruction of youth, there is a medium to be observed, between treating the subject in so extensive and minute a manner, as to embarrass and confuse their minds, by offering too much at once for their comprehension; and, on the other hand, conducting it by such short and general precepts and observations, as to convey to them no clear and precise information" (3). Walker recognized his need to strike such a balance, too, in presenting the complex subject of U.S. racial slavery and its many depredations. He acknowledges the intellectual and emotional complexity of his subject explicitly in his preamble: "The *causes*, my brethren, which produce our wretchedness and miseries, are so very numerous and aggravating, that I believe the pen only of a Josephus or a Plutarch, can well enumerate and explain them" (3).

Murray offers the following strategy for addressing the numerous and aggravating complexities of English grammar: "A distinct general view, or outline, of all the essential parts of the study in which they are engaged; a gradual and judicious supply of this outline; and a due arrangement of the divisions, according to their natural order and connexion, appear to be among the best means of enlightening the minds of youth, and of facilitating their acquisition of knowledge" (3). In the preamble, Walker similarly explains how he has ordered his *Appeal* using this divide-and-conquer approach: "The sources from which our miseries are derived, and on which I shall comment, I shall not combine in one, but shall put them under distinct heads and expose them in their turn" (5). The sources of misery he selects—slavery, ignorance, religion's perversion in service of slavery, and colonization—are the topics of the four chapters that follow his preface. And as I have suggested, by specifically titling this preface a "Preamble" and the four chapters as roman-numbered "Articles," Walker also reconstitutes what William Lloyd Garrison soon would come to reject as a proslavery document—the U.S. Constitution—into a foundational text in the histories of antislavery and antiracism.[15] Yet his *Appeal*'s piecemeal treatment of the subject and reconstitution of the Constitution do not come at the cost of underrepresenting the ultimate horror and irrationality of race-based slavery. Walker forewarns readers in the preamble—which he also refers to as his "remarks on the suburbs"—that when he enters "more fully into the interior of this system of cruelty and oppression" (8), the main causes of Black Americans' miseries that he presents in each article will be seen to "rage to such an alarming pitch, that they cannot but be a perpetual source of terror and dismay to every reflecting mind" (4).

In that English grammar likely was more difficult than perpetually terrifying and dismaying for most of the students Murray had in mind, he includes no such warning about his lessons rising to an alarming pitch. But he did recognize that, in seeking to establish a middle ground between overwhelming complexity and overly reductive simplicity with his *Grammar*, the middle would vary for readers at different levels in their education. Accordingly, he introduces the textual strategies he devised for reaching these different classes of readers where they are. Typography is central to Murray's strategies: "The more important rules, definitions, and observations, and which are therefore the most proper to be committed to memory, are printed with a larger type; whilst rules and remarks that are of less consequence, that extend or diversify the general idea, or that serve as explanations, are contained in the smaller letter." He advises beginning students to focus on the lessons printed in the largest type and to "postpone" the finer points he puts on them that are set apart in smaller type "till the general system be completed." And to adults who may be assisting younger learners in these lessons, either as parent-teachers or classroom teachers, Murray explains that he has included "notes and observations, in the common and detached manner, at the bottom of the page"—that is, footnotes. In adopting these textual strategies—different type sizes and footnotes to distinguish between main lessons and further elaboration—Murray explains, "care has been taken to adjust" his text "so that the whole may be perused in a connected progress, or the part contained in the larger character read in order by itself" (4). That is, some readers will be best served by reading only parts of his *Grammar* initially, then returning to it to read and learn more each time, and others by reading the whole of it. Either way, all readers will learn the same major lessons, with the most advanced readers learning them in greater detail.

While Walker takes advantage of typography (and footnotes) to add emphasis to messages that he wants to foreground in his *Appeal*, he does not follow Murray's model of presenting his main points for his least literate audience members in larger type and his subsequent elaborations of these points in smaller type.[16] Instead, he places the message he wants all readers to take away at the start of all but one of the text's five sections. The first paragraph of the preamble in all three editions features the principal claim of the *Appeal*: "that we, (coloured people of these United States,) are the most degraded, wretched, and abject set of beings that ever lived since the world began" (3rd ed., 3). In articles 1 and 3, the first paragraph contains his main point addressed to all audiences. Article 2—on what Walker terms "ignorance" and education—requires five paragraphs. For article 4—on the colonization debate—Walker abandons this structure and dives right into debates about what he calls the "colonizing trick" immediately after noting, with false modesty, that it "is a scheme on which so many able writers . . . have commented" that he feels a "delicacy about touching it" (49). In articles 1 through 3, Walker follows these argumentatively frontloaded introductions with lengthy discourses on the main topics, which he mostly addresses to his more educated free Black male readers, but also, at points, to White readers, whom he designates as Americans, Christians, and sometimes Christian Americans (and implies as male and educated) to indicate how slavery exposes their double hypocrisy with respect to their basic religious and secular values. As previously noted, article 4 lacks an introduction and is mostly dedicated to critiquing procolonization arguments through close reading; it ends with Walker's most succinct and damning indictment of White Americans by way of the Declaration of Independence's claim that all men are created equal.

In that his lengthy elaborations of his four articles' topics constitute the majority of the text of the *Appeal*, we can understand why Walker would have departed from Murray's model by choosing not to set them in smaller type. Scholarly readers who have been attentive to Walker's strategies for addressing different audiences in the same text do not seem to have discerned a pattern in how Walker divided up the text beyond its structure of a preamble and four articles.[17] Perhaps some of his nineteenth-century readers might have been quicker to isolate the main points at the beginning of most sections and abridge the text accordingly, either to suit their own more limited reading abilities, or to abridge it for reading aloud for easier consumption by others. Even if that were so, Walker suggests that his text does not need abridging for any readers; he concludes his *Appeal* by submitting it to his "brethren . . . in language so very simple, that the most ignorant, who can read at all, may easily understand—of which you may make the best you possibly can" (80).

In this closing statement of his pamphlet's legibility and his expectations of its readers, I want to suggest again that we should recognize the influence of Murray's *English Grammar* and the Enlightenment commitment to disciplined philosophical inquiry that it pedagogically exemplifies. Like Murray, Walker offered his whole book to readers at all levels of literacy, with the expectation that they would read it intensively, progressing in their education with each reading. While expecting such intensive engagement from enslaved readers might seem idealistic, if not impossible—given the strict controls on literacy, time, possessions, contact, mobility, and all other aspects of life in slavery—Walker was fully aware of these serious challenges to his aims for his pamphlet and its enslaved readers. In a December 8, 1829, letter that he included with copies of the pamphlet sent to Thomas Lewis in Richmond, Virginia, Walker establishes the terms on which he wanted his *Appeal* circulated: "the price of these Books is <u>twelve cents per Book,</u>—to those who can <u>pay for them,</u>—and if there are any who, cannot pay for a <u>Book</u> give them <u>Books</u> for nothing."[18] Understanding that making them freely available would not guarantee they would be read, Walker includes discussions at several points in the *Appeal* about how White southerners tightly restricted instruction in literacy to enslaved people, and how they violently punished enslaved people for trying to read or possessing printed materials.[19] And while we might be tempted to contradict his claim that the *Appeal*'s language is so very simple, some of it is, and a good deal of it is no more challenging than Murray's *English Grammar*. Recognizing this, I understand Walker to have been unwilling to concede to slavery that his *Appeal* would go unreceived, unread, and not understood by enslaved people, and as equally unwilling to expect anything less from his Black readers—including even the least literate enslaved adults—than White Americans (and Europeans) expected of their children, despite the age difference and their completely opposite circumstances. He wrote his *Appeal* with both the high-mindedness of a Diderotian philosophe and even tougher love than a stern pedagogue like Murray, setting the highest possible expectations for reading and learning not because he expected all of his readers to meet them immediately but because he wanted them to know that he was certain that all of them intellectually could, in time, through dedicated study, and with the right teachers, texts, and social and legal circumstances for learning.

In the next section, I focus on a major new addition that Walker included in the third and last edition of his pamphlet which foregrounds both his *Appeal*'s primary claim and his expectation that "all coloured men, women and children" will acquire a copy of the pamphlet and read it. This notice to readers, placed by Walker at the front of the pamphlet, is a very complicated addition to the text that deserves particularly close formal and textual analysis in the interest of understanding how Walker wanted his text to be read and what actions he wanted his readers to take after reading it.

Notice to Readers

Walker intended the text of the third edition of his *Appeal* to be the stable, final version of what had become an unusually dynamic text since its first edition as he kept up with slavery- and race-related legislation and discussions of his pamphlets in the popular press, and engaged both in numerous additions to the text in the second and third editions.[20] He indicated these intentions in a clarificatory note at the very end: "☞ It may not be understood, when I say my Third and last Edition, I [do not] mean to convey the idea, that there will be no more Books of this Third Edition printed, but to notify that there will be no more addition in the body of this Work, or additional Notes to this 'Appeal.'☜" (88).[21] (See Figure 1.)

Two paragraphs Walker added to the verso of the third edition's title page are the most obvious and important of these new additions. (See Figure 2.) In them, Walker reaffirms his pamphlet's primary audience, multiply asserts his primary claim, and speaks in several registers to readers within and beyond his main audience. Elizabeth McHenry refers to this addition as a "Pre-Preamble," understandably, because the first paragraph includes a verbatim statement of the preamble's—and the entire *Appeal*'s—primary message. She focuses exclusively, however, on the pre-preamble's second paragraph and its "direct address to the educated few who could themselves read the *Appeal*" and their "duty to deliver the text and its teachings to those less fortunate than themselves" (34). As we will see, there is much about how Walker wrote these paragraphs—what I read instead as a notice, in the literal and figurative sense, to readers—that specifically addresses the "men of colour, who are also of sense" to whom he more specifically dedicates the pamphlet within article 2 (33). But I argue that we can also see, literally and figuratively, how Walker truly meant for these very first words of his *Appeal* to be noticed and read by "all coloured men, women and children," just as he declares within the notice.

PART II.

11. For, God, they think, no notice takes,
    Of their unrighteous deeds;
    He never minds the suff'ring poor,
    Nor their oppression heeds.

12. But thou, O Lord, at length arise,
    Stretch forth thy mighty arm,
    And, by the greatness of thy pow'r,
    Defend the poor from harm.

13 No longer let the wicked vaunt,
    And, proudly boasting, say,
    "Tush, God regards not what we do;
    "He never will repay."—*Common Prayer Book.*

---

1 Shall I for fear of feeble man,
  The spirit's course in me restrain?
  Or, undismay'd in deed and word,
  Be a true witness of my Lord.

2 Aw'd by mortal's frown, shall I
  Conceal the word of God Most High!
  How then before thee shall I dare
  To stand, or how thy anger bear?

3 Shall I, to soothe th' unholy throng,
  Soften the truth, or smooth my tongue,
  To gain earth's gilded toys or, flee
  The cross endur'd, my Lord, by thee?

4 What then is he whose scorn I dread?
  Whose wrath or hate makes me afraid
  A man! an heir of death! a slave
  To sin! a bubble on the wave!

5 Yea, let men rage, since thou will spread
  Thy shadowing wings around my head:
  Since in all pain thy tender love
  Will still my sure refreshment prove.

  Wesleys Collection.

☞ It may not be understood, when I say my Third and last Edition, I mean to convey the idea, that there will be no more Books of this Third Edition printed, but to notify that there will be no more addition in the body of this Work, or additional Notes to this "Appeal."☜

THE END.

Figure 1. Note on additions to Walker's *Appeal*, 3rd ed. (1830), p. 88.

> ☞ It will be recollected, that I, in the first edition of my "Appeal,"* promised to demonstrate in the course of which, viz. in the course of my Appeal, to the satisfaction of the most incredulous mind, that we Coloured People of these United States, are, the most wretched, degraded and abject set of beings that ever lived since the world began, down to the present day, and, that, the white Christians of America, who hold us in slavery, (or, more properly speaking, pretenders to Christianity,) treat us more cruel and barbarous than any Heathen nation did any people whom it had subjected, or reduced to the same condition, that the Americans (who are, notwithstanding, looking for the Millennial day) have us. All I ask is, for a candid and careful perusal of this the third and last edition of my Appeal, where the world may see that we, the Blacks or Coloured People, are treated more cruel by the white Christians of America, than devils themselves ever treated a set of men, women and children on this earth.☜
>
> ☞ It is expected that all coloured men, women and children,† of every nation, language and tongue under heaven, will try to procure a copy of this Appeal and read it, or get some one to read it to them, for it is designed more particularly for them. Let them remember, that though our cruel oppressors and murderers, may (if possible) treat us more cruel, as Pharoah did the children of Israel, yet the God of the Etheopeans, has been pleased to hear our moans in consequence of oppression; and the day of our redemption from abject wretchedness draweth near, when we shall be enabled, in the most extended sense of the word, to stretch forth our hands to the LORD our GOD, but there must be a willingness on our part, for GOD to do these things for us, for we may be assured that he will not take us by the hairs of our head against our will and desire, and drag us from our very, mean, low and abject condition.☜
>
> *See my Preamble in first edition, first page. See also 2d edition, Article 1, page 9.
> † Who are not too deceitful, abject, and servile to resist the cruelties and murders inflicted upon us by the white slave holders, our enemies by nature.

Figure 2. Walker's notice to readers in place of a copyright notice on title page verso, Walker's *Appeal*, 3rd ed. (1830).

Beyond its priority at the very front of the text, we can imagine a number of reasons why this notice to readers could have been all that some readers may have read of the pamphlet. The title page could easily have been separated from the rest of the text through wear from multiple handlings and readings, especially if the pamphlet's semiprotective (and more noticeable) blue paper wrappers were removed as it passed from reader to reader. A single page containing the pamphlet's main point and a clear statement of its intended audience would also have been easier to circulate and secret away than the entire eighty-eight-page pamphlet for any readers who needed to do so.[22] However, either the entire pamphlet or this page alone might have reached "coloured men, women and children" with any degree of literacy; this notice to readers would have functioned for them much like the main lessons of Murray's *Grammar* that were set in larger type—by distinguishing the primary claims of Walker's *Appeal* from the rest of the text.

The first paragraph of the notice offers two iterations of the main lesson that Walker wanted Black readers of all abilities to take away from his

Appeal, plus a bit of exposition: "We Coloured People of these United States, are, the most wretched, degraded and abject set of beings that [e]ver lived since the world began, down to the present day, and, that, the white Christians of America, who hold us in slavery (or, more properly speaking, pretenders to Christianity,) treat us more cruel and barbarous than any Heathen nation did any people whom it had subjected, or reduced to the same condition, tha[n] the Americans (who are, not withstanding, looking for the Millennial day) have us." He then repeats a version of this claim in the sentence that follows (the last sentence of the first paragraph of the notice): "We, the Blacks or Coloured People, are treated more cruel by the white Christians of America, than devils themselves ever treated a set of men, women and children on this earth." With this second iteration, we see Walker offering a version of his *Appeal*'s primary claim "in language so very simple, that the most ignorant, who can read at all, may easily understand," whether they were trying to read it themselves or hearing it read aloud (80).

The crucial information in this claim sets up the equally crucial message that Walker communicates to all Black readers in the next paragraph: "The day of our redemption from abject wretchedness draweth near, when we shall be enabled, in the most extended sense of the word, to stretch forth our hands to the LORD our GOD." Much like the spirituals that were sung by enslaved people, Walker's ministerial message in his notice to readers reads in two ways: (1) God will soon deliver enslaved people who pray for relief from their plight in the worst form of slavery ever; and (2) enslaved people will soon be able to deliver themselves, through their own means with God's blessing—and possibly with other human allies' assistance—from this most terrible form of slavery. In explicitly stating that he is using the passive *enabled* "in the most extended sense," Walker implies both human agency and justification in this message to enslaved people. The second footnote to the notice makes these implications explicit and active to any who read it: having been awakened to the full injustice and indefensibility of U.S. racial slavery by Walker and his *Appeal*, enslaved people "who are not too deceitful, abject, and servile" will "resist the cruelties and murders inflicted upon us by the white slave holders, our enemies by nature" by whatever means necessary, and they will be fully justified in fulfilling this duty (title page verso).

As you can see, extracting these messages from the short but dense paragraphs and footnotes of Walker's notice to readers requires some significant close reading on my part. (Further below, we will see that this kind of laborious close reading is exactly what Walker demands of those most capable of performing it.) The text of the notice is set in significantly smaller type than the body text of the pamphlet (the reverse of Murray's strategy for reaching limited literacy readers), and there are footnotes that only advanced readers would have known how to read in relation to the body of the notice. Moreover, Walker cross-references previous editions of his pamphlet at the very beginning of the notice and in one of the footnotes. Given this textual intricacy, you might find it hard as you are reading this to imagine how Walker might reasonably have meant much of this notice to readers—or of the *Appeal* as a whole—for anyone other than the most advanced Black (and White) readers who had easy access to print and experience in navigating its conventions. But as I have read the notice to readers to you here—not aloud, but exegetically—then perhaps it is possible to imagine what parts might have caught the attention of Walker's most basically literate audiences, regardless of the textual complexity, and how they would have understood from them exactly what Walker wanted them to understand and do to resist slavery.[23]

No imagination and little effort are required, however, to recognize how Walker's more literate Black audiences likely read and understood what he wanted them to take from this notice. For those within his enslaved and free Black audiences in both the slaveholding and free states who had attained some degree of literacy, the first sentence of the second paragraph (emphasized with a pointing printer's index) makes clear that they should extend their advantages to any who are unable to read the pamphlet themselves, even as the sentence foregrounds the agency of the less literate. McHenry points to important evidence in a Boston newspaper that this part of the notice worked in prompting literate Black readers in the North to read it aloud to others soon after the publication of the third edition: "Since the publication of that flagitious pamphlet, Walker's Appeal," the article's author writes, "we have noticed a marked difference in the deportment of our colored population. It is evident they have read this pamphlet, nay, we know that the larger portion of them have read it, or *heard* it read, and that they glory in its principles, as if it were a star in the east, guiding them to freedom and emancipation."[24]

The first sentence of the previous paragraph of the notice (also emphasized with a printer's index) and the first footnote at the bottom would have been fully intelligible to his most advanced Black readers. In both, Walker refers this class of readers to previous editions of his pamphlet, citing specific page numbers for their reference in the footnote. And in the first sentence, he also specifically presumes, in notably genteel literary discourse, that they—and the most interested White readers in the South and North—have already read its first edition: "☞ It will be recollected, that I, in the first edition of my 'Appeal,'* promised to demonstrate in the course of which, viz. in the course of my Appeal, to the satisfaction of the most incredulous mind" his main claim of Black Americans' exceptional abjection under slavery. Whether or not these most advanced and engaged Black readers actually were keeping up with each new edition of Walker's pamphlet as highly attentive scholar-activists, we can see how these aspects of the third edition's notice to readers would have worked "to strengthen liaisons between" what Walker therein implies and McHenry cites as "the growing network of black reformers and intelligentsia in the South as well as the North" (34).

These most textually savvy Black (and White) readers also might have registered where Walker placed this notice to them: precisely where a copyright notice would be printed in a publication that has been registered for copyright. I read this as a deliberate placement and replacement by Walker. He never copyrighted his *Appeal*; instead, he prioritized its widest possible circulation to as many Black men, women, and children readers as possible over his authorial rights to the text, as the notice to readers makes explicit.[25] As we will see in the chapters that follow, some of the *Appeal*'s most engaged and literary Black and Indigenous readers responded to Walker's pamphlet, and particularly this notice, by publishing their own pamphlets, in some cases by presenting significant portions of Walker's text as their own. Along with these writers, I recognize that Walker sought instruction and activation of his readers, more than ownership of or personal profit from his pamphlet, in keeping with both his self-sacrificing activist work in Boston and his declared expectations for similarly advantaged Black readers to help the less fortunate.[26] Thus, I read this notice to readers in the third edition as much more than a pre-preamble for all of the work that it might have done—and actually did—in different ways for different readers. It emblematizes not only the *Appeal*'s main message but also how Walker put every possible print convention to work to instruct and activate these readers.

In the remaining sections of this chapter, I take on the body text of Walker's *Appeal*, focusing mostly on the third edition and, like Murray and Walker, employing a divide-and-conquer strategy to better understand how Walker carefully crafted his polemical and didactic text rhetorically and visually, to engage his different audiences, teach them important lessons, and move them to take the most powerful actions they could in their circumstances to end racial slavery and discrimination. I begin by examining specific passages in which Walker most clearly addresses his enslaved audience, analyzing how the text speaks to them in these moments, what he wants to teach them, and what he specifically directs them to do with this knowledge. Though these moments of direct address to enslaved people constitute a relatively small portion of Walker's *Appeal*, they gained the most attention from White readers who responded with significant and consequential alarm that Walker dared to communicate directly with enslaved people. Thus, I also briefly discuss the overrepresentation of this audience and these passages in the popular press and legislation and, thereby, this disproportionate response by White readers as part of my analysis.

Appealing to Enslaved People

Both the pamphlet's title and the third edition's notice to readers make clear that Walker wanted the broadest possible audience for his *Appeal*: the *Coloured Citizens of the World*, and even more broadly, "all coloured men, women and children, of every nation, language and tongue under heaven."[27] I read this as both politically strategic and philosophically ambitious of Walker. For him to situate U.S. racial slavery within a global political context, and Black Americans in relation to Africans and the Black global diaspora, in print was a powerful political act in itself—one that refused the politically isolating work done by American exceptionalist ideology. Moreover, to appeal to the "coloured people of the world" was, for Walker, to remind all White Americans that they were vastly outnumbered globally by people of color—a point that we will see William Apes make explicitly in his pamphlet.

I begin this section dedicated to how Walker addresses his enslaved audience by considering his broadest designations of his audience because it is always important to take Walker at his word. He meant everything that he asserted more than he cared whether it was practical or possible—where there's a will, there's a way is the implicit message within every lesson and message in his *Appeal*, and most significantly in those he directs to enslaved people. It is also the message within his prominent and ambitious designations of intended audiences—by declaring his will to reach the "coloured citizens of the world" and "very expressly" all Black men, women, and children in the United States, Walker would make it so.

With respect to reaching enslaved people specifically, we have seen how the notice to readers positions and articulates its primary messages of the exceptional cruelty and evil of U.S. racial slavery and the duty to resist this cruelty and evil in ways that increased the likelihood that enslaved people would receive them. The first paragraph of the preamble and the first two paragraphs of article 1 do the same, if somewhat more expansively. Another moment near the end of the first article reaffirms this primary message in ways that strikingly suggest how Walker was speaking to his enslaved audience from deeper within the text and using multiple textual strategies to reach them, even as he spoke to other readers. In a crucial passage near the conclusion of article 1, Walker both tells and shows all of his readers the action that he wanted all of his Black audience—and particularly those who were enslaved—to take in response to having read his *Appeal* and learned that their plight in America was so exceptional.

After noting that the growth of the United States, following its "*first* Revolution" (emphasis added), has led to a significant increase in the number of people being enslaved, Walker asks, "Are we MEN!!—I ask you, O my brethren! are we MEN?" (19). In the pamphlet's first edition, the sentence appears as "Are we men?—I ask you, O! my brethren, are we men?" (1st ed., 18). In this version, question marks follow both iterations of the rhetorical question "Are we men?" with emphasis signaled by the repetition of the question, by Walker's direct address ("I ask you") to his readers (his "brethren"), and by the interjection "O!" preceding this direct address. But in the second and third editions—as all silent readers would have seen, and those listening to the text being read and performed aloud clearly would have heard—Walker added further emphasis to the matter of the question. In the first iteration, "men" becomes "MEN" and the question mark has been replaced with two exclamation points. In the second part of the sentence, the exclamation point following "O" has been moved to follow "brethren" and the second "men" becomes the entirely majuscular "MEN."[28]

As I have begun to suggest here, and have examined at greater length previously, the typography of this passage as it was printed in the second and third editions not only gives it visual emphasis but also functions like dynamic markings in printed sheet music, signaling to those reading it aloud to an audience how to voice it, with the distinction between the small- and all-caps *men* suggesting its *fortissimo* (*ff*), then *fortississimo* (*fff*) performance.[29] Here, I further want to suggest that, by instructing his printer(s) to set the type as he indicated, Walker was able to signal the kind of complex emphasis Murray describes in his *Grammar*'s section on prosody: "Emphasis is of two kinds, simple and complex. Simple, when it serves to point out only the plain meaning of any proposition; complex, when, besides the meaning, it marks also some affection or emotion of the mind; or gives a meaning to words, which they would not have in their usual acceptation. In the former case, emphasis is scarcely more than a stronger accent, with little or no change of tone; when it is complex, besides force, there is always superadded a manifest change of tone" (233). How readers are to know just when and where to add emphasis while reading aloud is more complex, Murray admits: "In order to acquire the proper management of emphasis, the great rule, and indeed the only rule possible to be given, is, that the speaker or reader study to attain a just conception of the force and spirit of the sentiments which he is to pronounce." He also notes the high stakes of attaining this just conception of proper emphasis: "For to lay the emphasis with exact propriety, is a constant exercise of good sense and attention. It is far from being an inconsiderable attainment. It is one of the greatest trials of a true and just taste; and must arise from feeling delicately ourselves, and from judging accurately, of what is fittest to strike the feelings of others" (236).

The emphatic punctuation and typography in the "Are we MEN!!" passage, as it was printed in the second and third editions of Walker's pamphlet, work in multiple registers, much like several types of effects can be applied at once in amplified music to increase, modulate, and otherwise affect volume, pitch, and tone. So that readers do not have to judge for themselves, they clearly signal to readers what they should emphasize and how they should emphasize it. Even more broadly and significantly, they transform what was both a rhetorical and natural philosophical question about Black people's humanity into increasingly forceful—and expressly masculine—assertions of this humanity, and of what all Black men—most pointedly those who were enslaved—should do with it: resist manfully.[30] With the replacement of the first edition's question mark with two exclamation points in the first iteration, the question, graphically, is no longer a question. And as the sentence progresses from "MEN" to "MEN," that Walker was demanding an indignant affirmative response from all of his Black male readers is even clearer. I also read this visible increase in the typeface's height as signaling to Black and White readers alike that with their humanity so directly challenged, enslaved and free Black people must and will rise up—just as the typeface does—in a *second* Revolution, to prove their equal, if not superior, status to White people as "MEN."

While Walker had high expectations of all of his readers as readers, I read this passage as an example of him tempering these expectations of some of them, so that the words would have been noticed, read, voiced, and understood exactly as he wanted them to be. Using the lens of Murray's *Grammar*, I see Walker as offering these helpful typographical assists so that his less educated enslaved and free Black readers would not need to judge for themselves that what might be read—either silently or aloud to others—as a question is, in fact, an assertion, that the men in question needed to be doubly emphasized as such, and that Black men—especially those who were enslaved—should respond to this assertion by rising up, just as the type does.

In article 2, Walker offers specific advice to his enslaved audience about how to resist and the justice in their doing so:

> If you commence, make sure work—do not trifle, for they will not trifle with you—they want us for their slaves, and think nothing of murdering us in order to subject us to that wretched condition—therefore, if there is an *attempt* made by us, kill or be killed. Now, I ask you, had you not rather be killed than to be a slave to a tyrant, who takes the life of your mother, wife, and dear little children? Look upon your mother, wife and children, and answer God Almighty; and believe this, that it is no more harm for you to kill a man, who is trying to kill you, than it is for you to take a drink of water when thirsty; in fact, the man who would stand still and let another murder him, is worse than an infidel, and, if he has common sense, ought not to be pitied. (29–30)

By using plain language and simple analogy, Walker makes it clear here that enslaved men's violent resistance of their masters and defense of their families is a natural instinct and right, a masculine and spiritual duty, and an inevitably lethal confrontation. That this important message would have been readily understood by enslaved people, and was equally immediately understood by White people, is registered most clearly in how White southerners, and northerners, responded to it. While it contains very little of the eye-catching typography characteristic of the pamphlet's most rhetorically heated passages, this is the passage that most provoked southern—and some northern—newspapers to refer to the *Appeal* as that "incendiary pamphlet" and Walker as "sanguinary," "fanatical," and "diabolical," and southern authorities to convene emergency legislative sessions banning "insurrectionary" print and further restricting enslaved people's literacy, and enslaved and free Black people's contact and mobility throughout the South.[31] Put simply, those with the most to fear from this passage were certain that the enslaved people they owned would understand and act on it, with the humanity that Whites denied them, and without hesitation.

Again, none of this passage is emphasized typographically. To consider why that might be so, I again turn to Murray's *English Grammar*. Murray closes the section on emphasis within his lessons on prosody by cautioning against the error of adding too much emphasis by "multiplying emphatical words too much." As in music, "it is only by a prudent reserve in the use of them, that we give them any weight," Murray advises. "If they recur too often; if a speaker or reader attempts to render every thing which he expresses of high importance, by a multitude of strong emphases, we soon learn to pay little regard to them. To crowd every sentence with emphatical words, is like crowding all the pages of a book with Italic characters, which, as to the effect," he concludes, "is just the same as to use no such distinctions at all" (236). In light of Murray's caution, I read Walker's rendering of what is arguably the passage of highest importance to his enslaved audience in decidedly unemphatic type—thus, without any added textual effects—as another instance of his matching form to content: he presents clear and simple advice and reasoning about resistance in plain roman type punctuated only with periods.

Significantly, this clear and plain message immediately follows one of the most emotional and typographically emphatic passages in the *Appeal*: the part of article 2 where Walker responds to a newspaper account of a thwarted uprising of enslaved people in Ohio. From the dates of both the article's publication that Walker provides in the text and his *Appeal*'s composition that he included on its title page, we know that he had learned of this incident in a newspaper article that he read shortly before writing his *Appeal*.[32] This article and the circumstances it describes are likely what prompted Walker to write, and what nearly kept him from finishing it, as he tells readers in building up to the article and incident: "And when my curious observer comes to take notice of those who are said to be free, (which assertion I deny) and who are making some frivolous pretentions to common sense, he will see that branch of ignorance among the slaves assuming a more cunning and deceitful course of procedure.—He may see some of my brethren in league with tyrants, selling their own brethren into *hell upon earth*, not dissimilar to the exhibitions in Africa, but in a more secret, servile and abject manner. Oh Heaven! I am full!!! I can hardly move my pen!!! (25)." In my previous reading of this passage, I suggested that we might recognize in it a Romantic performance of the writer's experience of the sublime—which "characteristically begins with the interposition of an overwhelming force, which shatters equanimity and produces a feeling of blockage"—and understand it as such as part of Walker's extended engagement with Jefferson's *Notes on the State of Virginia*.[33] Here, I consider it in its more immediate context, in which Walker is directly confronting both his free and enslaved Black audiences about actions that some among them have taken to support, rather than resist, slavery. Walker performs this moment of shattered equanimity and a feeling of blockage, with matching textual effects, so that his primary audience—Black Americans—feels the full force of his horror in confronting the painful fact that some of them act more in solidarity with slavery and White supremacy than with other Black people to advance the liberation of the entire race.

In forging ahead with his writing after this eruption/interruption, Walker offers "a development of facts, which are already witnessed in the court of heavens," that culminates in his reprinting of a newspaper story about a "most shocking outrage," in the words of the article's presumably White author.[34] What specifically shocked, outraged, and overwhelmed Walker about the incident was the article mentioning that one of the enslaved women among a gang of sixty had helped the uninjured driver and owner of the group to escape the uprising and flee to safety—and that this driver and owner was himself Black.[35] While he directs most of his outraged commentary on the incident, and on the enslaved woman who aided her enslaver, to his most educated Black male readers (which I will address at greater length in the next section), Walker uses his commentary to present a crucial lesson for his enslaved readers/listeners as well. "Should the lives of such creatures be spared? . . . Ought they not to be destroyed?" he asks both his enslaved and free Black audiences who might have had moral reservations—and the White readers that he also knew were reading. In case anyone was uncertain of the right answer, he unambiguously declares, "Any person who will save such wretches from destruction, is fighting against the Lord, and will receive his just recompense." And to his enslaved brethren most specifically he asserts, "The black men acted just like *blockheads*. Why did they not make sure of the wretch? He would have made sure of them, if he could" (29). Noting the consequences of these enslaved men and women letting their oppressors live, Walker states, "They will have to suffer as much for the two whom, they secured, as if they had put one hundred to death" (29). This is the clause that immediately precedes his most direct, specific, and controversial advice to the enslaved to "make sure work" of their White and Black oppressors whenever they resist.

In presenting this negative example of thwarted resistance, the hardest lesson that Walker has learned for himself, and wants all of his Black readers and listeners to absorb and act on, is that racial solidarity and violent resistance are not instinctive but rather must be taught.[36] Thus, he adopts and performs the role of the stern teacher throughout article 2, and most prominently in these sections, to correct enslaved and free Black Americans' internalized racism and self-oppression—that is, their harmful misunderstandings, through systematic miseducation and undereducation, of their capacities and duties to themselves, each other, and God—and to goad them all to act powerfully on what he teaches them about racial solidarity and their natural right, spiritual duty, and fully human capacity to resist oppression, using whatever means are necessary to gain their due freedom.

The last passage in the *Appeal* in which Walker most directly and clearly addresses his enslaved audience occurs near the end of article 4, where he declares that he has written his *Appeal* in very simple language and advises them, "Make the best you possibly can" of it (80). In the sentence that immediately follows this advice, Walker speaks to the possibility of their gaining freedom by way of emancipation rather than resistance. "Should tyrants take it into their heads to emancipate any of you," he advises, "remember that your freedom is your natural right." In explaining the basis of this right, he returns to the typographically emphasized and realized claim of Black people's basic humanity that he made in article 1, stating it once more, but this time with further explanation instead of added visual and aural emphasis: "You are men, as well as they, and instead of returning thanks to them for your freedom, return it to the Holy Ghost, who is our rightful owner" (80–81). For those who were enslaved by White men who "do not want to part with your labours, which have enriched them," Walker significantly changes his advice from the rightful and dutiful resistance urged in article 2 to keeping faith in divine deliverance: "Let them keep you, and my word for it, that God Almighty, will break their strong band." In place of scriptural support for this promise of eventual deliverance, Walker offers more of his own words: "Do you believe this, my brethren?—See my Address, delivered before the General Coloured Association of Massachusetts, which may be found in Freedom's Journal, for Dec. 20, 1828.—See the last clause of that Address. Whether you believe it or not, I tell you that God will dash tyrants, in combination with devils, into atoms, and bring you out from your wretchedness and miseries under these *Christian People!!!!!!*" (81).

Walker of course knew that enslaved people would have an extremely difficult, if not impossible, time obtaining a copy of *Freedom's Journal* to read his speech, and an even more difficult, if not impossible, time surviving slavery and keeping faith in their eventual deliverance. I read this self-citation within his specific advice to enslaved people, then, as another instance of Walker speaking to multiple audiences at once. With this reference, he more likely was directing his most literate Black readers—and most specifically Black activists in the North who had access to Black-published periodicals like *Freedom's Journal*—to track down his speech. He also likely was establishing for them his bona fides as an activist. With that in mind, we should also read it as a subtle reassurance to his enslaved audience that Black activists in the North were organized and publicly championing their cause, in antislavery newspapers that they published themselves and in large meetings with each other—that is, using their advantages to work for their enslaved brothers' and sisters' freedom, not just waiting for God to intercede or forgetting them and their plight.

In the paraphrase of his closing promise in his speech before the General Coloured Association of Massachusetts, which he offers in his *Appeal*, Walker significantly does not suggest when his enslaved readers should expect this ultimate divine intervention on their behalf. He knew—from both the American and Haitian Revolutions, both of which he invokes repeatedly in the *Appeal*—that self-liberating uprisings by oppressed people—be they White or Black, and much differently oppressed—were no more immediate than divine intervention. By contrast, in the speech he had delivered before a meeting of free Black activists in Massachusetts, and that free Black northerners read in *Freedom's Journal*, he suggests that God will end slavery in "a not very distant period," but also specifically acknowledges that "this, and perhaps another, generation may not experience the[se] promised blessings of Heaven."[37] In these differences between the two texts, we can clearly see how Walker tailored both his message and its delivery to his different audiences in their different circumstances. When speaking most directly to free Black activists in the North, he is more specific in his suggestion that the liberation of the enslaved may not come in either their lifetimes or those of the next generation. But when addressing enslaved people most directly, and White slaveholders and their abettors implicitly, he shifts from predicting the disheartening time frame of this millennial deliverance to emphasizing the force with which God will obliterate slavery and their enslavers, declaring that these sinful Christians will be smashed to atoms, and reinforcing this force with ironic italics and emphatic exclamation points.

In the next section, I turn to consider several passages in which Walker directly addresses and instructs his most literate free Black male readers to act in solidarity with both enslaved and free Black people who were less educationally and economically advantaged. As with the specific moments of addressing his enslaved audience, Walker knew that other audiences were reading these passages, too. Thus, we will see again how the text both mixes its messages and communicates clearly to different readers at the same time.

Appealing to "Men of colour, who are also of sense"

When Walker directly addresses the readers of his pamphlet who were most like himself—"men of colour, who are also of sense," as he designates them in article 2—he typically engages them textually, by invoking a specific text and reading it both with and for them. We have begun to see this pattern in the previous three sections of this chapter. In the notice to readers that he added to the third edition, he refers this class of readers to the two previous editions of his pamphlet. In exposing them to how much work there is to be done in educating their nominally free brethren and their children about the importance of education, and in calling on them "to do your utmost to enlighten them—*go to work and enlighten your brethren!*" he specifically invokes Murray's *English Grammar* as the necessary textbook for doing this work (33). And as we have just seen, when he addresses the painful problem of how some Black people are collaborating with White oppressors for their own profit at the expense of the entire race, he reprints a newspaper article.

These represent only a few of Walker's numerous textual engagements with his more educated and informed Black male readers that we find throughout the *Appeal*. In each of them, Walker models reading itself as a politically necessary and powerful act. In doing so, I want to suggest, Walker was himself working from a model of intellectual inquiry through close reading and textual engagement: Thomas Jefferson, and specifically query 6 in his *Notes on the State of Virginia*, which includes Jefferson's readings of and responses to European natural philosophers' writings about the fauna, flora, and peoples of the Americas as well as his most vigorous defense of

Americans of European descent as equal, if not superior to, Europeans.[38] In what follows, I focus on several of Walker's textual engagements, including with Jefferson's *Notes*, and offer close readings of Walker closely reading himself, as he wants his readers who are most like him to do.

I begin by returning to the newspaper article about the thwarted uprising of enslaved people in article 2, connecting it to Walker's explicit engagement with Jefferson's *Notes* in article 1. As noted previously, Walker dedicates much of his commentary on this incident, and specifically on the enslaved woman who assisted her White oppressors, perhaps surprisingly, to his most educated free Black male audience in the North. It is important to recall that the newspaper article and commentary come within article 2, which Walker devotes to the liberatory power and necessity of education and to the consequences of what he terms *ignorance*. While the story and incident overwhelm Walker affectively and occasion his most pointed advice to enslaved people to kill or be killed in their resistance, they also form a subtle but important part of Walker's extended engagement with Jefferson's widely read and influential claims in queries 6 and 14 of *Notes* about the intellectual, affective, moral, and political differences among Indigenous Americans and Americans of European and African descent.

In singling out the enslaved woman who helped her White owner and driver over her fellow Black and enslaved people in the incident, Walker holds her up not just for harsh criticism but also to his most advanced Black (and White) readers for intellectual consideration—specifically, as a specimen for testing Jefferson's claim that the "existence" of people of African descent in the United States "appears to participate more of sensation than reflection" (206). Walker begins his commentary on the newspaper article, "Here my brethren, I want you to notice particularly in the above article, the *ignorant* and *deceitful actions* of this coloured woman. I beg you to view it candidly, as for ETERNITY!!!!" After offering his synopsis of the incident, he asks, "Brethren, what do you think of this? Was it the natural *fine feelings* of this woman, to save such a wretch alive?" He makes it clearer that Jefferson's comparative claims about White Europeans and Americans in query 6 of *Notes* are driving this inquiry in the sentence that follows: "I know that the blacks, take them half enlightened and ignorant, are more humane and merciful than the most enlightened and refined European that can be found in all the earth" (28).[39]

Walker first invokes Jefferson in article 1 as important evidence for his argument about the exceptional evil of U.S. racial slavery, as part of his observation that no enslaved people in history have been told "that they were not of the *human family*" (12). While these early ethnological claims were made by several White European and American Enlightenment natural philosophers, Walker specifically pins them on Jefferson and his *Notes*, due to Jefferson's broad cultural influence as a natural philosopher and Founding Father and his own careful reading of Jefferson's book, not just for its arguments but also for how Jefferson thought and wrote. As Cheryl A. Wall puts it, "Above all other Americans, Jefferson personifies [the] denial" of "black people's humanity" for Walker (48). By way of a rhetorical question, Walker declares, "Has Mr. Jefferson declared to the world, that we are inferior to the whites, both in the endowments of our bodies and of minds?" Immediately following, he offers what I read as a moment of knowing condescension that he shares with his most learned Black peers toward the recently deceased Jefferson: "It is indeed surprising, that a man of such great learning, combined with such excellent natural parts, should speak so of a set of men in chains. I do not know what to compare it to, unless, like putting one wild deer in an iron cage, where it will be secured, and hold another by the side of the same, then let it go, and expect the one in the cage to run as fast as the one at liberty" (12–13).[40] Walker's model for what Ian Finseth calls this "parodic inversion of Jefferson's 'suspicion' regarding blacks' inferiority" (353), and, I would add, undermining Jefferson's authority with ironic praise was none other than Jefferson himself—particularly this challenge to George-Louis Leclerc, comte de Buffon, in query 6 of *Notes*: "I am induced to suspect, that there has been more eloquence than sound reasoning displayed in support of this theory [of species' degeneration in warmer climates]; that it is one of those cases where the judgment has been seduced by a glowing pen; and whilst I render every tribute of honor and esteem to the celebrated zoologist [Buffon], who has added, and is still adding so many precious things to the treasures of science, I must doubt whether in this influence he has not cherished error also, by lending her for a moment his vivid imagination and bewitching language" (97). Walker, by similarly feigning praise of Jefferson's sound reasoning abilities, but also affecting his own incomprehension—both of which Walker's peers immediately would have recognized as ironic—damningly critiques both the patent irrationality of Jefferson's own observations about racial difference in *Notes*, and how Jefferson uses Enlightenment scientific authority to represent the effects of the man-made institution of slavery as natural biological differences. After several more pages of engaging and countering these claims, Walker remarks to his most intellectual Black readers—again with an obviously affected modesty that they immediately would have recognized, or learned through his example, as a convention of gentlemanly scholarly discourse—that "Mr. Jefferson's very severe remarks on us have been so extensively argued upon by men whose attainments in literature, I shall never be able to reach." He then more pointedly informs his readers, "I would not have meddled with it, were it not to solicit each of my brethren, who has the spirit of a man, to buy a copy of Mr. Jefferson's 'Notes on Virginia,' and put it in the hand of his son," so that "blacks *themselves*," not Whites, will most powerfully refute its racist claims (17–18, emphasis in the original).

With this solicitation, we see Walker challenging his Black male readers and their sons with some education to advance their intellectual activism, by carefully reading and responding to this key text in racial and political science with their own contributions to learned discourse and debate. He is also inciting them to meet, if not exceed, the example that he is setting—for both them and Whites—as a living contradiction to Jefferson's claims of the natural inferiority of people of African descent. As Jarrett understands this incitement, Walker's "refutation of black inferiority per se was the least of his concerns. . . . After all, he already embodied the refutation. More salient was his critique of the cultural and political implications" of Jefferson's claims (30).

When we connect this initial, explicit engagement with Jefferson's *Notes* in article 1 to Walker's engagement with the newspaper story of the frustrated slave revolt in article 2, we can better understand how Walker uses the newspaper article to reach and teach his least educated Black readers a version of the same lesson. Through negative example, he instructs his enslaved readers in the best and only way to resist: they must kill or be killed, just as White Americans did in the Revolutionary War, not aid their oppressors out of sympathy for their suffering. And to his free and most educated Black readers he holds up the example of the enslaved woman–collaborator not just to challenge Jefferson's claims about essential racial difference but also, ultimately, to confront these readers with their own internalized racism. With his commentary, he seeks to disabuse them of any thoughts they might harbor that any Black people actually are essentially inferior to White people, that they as elites are fundamentally different from their enslaved sisters and brothers, or that any Black Americans are any less justified in resisting oppression for liberty than White Americans had been. Rooting out all such thoughts are the actions that Walker wants these "men of sense," most like himself, to take on themselves, so that they can lead the race to freedom by the example they set as intellectuals, and by putting their advantages to work on behalf of the entire race.

To drive this point home, and further rally all of his Black readers by way of negative textual example, Walker explicitly returns to Jefferson's *Notes* immediately after his kill-or-be-killed advice in article 2. After asking "What set of men can you point me to, in all the world, who are so abjectly employed by their oppressors, as we are by our *natural enemies?*" he quotes, cites, and adds typographical emphasis to Jefferson's most racist and consequential claims in *Notes*: "How could Mr. Jefferson but say, *'I advance it therefore as a suspicion only, that the blacks, whether originally a distinct race, or made distinct by time and circumstances, are *inferior* to the whites in the endowments of body and mind?'—'It,' says he, 'is not against experience to suppose, that different species of the same genius, or varieties of the same species, may possess different qualifications.' [Here, my brethren, listen to him.] ☞ 'Will not a lover of natural history, then, one who views the gradations in all the races of *animals* with the eye of philosophy, excuse an effort to keep those in the department of MAN as *distinct* as nature has formed them?'" (30–31). Again, by adding such emphasis, Walker is not merely quoting Jefferson but also guiding his more literate Black readers, who did not necessarily consider themselves to be intellectuals, in how to read and understand the logic and import of Jefferson's natural philosophical claims about racial difference and segregation in query 14. His effects here are adding strategic italics and small capitals to Jefferson's words, and intervening with his own words enclosed in brackets and a printer's index, both of which direct readers' attention to what he sees as the most crucial part of the argument. Notably, he also stops short of doing all the work for these readers, giving them, instead, an important homework assignment for further thinking and, likely, research: "I hope you will try to find out the meaning of this verse—its widest sense and all its bearings," following this hope with a stern warning "Whether you do or not, remember the whites do" (31).

We find another important such moment of guided textual analysis and politically engaged critique as its end in article 4, in which Walker argues against the colonization movement by closely reading not only several published procolonization speeches and an important Black counterargument but also, and first, his own text. To his introduction of an excerpt from a speech Henry Clay delivered at the founding meeting of the American Colonization Society (ACS), Walker added a footnote in the second and third editions, correcting the date of the meeting from 1826, as it was printed in the first edition, to 1816. This footnote serves as an important correction that makes clear just how long the colonization movement has been underway. It also reads as an example for his more educated readers of just how important it is to read closely, and find meaning in, all texts, including dates in his own pamphlet. With respect to reading more broadly, but still closely, he notes, "I have been for some time taking notice of this man's [Henry Clay's] speeches and public writings, but never to my knowledge have I seen any thing in his writings which insisted on the emancipation of slavery, which has almost ruined his country" (56). With this critique of Clay's political investments, Walker adds to the model of intellectual political activism for his more educated Black readers that he has prepared them for with his footnote: to be most effective, they must read not just closely but also widely and constantly to keep tabs on their opponents' public discourse and counter it with their own, accurate commentary.

After briefly challenging some passages in Clay's speech, Walker turns to a speech by "Mr. Elias B. Caldwell, Esq. of the District of Columbia, extracted from the same page on which Mr. Clay's will be found," and gets to even more impassioned exegetical work:

> Mr. Caldwell, giving his opinion respecting us, at that ever memorable meeting, he says: "The more you improve the condition of these people, the more you cultivate their minds, the more miserable you make them in their present state. You give them a higher relish for those privileges which they can never attain, and turn what we intend for a blessing into a curse." Let me ask this benevolent man, what he means by a blessing intended for us? Did he mean sinking us and our children into ignorance and wretchedness, to support him and his family? What he meant will appear evident and obvious to the most ignorant in the world ☞ See Mr. Caldwell's intended blessings for us, O! my Lord!! "No," said he, "if they must remain in their present situation, keep them in the *lowest state of degradation and ignorance*. The nearer you bring them to the condition of brutes, the better chance do you give them of possessing their *apathy*." (57–58)

Walker clearly means to infuriate his most educated and politically engaged Black readers with Caldwell's remarks; they reveal, even more explicitly than Jefferson's *Notes*, the extent to which White supremacy was deliberately weaponizing the brutalization of Black people in the United States to reinforce its effects as evidence of natural inferiority. He also makes explicit that this kind of engaged and outraged close reading is, and should be, hard work for even the most highly literate, including intellectuals: "Here I pause to get breath," he says immediately after quoting Caldwell, "having labored to extract the above clause of this gentleman's speech, at that colonization meeting." And he pointedly adds, "I presume that every body knows the meaning of the word '*apathy*,'—if any do not," he directs his somewhat educated Black readers who had access to books, "let him get Sheridan's Dictionary, in which he will find it explained in full" (58).

Walker continues this argument about the power of close and effortful intertextual reading by making it clear how White people were also weaponizing rhetoric and grammar as part of their efforts to ensure White supremacy: "To what length will not man go in iniquity when given up to a hard heart, and reprobate mind, in consequence of blood and oppression? The last clause of this speech, which was written in a very artful manner, and which will be taken for the speech of a friend, without close examination and deep penetration, I shall now present" (58). He then quotes the misleading passage in Caldwell's speech: "Surely, Americans ought to be the last people on earth, to advocate such slavish doctrines, to cry peace and contentment to those who are deprived of the privileges of civil liberty, they who have so largely partaken of its blessings, who know so well how to estimate its value, ought to be among the foremost to extend it to others."[41] Walker comments: "The real sense and meaning of the last part of Mr. Caldwell's speech is, get the free people of colour away to Africa, from among the slaves, where they may at once be blessed and happy, and those who we hold in slavery, will be contented to rest in ignorance and wretchedness, to dig up gold and silver for us and our children. Men have indeed got to be so cunning these days, that it would take the eye of a Solomon to penetrate and find them out" (58). That Walker has just such a Solomonic eye himself— and that he has used it not just to find out Caldwell but also to discover recent legislation that was passed and published in response to discoveries of his pamphlet circulating in the South—becomes even more apparent in a lengthy addition to the third edition that immediately follows this commentary.

Within this addition, Walker declares that, "very recently," God has "published some of their [White Christian Americans'] secret crimes on the house top, that the world may gaze on their Christianity and see of what kind it is composed" (59). He means *publication* here both figuratively and literally, drawing the following from newspapers (which he does not cite explicitly, because he is summarizing): "A law has recently passed the Legislature of this *republican* State (Georgia) prohibiting all free or slave persons of colour, from learning to read or write; another law has passed the *republican* House of Delegates, (but not the Senate) in Virginia, to prohibit all persons of colour, (free and slave) from learning to read or write, and even to hinder them from meeting together in order to worship our Maker!!!!!!" (59–60). With this, Walker not only reaffirms how alert his most educated and engaged Black readers must stay so that they can confront all the latest developments in White Americans' efforts to oppress Black Americans. He makes it clear that they must read *all* the news in newspapers and other periodicals, to discover and digest both the obvious and subtle means through which White supremacy is being reinforced and expanded throughout the United States and the world.

When the text returns to closely reading the book of American Colonization Society speeches after the inserted addition, Walker engages a speech by John Randolph in which Randolph raised the "very important and delicate question, which ought to be left as much as out of view as possible, (Negro Slavery.)*"[42] Within these parentheses, Walker makes visible precisely what Randolph wanted left out of view at the founding of the ACS. And to make it even more prominent that it is not just slavery, but also race and racism, that the colonization movement wished to hide in their motivations, Walker adds a note, signaled by the asterisk and first printed in the second edition: "*'Niger,' is a word derived from the Latin, which was used by the old Romans, to designate inanimate beings, which were black: such as soot, pot, wood, house &c. Also, animals which they considered inferior to human species, as a black horse, cow, hog, bird, dog, &c." After this etymology of *negro*—which he pointedly makes *nig[*]er*, instead of *negro*, in the footnote— he adds his own commentary: "The white Americans have applied this term to Africans, by way of reproach for our colour, to aggravate and heighten our miseries because they have their feet on our throats" (61).[43] In the second edition, this sentence ends with an additional clause: "and we cannot help ourselves" (2nd ed., 58). In the third edition, Walker deleted this clause. I read him as having done this, so that the footnote did not contradict his insistence throughout the *Appeal* that all Black Americans could and must help themselves.

In both the body of the text of article 4 and its footnotes, we thus see Walker modeling not just close but also intertextual encyclopedic reading—poring over the book of ACS speeches with a dictionary at hand (not the previously referenced Sheridan's, however, and uncited otherwise).[44] Through the example of himself, he makes it clear that these are the kinds of close, exhaustive, and exhausting readings that are required of his most educated Black readers as well—not just so that they are able to get to the root of the problem, linguistically, ideologically, and politically but also to discover what it will take to completely eradicate White supremacy, and not Black people, from the United States. As he concludes from his readings of the ACS speeches, "Here is a demonstrative proof, of a plan got up, by a gang of slaveholders to select the free people of colour from among the slaves, that our more miserable brethren may be the better secured in ignorance and wretchedness." This gang of slaveholders, of course, included Thomas Jefferson, whose consideration of emancipation in Virginia and the colonization of emancipated Black Virginians in query 14 of *Notes* occasions his most racist claims about racial difference in *Notes*. "This country is as much ours as it is the whites, whether they will admit it now or not, and they will see and believe it by and by," Walker ominously asserts at the end of his close readings of the ACS speeches, implicitly alluding to the apocalyptic race war that Jefferson anticipates in query 14 as inevitable if colonization does not follow emancipation (62).

So that racist White slaveholders and colonization supporters do not have the last word on the question of colonization in either public debate or his pamphlet, Walker reproduces part of a letter written by Bishop Richard Allen, founder of the African Methodist Episcopal Church, reverend of Mother Bethel Church in Philadelphia, and a major Black intellectual and political activist. Walker reproduces the letter from *Freedom's Journal*, the first Black-edited and Black-published newspaper and an important forum and resource for Black public intellectual and political debate, to which he was a contributor and for which he served as a subscription agent.[45] Allen's letter makes for *Freedom's Journal* and its readers a fuller version of the argument that Walker has just offered against colonization. Allen closes it by declaring, "This land which we have watered with our *tears* and *our blood*, is now our *mother country*, and we are well satisfied to stay where wisdom abounds and the gospel is free."[46] Walker—acknowledging that "thousands, and perhaps millions of my brethren in these States, have never heard of such a man as Bishop Allen"—lifts Allen and his work up after reprinting his letter: "Richard Allen! O my God!! The bare recollection of the labours of this man, and his ministers among his deplorably wretched brethren, (rendered so by the whites) to bring them to a knowledge of God and Heaven, fills my soul with all those very high emotions which it would take the pen of an Addison to portray" (65).

Here, again, we see Walker nearly overwhelmed by powerful emotions, but in this case, by positive ones because Allen exemplifies godly spiritual, intellectual, and political work for the entire race, rather than craven, "ignorant" work against it. Upon recovering, Walker continues: "My brethren, search after the character and exploits of this godly man among his ignorant and miserable brethren, to bring them to a knowledge of the truth as it is in our Master" (66). This, as I now see it, is the more traditional Romantic sublime moment in Walker's *Appeal*, in which "inertia becomes transport" and he is "hurried on as if 'by an irresistible force,'" leaving "behind a newly invigorated sense of identity" as the "experience recedes."[47] But here, as with every literary model on which he draws, Walker does not simply reproduce Romantic sublimity in his textual performance of it, he also subtly and significantly alters it—affectively and typographically so that he and the text respond powerfully to Allen's moving example—so that such sublimity fully represents the feelings, experiences, and potential of Black, and not just White, people.

In early 1831, the *Liberator* featured a spirited debate about Walker's pamphlet between two of the *Liberator*'s—and the *Appeal*'s—most educated and politically active Black readers writing to the *Liberator*, with Garrison commenting. This three-letter exchange, between a pseudonymous Leo of Philadelphia and J. I. W., who chose not to divulge his location, evinces how Walker's demonstrations of close reading worked to provoke these readers just as Walker sought, even as they debated whether he could have been the *Appeal*'s author. A January 21 letter from Leo to Garrison initiates the debate, with Leo explaining his reasons for doubting Walker as the *Appeal*'s author. He cites not only the capacious reading that it displays but also "the excellent criticisms upon the speeches of the most talented men of the age—all of which discover to us a greater degree of education than we have any reason to believe that he [Walker] possessed." He also specifically singles out the pamphlet's "unbounded praise" for Richard Allen, which we have just seen, as reason to doubt the literary judgment of its author, suggesting, without naming him, that Allen was "one whose name the political, the moral, and the religious world will be found equally indifferent about." With these specific references to the close readings of the ACS speeches and Allen's letter in article 4, Leo reveals that he has been closely reading Walker's performances of critique in the *Appeal*—not to take on White public intellectuals, but to discern whether the man reading and writing so encyclopedically and critically could have been the same man who has been represented to him as "vulgar."[48]

In the first issue of the *Liberator*, Garrison had praised Walker's *Appeal* as "one of the most remarkable productions of the age."[49] In replying four issues later to Leo's "incredulity," and vigorously defending Walker—because Walker was no longer alive to do so himself—Garrison expands on what he found exceptionally remarkable about the *Appeal*, noting that "Mr. Walker was personally unknown to us; but we are assured, by those who intimately knew him, that his Appeal was an exact transcript of his daily conversations." In specifically defending Walker's erudition, he declares that, "within the last four years, he was hurtfully indefatigable in his studies."[50] With this, Garrison suggests that Walker literally read and wrote himself to death—a claim that suggests how Garrison, too, was very closely reading this same section in article 4 of the *Appeal* and took particular note of the moment where Walker "pause[ed] to get breath, having labored to extract" the implied messages of the colonization speeches. Garrison likely knew from those who knew Walker personally that he had died of tuberculosis and, therefore, read Walker's pausing to get breath literally, as his response to Leo suggests.

A response from J. I. W. in the next issue of the *Liberator* goes even farther than Garrison's suggestion of self-sacrificing intellectualism, offering Walker's erudition and athletic displays of critical reading and intellectual debate as signs of his having been a heaven-sent messenger and martyr. "It seems to me that this writer [Leo] does not see in what manner God intends to perform his promises," J. I. W. writes before invoking Matthew 11:25: "'Thou hast hid these things from the wise and prudent, and hast revealed them unto babes.'"[51] In this brief but significant debate, conducted entirely in print and calling on print's authority, we see clearly how at least three of Walker's most educated and politically engaged Black and White readers deeply absorbed his *Appeal*'s lessons in close reading, applied them to the text itself, and put these skills to use in public political debate, even if to much different ends than Walker had intended.

Appealing to Barbers and Bootblacks

In contrast to the awe-inspiring example of Richard Allen, free Black working men "who are actuated by avarice only" particularly exasperate Walker with their self-satisfied contentment (34). He directs some of the most difficult messages in his *Appeal*, and some of his fiercest ire, in article 2, to this audience—free Black men who have achieved some degree of economic stability and established families, and who consider themselves and their families "free and happy" and ask "What have [I] to do with the wretched slaves and other people?" "Look into our freedom and happiness, and see of what kind they are composed!! They are of the very lowest kind—they are the very *dregs!*—they are the most servile and abject kind, that ever a people was in possession of!" he vehemently declares (33).

In this last section of article 2, Walker confronts an activist's most difficult task short of achieving the ultimate goal: unsettling those who have made some gains, become content, and settled, and who have thus separated themselves from the struggle of others who are not so modestly fortunate. As Walker recognizes, they also actively resist being politically disturbed and made discontent in their situation for fear of losing their hard-won, if modest, gains and their hopes of gaining more. His strategy for moving them is two-pronged: shake nominally free Black working men out of this contentment by confronting them with evidence of their unfreedom and insist on a liberal education as the true path for attaining "the salvation of our whole body"—that is, not just of the hands but also the heart and head, and not just enslaved people but all Black Americans (35).

Walker mostly tells this audience within his Black audience just what and how they should think. But he also shows them, specifically through negative examples that he presents through anecdotes. These anecdotes contrast with Walker's preferred mode of inquiry in most of the rest of the *Appeal*, which is decidedly empirical. He peppers the text with references to an "observer" who he imagines and presents as his Enlightenment-minded ideal reader for his "penetrating" first-person observations of life under slavery, and for his scholarly survey and exegesis of history books, the Bible, and many other forms of print. Of the signals that Walker sends with such language and their frequency in the text, Finseth argues that "from start to finish . . . the reader knows that the *Appeal* is not to be merely a fiery screed, though it is that, but a reasoned argument proceeding according to principles of evidence, induction, and analysis" (350). But just which readers specifically know this? As we have seen, Walker addresses the bulk of his findings to his most highly educated and more politically engaged Black men, writing more formally as he encourages these "men of sense" to work in the same mode, both to confirm his inquiries and conclusions as repeatable and to advance the work. In his most direct appeal to free Black working men, Walker offers anecdotal evidence, in the form of other ordinary working-class Black men he knows or has met in everyday life, to make his arguments about unfreedom and undereducation. He also writes in a markedly more conversational style. I read these strategic shifts as Walker's rhetorical equivalents of the spoonful of sugar that help his harshest lessons for this class of readers of his *Appeal* to go down more easily.[52]

The first anecdote Walker introduces is the story of a recent encounter with a bootblack: "I met a coloured man in the street a short time since, with a string of boots on his shoulders; we fell into conversation, and in the course of which, I said to him, what a miserable set of people we are! He asked, why?—Said I, we are so subjected under the whites, that we cannot obtain the comforts of life, but by cleaning their boots and shoes, old clothes, waiting on them, shaving them &c. Said he, (with the boots on his shoulders) 'I am completely happy!!! I never want to live any better or happier than when I can get a plenty of boots and shoes to clean!!!'" (34). Here, Walker holds up the bootblack as the representative of the nominally free Black working class and its contentment. That he is not just a didactic representative example or intellectual specimen but also an actual person Walker personally met in his daily life, is suggested in Walker's mention of dealing in used clothing among the forms of free Black men's subjection as workers. Walker ran a used clothing shop in Boston for income for himself and his family and worked as an activist—including researching, writing, editing his *Appeal*, and spending much of his earnings assisting Black people in need—in his free time.[53] When White critics of the *Appeal* publicly questioned whether Walker could have been its author, they pointed to his trade as evidence that it must have been written instead by a highly educated White person masquerading as Walker. An article in the March 22, 1830, *Boston Daily Courier* claimed that curiosity inspired by the panicked southern response to the pamphlet prompted the paper to seek out a copy. The article's author concludes,

> The thing is inflammatory enough, in all conscience; but he who believes it to have been written by David Walker, the dealer in old clothes in Brattle street, must have more abundant faith than falls to our humble share. It is not, cannot have been, the work of that man. There are too many allusions to names and incidents in ancient and classical history scattered through the pamphlet, to admit of such a belief. It has the appearance of being the work of an educated and well-read writer, endeavoring to conceal his real character, by affecting the style of an illiterate man, and endeavoring to keep down to the supposed level of the negro; but there is nothing which, in our apprehension, indicates the mind or the hand of an ignorant or unlearned man.[54]

The *Daily Courier* article underscores the truth of the claim that Walker makes immediately prior to the anecdote about the bootblack: "I am not a living man: or any man of colour, immaterial to who he is, or where he came from, if he is not *the fourth from the negro race!!* (as we are called) the white Christians of America will serve him the same they will sink him into wretchedness and degradation for ever while he lives" (33).

Walker makes clear here that he understands how White people see and treat all Black people monolithically.[55] He also confronts free Black working-class men for not understanding this—or for refusing to admit as much. Thus, we see him as sensitive—to a degree—to how they will receive both this message and the messenger: "Understand me, brethren, I do not mean to speak against the occupations by which we acquire enough and sometimes scarcely that, to render ourselves and our families comfortable through life. I am subjected to the same inconvenience, as you all" (34). With this, Walker both identifies himself and identifies with them, as a fellow worker. He knows of what he speaks, and speaks to them from the same place. But in that he refers to work as an "inconvenience" and writes here in more formal language than within the conversational anecdote, he sets himself apart at the same time. I read him as distinguishing himself no less purposefully than he deliberately identifies as and with the working class, so that he can offer himself as the positive workingman counterexample to the negative example of the bootblack and, thereby, deliver his most challenging messages about uplift:

> My objections, are to our *glorying* and being *happy* in such low employments; for if we are men, we ought to be thankful to the Lord for the past, and for the future. Be looking forward with thankful hearts

to higher attainments than *wielding the razor* and *cleaning boots and shoes*. The man whose aspirations are not *above*, and even *below* these, is indeed, ignorant and wretched enough. I advance it therefore to you, not as a *problematical*, but an unshaken and immoveable *fact*, that your full glory and happiness, as well as all other coloured people under Heaven, shall never be fully consummated, but with the *entire emancipation of your enslaved brethren all over the world*. . . . For I believe it is the will of the Lord that our greatest happiness shall consist in working for the salvation of our whole body. (34–35)

In this, we see Walker's shift from personal anecdote back to a statement of a priori fact—from telling the story of a representative contented Black bootblack to declaring it as an absolute fact that true freedom and happiness are impossible in a White supremacist slaveholding society/world. Only by working in solidarity to save the whole body—again, their minds as well as their hands, and enslaved and otherwise oppressed Black people—can all Black people hope to gain the ultimate salvation, Walker teaches here from what he has learned in both his trade and his studies.

After figuring this ultimate goal metaphorically—that is, Black solidarity and uplift as the "whole body"—shifting argumentative modes from a posteriori to a priori, and lecturing with authority at some length, Walker returns again to a conversational anecdote, this time to communicate his lesson about the critical importance of a liberal education. Casually noting that he "promiscuously fell in conversation once, with an elderly coloured man on the topics of education, and of the great prevalency of ignorance among us," he introduces the next class within the class of nominally free working-class Black men—those who have higher, but not quite high enough, hopes for the next generation and their education. He quotes this subclass's representative thus: "Said he, 'I know that our people are very ignorant but my son has a good education: I spent a great deal of money on his education: he can write as well as any white man, and I assure you that no one fool him,' &c." To correct the elderly man and his peers' simplistic—and likely generational—idea of what counts as an education, Walker turns the casual conversation into an aggressive interrogation of the elderly man that culminates in a harsh indictment: "Said I, what else can your son do, besides write in a good hand? Can he post a set of books in a mercantile manner? Can he write a neat piece of composition in prose or in verse? To these interrogations he answered in the negative. Said I, did your son learn, while he was at school, the width and depth of English Grammar? To which he also replied in the negative, telling me his son did not learn these things. Your son, said I, then, has hardly any learning at all—he is almost as ignorant, and more so, than many of those who never went to school one day in all their lives" (36). Walker closes the anecdote by noting that his "friend got a little put out" and "so walking off, said that his son could write as well as any white man." With this, Walker demonstrates by way of anecdotal example not just his lesson but also its reception and its ultimate rejection, due to both the unsettling nature of the message and its tough-love delivery by a younger, and more educated, man to an elder friend. Yet, rather than moderating his message and how he delivers it in response to this negative reaction, Walker doubles down on his indictment and his harsh tone, by generalizing from his elder friend to "most of the coloured people" who mistake good penmanship and its praise for a thorough education, and by unfolding the dire consequences of this mistake: "The poor, ignorant creature, hearing" that a good hand is a significant educational accomplishment, "is ashamed, forever after, to let any person see him humbling himself to another for knowledge but going about trying to deceive those who are more ignorant than himself, he at last falls an ignorant victim to death in wretchedness" (36–37).

After thus rhetorically reducing this partially educated and proud class within his Black audience to the lowest possible point, Walker offers up a prayer on their behalf that also serves as a lesson to them: "I pray that the Lord may undeceive my ignorant brethren, and permit them to throw away pretensions, and seek after the substance of learning." Then he offers himself as the model supplicant for such enlightenment: "I would crawl on my hands and knees through mud and mire, to the feet of a learned man, where I would sit and humbly supplicate him to instil into me, that which neither devils nor tyrants could remove, only with my life—for colored people to acquire learning in this country, makes tyrants quake and tremble on their sandy foundation" (37). Knowledge, as Walker presents it here to those too "ignorant" or proud to attempt anything beyond a basic education, is not only holy but also a powerful weapon that White Americans want to keep from all Black people to maintain their own supremacy. He also makes it clear how this weapon can and should be wielded, and by whom. He begins with educated Black men, who will make White Americans' "infernal deeds of cruelty . . . known to the world," just as Walker is doing with the pamphlet his readers have in hand. Then, by way of a rhetorical question, he presents education as the great equalizer and, thereby, what ultimately unsuits any man for chains and compels him to resist mercilessly: "Do you suppose one man of good sense and learning would submit himself, his father, mother, wife and children, to be slaves to a wretched man like himself, who, instead of compensating him for his labours, chains, and hand-cuffs and beats him and his family almost to death, leaving life enough in them, however, to work for, and call him master? No! no! he would cut his devilish throat from ear to ear, and well do slave-holders know it. The bare name of educating the coloured people, scares our cruel oppressors almost to death" (37). Having thus appealed directly to the masculinity of his free Black working-class audience, Walker returns to intellectual indictments, focusing next on prideful resistance to further education from some of the most educated among his Black readers, particularly indicting those who fancy and present themselves to others as know-it-alls.

The particular transgression for which Walker specifically and resentfully brands this class as "ignorant, vicious, and wretched men" is refusing to listen to him and other Black intellectuals like him. In their affected haughtiness, they set a powerful negative example for the most promising youth of the race, thereby "contribut[ing] almost as much injury to our body as tyrants themselves, by doing so much for the promotion of ignorance amongst us; for they, making such pretensions to knowledge, such of our youth are seeking after knowledge, and can get access to them, take them as criterions to go by." Rather than know-it-alls, Walker wants them to be—for themselves, future generations, and the good of the whole race—men of "good-breeding, sense and penetration"—the kind of intellectuals who, "if he had heard a subject told twenty times over, and should happen to be in company where one should commence telling it again, he would wait with patience on its narrator, and see if he would tell it as it was told in his presence before—paying the most strict attention to what is said, to see if any more light will be thrown on the subject" (38).

Here, we see Walker teaching close listening in addition to close reading, in recognition of how much knowledge was circulated and acquirable in conversation and in public, and not just in print and in classrooms—sites where structural and institutional racism limited access and participation. In doing so, he also acknowledges not just different learning opportunities and styles but different competencies as well, noting that "all men are not gifted alike in telling, or even hearing the most simple narration" (38). For his most intellectual readers, Walker also puts a further, finer point not only on his observation here but also on one of Jefferson's most significant claims about the intellectual—and, specifically, literary—limitations of people of African descent: "But never yet could I find a black that had uttered a thought above the level of plain narration."[56] Like Jefferson, Walker acknowledges that men have different God-given capacities in both narrating and listening to narrations. But unlike Jefferson, Walker makes it clear to his readers that these essential capacities are due to differences in individual minds, not distinctions between the races. Even so, Walker suggests, anyone with the will to practice the critical close listening and reading that he teaches here and throughout the *Appeal*—and to undertake wide and deep study of Murray's *English Grammar*, which he invokes in the next and last paragraph of article 2—can learn and improve their capacities, even to the astonishing heights that he models in what they are reading.

Appealing to "Americans"

As we have seen through this series of close readings, Walker is careful to distinguish among the several different audiences within his main audience of Black Americans and adapt his strategies for appealing to them accordingly. He makes no such fine distinctions within his White audience (except for his engagements with Jefferson), instead more frequently addressing them directly and generally as "Americans." This mode of address is no less strategic—it is Walker's rhetorical refusal to let White northerners off the hook for the national problems of slavery and racism. We see this broad indictment clearly at the beginning of article 1: "The white Americans having reduced us to the wretched state of *slavery*, treat us in that condition *more cruel* (they being an enlightened and Christian people,) than any heathen nation did any people whom it had reduced to our condition" (9). As this instance of what is also Walker's main indictment makes clear as well, the founding of the United States on both Enlightenment principles of natural rights and basic Christian principles makes all White Christian Americans exceptionally damnable for the great sacred and secular sin of racial slavery. Although he refers eight different times in the *Appeal* to White people as Black people's "natural enemies," and is no less inclined than Jefferson to make claims about the transhistorical, essential characteristics of people grouped by skin color—as we see when he declares that "whites have always been an unjust, jealous, unmerciful, avaricious and blood-thirsty set of beings, always seeking after power and authority" (20)—he also believes that White Christian Americans can be reformed and save themselves from divine judgment by ending slavery, as we see when he unambiguously states "I should like to see the whites repent peradventure God may have mercy on them" (24).[57]

Walker directs and repeats these primary messages of repentance and reform to his White audience several times.[58] He delivers the sacred message of repentance in some of the most jeremiadic passages in the *Appeal*, most prominently those in article 3, dedicated to "Our Wretchedness in Consequence of the Preachers of the Religion of Jesus Christ." Walker's debt to sensational evangelical preaching styles and theology—characteristic not only of Calvinism but also and more immediately the Methodism of the Second Great Awakening—is noticeably audible and visible in the following passage.[59] It comes immediately after Walker specifically indicts the White religious press for not addressing the sin of slavery in the pages of their "newspapers and monthly periodicals, which they receive in continual succession."

> Perhaps they will laugh at or make light of this; but I tell you Americans! that unless you speedily alter your course, *you* and your *Country are gone!!!!!!* For God Almighty will tear up the very face of the earth!!! Will not that very remarkable passage of Scripture be fulfilled on Christian Americans? Hear it Americans!! "He that is unjust, let him be unjust still:—and he which is filthy, let him be filthy still: and he that is righteous, let him be righteous still: and he that is holy, let him be holy still."* I hope that the Americans may hear, but I am afraid that they have done us so much injury, and are so firm in the belief that our Creator made us to be an inheritance to them for ever, that their hearts will be hardened, so that their destruction may be sure. This language, perhaps is too harsh for the American's delicate ears. But Oh Americans! Americans!! I warn you in the name of the Lord, (whether you will hear, or forbear,) to repent and reform, or you are ruined!!! (45)

Just as in his more secular didactic messages directed to his Black readers, his pastoral message here to White Americans includes both authoritative information and instructions for specific action, with both put in terms that this audience would readily understand, but also leaving them some interpretive work to do for themselves. By citing Revelation 22:11 in his asterisked footnote, Walker also implies to people who were well versed in the Bible the preceding and subsequent verses. Verse 10—"And he saith unto me, Seal not the sayings of the prophecy of this book: for the time is at hand"—suggests that the millennium is imminent. And verse 12—"And, behold, I come quickly; and my reward is with me, to give every man according as his work shall be"—contains Christ's promise of judgment and its consequences for all.[60] For a Black man to be preaching repentance so sensationally to White Americans, and both implying and promising that their demise was imminent unless they immediately end the sin of racial slavery, was provocative in itself, as Walker himself acknowledges within the passage—"This language, perhaps is too harsh for the American's delicate ears." But in that the language he specifically calls them to hear is familiar scripture and the affect with which it is preached is also familiarly evangelical, he ensures that their rejection of this message and call to spiritual duty will be a refusal of Christ's words and church, not of a specific Black man's words and his individual style of delivery.

At the culmination of the *Appeal*, Walker once again commands White Americans to "hear"—and this time to "see" as well—as he cites chapter and verse. In his closing lesson to them on the great wrongs of slavery and racism, the scripture he invokes is secular—the Declaration of Independence. As a founding text, its authority is thus no less venerated by his White audience.[61] What he initially reprints from the Declaration is typographically unremarkable in all three editions of the *Appeal*. (See Figure 3.) But immediately following the sentence claiming Americans' right and duty to revolt against absolute despotism with which the excerpt concludes, Walker's text restarts with rhetorical, punctuational, and typographical fireworks as he repeats passages from the Declaration:

> See your declaration Americans!!! Do you understand your own language? Hear your language, proclaimed to the world, July 4th, 1776—☞ "We hold these truths to be self evident—that ALL MEN ARE CREATED EQUAL!! that they *are endowed by their Creator with certain unalienable rights*; that among these are life, *liberty*, and the pursuit of happiness!!" Compare your own language above, extracted from your Declaration of Independence, with your cruelties and murders inflicted by your cruel and unmerciful fathers and yourselves on our fathers and us—men who have never given your fathers or you the least provocation!!!!!!

Hear your language further! ☞ "But when a long train of abuses and usurpation, pursuing invariably the same object, evinces a design to reduce them under absolute despotism, it is their *right*, it is their *duty*, to throw off such government, and to provide new guards for their future security" (85).

These accusing indexes and exclamation points—at their most imperative, emphatic, outraged—are consistent across the three editions, as are Walker's typographical alterations of the text of the Declaration. The all caps and small caps and the italics visually signal how Walker voiced its key words that all Americans—Black and White—needed to hear when he spoke them.[62]

As I have argued previously, these typographic effects allow Walker to effectively rewrite the Declaration according to his interpretation, even as he quotes its language word for word.[63] They also graphically effect on the page Walker's demand that White Americans both "hear" and "see" their Declaration as he does and, thus, understand it as he does: the full capitalization of "all" and "equal" visually distinguishes the two most important words in the most important sentence of the document; "men are created" in small caps heightens the clause's significance as well, but without diminishing visually or argumentatively the equivalence of "all" and "equal."

"Do you understand your own language?" Walker demands of White Americans as a whole and—given his previous challenges to Jefferson in the *Appeal*—of the Declaration's author specifically, if only rhetorically, given Jefferson's death in 1826. So that misunderstanding would no longer be possible for either White or Black audiences, Walker again typographically stresses how this crucial language should be properly emphasized when reading—particularly those reading it aloud ("Hear your language"). Italicizing the claim that these all-equal men are divinely endowed with unalienable rights, "liberty" alone among these rights, and "right" and "duty" in the charge to overthrow despotic governments further rules out any confusion, deliberate or accidental. Here, at the conclusion of his *Appeal*, both seeing and hearing this all-important language, as Walker both visually and verbally emphasizes in his reprinting of the Declaration, are key to all of Walker's readers understanding its incontrovertible meaning. For Walker, the verbatim language of the nation's founding—activated by the graphic form that this language takes

Not satisfied with this, my Lord!
They throw us in the seas:
Be pleas'd, we pray, for Jesus' sake,
To save us from their grasp.

We believe that, for thy glory's sake,
Thou wilt deliver us;
But that thou may'st effect these things,
Thy glory must be sought.

In conclusion, I ask the candid and unprejudiced of the whole world, to search the pages of historians diligently, and see if the Antideluvians—the Sodomites—the Egyptians—the Babylonians—the Ninevites—the Carthagenians—the Persians—the Macedonians—the Greeks—the Romans—the Mahometans—the Jews—or devils, ever treated a set of human beings, as the white Christians of America do us, the blacks, or Africans. I also ask the attention of the world of mankind to the declaration of these very American people, of the United States.

A declaration made July 4, 1776.

It says, *"When in the course of human events,
"it becomes necessary for one people to dissolve
"the political bands which have connected them
"with another, and to assume among the Powers of
"the earth, the separate and equal station to which
"the laws of nature and of nature's God entitle
"them. A decent respect for the opinions of mankind
"requires, that they should declare the causes which
"impel them to the separation.—We hold these
"truths to be self evident—that all men are created
"equal, that they are endowed by their Creator
"with certain unalienable rights: that among these,
"are life, liberty, and the pursuit of happiness that,
"to secure these rights, governments are instituted
"among men, deriving their just powers from the

---

* See the Declaration of Independence of the United States.

AN APPEAL, ETC. 85

" consent of the governed; that whenever any form
" of government becomes destructive of these ends, it
" is the right of the people to alter or to abolish it,
" and to institute a new government laying its
" foundation on such principles, and organizing its
" powers in such form, as to them shall seem most
" likely to effect their safety and happiness. Pru-
" dence, indeed, will dictate, that governments long
" established should not be changed for light and
" transient causes; and accordingly all experience
" hath shewn, that mankind are more disposed to
" suffer, while evils are sufferable, than to right
" themselves by abolishing the forms to which they
" are accustomed. But when a long train of abu-
" ses and usurpations, pursuing invariably the same
" object, evinces a design to reduce them under abso-
" lute despotism, it is their right it is their duty to
" throw off such government, and to provide new
" guards for their future security." See your Declaration Americans!!! Do you understand your
own language? Hear your language, proclaimed
to the world, July 4th, 1776— ☞ " We hold these
" truths to be self evident—that ALL MEN ARE
" CREATED EQUAL!! that they *are endowed by*
" *their Creator with certain unalienable rights;* that
" among these are life, *liberty*, and the pursuit of
" happiness!!" Compare your own language
above, extracted from your Declaration of Independence, with your cruelties and murders inflicted by your cruel and unmerciful fathers and
yourselves on our fathers and on us—men who have
never given your fathers or you the least provocation!!!!!!

Hear your language further! ☞ " But when a
" long train of abuses and usurpation, pursuing
" invariably the same object, evinces a design to re-
" duce them under absolute despotism, it is their
" *right*, it is their *duty*, to throw off such govern-
" ment, and to provide new guards for their future
" security."

Figure 3. Walker's *Appeal*, 3rd ed. (1830), pp. 84–85.

as he directed it to be reprinted and read aloud—stand as both the final lesson of and ultimate authority for his *Appeal*: it is White Americans' duty to make good on their own Declaration's statement of Black people's equality and liberty by putting an end to the "long train of abuses and usurpation" of slavery, thereby "throw[ing] off" their own "absolute despotism" over Black Americans before Black Americans fulfill this "*right*" and "*duty*" themselves in a necessary, and divinely inspired and sanctioned, second American Revolution.[64]

Responses to Walker's *Appeals*

All of these rhetorically strategic aspects of Walker's pamphlet—and especially his implicit messages to White slaveholders in his direct addresses to enslaved people and the graphically confrontational appearance of the printed text—moved it to the center of southern legislation and northern debates regarding resistance to slavery. That is to say, the didactic and specifically textual strategies that Walker used to address his different audiences, convey his lessons, and call them to specific actions produced real-world effects, including significant legislation by powerful White people to limit freedoms of speech and mobility for enslaved and free Black people in the South. In a lengthy footnote he added near the conclusion of the final edition of his *Appeal*, Walker directly acknowledges and touts the impact that his pamphlet had already made:

> Why do the Slave-holders or Tyrants of America and their advocates fight so hard to keep my brethren from receiving and reading my Book of Appeal to them?—Is it because they treat us so well?—Is it because we are satisfied to rest in Slavery to them and their children?—Is it because they are treating us like men, by compensating us all over this free country!! for our labours?—But why are the Americans so very fearfully terrified respecting my Book?—Why do they search vessels, &c. when entering the harbours of tyrannical States, to see if any of my Books can be found, for fear that any of my brethren will get them to read? Why, I thought the Americans proclaimed to the world that they are a happy, enlightened, humane, and Christian people, all the inhabitants of the country enjoy equal Rights!! America is the Asylum for the oppressed of all nations!!! (82)

Here—once again directly addressing his Black audience and, thereby, indirectly addressing White southerners—Walker represents his "Book" not so much as a weapon but as a personified agent in itself, stealthily traveling into the South to speak directly with enslaved people and, by doing so, provoking White Americans to restrict civil liberties in ways that exposed slavery's perversion of the nation's most basic founding principles.

After paraphrasing these principles, he then posits that the most dangerous thing contained within his *Appeal* is not his words but rather White Americans' own—specifically the language of the Declaration of Independence, which he quotes again in the footnote to make it clear that his pamphlet has only made its, and not his, message of the duty of resisting tyranny more widely available with its partial reprinting in article 4. "But perhaps the Americans do their very best to keep my Brethren from receiving and reading my 'Appeal' for fear they will find in it an extract which I made from their Declaration of Independence," he pointedly speculates. Lest an opportunity be missed to restate and, thus, reactivate both that text's and his text's fundamental statements of equality, he repeats the former: "'We hold these truths to be self-evident, that all men are created equal,' &c. &c. &c." (82). In this note added to the third edition, Walker presents the declared truth of God-given equality as self-evident—that is, without adding any special typographical effects. That he was able to do so points up the confidence that he had not only in the validity of the nation's founding principles, even if they had yet to be fully realized, but also in his *Appeal*'s success in already having realized many of his most important aims before he published its final edition.

Although many of the *Appeal*'s readers—from fearful nineteenth-century slaveholding White Americans to some recent editors and scholars of the pamphlet—have focused primarily on the threat of violent action in and promoted by it, we have seen how carefully Walker crafted it to communicate other primary lessons and to provoke a range of meaningful and powerful actions in response from its different audiences.[65] In looking beyond violence, scholars have come to an array of conclusions about both the means and ultimate ends of Walker's *Appeal*. With respect to the latter, Finseth argues that the *Appeal* is "a text intended to provoke its readers to practical action," but concludes that "Walker really was not certain in his own mind what he envisioned"—a violent revolution by the enslaved or their divine deliverance—and sees an "ambiguity in the text [that] is heartfelt but not deliberate, a product of the horizons he described in his own argument" (355, 358). Robert S.

Levine suggests that "there is virtually nothing in the *Appeal* suggestive of U.S. whites' willingness or ability to conceive of blacks as human beings, to listen to what they have to say, or to consider them as possible friends or fellow citizens." From this, he concludes, "Walker's avowed hopes for a development that he must know will not occur in the immediate future can be interpreted as a moment of counterfactual narration, an attempt to imagine or create a different history from what he suspects will be the social reality at the time of the *Appeal*'s publication."[66] Tara Bynum puts Walker's aims and his texts' effects more positively, immediately, and concretely: Walker's "anger and his call for anger pursue a reconciliation that promises a way to feel good," and his *Appeal* "compels readers to accept what makes life real, material, and worth living" (14). And Elizabeth McHenry argues that Walker succeeded in not simply imagining and promising a different history but also in creating one: "the impact of the *Appeal* on the black population in the United States was irrefutable, regardless of whether it was read privately by a literate individual or heard by one without the ability to read" (36). Douglas A. Jones Jr. expands this claim significantly to assert that "the *Appeal* and its popularity signify the antebellum black public sphere's horizon of possibility and its ever-forming national collectivity" (63).

This range of scholarly responses to Walker's *Appeal* and its effects, I conclude, are themselves effects of reading more generally than closely to distinguish among Walker's subaudiences, his rhetorical strategies for reaching them, and the specific actions he wanted them to take to achieve different goals. Reading closely allows us to discern his *Appeal* as both a grammar and an encyclopedia of slavery and racism. As we have seen in this chapter, the striking punctuation and typography of the *Appeal* are only the most visible sites and signs of Walker's textual strategies for reaching different readers and moving them to resist. I hope this more comprehensive analysis of the text's multifaceted strategies helps us understand with greater nuance the different ways that Walker's *Appeal* worked to reach, teach, and motivate his multifaceted audiences to do the work of resisting powerfully and making a different social reality. For Walker and his readers, this work includes reading, listening, studying, critiquing—all done as athletically and exhaustively as possible—and resisting violently, if necessary.

Near the conclusion of her reading of Walker's *Appeal*, McHenry tantalizingly suggests that "the story of the *Appeal* points to the tentative beginnings of a cooperative system for the distribution of knowledge and pertinent information in antebellum black communities" (36–37). With this in mind, I also hope that the close readings presented in this chapter help us begin to understand in more detail just how Walker's *Appeal* specifically worked to move several writers of color to get to work themselves, on behalf of others like them. The chapters that follow are dedicated to these writers, their pamphlets, and the significant individual and collective work done in and by these works.

CHAPTER 2

Immediate Effects

William Lloyd Garrison's *Liberator* and Maria W. Stewart's
Religion and the Pure Principles of Morality

This chapter focuses on the most local and immediate, yet substantial textual responses to Walker's *Appeal*: William Lloyd Garrison's antislavery newspaper the *Liberator* and Maria W. Stewart's pamphlet *Religion and the Pure Principles of Morality: The Sure Foundation on Which We Must Build*, both published by Garrison in Boston in 1831. Scholars regularly associate Walker, Garrison, and Stewart as Boston contemporaries and the *Appeal*, the *Liberator*, and Stewart's publications and lectures as pivotal texts in the shift to radical antislavery.[1] This chapter goes deeper than their temporal, geographic, and political proximity, looking closely and comparatively at Walker's and Stewart's pamphlets and Garrison's newspaper to examine how Stewart and Garrison differently managed the powerful influence of Walker's *Appeal* in the texts they produced after encountering the pamphlet. In doing so, I recover a more complex relationship among these publications and their audiences than has been recognized. I argue that we should consider them not just as locally and politically associated but as inextricably, if figuratively, bound together—by their shared words and arguments, their rhetorical and visual resemblance to each other, and the material and legal conditions of printing and circulating antislavery and antiracism texts in the wake of both the last edition of Walker's *Appeal* in 1830 and the uprising led by Nat Turner in August 1831. We will also see how these writers and their works not only maintained but also foregrounded important distinctions among them in the interest of advancing specific political and moral arguments that spoke to and for different audiences within antislavery and

African American print cultures, even as they visibly manifest a shared connection to Walker's *Appeal* and its radicalism.

In the first half of the chapter, I look closely at specific articles and numbers of the *Liberator* from the first year of its publication in which Garrison strategically incorporated elements of Walker's pamphlet in his newspaper's pages by both reprinting excerpts from the *Appeal* as part of the *Liberator*'s early content and imitating the rhetorical style and the visual appearance of Walker's pamphlet, even as he condemned its message. In articles responding to the uprising of enslaved people led by Turner and covering heated southern discussions about "incendiary" publications, Garrison's insistent association of the *Liberator* with Walker's *Appeal* becomes especially visible. While antebellum southerners and later historians have recognized the geographical, temporal, activist community connections between Walker's pamphlet and Garrison's paper, I will show how Garrison specifically and deliberately imitated both the look and rhetoric of Walker's *Appeal* to draw greater attention to his fledgling paper, regardless of whether it took the form of scorn or support. These efforts provoked concrete and important responses from southern and northern, and White and Black, readers: southern states passed laws attempting to restrict the circulation of so-called incendiary print originating from the North, specifically pairing and citing Walker's *Appeal* and Garrison's *Liberator* as evidence of a concerted northern effort to infiltrate their states and foment slave rebellion.[2] At the same time, Black readers sustained Garrison's paper during its vulnerable first year, not only as the majority of the *Liberator*'s paying subscribers but also as substantial contributors to its content.[3] With the only Black-published newspapers recently having ceased publication due to financial hardship, the *Liberator* filled a significant void for Black readers and writers who had the means to be paying subscribers. One of these Black Bostonian readers, Maria Stewart, personally visited Garrison to ask if he would read and publish her Walker-influenced writings aimed at Black women, which he enthusiastically printed as the pamphlet *Religion and the Pure Principles of Morality* in October 1831 and sold from the *Liberator*'s office.[4]

In transitioning to focus on Stewart's pamphlet in the second half of the chapter, I briefly consider how *Religion and the Pure Principles of Morality* provided Garrison with a unique opportunity to deepen his and his newspaper's association with Walker and his *Appeal* while maintaining a strategic distance from both. As Cheryl A. Wall has observed, "Walker's rhetoric, no less than his personal example, inspired [Stewart]. Her words, like his, inscribed an unbreakable connection between the spiritual and political realms."[5] Even so, the impassioned pamphlet she wrote in response to his is also significantly distinct in being written by a woman and focusing on Black women's religious practice, morality, and gender roles more than on militant Black masculinity and White Christian hypocrisy. As we will see, Garrison recognized in Stewart not just a female version of Walker but also a potential Phillis Wheatley he would be both credited with discovering and condemned for publishing.

For her part, Stewart wrote with the same motive and with no less urgency than Walker. Her call to action specifically addresses free Black women in the North—a population within the "coloured citizens of the world" that Walker largely had neglected. The second half of the chapter is dedicated to Stewart's didactic pamphlet and foregrounding the specific set of actions she urges these Black women to take to improve and ultimately free themselves spiritually, morally, and intellectually, following the same path she had taken in becoming a Christian, activist, and published writer. In our time, feminist scholars have recognized Stewart as "the founding voice of feminist theory" whose "work is beginning to command its own canon of interpretation."[6] With respect for Stewart's feminism, I offer a new reading of her program for liberation specifically in light of her connection with both Walker and Garrison, which made it possible for her message to be brought into print.

More specifically, at several points in the text of *Religion and the Pure Principles of Morality*, Stewart both argues for and models different kinds of imitation—spiritual, pedagogical, and aesthetic—of the virtuous examples of others as necessary transitional steps on the path to ultimate spiritual, intellectual, and practical self-liberation. She urges Black women to "imitate the character of the meek and lowly Jesus" according to the Christian tradition of imitatio Christi that Methodism encouraged (6). Like Walker, she also presents earthly examples of exceptionally good behavior, earnest labor, and intellectual development as worthy of pedagogical and aesthetic imitation—most notably, David Walker himself. At the same time, Stewart is careful to establish limitations on the imitation of even the most virtuous human examples, in that all men and women necessarily fall short of the example of Christ. As she sees it, the "daughters of Africa" must transition from "slumber" to being fully "awake!" through their strategic imitation of worthy role models that allows them to develop and fulfill their own "noble and exalted faculties" and, ultimately, "distinguish [them]selves" (3). With this, we see how, for Stewart, "the gap between promise and fulfillment registers as a primarily female space sustained by women's work and women's culture," as Carla L. Peterson has argued.[7] As we will see in *Religion and the Pure Principles of Morality*, Stewart concludes that the fulfillment of Black people's potential is free northern Black women's ultimate work. By learning through their imitation of powerful examples of self-assertion—not only to realize their own spiritual and intellectual self-development but also to exemplify it for their children, who will reproduce their mothers' examples—Black women have the power to liberate the entire race, Stewart asserts.

With respect to Stewart's practice as an activist-writer and how it relates to her feminist claim about Black women's power, I closely examine how she followed Walker's model of fierce commitment to the cause of Black liberation and of the significant self-education and intellectual inquiry that underwrites his activism and his *Appeal*. We will also see how she borrowed aspects of the *Appeal*'s language and rhetoric in writing her own pamphlet with its distinct message. I argue that Stewart, through her close study of the *Appeal*, developed her own powerful rhetorical voice but also came to recognize that even the "noble, fearless, and undaunted DAVID WALKER" was fallible, specifically because he only imagined Black men as the ultimate agents of Black liberation. Put most simply, by both following and moving away from Walker's powerful but limited example with her own pamphlet, Stewart not only appeals to Black women as the unaddressed half of Walker's "coloured citizens of the world" but also realizes her crucial feminist revision of his main argument: that Black women, more than Black men, will be the main agents of Black liberation, as God's instruments.

I have organized this chapter chronologically, starting with Garrison's *Liberator* as a response to Walker's *Appeal*, followed by Stewart's *Religion and the Pure Principles of Morality* as a response to both Walker's pamphlet and Garrison's newspaper. Yet neither the chapter's organization, nor its main argument about the utility of imitation to Stewart as a writer and activist, should be understood to make Stewart's theories of Black liberation or her literary and political work secondary or inferior to those of her male peers. I want to underscore here how her pamphlet both argues for and exemplifies a feminist theory of self-assertion that is founded on connections with others and ultimately strengthens these connections and community through productive recognitions and negotiations of difference. Thus, in this chapter, I apply Stewart's own feminist theory of imitation and differentiation to recognize and negotiate the important connections and productive differences among Walker's, Garrison's, and her works.

Garrison's and the *Liberator*'s Debts

Garrison published the first number of the *Liberator* in Boston on New Year's Day in 1831, just nine months after Walker published the third and last edition of his *Appeal* in early March 1830.[8] Garrison had returned to his native Massachusetts from Baltimore where he had been editing and publishing the *Genius of Universal Emancipation* with Benjamin Lundy. In deciding to publish his own antislavery newspaper, he had initially planned to do so from Washington, D.C., but Walker's *Appeal* had trained all eyes on Boston as a hotbed of antislavery print and activism, and the controversy over the *Appeal* surely factored in Garrison's decision to publish the *Liberator* there instead.[9] The *Liberator* filled a void for the free Black communities of the North by advocating the antislavery cause after the first Black-published newspaper, *Freedom's Journal*, and its successor, *Rights of All*, had ceased publication in New York City in 1829 and 1830, respectively.[10] In the first number of the paper, Garrison announced of his purpose, "I am in earnest—I will not equivocate—I will not excuse—I will not retreat a single inch—AND I WILL BE HEARD."[11] On its third page, he also included a brief notice titled "Walker's Pamphlet," reporting on North Carolina's legal response to the best-known Black publication up to that point, and promising his own response to it in a future number of the *Liberator*: "The Legislature of North Carolina has lately been sitting with closed doors, in consequence of a message from the Governor relative to the above pamphlet. The south may reasonably be alarmed at the circulation of Mr. Walker's Appeal; for a better promoter of insurrection was never sent forth to an oppressed people. In a future number, we propose to examine it, as also various editorial comments thereon—it being one of the most remarkable productions of the age. We have already publicly deprecated its spirit."[12] With what effectively functions as an advertisement for both Walker's pamphlet and his own newspaper, Garrison here yokes together what he presents as Walker's already-familiar *Appeal* and his fledgling *Liberator* as well as the *Liberator* and the earliest and then longest-running U.S. antislavery periodical, Lundy's *Genius of Universal Emancipation*, in which Garrison had "publicly deprecated" the spirit of Walker's pamphlet as its interim editor in 1830.[13]

Garrison made good on his promise to return to Walker's *Appeal* just a week later in the second number of the *Liberator*. There, he again "deprecate[s] the spirit and tendency of this Appeal," only to make a startling claim for someone committed to moral suasion as the only justifiable means of ending slavery: "Nevertheless, it is not for the American people, as a nation, to denounce it as bloody or monstrous. Mr. Walker but pays them in their own coin, but follows their own creed, but adopts their own language." Garrison continues with his mixed message that simultaneously invokes and condemns violence:

> *We* do not preach rebellion—no, but submission and peace. Our enemies may accuse us of striving to stir up the slaves to revenge: but their accusations are false, and made only to excite the prejudices of the whites, and to destroy our influence. We say, that the possibility of a bloody insurrection at the south fills us with dismay; and we avow, too, as plainly, that if any people were ever justified in throwing off the yoke of their tyrants, the slaves are that people. It is not we, but our guilty countrymen, who put arguments into the mouths, and swords into the hands of the slaves. Every sentence that they write—every word that they speak—every resistance that they make, against foreign oppression, is a call upon their slaves to destroy them.[14]

In speaking here in the first person plural ("Our enemies"), Garrison speaks for all antislavery print, thereby firmly, if prematurely, associating himself and the *Liberator* with Walker and his *Appeal*. Given the notoriety of Walker's *Appeal* in southern and northern newspaper coverage, editors of the one hundred newspapers with which Garrison had strategically established an exchange relationship—particularly those that supported slavery—would have been acutely sensitive to the *Liberator*'s coverage of the pamphlet.[15] Yet, with only one number of the *Liberator* having been published at that point, and only a week before the publication of this article, there would have been little time for "enemies" to assert themselves as Garrison's specifically.[16]

When southern newspapers and legislatures began to recognize and challenge Garrison as an enemy and the *Liberator* specifically as a firebrand in late January 1831—and even more so after Nat Turner's uprising in August 1831—they, too, insistently connected Walker's pamphlet and Garrison's newspaper as invasive and dangerous print. Garrison frequently and eagerly reprinted reports of this suppression in the *Liberator*. One appears under the *Appeal*-like headline "**THREE CURIOSITIES!!!**" in the October 22, 1831, number, quoting an article from the Charleston *Mercury*: "'The "Vigilance Association of Columbia," S.C. composed of gentlemen of the first respectability have offered a reward of FIFTEEN HUNDRED DOLLARS for the apprehension and prosecution to conviction, of any white person who may be detected in distributing or circulating within that State the newspaper called "The Liberator," printed in Boston, or the pamphlet called "Walker's Pamphlet," or any other publication of seditious tendency.'" Never missing an opportunity to convert bad publicity into good, or to make a pitch for more subscribers, Garrison follows the reprinted story with his editorial estimation of the offered reward: "'Fifteen hundred dollars!' A pretty liberal sum. But, without vanity or boasting, we think the numbers of the Liberator are worth more money, although we charge only two dollars per annum! We shall expect a large increase of subscribers forthwith."[17] With such articles, Garrison strategically forged, not simply reported on, this link between Walker's *Appeal* and his *Liberator*. By regularly including such news about attempts to restrict the circulation of both publications throughout the rocky first year of the *Liberator*'s existence, he successfully provoked both southern ire and further legislation that Walker's *Appeal* had incited and, in turn, attracted northern Black and White supporters interested not only in antislavery but also in defending a free press.[18]

Garrison solidified the link between Walker's well-known pamphlet and his ambitious newspaper by imitating the striking look of the *Appeal* in the pages of the *Liberator*. He was both the paper's editor and one of its compositors in its earliest days, and in both roles, I argue, he adopted Walker's characteristic use of italics, all capitals, multiple exclamation points, and pointing indexes—as we saw in the headline above and in the other examples pictured here (see Figures 4 and 5)—to add emphasis to some of the most sensational news about slavery to which he wanted to draw readers' attention and indignation. As Augusta Rohrbach has observed, "Form follows content in the *Liberator*." "One of the first things that a nineteenth-century reader would have noticed is the use of italics, boldface, and capital letters," she rightly suggests. Yet, while Rohrbach sees "Garrison's efforts [as] carefully calculated according to the emerging principles of advertising," I contend that Walker's striking use of punctuation and typographical emphasis, discussed in the previous chapter, was both a more immediate and relevant influence on Garrison.[19] This is not to suggest that Garrison and Walker were not both drawing from the sensationalism of antebellum print advertising to some degree in attending to the visual registers of their texts. But I do want to foreground Walker's integration of his text's striking rhetoric and visual form as directly affecting how Garrison sensationalized not only the controversial contents but also the confrontational typesetting of the *Liberator* on the model of Walker's "remarkable" *Appeal,* even as he "deprecated its spirit."[20]

That Garrison strategically forged an identity between the *Liberator* and Walker's *Appeal* that could be perceived with just a glance made them equally deadly weapons in the eyes of southerners. Lawmakers and vigilantes alike were anxious to control the entry and circulation of what they saw as such potentially dangerous publications in their states if they could not legally thwart their publication in the North. Upon discovering copies of

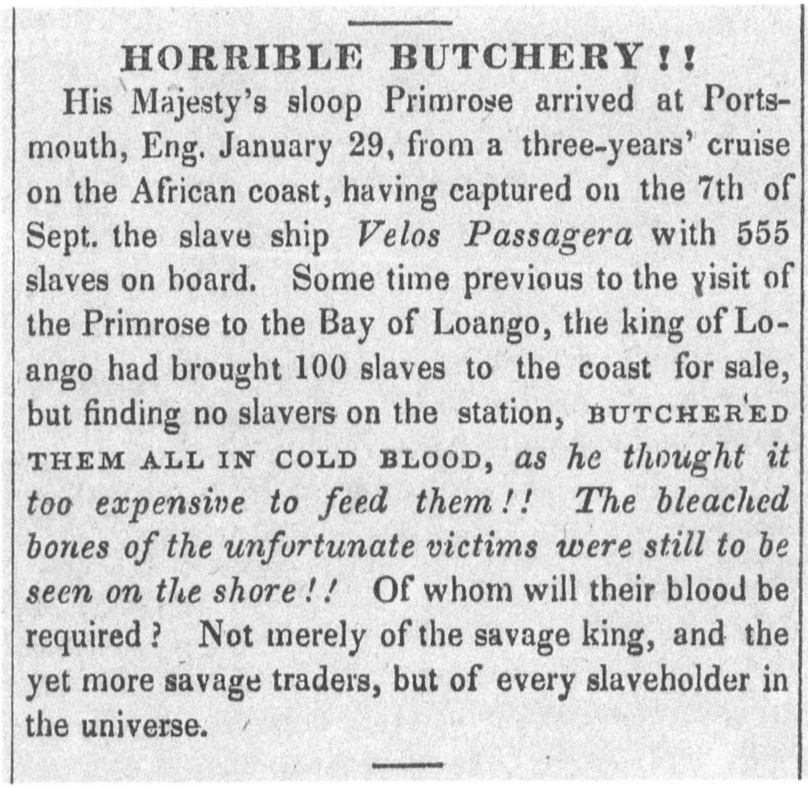

HORRIBLE BUTCHERY!!

His Majesty's sloop Primrose arrived at Portsmouth, Eng. January 29, from a three-years' cruise on the African coast, having captured on the 7th of Sept. the slave ship *Velos Passagera* with 555 slaves on board. Some time previous to the visit of the Primrose to the Bay of Loango, the king of Loango had brought 100 slaves to the coast for sale, but finding no slavers on the station, BUTCHERED THEM ALL IN COLD BLOOD, *as he thought it too expensive to feed them!! The bleached bones of the unfortunate victims were still to be seen on the shore!!* Of whom will their blood be required? Not merely of the savage king, and the yet more savage traders, but of every slaveholder in the universe.

Figure 4. Detail of *Liberator*, March 12, 1831, p. 43. Courtesy of the American Antiquarian Society.

Figure 5. Detail of *Liberator*, May 12, 1832, p. 74. Courtesy of the American Antiquarian Society.

SLAVERY RECORD.

LOOK AT THIS!

☞ Somebody has forwarded to us a copy of the Georgia Journal, printed at Milledgeville, in which we find Judge Thacher's presumptuous and anomalous Charge to the Grand Jury in this city, respecting incendiary publications, accompanied by the following unfortunate panegyric:

'It is with no common feeling of approbation and of pleasure, that we copy from a northern paper the following extract of a late excellent charge of Judge Thacher to a grand Jury in Boston.—Such doctrines will stand the test of all time; and in extending their circulation, we believe we are rendering an essential service to the country.'

How flattering is the praise of men-stealers, and how highly it is merited in the present instance! Verily, this is 'confirmation strong' of the soundness of Judge Thacher's opinions, and must hasten an indictment from the Grand Jury.

In the same number of the Georgia Journal, we find the following——cattle?—no, HUMAN BEINGS, advertised to be sold at public auction, having been levied on by the sheriff as the PROPERTY of certain individuals, 'to satisfy a fi. fa.' in favor of certain creditors. The ruinous tendency of slavery is visibly manifested in this revolting exhibition. New-England mothers! think of an infant, only FOUR WEEKS old, and another eighteen months old, seized for debt, and sold to the highest bidder!!! O, certainly, we ought to abolish a system, which permits this horrible violence, by a very slow process!

One negro woman, by the name of Sylvia, about 33 years of age.
Three negroes, to wit—Jim about 40 years old, Peter about 15 years old, and Jacob about 14 years old.
Three negroes, viz.—Jude 15, Creed 12, and Delpha 10 years old.
One negro man named Dick.
One negro man named Lewis, 22 years old.
One negro man by the name of Roger.
One negro woman by the name of Betty.
Two negroes, Tab a woman, and Tabitha a girl.
Two negroes, viz.—Cato a man, and Rhoda a girl.
One negro girl by the name of Sophia, about 11 years of age.
One negro girl by the name of Kizzy, about 9 years of age.
A negro man by the name of Milledge, about 22 years of age.
A negro man by the name of Nathan, about 30 years of age.
One negro man named Jack, about 34 years old.
One negro man by the name of David.
Four negroes, to wit—Sam a boy about 12 or 14 years old, Sarah a girl 8 years old, Nancy a girl 6 years old, and Matilda *a girl 2 years old.*
Sukey a woman about 30 years of age.
Harry a boy about 7 years of age.
Lymus a boy about 3 years of age.
Buck a boy about 5 years of age.
☞ Angeline a girl *about 18 months old!!*
☞ A negro child by the name of James, ABOUT FOUR WEEKS OLD!!!

the *Appeal* circulating in their states in late 1829 and throughout 1830, authorities in Georgia, South Carolina, Virginia, North Carolina, and Louisiana reacted quickly and severely to suppress Walker's pamphlet, to prohibit the entry and circulation of similarly "seditious" slavery-related print, and to restrict the literacy and mobility of enslaved people and free Blacks.[21] With the *Liberator* following hard on the heels of Walker's *Appeal* in 1831, southern authorities found copies of Garrison's paper circulating in their states despite the restrictions that were quickly adopted in response to Walker's *Appeal*. The Turner uprising in August and other resistant organizing and actions by enslaved people in Virginia and North Carolina between 1829 and 1831 occasioned even more severe restrictions aimed not just at Walker's *Appeal* but now also at the *Liberator* and Garrison himself. In October 1831, a North Carolina grand jury indicted Garrison and his partner Isaac Knapp for circulating the *Liberator* in Raleigh. In December, Virginia's governor John Floyd and South Carolina's governor James Hamilton encouraged their respective legislatures to pass laws restricting antislavery print, with Hamilton including copies of the *Liberator*, Walker's *Appeal*, and other specimens of "incendiary newspapers and other publications, put forth in the non-slave-holding states" as evidence of the urgent threat in his letter to the legislature.[22] And the state of Georgia offered five thousand dollars "to be paid to any person or persons who shall arrest, bring to trial and prosecute to conviction ... the editor or publisher of a certain paper called the *Liberator*" as well as "any other person or persons who shall utter, publish, or circulate ... the *Liberator*, or any other paper, circular, pamphlet, letter, or address of a seditious character."[23] Like Walker's *Appeal*, Garrison's editorial voice in the *Liberator* was adamantly in the first person; he declared in the first issue, "I will be as harsh as truth, and as uncompromising as justice. On this subject, I do not wish to think, or speak, or write, with moderation. No! no! Tell a man whose house is on fire to give a moderate alarm; tell him to moderately rescue his wife from the hands of the ravisher; tell the mother to gradually extricate her babe from the fire into which it has fallen;— but urge me not to use moderation in a cause like the present."[24] Yet his and White southerners' insistent association of his paper with Walker's *Appeal* points up the bivocality of Garrison's rhetoric—immoderate even as he preaches a nonviolent end to slavery—and his necessary dependence on others, including Walker and Black subscribers and contributors, for the *Liberator*'s existence.

That the *Appeal* and *Liberator* resembled each other argumentatively, rhetorically, and visually must have been immediately apparent to members of Boston's Black activist community, including Stewart, who had known Walker personally and were very familiar with his thoughts, rhetorical style, and the forms they took in his pamphlet.[25] For other curious readers in Black communities in Boston and the North more broadly who may only have heard of Walker and his pamphlet without knowing him or reading it, Garrison's frequent coverage of its circulation and his publication of excerpts of the text and *Liberator* readers' debates about the text might have attracted both the attention and support of such readers as a means of accessing at least portions of Walker's message. As Jacqueline Bacon has observed of Black activists' and subscribers' crucial contributions to the publication, Garrison was "strongly influenced by the views of African Americans" and "embraced at the time by people of color, whose support was crucial to the initial success of the *Liberator*. African Americans worked as agents and placed advertisements in the paper. In its early years, African Americans were a large majority [of the paper's subscribers]—eighty percent at the outset" (267).[26] Black writers also contributed poetry and other substantial content to the *Liberator*'s pages.[27]

But support from the Black communities of Boston, Philadelphia, and New York were not alone enough to sustain the *Liberator* and Garrison actively solicited and received contributions from wealthy White abolitionists to keep the publication afloat in its first year.[28] He was frequently short on both time and money, as he explained in February 1831 to his fellow abolitionist and former newspaper editor Samuel J. May (to whom Garrison also sent a copy of the third edition of Walker's *Appeal*, as his "friend and admirer"): "I am ashamed of the meagre aspect which the paper presents in its editorial department; because the public imagine that I have six days each week to cater for it, when, in fact, scarcely six hours are allotted to me, and these at midnight. My worthy partner [Isaac Knapp] and I complete the mechanical part; that is to say, we compose and distribute, on every number, one hundred thousand types, besides performing the press-work, mailing the papers to subscribers, &c., &c. In addition to this, a variety of letters, relative to the paper, are constantly accumulating, which require prompt answers."[29] When we consider these circumstances, it seems even less likely that Garrison would have made the time or taken the financial risk to publish a first-time writer's work as he did just eight months into the *Liberator*'s existence with Stewart's pamphlet *Religion and the Pure Principles of Morality* unless he had good reason to believe he could capitalize on his and his paper's association with Stewart and her work.³⁰

Scholars have noted that Garrison was responsible for bringing Stewart into print and that he sold copies of the pamphlet at the *Liberator*'s offices, but the material circumstances of his doing so have gone unconsidered, most likely because we tend to think of Garrison and the *Liberator* as the powerful forces they came to be instead of at their most vulnerable. As a result, scholarship on Stewart has neglected reciprocally considering the significance of Stewart's writings to Garrison and the early *Liberator*. Stewart's Walker-inspired appeal to free northern Black women, I contend, allowed Garrison to associate himself and his press with a direct intellectual and rhetorical descendant of Walker, yet whose fire was moderated by Stewart's gender, the ardor of her faith, and her insistence on propriety as the key to freedom and equality. That is to say, Stewart's pamphlet allowed Garrison to continue having it both ways with Walker's *Appeal*: it offered him an opportunity to print and put into circulation himself a defiant essay by a Walker-influenced Black Bostonian. At the same time, it allowed him to maintain a strategic moral distance from Walker's justifications of violent resistance—especially after Turner's 1831 rebellion—in that the pamphlet was penned by a pious Black widow in the North who passionately urged resistance, but primarily through faith and propriety. Thus, while Garrison sold Stewart's pamphlet for six cents a copy from the *Liberator*'s office—half the price of Walker's *Appeal*—we should think of the indirect, yet significant gains it provided him. As Stewart's publisher, Garrison was able to represent himself to the educated and "respectable" Black communities of the North as a committed ally. At the same time, known to an ever more fearful South as an inexorable "incendiary," the publisher Garrison was only increasing the output of antislavery and antiracism print in the wake of Walker's *Appeal*, the Turner uprising, and vigorous southern attempts to suppress "seditious" print and slave resistance.

This close interrelationship of Stewart's pamphlet, Garrison's *Liberator*, and Walker's *Appeal* is particularly visible in the October 8, 1831, number of the *Liberator*. In the second column on its first page, immediately below a printer's index that points to Garrison's editorial refusal to reply to a "murderous and abominable article" that had been published in the *National Intelligencer*, the bold headline "**INCENDIARY PUBLICATIONS**" reminds readers about southern responses to the discovery of the *Appeal* circulating in their states and about the recent uprising in Southampton, Virginia, led by Nat

Turner.³¹ Once again, Garrison uses Walker's *Appeal* as an occasion to insert the *Liberator* into the most pitched conversation following Turner's revolt. He does so here by reprinting a letter from a resident of Washington, D.C., to the *Tarborough (NC) Free Press* via the *National Intelligencer*. It reads, "An incendiary paper, 'The Liberator,' is circulated openly among the free blacks of this city; and if you will search, it is very probable you will find it among the slaves of your county. It is published in Boston or Philadelphia by a white man, with the avowed purpose of inciting rebellion in the South; and I am informed, is to be carried through your county by secret agents, who are to come amongst you under the pretext of pedling [sic], &c. Keep a sharp look out for these villains, and if you catch them, by all that is sacred, you ought to barbacue [sic] them. Diffuse this information amongst whom it may concern." Garrison follows the letter with the *National Intelligencer*'s editorial response which "appeal[s] to the worthy Mayor of the City of Boston, whether no law can be found to prevent the publication, within the City over which he presides, of such diabolical papers as we have seen a sample of here in the hands of slaves, and of which there are many in circulation to the South of us." He also includes the *Intelligencer*'s editors' acknowledgment that their appeal will likely go unanswered "because the nuisance is not a nuisance, technically speaking, within the limits of the State of Massachusetts."³²

To the South—including in the near-South Washington, D.C., where slavery was legal and the *Intelligencer* was published—any slavery- and race-related print issuing from Boston was considered a "nuisance." Knowing this, Garrison persisted in, if not amplified, both his frequent and forked-tongue coverage of Walker's *Appeal* in the *Liberator* and his deliberate fashioning of his paper's confrontational rhetoric and visual text after Walker's pamphlet, even after Nat Turner's Rebellion and despite his continued insistence on a nonviolent end to slavery. The strategy worked to make his newspaper as much of a fearsome nuisance to southerners—and almost as much of a champion of Black rights to free Black subscribers—as the *Appeal*.³³ It also drew greater financial and political support from wealthy White antislavery activists who saw themselves and their interests as vulnerable to expanding southern power, and from White readers in the North who were increasingly concerned about a free press but otherwise ambivalent about slavery.

Most remarkable—particularly in the aftermath of the Southampton uprising and before Turner's capture at the end of October—is Garrison's most Walker-like headline in the same October 8 issue—"BLOOD! BLOOD!! BLOOD!!!"—with its intensifying exclamation points, followed by the bold, small caps subhead "ANOTHER INSURRECTION." In the column adjacent to the beginning of "Blood! Blood!! Blood!!!" a pointing printer's index draws attention to what its context makes clear is a comparatively modest notice: "☞ For sale at this office, a tract addressed to the people of color, by Mrs. Maria W. Steward [sic], a respectable colored lady of this city. Its title is, 'Religion and the pure principles of Morality, the sure foundation on which we must build.' The production is most praiseworthy, and confers great credit on the talents and piety of its author. We hope she will have many patrons. Extracts in the paper hereafter. Price 6 cents."[34] (See Figure 6.) With this, Garrison introduces Stewart—whose married name he spells as "Steward"—to the reading public for the first time as a respectable, talented, and pious new writer whose works he not only recommends but also sells at the *Liberator*'s office. Again, the context of the notice is significant: in the same issue that contains two related pieces featuring southern indictments of the *Liberator* and Walker's *Appeal* as incendiary publications and Garrison's defense of his paper, Garrison inserts an advertisement, right next to the second of those pieces, for an unambiguously nonincendiary publication he has printed on the same press as the *Liberator* and seeks to circulate from its office. Which is to say that in this post–Turner's Rebellion issue of the *Liberator* that is so focused on incendiary publications while Turner was still at large, we should read Garrison's advertisement for Stewart's pamphlet not just as endorsing a new work by a new author. The ad also strategically positions Stewart and her pamphlet as reciprocal endorsements of Garrison and his paper's respectability and religiosity against proslavery indictments of them as infernal inciters of further revolutionary violence.

More specifically, Garrison advertising Stewart's pamphlet as a "tract" signals it as belonging to the evangelical reform writing that saturated the 1830s United States with the mass production and circulation of instructional pamphlets by reform-minded religious organizations.[35] His additional designation of the text as a praiseworthy "production" that "confers great credit on the talents and piety of its author" also makes it something more: an original work of literature by an intellectually gifted author. Recall that Garrison also deemed Walker's *Appeal* "one of the most remarkable productions of the age." Noah Webster's 1828 dictionary defines *production* as "1. The act or process of producing, bringing forth or exhibiting to view. 2. That which is produced or made; as the productions of the earth, comprehending all vegetables and fruits; the productions of art, as manufactures of every kind, paintings, sculpture, etc.; the productions of intellect or genius, as poems and

Figure 6. Detail of *Liberator*, October 8, 1831, p. 163, with advertisement for Stewart's *Religion and the Pure Principles of Morality* in the right-hand column. Courtesy of the American Antiquarian Society.

prose compositions."³⁶ Here, I mean to suggest that, in view of both of Webster's definitions, we can read both Garrison's ad and the title of Stewart's pamphlet as very subtly but distinctly introducing her in the image of the best-known Black Bostonian female author, Phillis Wheatley, whose religious poetry abolitionists had praised and Jefferson had famously dismissed in *Notes on the State of Virginia*. Both the familiar frontispiece portrait and the title page of Wheatley's *Poems on Various Subjects Religious and Moral* (1773) introduce Wheatley as a "negro servant," a Bostonian, and, most significantly, an author.³⁷ Garrison's ad suggests the same of "Steward," identifying her as "a respectable colored lady of this city" and, perhaps unintentionally, presenting her as the domestic worker she had been prior to becoming an activist by spelling her name as *Steward*.³⁸ The ad also specifically encourages the *Liberator*'s readers to become Stewart's patrons, calling to mind how the Countess of Huntingdon's and others' patronage of Wheatley brought her works to public view. By presenting Stewart in these ways, Garrison's brief notice effectively, if ever so implicitly, offers her up as counterevidence to Jefferson's influential claims that people of African descent were incapable of intellect or genius, particularly so with respect to literary production.³⁹ Garrison's introduction did much to bring a first-time writer to public notice as a talented author as worthy of patronage as any other—if not as more deserving than many talented others because of her additional piousness, respectability, race, and status as a widow. Yet we can and should also see Stewart as having offered Garrison an opportunity to bring both the newest potential Wheatley—and Walker—into print, thereby further enhancing his status among Black and White abolitionists and goading his proslavery enemies.

Stewart's Principles and Practices of Imitation in *Religion and the Pure Principles of Morality*

Neither Garrison's advertisement nor the title of Stewart's pamphlet would have given readers any reason to suspect that the nonviolent abolitionist was printing and selling a work that had been directly inspired by Walker's *Appeal*. The ad also paints a much different portrait of the author, who represents herself within her pamphlet as no less a martyr to the cause than Walker, and who warns White America that Black Americans' "souls are fired with the same love of liberty and independence with which your souls are fired... AND WE CLAIM OUR RIGHTS," unafraid "of them that kill the body, and after that can do no more."⁴⁰ Yet the *Liberator* ad and the title of Stewart's pamphlet are not actually misleading, in that Stewart primarily focuses on religion, morality, and education in her essay addressed to a Black female audience. Even so, she addresses all Black readers in her introduction with a Walker-sounding and Garrison-like mixed message on resistance: "Far be it from me to recommend to you, either to kill, burn, or destroy," she declares in the pamphlet published just over a month after Turner's uprising and before his capture. "But," she significantly adds, "I would strongly recommend to you, to improve your talents: let one not lie buried in the earth. Show forth your powers of mind" (2). With this rhetorical move clearly modeled after both Walker and Garrison, Stewart at once directs the powerful imperatives "kill," "burn," and "destroy" to Black readers only to quickly distance herself from inciting them to take these actions, in case White people are also reading. Rather than acting violently toward White people, Black women and men should act on themselves in productive efforts at self-improvement, Stewart urges.⁴¹ As with Walker, racial uplift is her primary message.

Stewart opens her essay by implicitly building on the *Appeal* for Walker's evidentiary work in establishing the causes of Black people's abjection in the United States. With Walker already having done this work, she is able to assume her readers' familiarity with it and simply states this abjection as a given, then move quickly to her focus on strategies for its remediation: "in view of our wretched and degraded situation, and sensible of the gross ignorance that prevails amongst us," she begins, "I have thought proper thus publicly to express my sentiments before you." Here, we notice that the first sentences of Stewart's and Walker's body texts share two adjectives for describing the condition of Black people: *wretched* and *degraded*. Thus, while Garrison advertised Stewart's originality as an author, we can see how Stewart herself openly admired, depended on, and borrowed from Walker in her writing. She also echoes Wheatley in adopting the conventional authorial humility trope with her hope that her "friends will not scrutinize these pages with too severe an eye, as [she has] not calculated to display either elegance or taste in their composition, but [has] merely written the meditations of [her] heart as far as [her] imagination led." Yet Stewart also makes it clear that she has made herself vulnerable in these expected ways as a novice author for an exceptional purpose: "in order to arouse you [here, her Black female and male readers] to exertion, and to enforce upon your minds the great necessity of turning your attention to knowledge and improvement" (1). Thus, Stewart uses both her race's and her own "degraded" states as rhetorical starting and pivot points, to articulate their dire need for improvement and to urge them to action to fulfill their significant potential.

In the paragraph that follows, Stewart explains further that the need to imitate role models and humble herself is not only a conventional requirement for a fledgling author but also and specifically the direct result of living in a patriarchal White supremacist society. Because she was a poor, Black orphan she was "deprived of the advantages of education, though [her] soul thirsted for knowledge." By including these autobiographical details, Stewart further converted her acknowledgment of her own and her race's vulnerabilities and shortcomings into evidence of the racism of a White patriarchal society that denies her and all Black people—and especially Black women and children—not only educational opportunities but also the basic possession of a human soul. To overcome these imposed disadvantages and inevitable disappointments, she explains, she has recently converted from an enforced and frustrated material dependence on Whites to an elected and fulfilling spiritual reliance on God alone. As a result of her conversion, she "now possess[es] that spirit of independence, that, were [she] called upon, [she] would willingly sacrifice [her] life for the cause of God and [her] brethren" (1). With this declaration Stewart conforms to the generic characteristics of the spiritual autobiography that religious societies began printing in bulk and circulating as tracts in the 1820s and 1830s. Moreover, she offers herself up as an example to her readers of how accepting Christ as she has will bring them the same spirit of independence that can be achieved if they give up their faith in White people and instead believe in themselves and God, and sacrifice themselves for God alone.[42]

At several points in the body of her essay, Stewart articulates her insecurities and reluctance as a recent Christian convert, an activist, and an author, acknowledging the high stakes of speaking out and exposing herself not only to criticism and scorn but also to violent attack for doing so. Addressing her "respected friends," Stewart admits that she "feel[s] almost unable to address [them]; almost incompetent to perform the task" of urging Black people to unite to break "the chains of slavery and ignorance" as one "sensible" of her own "ignorance" (2–3). Yet, as before, she makes it clear that these are not individual or biological failings but rather the product of limitations that have been imposed on her by others—not just by White but also by Black people, like those Walker confronts—and that these limits can only be transcended with God's help. In modeling this faithful resistance, Stewart presents herself as ready to "suffer for pleading the cause of oppressed Africa," proudly affirming that she "shall glory in being one of her martyrs" (2). She also speaks directly to her potential detractors among her Black readers, whom she anticipates will condemn her for thinking of herself as better than them. It "is high time for prejudices and animosities to cease from amongst us," she declares. Freed from them by her faith and Walker's example and encouragement, she "speak[s] as one that must give an account at the awful bar of God" and as a "dying mortal, to dying mortals" without being subject to "calumny and reproach" and their "scoffs and frowns" (3).

Stewart's sense of the high stakes of writing might be read as a novice author's tendency toward overdramatization, a recent convert's typical evangelical enthusiasm, or a Black female writer's extraordinary need for self-justification for speaking up instead of remaining quiet in a patriarchal White supremacist society. Yet, when we recognize the immediate context of Stewart's expressions of anxiety and vulnerability, we see how they give exceptional life to these otherwise conventional feelings. David Walker had died under mysterious circumstances soon after publishing the last edition of his *Appeal*, just a little over a year before Garrison published Stewart's pamphlet. In paralleling herself with Walker as a ready martyr to the cause of oppressed Africa, Stewart imagines herself to be in similar jeopardy: "I am firmly persuaded, that the God in whom I trust is able to protect me from the rage and malice of mine enemies, and from them that will rise up against me," she affirms before offering that "if there is no other way for me to escape, he is able to take me to himself, as he did the most noble, fearless, and undaunted DAVID WALKER" (2).

Surely adding to these fears, after Walker's death and immediately following the Turner-led resistance in late August 1831, were the death threats that Garrison had received and to which he dedicated the front page of the September 10 number of the *Liberator*. In his editorial remarks prefacing these letters, Garrison explains, like Stewart, how he had anticipated ridicule and physical harm in publishing for the cause: "In attacking the system of slavery, I clearly foresaw all that has happened to me. I knew, at the commencement, that my motives would be impeached, my warnings ridiculed, my person persecuted, my sanity doubted, my life jeoparded [*sic*]: but the clank of the prisoner's chains broke upon my ear—it entered deeply into my soul—I looked up to Heaven for strength to sustain me in the perilous work of emancipation, and my resolution was taken." The letters he has received after the Southampton uprising only "infuse new blood into [his] veins," Garrison affirms. "Sure I am," he declares, "that, if the sacrifice of my life be required in this great cause, I shall be willing to make it; only regretting the meanness of the offering, and the want of a thousand lives to lay down in the same enterprise." Further fanning the flames, Garrison effectively offers himself up for assassination, and his death as the triggering event that would end slavery: "Sure I am, that the progress of liberty cannot be arrested by the dagger of the assassin" and that "the murder of one *white man*,—however insignificant he might be,— ... would kindle a fire of indignation and sympathy in the breasts of the people, intense enough to melt every chain."[43]

Garrison printed these threats and his response less than a month before he published Stewart's pamphlet. Even if Stewart had written the majority of it earlier in the year—as Garrison retrospectively recalled in an 1879 letter to her—it is likely that she wrote the pamphlet's introduction—in which she similarly anticipates and embraces martyrdom—closer to the time of publication. Given the intensity of these very real threats to both Walker's and Garrison's lives—and Stewart's even greater vulnerability as a Black woman not only for daring to speak but also for doing so boldly in front of a "mixed audience" (that is, both men and women)—we should read Stewart's articulations of her feelings of insecurity as deeply felt and not just as mere literary convention.[44]

After each such expression of vulnerability in her essay, Stewart consistently pivots to a position of strength. Carla Peterson has attributed Stewart's entire publishing career to this strong sense of the need "to transform herself . . . from a position of humility to one of greater self-assertion" so that she would be better able to serve as a "'humble instrument in the hands of God.'"[45] We see this dynamic at work from the beginning of her career, in her introduction to *Religion and the Pure Principles of Morality,* where she prefaces her certainty that she will be attacked with her confidence that God will protect her and concludes that this protection may take the form of bodily releasing her from mortal concerns, as she has seen in the example of the martyred Walker.

While Stewart only speaks of Walker explicitly in two moments in the brief twelve-page pamphlet, his influence on her words and arguments is apparent throughout the essay, most overtly so in her observations about White America and when she directly addresses White Americans. At the same time, the writing is also very much Stewart's own, asserting her necessarily different situation and experiences as a free Black woman in the North while suggesting that this different path has brought her to the same conclusions as Walker about White supremacy and its effects on Black women and men. We see this dynamic clearly in the fourth section of her essay, where Stewart presents herself as no less an encyclopedic and critical observer of White people in the United States than Walker as he presents himself in his preamble. Walker begins, "Having travelled over a considerable portion of these United States, and having, in the course of my travels, taken the most accurate observations of things as they exist" (1). Stewart similarly, if more simply, declares, "I have been taking a survey of the American people." Unlike Walker, though, her survey has been mental, taken in her "own mind" rather than through actual travel. Though she does not state the reason explicitly, we know that her status as both a widow and a working woman would have made solitary travel even more difficult, if not impossible even though she was free and lived in the North. In spite of these intersectional limitations, she arrives at the same conclusion as Walker, seeing "very few . . . amongst [White people] that bestow one thought upon the benighted sons and daughters of Africa, who have enriched the soils of America with their tears and blood!" (6). With this, Stewart purposefully echoes the beginning of the *Appeal*'s article 1, where Walker objects to Black people "dig[ging] their [White people's] mines and work[ing] their farms; and thus go on enriching them, from one generation to another with our *blood* and our *tears!!!!*" (9).

Despite the rhetorical similarity, we notice that Stewart's emotions and her pamphlet's punctuation are more restrained than Walker's. I read this as Stewart consciously moderating the distinctive typographic tone of Walker's pamphlet, just as Walker also did in some parts, so that her punctuation matches her message of propriety as the key to uplift—but only visually.[46] Stewart is anything but moderate or delicate rhetorically when she is arguing that Black Americans have the same desire for and right to freedom that White Americans had in revolting against Great Britain, pointing up White people's hypocrisy for subsequently "depriv[ing] [their] fellow man of equal rights and privileges," and introducing the specific effects of these deprivations on Black women. "Oh, America, America, foul and indelible is thy stain!" she declares, again with comparatively restrained punctuation for as bold an indictment as Walker's of White America. She continues: "Dark and dismal is the cloud that hangs over thee, for thy cruel wrongs and injuries to the fallen sons of Africa. The blood of her murdered ones cries to heaven for vengeance against thee. Thou art almost become drunken with the blood of her slain; thou hast enriched thyself through her toils and labours; and now thou refuseth to make even a small return. And thou hast caused the daughters of Africa to commit whoredoms and fornications; but upon thee be their curse" (10). While Walker's influence is again both legible and audible here, even without his emphatic italics or punctuation, we see that Stewart significantly departs from his example by frankly addressing the effects of slavery and racism on Black women's sexual lives. Throughout his *Appeal*, Walker merely implies Black women's sexual victimization in his catalogs of the injustices and harms of slavery by narrowly representing Black women only as vulnerable wives and mothers. And as we have seen, all of Walker's justifications for Black people's right to revolt only and emphatically address men—as in "Are we MEN!!—I ask you, O my brethren! are we MEN?" (19). The passage above suggests that she recognized how Walker's graphic assertions of Black masculinity effectively displaced Black women's sexual vulnerability and violation in favor of foregrounding the emasculation that Black men have endured from White people as what must be overcome through violent physical resistance. Here, Stewart foregrounds the specific consequences for Black women and their bodies.

I also read Stewart addressing the specific bodily and moral consequences of slavery and racism for women as further demonstrating her repeated conversion of aspects of Black women's White-imposed abjection into grounds for individual and communal self-assertion. By adopting Walker's language and tone to speak from her own observations and experiences, Stewart is able not only to boldly address the specific plight of Black women under racism and slavery but also to curse White women to suffer the punishment that Black women would suffer under ordinary moral circumstances. Again, despite Walker's reputation as a firebrand, he is never so bold as Stewart is in asserting the most damaging effects of slavery and racism on Black women's bodies and souls. Whereas he is silent about unmarried sex, sex work, or other forms of bodily sacrifice for self-protection or advancement for Black women, she speaks them with what would have been shocking language ("whoredoms" and "fornications") to most readers—and to female ones most of all. Under ordinary circumstances, the religious morality and feminine propriety that Stewart seeks to instill in Black women throughout her essay would restrain her from speaking so bluntly about sexuality. But the extraordinary circumstances of slavery and racism as well as Walker's silence on women's different experiences of them in his otherwise bold indictment compel Stewart to risk censure by using graphic language that is just as appropriate as the graphic typographic emphases in Walker's text.[47] One further rhetorical move insulates Stewart and her sisters alike from punishment for these rhetorical and moral transgressions: she insists that White people alone should bear punishment for Black women's wrongs because the sin originates with them, not Black women. In this, we also see Stewart's confidence that God will recognize that White men and women have forced all Black American women—including herself—into the desperate physical, moral, and/or rhetorical positions that they have no choice but to inhabit.

How Stewart represents her own relationship to God suggests how she likely thought about Walker's omission of Black women and the specifics of their plight from his *Appeal*. While she declares herself a "feeble instrument" as a novice female author, as a Christian, she also clearly recognized that Walker was also God's instrument, and no less feeble as such, even as he was also "most noble, fearless, and undaunted." We see as much when she represents not just Walker but also her publisher Garrison, as embodiments of divine favor and God's earthly agents who act with the pen instead of the sword, as she urges Black men to await divine vengeance against White Americans instead of seeking it themselves: "Then, my brethren, sheathe your swords, and calm your angry passions. Stand still, and know that the Lord he is God. Vengeance is his, and he will repay. . . . God hath raised you up a Walker and a Garrison. Though Walker sleeps, yet he lives, and his name shall be had in everlasting remembrance" (11).

Walker lives not only through the words of his still-available *Appeal*, but also through Stewart, whom he has inspired to write the essay and memorial that readers have in hand. Yet, even as she implies herself as Walker's successor, we see that she is once again careful to assert and distinguish herself. Stewart does so, in this case, by paraphrasing Psalms 37:35–36 and using the scripture's first person to represent both Walker and herself speaking with one voice: "I have seen the wicked in great power, spreading himself like a green bay tree, and lo, he passed away; yea, I diligently sought him, but he could not be found" (11). But in place of verse 37—which reads in the King James Bible as "Mark the perfect man, and behold the upright: for the end of that man is peace"—Stewart writes, "It is God alone that has inspired my heart to feel for Afric's woes" (11). With this revision, Stewart both crucially asserts herself and insists on God's influence over that of any others. Moreover, the scripture allows her to imply that neither Walker nor Garrison is perfect, and to assert that the only perfect man is Christ, whom biblically versed readers would recognize as the sought-after man in the quoted verses even without her including verse 37. While her words may have been influenced by Walker and brought into public view by Garrison, she thus makes it clear that it is ultimately God who has made it possible for all of them to write. That she writes as a woman makes her no less worthy an instrument than Walker or Garrison, she also implies.

Recognizing how Stewart understood herself, Walker, and Garrison as God's instruments further helps us understand why she theorized specific forms and practices of imitation as all Black women's best route to depending only on themselves, each other, and ultimately God. At several points in the essay, Stewart proposes the imitation of Christ's example as an important action that all Black people can and should take toward overcoming the effects of slavery and racism. She first introduces this advice in the prayer she includes in her essay, asking God to "clothe us with humility of soul, and give us a becoming dignity of manners: may we imitate the character of the meek and lowly Jesus; and do thou grant that Ethiopia may soon stretch forth her hands unto thee" (6). Here, Stewart specifically invokes the principle of imitatio Christi, "made popular in the spiritual biography and autobiography of the sixteenth and seventeenth centuries."[48] This path emerged for Stewart as part of what Marilyn Richardson describes as her powerful "conversion or 'born again' experience which deepened her religious commitment" following the deaths of both her husband, James W. Stewart, in 1829 and their mutual friend Walker in 1830. While Stewart does not specify which Christian denomination informs her theology, she draws on John Wesley–inspired American Methodism, which specifically emphasized Christian self-improvement via the imitation of Christ as a powerful alternative to both the moral temptations of sin and the material conditions of degradation.[49]

"Why is it," Stewart asks, "that thick darkness is mantled upon every brow, and we, as it were, look sadly upon one another?" "It is on account of sin," she mournfully answers (6–7). Instead of capitulating, assuming that Black men will save the race (as Walker does), or waiting on God's eventual redemption, Stewart asserts that Black mothers possess the immediate and ultimate power to redeem the race from this sin and to restore people of African descent to God's favor. They can and must do so by establishing their own Christian subjectivities and instilling the same in their children. She appeals: "O, ye mothers, what a responsibility rests on you! You have souls committed to your charge, and God will require a strict account of you.... It is no use to say, you can't do this, or, you can't do that: you will not tell your Maker so, when you meet him at the great day of account. And you must be careful that you set an example worthy of following, for you they [your children] will imitate" (7). According to Stewart's Black feminist theory of liberation, those Black mothers who have not been forcibly separated from their children must become Christian mothers to set an example worthy of their children's imitation. To become such powerful role models, they must imitate Christ and Christian principles more than the standards of White femininity, propriety, and faith in the nineteenth century "cult of true womanhood" to which free Black women simultaneously were held and from which they were excluded, as Stewart here recognizes and Hazel V. Carby has shown historically.[50]

Stewart does admit one earthly example worthy of free Black women's imitation: the hard and dedicated physical labor exemplified by a specific group of White Christian women seeking to build a church of their own. "The good women of Wethersfield, Connecticut," she writes, "toiled in the blazing sun, year after year, weeding onions, then sold the seed and procured money enough to erect them a house of worship." "Shall we not imitate their examples," Stewart asks of her Black female readers—significantly adding "as far as they are worthy of imitation?" (8). While the Wethersfield women's aim is a holy one, Stewart here is careful to limit her recommendation to imitate them specifically to their examples of hard work and saving to build a church—in this case, so that free Black communities can have churches of their own. That is, Stewart clearly does not present White womanhood as the ideal to which Black women should aspire and that they should imitate in all respects. These particular White women's actions may be Christian, Stewart suggests, but neither the Christian mothers of Wethersfield nor any White women should be mistaken for the ultimate role model of Christ—no matter how frequently they were represented, or were representing themselves, as closer to God's image because of their race.[51]

With respect to the issue of labor more broadly, Stewart notes that the division between mental and physical work in the United States has historically been made along racial lines. Once again, she advocates a limited form of imitation as the best strategy for free Black women overcoming this division. "The Americans have practiced nothing but head-work these 200 years" while both enslaved and free Black people "have done their drudgery," she laments. "And is it not high time for us to imitate their examples, and practice head-work too, and keep what we have got, and get what we can?" she insists by way of a rhetorical question (9). In Stewart's last argument in her essay for pedagogical imitation as a necessary stage of Black self-development toward ultimate liberation, she here urges both free Black women and men to think more about working for themselves and keeping what they have worked for, and to gain more by working smarter. And lest this emphasis on "head-work" and self-interest lead readers too far from her primary advice to imitate Christ's moral example, she concludes this section on labor by returning to the ultimate goal: "That day we, as a people, hearken unto the voice of the Lord our God, and walk in his ways and ordinances, and become distinguished for our ease, elegance and grace, combined with other virtues,— that day the Lord will raise us up, and enough to aid and befriend us, and we shall begin to flourish" (9).

For each of her suggestions that Black Americans should imitate specific virtues and practices of White Americans, then, we see that Stewart is careful to follow this advice with a version of the imitatio Christi principle, reminding her readers that only the son of God is the perfect man and role model. Through her own strategic and transitional imitation of David Walker's principles and practices, she further models how Black women should follow the most virtuous earthly role models only to move beyond them and, thereby, achieve the ultimate goals in this life: educating themselves and their children, uniting with others in worship in a church of their own, and performing better work for greater pay. Thus, in both literature and life, as Stewart understands and models as a Christian author, true independence can be gained only through the limited imitation of other virtuous Christians' principles and practices as part of transitioning to depending ultimately on oneself and God alone to set one's mind, body, and race free.

* * *

For such devotion, Stewart won the notice—and the high literary praise—of an unnamed "highly respectable clergyman" who, Garrison claimed, wrote to him shortly after the publication of *Religion and the Pure Principles of Morality*: "Mrs Steward [sic] has sterling wit—is practical—and in some instances is truly eloquent. Her praise will be in all the circles of her people, and our country will yet place her name among the few and not among the many."[52] Garrison may have written this puff himself, as was common practice for publishers at the time. He printed it among notices of other publications worthy of *Liberator* subscribers' support. In this context, it effectively functions as one of three advertisements he published for Stewart's pamphlet in October and November 1831. In the first issue of the *Liberator* in the new year, he made good on his promise to publish an extract from Stewart's pamphlet available in his paper, dedicating nearly half of the new "Ladies' Department" to Stewart's "spirited" words, as he characterized them.[53]

The excerpt Garrison selected for reprinting begins with Stewart's "strong opinion, that the day on which we unite, heart and soul, and turn our attention to knowledge and improvement, that day the hissing and reproach amongst the nations of the earth against us will cease," then turns to Stewart's suggestion that Black women should imitate White women "as far as they are worthy of imitation" (2). It also includes Stewart's urging Black Americans to imitate their White counterparts' "head work" and concludes with her circling back to imagine the day that they begin to flourish by embodying Christian virtues and being lifted up by God in recognition of their worthiness (3). Significantly, Garrison printed this excerpt foregrounding Black intellectual self-assertion immediately after his reprinting of the constitution of the newly founded Afric-American Female Intelligence Society of Boston. But Stewart had met with a chilly, if not hostile, reception by the society when she spoke before them in March 1832. As Elizabeth McHenry has concluded of the speech and its reception, Stewart's unwillingness to "remain quietly at home, or adopt more 'feminine' and thus more acceptable means of acquiring public voice . . . made her public presence intolerable"— to the point that Stewart left Boston and suspended her career as a public author until 1879 (71).[54]

Given this "hissing and reproach" Stewart suffered from fellow Black Christian women for her public activism, I want to suggest that we should read Garrison's reprinting of a portion of Stewart's pamphlet in the *Liberator*'s Ladies' Department as another instance of Garrison attempting to have it both ways with a "spirited" Black author. That is, just as he had done with Walker's *Appeal* in the *Liberator*, he reprinted and further circulated Stewart's words even as he contained them. And whereas he had deprecated Walker's spirit, he departmentalized and gendered Stewart's, by printing her words next to and below the constitution of a society composed of "a large number of the most respectable females of color," as he noted in his editorial preface to the Intelligence Society's constitution.[55]

Stewart, though, would not be contained, as she made clear in her speech to the Intelligence Society in which she boldly asserted, "Be not offended because I tell you the truth; for I believe that God has fired my soul with a holy zeal for his cause. It was God alone who inspired my heart to publish the Meditations thereof; and it was done with pure motives of love to your souls, in the hope that Christians might examine themselves, and sinners become pricked in their hearts. It is the word of God, though men and devils may oppose it." The words she had written in *Religion and the Pure Principles of Morality* are "the word of God," Stewart reiterated and reaffirmed, "and little did I think that any of the professed followers of Christ would have frowned upon me, and discouraged and hindered its progress."[56] Yet Stewart's seeming peers did just that, thereby frustrating on one front the realization of her pamphlet's ultimate message: that Black women's solidarity, achieved through self-development and self-assertion, would earn God's favor and all Black people's freedom.

Garrison, in response to the Intelligence Society's rejection of Stewart's public activism and confrontational rhetoric, printed Stewart's address again in the Ladies' Department of the April 28, 1832, issue. In this instance, we might read his placement of Stewart's address in the Ladies' Department as both a subtle editorial scolding of the Intelligence Society for their hostile reception of Stewart, and a defense of the feminine propriety of spirited public activism. His disagreement becomes more explicit in the editorial notice he printed two columns over from the address: "☞ It is proper to state that the Address of Mrs. Stewart, in our Ladies' Department to-day, is published at her own request, and not by desire of the Society before whom it was delivered. Mrs. S. uses very plain, some may call it severe language; but we are satisfied that she is actuated by good motives, and that her only aim is to rouse a spirit of virtuous emulation in the breasts of her associates, and to elevate the whole colored population. 'Faithful are the wounds of a friend, but the kisses of an enemy are deceitful.'" These remarks evince the characteristic Garrisonian double move, in this case allowing him to acknowledge the Intelligence Society's disapproval of Stewart even as he reaffirms her virtue. Furthermore, by acknowledging that he has published Stewart's lecture at her request and without the Intelligence Society's endorsement, he is careful not to alienate the society's members and, thus, maintains his relationship with an important constituency within the diverse Black community and his readers.

Stewart proved unwilling either to perform or endure such ambivalence. Soon after delivering her farewell address, she withdrew not only from public speaking but also from Boston entirely. In New York, she joined a literary society of "young women who, like herself, were 'full of the greed for literature and letters.'"[57] With these like-minded women, it seems she found peers who were committed to the program of self-development through encyclopedic study and continuously learning through imitating the most virtuous examples encountered in these readings. She did not lecture publicly ever again, nor did she publish any writings between 1833 and 1879, until she published *Meditations from the Pen of Mrs. Maria W. Stewart* herself. During this extended period of study—both independently and in literary societies—and working as a teacher, Stewart "developed into a much more practiced and skillful writer," McHenry notes (77). In doing so, she was continuing to evolve from the powerful example that Walker set with his *Appeal*, thereby fulfilling the tremendous potential that she saw in all Black women, and that we recognize emerging in her in *Religion and the Pure Principles of Morality*.

CHAPTER 3

Taking the Texts

William Apes's "An Indian's Looking-Glass for the White Man"

We have seen how Maria Stewart both admired David Walker for his fearless indictment of white supremacy and saw the limitations of his *Appeal to the Coloured Citizens of the World* for mostly addressing Black men, and also how she seized on this omission as an opportunity to address Black women's distinct experiences of racism and slavery in a bold pamphlet of her own in 1831. In this chapter, I turn to the Pequot minister William Apes, who similarly built on the notoriety and confrontational rhetoric of Walker's *Appeal* to challenge White Americans' racism against Indigenous Americans with his 1833 essay "An Indian's Looking-Glass for the White Man."[1] Less than two months after Walker's publication of the last edition of his *Appeal*, Andrew Jackson signed the Indian Removal Act of 1830, and in 1831 and 1832, two Supreme Court cases—*Cherokee Nation v. Georgia* and *Worcester v. Georgia*—sought to delimit Indigenous people's rights as both U.S. citizens and sovereigns of their own lands.[2] In addition to forced relocation and such significant legal challenges to Indigenous Americans' citizenship and sovereignty, worsening conditions on existing reservations gave Apes immediate and urgent reasons to apply Walker's words to Indigenous Americans and declare them the "most mean, abject, miserable race of beings in the world."[3]

As this passage from the beginning of Apes's essay shows, and as a number of scholars have noted, the influence of Walker's *Appeal* on Apes's self- and Boston-published "Looking-Glass" is immediately apparent, extending to the essay's language and its rhetorical strategy of directly addressing and indicting Whites for their racist discrimination of Indigenous Americans.[4] What has gone unnoticed is Walker's influence on Apes as a reader, specifically with respect to Jefferson's *Notes on the State of Virginia*. As we will recall, Walker "solicit[s] each of [his] brethren, who has the spirit of a man, to buy a copy of Mr. Jefferson's 'Notes on the State of Virginia,' and put it in the hand of his son" so that the rising generation would prove Black people equal, if not superior, to White people (17). Apes—a "Son of the Forest," as he designated himself with the title of his self-published 1829 autobiography—heeded Walker's advice, but with a much different result. We see this most clearly in his "Looking-Glass" when Apes adopts Jefferson's claims that Indigenous people "are the most ingenious people amongst us" and "men of talents," as he paraphrases Jefferson's admiration of Indigenous Americans and theories of the different races' comparative intellectual and creative abilities that so incensed Walker.[5]

In this chapter, I examine how Apes drew not only from the Bible and his experiences as a Methodist minister but also from both Walker's *Appeal* and Jefferson's *Notes on the State of Virginia* to compose "An Indian's Looking-Glass for the White Man." Using Walker's words and rhetorical style in combination with Bible verses and Jefferson's admiration for Indigenous Americans and claims of their racial superiority to people of African descent, Apes boldly exhorts White Christian Americans to recognize Indigenous Americans as their equals and practice the basic Christian principle of mutual respect, to disown their prejudice against Indigenous people.[6] By doing so, Apes and his "Looking-Glass" achieve a similarly complex synthesis of texts and forms of authority to that of Walker's original *Appeal* to confront inequality.

More specifically, to make his argument that White Americans should not discriminate against Indigenous Americans, Apes fused the Christians' Golden Rule—"All things whatsoever ye would that men should do to you, do ye even so to them" (Matthew 7:12)—with Jefferson's secular, natural philosophical hierarchy of the races that positioned Indigenous people as essentially equal, if not superior in some respects, to White Americans and Europeans. In his text, Apes exhorts White Americans to understand that taking both principles to heart makes it not only moral and rational but also easy for them to treat Indigenous Americans as White Americans wish to be treated themselves.

He also confronts Whites as Christians and Americans with their double hypocrisy by using language and rhetoric from specific passages in

Walker's *Appeal* where Walker directly addresses his White readers—including, specifically, the recently deceased Jefferson—to confront their religious and political sins as a race. Apes took a significant risk by doing so. As we have seen, William Lloyd Garrison had "deprecated" the "spirit" of Walker's *Appeal* on multiple occasions, and a majority of the press coverage it received more broadly in Boston and the rest of the North was hardly more positive than its reception in the South. But Apes, no less than Garrison and Stewart, recognized from both newspapers and Walker's own discussion of the fear-provoking power of his pamphlet in its third edition that Walker's confrontational and ministerial rhetorical style and arguments got White people's attention and moved them to act.

As a Methodist minister, Apes had significant experience in directly confronting sinners about their sins with attention-getting rhetoric, then citing principles from scripture to show them the path to reform. As a Methodist bookseller (colporteur) as well, he undoubtedly recognized how Walker was effectively preaching through print and the power of his *Appeal* to reach a nationwide audience. When he turned to print himself to preach the sin of Whites' discrimination against Indigenous people and urge their reform, Apes effectively extended Walker's *Appeal* not only into the multicultural history of the early American Methodist Church but also further into the unprecedented volume of religious print published in the first half of the nineteenth century. He did so in this case by including his political and polemical "Looking-Glass" within a tract of religious conversion narratives titled *The Experiences of Five Christian Indians*. (See Figures 7 and 8.)

I see Apes's placement of his essay at the end of this religious tract as a strategic choice—one that gave it a better chance of reaching the White readers who were more likely to be moved by what Apes had to say to them and how he said it. That is, if he had published "An Indian's Looking-Glass for the White Man" on its own as an overtly political pamphlet addressed to a White audience, it would have been much more vulnerable to neglect, outright rejection, or even destruction. Even for readers who might not have recognized its apparent debt to Walker's *Appeal*, such a bold indictment of Whites for betraying their basic principles would have been hard to swallow coming from an Indian, given the negative popular representations of Indigenous people in a nation set on their extermination.[7] As a self-published, twelve-page pamphlet, it could easily have been lost in the shuffle of millions of religious and reform tracts that were circulating at the time, and the essay's sermonlike brevity would have added to its physically vulnerability.

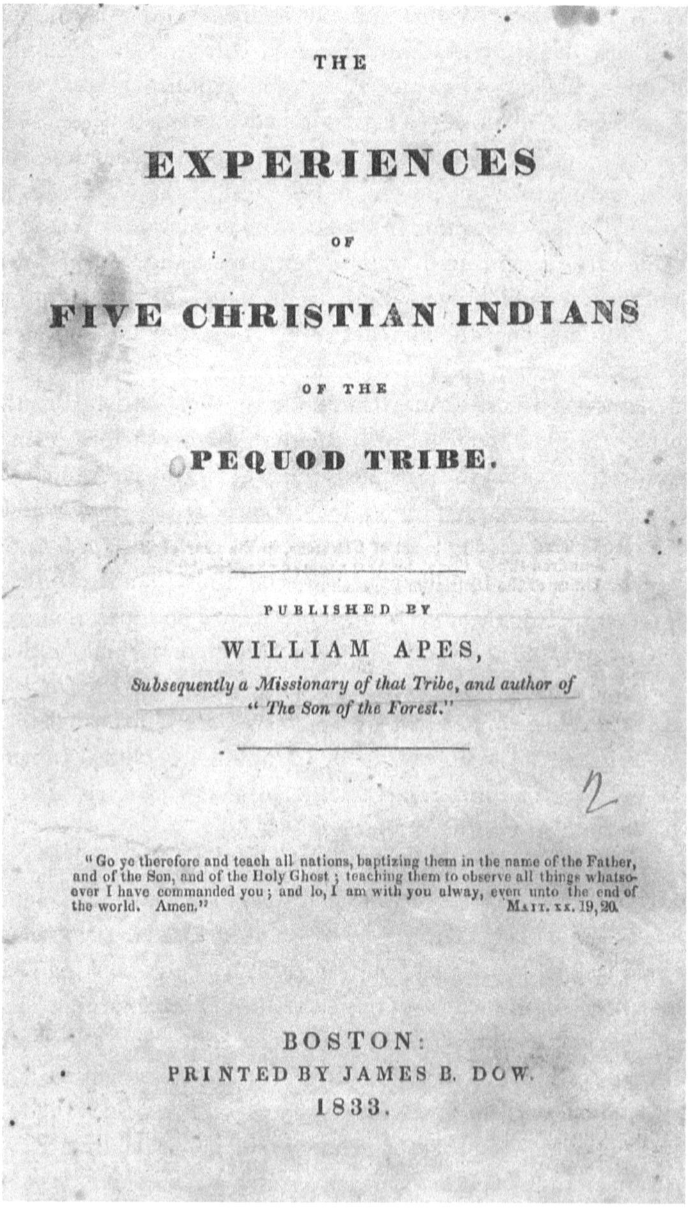

THE

EXPERIENCES

OF

FIVE CHRISTIAN INDIANS

OF THE

PEQUOD TRIBE.

PUBLISHED BY
WILLIAM APES,
*Subsequently a Missionary of that Tribe, and author of
"The Son of the Forest."*

"Go ye therefore and teach all nations, baptizing them in the name of the Father, and of the Son, and of the Holy Ghost; teaching them to observe all things whatsoever I have commanded you; and lo, I am with you alway, even unto the end of the world. Amen." MATT. xx. 19, 20.

BOSTON:
PRINTED BY JAMES B. DOW.
1833.

Figure 7. Title page, William Apes, *The Experiences of Five Christian Indians of the Pequod Tribe* (Boston, MA: James B. Dow, 1833). Library Company of Philadelphia.

Figure 8. Internal title page for William Apes, "An Indian's Looking-Glass for the White Man," unnumbered p. 51. Library Company of Philadelphia.

Publishing his "Looking-Glass" instead as part of a more substantial sixty-two-page tract gave it significantly more material heft, and specifically publishing it at the end of five conversion narratives likely attracted the attention of potentially sympathetic White Christian readers who were interested not only in their own but also in Indigenous people's spiritual salvation. (In Chapter 5, we will see how Henry Highland Garnet pursued a similar publishing strategy for giving his "Address to the Slaves of the United States of America" material heft.) However readers came to his pamphlet, once Apes had them reading his, his wife's, and three other Indigenous women's conversion stories, he deftly turned what was otherwise a tract into a figurative mirror so that Whites had to look at their own urgent need for reform, not just spiritually but also democratically, as Christian Americans.

With respect to Apes's compositional practice, we might think of him as having adapted the basic Christian principle for the treatment of other people to his treatment of Walker's text in his "Looking-Glass." Following Walker, Apes holds White Christian Americans to their best sacred and secular principles. In doing so, he not only continues the important reform mission of Walker's *Appeal* after Walker's death but also extends it to apply to Indigenous people. At the same time, repurposing Walker's powerful appeal to advocate for Indigenous Americans effectively allowed Apes to do what Walker might and should have done himself more powerfully and fully.

That Apes argued against discrimination against Indigenous people by drawing on, rather than contradicting, Jefferson's hierarchy of the races in the United States further suggests that Apes saw equal opportunity in the influential arguments of both Walker's *Appeal* and Jefferson's *Notes* for invoking aspects of each that would help him make his best case to White Christian Americans. To understand this aspect of his compositional practice, it is necessary to understand both Apes's uncertain standing in the Methodist Church and Methodist preaching styles at the time. Apes had been baptized as a Methodist in late 1818 and soon after became an exhorter in a small Methodist community in Colrain, Massachusetts. Itinerant for much of the 1820s, Apes also worked as a colporteur, selling Methodist books and tracts to support his family as he struggled with racist White church officials over being officially ordained as either an exhorter or preacher in the church.[8] Of the church's ministerial hierarchy and its relationship to Methodist textual practices, John H. Wigger explains that nineteenth-century American Methodists "drew a distinction between exhorting and preaching, and between local and itinerant preachers. In theory, exhorting consisted of simply telling one's testimony of conversion or relating life experiences in the faith, with the goal of imploring one's listeners toward greater holiness and fuller service. . . . Preaching, on the other hand, consisted of 'taking,' or reading, a text of scripture and then explaining the meaning of that passage." "Only licensed preachers were supposed to exercise the privilege of taking a text," but in practice, according to Wigger, "this distinction often became blurred almost beyond meaning. Preachers sometimes chose perfunctory texts that served only as launching pads for what were really exhortations."[9]

Alfred Brunson, an itinerant Methodist preacher and exhorter and a contemporary of Apes, more colorfully describes this blurring in practice: "My gifts, whatever they may be, are for textual preaching—to take a text, and explain it. Topical preaching and exhortation are so nearly allied as to be inseparable. After much discussion with preachers and people, the grave conclusion was, that an exhorter might *steal* a text. That is, he had no right to sing and pray and take a text, giving book, chapter, and verse: but might, after singing and prayer, begin to introduce a subject, and bring in a text that he wished to explain, but not tell where it could be found. He must not divide it into heads and points, but might, topical fashion, take up one at a time, till he gets through the heads and points of it."[10] Within Methodist print history, a tradition of appropriating others' texts as one's own as a minister and writer began with John Wesley, as we will see further in Chapter 4. Here, I apply Brunson's concept of "stealing" a text to understand how Apes brought certain passages from Walker's *Appeal* and Jefferson's *Notes* into his "Looking-Glass" without telling his audience where he found them. That is, in addition to scripture, Apes drew language and arguments from what he recognized as authoritative secular texts—both Jefferson's and Walker's—as the basis for his powerful print exhortation to White Christian Americans to treat Indigenous Americans as their equals. Just as he would have done with scripture as either an exhorter or a preacher, he carefully selected the aspects of each text that best supported his ultimate message, taking them up one at a time in his "Looking-Glass" to get through the "heads and points" of his argument, as Brunson describes, in print.

Karim M. Tiro has argued that "it was by writing and speaking within the discourse of an existing Euro-American religious movement whose primary appeal was to lower-class youths like himself that Apess managed to articulate to a broad audience a critique of the dominant culture and a vindication of the indigenous one."[11] I see Tiro's argument as extending to why Apes specifically chose to confront White Christians in print with his "Looking-Glass." He not only understood the dominant discourse but, from the powerful examples of the Bible, Jefferson's *Notes on the State of Virginia*, and Walker's *Appeal*, he also recognized and harnessed the power of its most authoritative medium—print—for how it would allow his antidiscrimination sermon to reach, register with, and be adopted by a wider White audience.

I begin with the immediate and historical context of Apes's "Looking-Glass," considering its relationship to the religious conversion narratives with which he published it, how Apes positioned the confrontational essay at the end of a collection of these narratives, and the essay's debt to a centuries-old tradition of using this titular metaphor in religious and political reform literature.

Situating Apes's "Looking-Glass"

Much like Stewart's *Religion and the Pure Principles of Morality*, the title of Apes's *Experiences of Five Christian Indians* offers no suggestion of the political polemic contained within—in this case, in the pamphlet's last eight pages. And while the pamphlet's title page indicates Apes was the publisher, his designation as "a Missionary of that Tribe" (Pequot), and the epigraph from scripture about missionary work (Matthew 20:19–20), both signal that it is an evangelical publication. As such, *Experiences* contributed to the outpouring of official and popular religious tracts during the Second Great Awakening that coincided with the rise of technologies of mass print production and included Stewart's and, as we will see, William Paul Quinn's pamphlets.[12] Apes begins the pamphlet with "The Experience of the Missionary," an abbreviated story of his own youth, his introduction to Christianity, and his struggles with faith as a new convert. He follows his story with the spiritual autobiography of his wife Mary, then the spiritual biographies of Hannah Caleb, Sally George, and Anne Wamply, respectively—all of which Apes also authored.

Several aspects of Apes's brief story of his life and conversion quickly alert readers that what they have in hand is not only a religious tract but also a political pamphlet. In the first sentence of his "Experience," Apes specifically labels the text as a "pamphlet" rather than a tract.[13] While contemporary scholars often use the words interchangeably, pamphlets, in the wake of the American Revolution and, more immediately and specifically, of Walker's *Appeal*—which newspapers frequently referred to as "Walker's pamphlet" or simply the "incendiary pamphlet"—had recovered their association with politics, particularly political radicalism and controversy.[14] Following the founding of the New England Tract Society in Boston in 1814 and the American Tract Society in New York City in 1825 to mass-produce religious readings cheaply and circulate them as widely as possible, the tract was more commonly and closely associated with evangelical religious content, including spiritual autobiographies.

That Apes was mixing both print formats and genres becomes clear when he directly addresses his audience at the beginning of his narrative. He at once instructs and reprimands White Christian Americans, "When you read this, ask yourselves if you ever had such trials? If not, begin now to prize your privileges, and show pity to those whose fates are wretched and cruel" (4). With this use of direct address, we recognize an early suggestion of Walker's influence not only on Apes's rhetoric but also on his choice of words ("wretched and cruel"). Walker's influence is also apparent when Apes exclaim-asks, "O white man! how can you account to God for this [the sufferings of Indigenous children]? Are you not afraid that the children of the forest will rise up in judgment and condemn you?" (5–6). He also deploys Walker-like rhetorical—though not typographic—finger-pointing: "Shame! shame! shame! to be so indecent, who boast of so much correctness and p[u]rity!" (13). With this, we begin to see how Apes's narrative blends the genres of spiritual autobiography, reform literature, and political polemic as well as his own words and Walker's. "The Experience of the Missionary" thus offers an important preview of his "Indian's Looking-Glass for the White Man," which he places immediately after the five conversion narratives.[15]

The title of Apes's essay ("An Indian's Looking-Glass for the White Man"), unlike that of the pamphlet (*Experiences of Five Christian Indians*), clearly indicates that Apes is writing polemically to a White audience. Metaphorically making it a "Looking-Glass" places his essay in both a centuries-old tradition of radical political protest published in pamphlet form and a specific genre within the format: the didactic pamphlet, a genre it shares with both Walker's *Appeal* and Stewart's *Religion and the Pure Principles of Morality*. Even more specifically, Apes's use of what Herbert Grabes calls the "titular metaphor for the unmasking of concealed ills"—the mirror, or looking glass—places it within a subgenre of didactic literature that spans from the *specula* of antiquity and the Middle Ages through seventeenth-century broadsides and pamphlets titled *mirrors* and *looking-glasses*.[16]

With respect to the metaphor's significance in aesthetic theory and its relationship to the moral principle of imitation, Grabes explains that the "preference for the mirror was, for one thing, fostered by the universal validity of the principle of *imitatio* throughout the Middle Ages and the Renaissance. Central here was the re-creation of the pre-existent: in aesthetic theory, imitation of *natura* by the *artes*; in the earlier neoclassical theory, imitation of models." In the Middle Ages and Renaissance, writers of didactic pamphlets extended this aesthetic principle to religious morality: "It was believed that acquaintance with the largely didactic literature of the time could and would bring about moral improvement. Moral purpose is clearly manifested in the frequency with which the mirror-metaphor occurs as a designation for exemplary texts and for human beings as positive or negative models of behaviour." In this logic, "the use of a looking-glass for physical correction would serve as a self-evident metaphor for introspection leading to moral purification" (228). While Grabes does not discuss the moral principle of imitatio Christi specifically, it is both implied in and central to this understanding of moral reform via imitation; early modern Christians, seeing their moral failings accurately reflected, looked to mirror Christ as the perfect model.[17] John Wesley renewed this tradition in eighteenth-century evangelical Christianity, and Methodists in the United States made the imitation of Christ part of their evangelism, as we saw in the previous chapter.

By specifically making his essay a "Looking-Glass," Apes draws on the popular understanding that mirrors accurately represent what is in front of them, without exaggeration. By doing so, he is able to present white Christian Americans' faults to them so that his "Looking-Glass" prompts their reform, not their rebuttal or refusal as misrepresentational. His title also evokes the popularity and power that the mirror metaphor in pamphlet titles had maintained in the nineteenth century United States. *The Clergyman's Looking Glass* (published throughout New England between 1803 and 1805), *A Mirror, or Looking Glass for the Rising Generation and Young Convert* (New York, 1804), and *The Drunkard's Looking Glass* (widely reprinted between 1813 and 1818) are just a few examples of the many such moral and social reform pamphlets.[18] It is likely that Apes encountered these or similar "looking glasses" in his itinerancy as a Methodist minister and colporteur, and as part of his project of self-improvement not just as an Indigenous convert to Christianity but also as a nineteenth-century subject living in an era of religious revival and reform.[19]

Thus aware of the power and familiarity of this metaphor for both spiritual and political reform, Apes extends it beyond the title into his text, comparing his "surprising and horrible" words to a mirror that reflects back to White Christian Americans what he, as an Indigenous American, can see of and in them but what they apparently are not able see self-reflexively (55). He explains that with his pamphlet he is "merely placing before [Whites] the black inconsistency that [they] place before [him]—which is ten times blacker than any skin that you will find in the universe" (55). Here, we see that Apes's metaphorical looking glass draws on popular imaginative representations of the mirror's introspective power, in this case to surface and reflect back White Americans' apparent hatred of Indigenous Americans even though they, as Christians, should understand that God is "the maker and preserver both of the white man and the Indian" (53).[20] Significantly, Apes figures this "inconsistency" between White people's basic principles as Americans and Christians and their inner hatred of Indigenous people as visibly "black," thus maintaining the long-standing association of the color with evil. But at the same time, he also dissociates so-called black skin color from this interior evil of character when he emphasizes that this blackness is manifested through deeds, not pigment. White people's moral blackness, as Apes's mirror both sees and shows it, thus is "ten times blacker than any skin that you will find in the Universe" (55).

By thus figuratively holding up his looking glass so that White Christian Americans can clearly see and must confront the hypocrisy and sin of racial discrimination, Apes draws from not just the jeremiad and its "traditional mode of denunciation" derived from Calvinism and favored by Walker, but also popular figurations of the spiritual self-reflection and reform characteristic of Methodism and its focus on the moral exercise of an individual's will.[21]

Resemblance Without Exact Likeness

At the level of both language and argumentation, Apes's "Looking-Glass" is not a mirror, in that it does not reproduce either Walker's words or arguments exactly as they appear in the *Appeal*. As I have suggested, Walker only discusses Indigenous Americans in passing in his essay. Apes also understood that Black and Indigenous people in the United States were not viewed in the same way by White people, and, consequently, that Black and Indigenous people experienced discrimination differently. Thus, a strict mechanical copying of any lengthy passages from Walker's *Appeal* would not have allowed Apes to address Indigenous Americans' necessarily different plight. Yet Apes recognized enough similarity in Black and Indigenous experiences of racism as well as the relevance of many antislavery and antiracism arguments to Indigenous people to create a distinct echo of Walker's *Appeal* in his "Looking-Glass." This echo effect was also likely legally strategic on Apes's part: exactly copying any significant part of Walker's *Appeal* would have made it more difficult for him to copyright his pamphlet as his own creation, which he took the trouble to do in notable contrast to Walker. Phillip Round has considered at length Apes's idea of proprietary authorship, arguing that "copyrighted authorship offered unique 'rights and privileges' protected by the Constitution and sanctioned by the new social status being accorded professional authors" (153). In the case of *Experiences*, and more specifically "Looking-Glass," we can see how linguistic and rhetorical resemblance without exact likeness to Walker's *Appeal* allowed Apes to secure this protection and to conjure both the fury of Walker's pamphlet and the anxious attention it received in response, even as he significantly modified his argumentative basis for confronting and reforming Whites about another aspect of their racist discrimination. Through this repetition with important differences, Apes's "Looking-Glass" thus became both an inventive and alienable adaptation of Walker's *Appeal* and a powerful appeal in its own right on behalf of Indigenous people.

This dynamic of resemblance with some notable differences is immediately visible in the first paragraph of Apes's "Looking-Glass." The essay begins,

> HAVING a desire to place a few things before my fellow creatures who are travelling with me to the grave, and to that God who is the maker and preserver both of the white man and the Indian, whose abilities are the same, and who are to be judged by one God, who will show no favor to outward appearances, but will judge righteousness. Now I ask if degradation has not been heaped long enough upon the Indians? . . . Let me for a few moments turn your attention to the reservations in the different states of New England, and, with but few exceptions, we shall find them as follows: The most mean, abject, miserable race of beings in the world—a complete place of prodigality and prostitution. (53)

Whereas Apes implicitly addresses a White audience from the outset of his "Looking-Glass," Walker explicitly addresses the preamble of his *Appeal* to his "*dearly beloved Brethren and Fellow Citizens*" (3, emphasis in the original). But the verbal similarity between their two opening paragraphs is otherwise striking, starting with a shared first word in small caps. Here is Walker's:

> HAVING travelled over a considerable portion of these United States, and having, in the course of my travels, taken the most accurate observations of things as they exist—the result of my observations has warranted the full and unshaken conviction, that we, (coloured people of these United States,) are the most degraded, wretched, and abject set of beings that ever lived since the world began; and I pray God that none like us ever may live again until time shall be no more. (3)

As we can see, Apes's claim that the Indigenous people on New England's reservations are the "most mean, abject, miserable race of beings in the world" very nearly repeats Walker's claims about Black people's state as a race under slavery and discrimination. It also suggests that Walker's prayer has gone unanswered and, moreover, that Indigenous people's abjection on the reservations set aside for them in 1825 is worse than Black people's in slavery, in that Apes declares Indigenous Americans the "*most* mean, abject, and miserable race" (emphasis added). Apes further distinguishes his text from Walker's by not repeating Walker's words or word order exactly; he describes Indians as suffering "degradation" and as "mean" instead of as "degraded," and as "miserable" instead of "wretched."

The noticeably awkward syntax in the last sentence of Apes's opening paragraph draws our attention to how he both adopted and adapted Walker's language and arguments to bring notice to Indigenous Americans' necessarily different plight. Into the middle of a sentence about the condition of Indian reservations as unseen places within New England, Apes abruptly introduces a Walker-like claim about Indigenous people's abjection as a race. That he has only lightly revised Walker's words to do so suggests not only the power, but also the resonance of Walker's phrase, which Walker repeats with some slight variations three times at the beginning of the third edition of his *Appeal*. As we have seen, this claim first appears in the notice to readers that Walker inserts in place of a copyright in the third edition: "☞ IT will be recollected, that I, in the first edition of my 'Appeal,'* promised to demonstrate in the course of which, viz. in the course of my Appeal, to the satisfaction of the most incredulous mind, that we Coloured People of these United States, are, the most *wretched, degraded and abject* set of beings that [e]ver lived since the world began, down to the present day" (emphasis added). As we have also seen, in the footnote signaled by the asterisk, Walker circularly cites himself, sending readers to both the "Preamble in first edition, first page" and "2d edition, Article 1, page 9" for two more versions of his primary claim. And in article 3 of the third edition, he again included a variant of this claim, declaring, "There are not a more *wretched, ignorant, miserable, and abject* set of beings in all the world, than the blacks in the Southern and Western sections of this country" (46, emphasis added). Again, all of Walker's repetitions of this emphatic and similarly worded assertion of Black people's extreme suffering—both within the text of the *Appeal* and among its different editions—surely registered this primary claim with all the pamphlet's readers, especially such a trained exegetical and interested reader as Apes. Given Apes's training and experiences as a minister, he would have been unusually sensitive to how repeating a variant of this phrase himself would call attention to Indigenous people's extreme suffering while also calling up Walker's text and similar claim about Black suffering in his readers' minds, just as a minister's paraphrased oral repetition of a Bible verse would register in listeners' minds during a sermon.

The other resonant phrase that Apes borrowed from Walker is "by the inches"—or as Apes modifies it, "by inches"—to describe how White Americans incrementally, yet relentlessly distress and murder Indigenous Americans just as they do Black Americans. Walker repeats "by the inches" three times in his *Appeal*; he may have drawn it from Shakespeare's *Coriolanus*— "They'll give him death by inches" (act 5, scene 4). Given Apes's restoration of Shakespeare's original wording, it is possible that he meant to allude to both Walker and Shakespeare here, thinking that both might resonate— though very differently so—with a White audience. Either way, the phrase evokes White Christian Americans' systematic microtortures of both Black and Indigenous Americans—the rhetorical equivalent of our modern colloquial expression "death by a thousand paper cuts" and similar to the concept of racial microaggressions—in violation of both the democratic principle of equality and the Christian Golden Rule. (I will return to this passage below in discussing Apes's engagements with Thomas Jefferson.)

Apes's text most clearly resembles Walker's in its direct argumentative and rhetorical confrontations of White people with their hypocrisy as Christian Americans, almost as if Apes had annotated and abridged his copy of Walker's *Appeal* to keep only the sections in which Walker explicitly addresses his White readers as the model for his "Looking-Glass." We remember that these are also the most jeremiad-like sections of the *Appeal*, in which Walker focuses on Christianity and ministerially cites scripture to point up White Americans' contradictions of their professed faith and the peril they face in provoking divine retribution.[22] Apes the Methodist minister is no less confrontational than Walker, but as I have suggested, his "Looking-Glass" works to provoke self-reflection and spiritual reform so that White American Christians' practices match their sacred and secular principles and they thereby redeem themselves.

In showing White Christian Americans the errors of their ways, both Walker and Apes are motivated by the simple question that Walker asks about whether there is any biblical basis for Whites' racial discrimination: "Does [the Bible] teach them any distinction on account of a man's colour [sic]?"[23] For both Walker and Apes, *distinction*—or differentiation according to race—is a key word and the principle upon which the sins of discrimination, oppression, and slavery are based. Walker derives the word from Jefferson's assertion in *Notes* that "it is not their *condition* then, but *nature*, which has produced the distinction" among the races.[24] Like Walker, Apes emphasizes that distinction has less to do with Black and Indigenous bodies and minds than with White people's ideas and actions, as we see when Apes declares, "I am not talking about the skin, but about principles." "And let me ask," he continues, "is it not on the account of a bad principle, that we who are red children have had to suffer so much as we have? And let me ask, did not this bad principle proceed from the whites or their forefathers?" (54). Without naming it, Apes describes distinction as "a most unrighteous, unbecoming and impure black principle" that is "as corrupt and unholy as it can be," and defines it as whites "tak[ing] the skin as a pretext to keep [Indians] from [their] unalienable and lawful rights" (55). He first uses the word in asking, "Why is all this distinction made among these christian [sic] societies?" (58). And in the culminating last sentence of the essay, he prays that "this tree of distinction shall be levelled [sic] to the earth, and the mantle of prejudice torn from every American heart" (60).

Walker surveys White peoples' history as a race in making his case against distinction and, in the process, makes some distinctions himself within the race. In concluding his survey of histories of ancient Greece and Rome, he determines that White people "have always been an unjust, jealous, unmerciful, avaricious and blood-thirsty set of beings." "But we will leave the whites or Europeans as heathens, and take a view of them as Christians," Walker explains of the next stage of his inquiry. As Christians, he observes, Whites are "as cruel, if not more so than ever." In Walker's view, White, Enlightenment-minded Christians' innovation of racial slavery has made them *"ten times more cruel, avaricious and unmerciful than they ever were"* (20, emphasis added).

Apes uses the same scale as Walker to measure White American Christians' sin of racism when he says that his "Looking-Glass" is "merely placing before you [his White audience] the black inconsistency that you place before me—which is *ten times* blacker than any skin that you will find in the Universe" (55, emphasis added). With this comparison, Apes alludes to the story in Genesis of Cain and Abel and the mark that God placed on Cain as part of cursing Cain as punishment for murdering his brother, and to White Americans' use of this story as a justification for racial discrimination and slavery. (Walker also directly addresses the Cain and Abel story in his *Appeal*'s fourth article, as we will see below.[25]) Interestingly, Apes uses Walker's measurement of White Christian Americans' sinfulness rather than the original proportion set forth in Genesis 4:15: "And the LORD said unto him, Therefore whosoever slayeth Cain, vengeance shall be taken on him sevenfold. And the LORD set a mark upon Cain, lest any finding him should kill him." Apes repeats Walker's math when he "exhort[s] [White Americans] to do away [with] that principle [of distinction], as it appears *ten times* worse in the sight of God and candid men, than skins of color—more disgraceful than all the skins that Jehovah ever made" (55, emphasis added).

Recognizing, though, that this logic comes dangerously close to reinscribing skin color rather than racial discrimination as the source of sin, as Walker does in his essay's most ethnological moment, Apes recalculates. He switches from the powers of ten—also commonly used in lens-based observation and the magnifying powers of microscopes and telescopes—to ratios, which are more suitable for a comparative statistical view of the earth's human population: "If black or red skins, or any other skin of color is disgraceful to God, it appears that he has disgraced himself a great deal—for he has made fifteen colored people to one white, and placed them here upon this earth" (55). By thus presenting—through argumentative resemblance to Walker's text without exact likeness—the overwhelming odds against God's having made people of color inferior, given their significant majority, Apes makes the same point as Walker—that White Americans have corrupted Christian principles in service of racism—while compelling these same White Christian Americans to see both the irrationality and sin of using a visibly different skin color as a basis for discrimination and to change their ways.

Apes's ministerial experience had conditioned him to anticipate objections from sinners looking for every opportunity to continue on the road to ruin rather than take the harder route of reform and righteousness. Thus, he broadens his essay's view from the mirror metaphor to other ways of looking and seeing, staying with the theme of skin to imagine that he is "look[ing] at all the skins" of the peoples of the world as the medium for recording the historical deeds of the different races. "When I cast my eye upon that white skin, and if I saw those crimes written upon it," he declares, "I should enter my protest against it immediately" (56). With this, Apes imagines white skin not just as a writing surface, like the white pages of his manuscript and the pamphlet that readers have in hand, but also as itself surfacing the entire history of White people's wrongdoings as a race, just like the introspective metaphorical mirror that he holds up for White American Christians to see themselves as he does.

Though he says he will "ask one question more," he asks several more that answer the question about which race and nation will record the greatest number of crimes: "Can you charge the Indians with robbing a nation almost of their whole Continent, and murdering their women and children, and then depriving the remainder of their lawful rights, that nature and God require them to have? And to cap the climax, rob another nation to till their grounds, and welter out their days under the lash with hunger and fatigue under the scorching rays of a burning sun?" (56). Here, again, Apes's text and logic closely resemble Walker's, specifically where Walker directly addresses White American Christians' appropriation of the story of Cain and Abel as a justification for racial slavery in article 4. There, Walker asserts that

> some ignorant creatures hesitate not to tell us that we, (the blacks) are the seed of Cain the murderer of his brother Abel. But where or of whom those ignorant and avaricious wretches could have got their information, I am unable to declare. Did they receive it from the Bible? I have searched the Bible as well as they, if I am not as well learned as they are, and have never seen a verse which testifies whether we are the seed of Cain or of Abel. Yet those men tell us that we are the seed

> of Cain, and that God put a dark stain upon us, that we might be known as their slaves!!! Now, I ask those avaricious and ignorant wretches, who act [sic] more like the seed of Cain, by murdering the whites or the blacks? How many vessel loads of human beings, have the blacks thrown into the seas? How many thousand souls have the blacks murdered in cold blood, to make them work in wretchedness and ignorance, to support them and their families?—However, let us be the seed of *Cain, Harry, Dick,* or *Tom*!!! God will show the whites what we are, yet. (68)

Whereas Walker concludes this section by threatening White Americans with Black Americans' divinely sanctioned vengeance in a second revolution, Apes encourages his White readers to complete his logic and, thereby, to realize for themselves the full force of what he is saying. This is where he declares: "I should look at all the skins, and I know that when I cast my eye upon that white skin, and if I saw those crimes written upon it, I should enter my protest immediately, and cleave to that which is more honorable" (56). By representing himself here as looking at the written record of all White people's crimes and responding in protest, Apes further invites his White readers to reflect on how the white pages they have in hand also record Apes's justified protest. And again, the skin-as-parchment implicitly recalls Apes's pamphlet-as-mirror conceit, in that both media capture Whites' ugly history, compelling them to see themselves as they really are, rather than as they idealize themselves to be.

Both Apes and Walker base this idea of the inevitable publication—in the broad sense of making public—of the White race's sins on Matthew 10:27: "What I tell you in darkness, *that* speak ye in light: and what ye hear in the ear, *that* preach ye upon the housetops." As they respectively "steal" this verse (in Brunson's sense), we again notice the resemblance without exact likeness among the texts—here, the Bible, Apes's "Looking-Glass," and Walker's *Appeal*—that is characteristic of such ministerial stealing. Walker twice alludes to Matthew 10:27 and, in both instances, specifically changes preaching to publishing. The first time he asks his White readers, "Will he not publish your secret crimes on the house top?" (45). Later, we recall, Walker notes, "These and similar cruelties"—specifically, North Carolina having criminalized teaching anyone Black to spell, read, and write—"*Christians* have been for hundreds of years inflicting on our fathers and us in the dark, God has however, very recently published some of their secret crimes on the house top, that the world may gaze on their Christianity and see of what kind it is composed" (59, emphasis in the original). With this, Walker refers his readers to the printed proceedings of the Georgia, Virginia, Florida, South Carolina, and Kentucky legislatures—publishing these states' names with eye-catching all capital type in his own text—for their debates over legislation to restrict Black people from reading, writing, and meeting to worship. Thus, we can see how, for Walker, print served as both a material means for, and material evidence of, God bringing Whites' secret crimes to light.

With this Walker's *Appeal* becomes more visible as Apes's secular source for likening White skin specifically to paper that records and publicizes Whites' crimes as a race.[26] Apes also stays close to Walker by similarly pointing White readers to their self-publication of their sins when he refers specifically to the "disgraceful act in the statute law passed by the Legislature of Massachusetts" regarding intermarriage as proof of the same moral crimes made public (59). Walker, as part of his exposure of Whites' self-indictment in print, declares, "I tell you that God works in many ways his wonders to perform, he will unless they repent, make them expose themselves enough more yet to the world" (60). Here we might read Walker as exhorting his readers—including Apes—to read White Americans' law books (or at least newspaper articles about this legislation), Jefferson's *Notes*, his *Appeal*, and, unknowingly, Apes's "Looking-Glass" as evidence of God's work in many ways to expose the White race's sins. While men may have written all of these texts that publish the White race's sins for all to see, we see here how Walker, like the recent converts Stewart and Apes, understood that God is the original author, and that all mortal authors—be they White, Black, or Indigenous—are only God's agents.[27]

Apes's and Walker's Different Engagements with Jefferson

In contrast to the sinful racial distinctions made by White Christians, Apes points out, "Jesus Christ and his Apostles never looked at the outward appearances." Instead, like Apes and his mirror, Jesus "looked at the hearts, and his Apostles through him being discerners of the spirit looked at their fruit without any regard to the skin, color or nation" (57–58). In displaying this distance between White Christian Americans and Christ and his apostles, Apes aims for his mirror to spur the moral purification that Grabes describes as typical of the tradition of didactic mirror pamphlets, specifically by way of the imitatio Christi principle. By seeing so clearly how little they resemble Christ, White Christian Americans should be compelled to reform themselves in his image, which necessarily would include loving Indigenous Americans as fellow Christians without concern for their skin color. To do so, they once again must turn from seeing only others' skin to considering their own. Thus focusing their gaze, Apes returns to the essay-as-looking-glass metaphor, declaring, "By what you read, you may learn how deep your principles are. I should say they were skin deep" (60). This compact and powerful rebuke requires some unpacking.

In this instance, Apes's figurative looking-glass only shows White Christian readers their outer appearance, but not because it is limited to reflecting this outer appearance (figured here as their skin) like an actual mirror would be. Rather, Apes's metaphorical mirror is able to penetrate more deeply to surface how Whites lack a moral character as either Christians or Americans; it has such insightful power precisely because it is a metaphorical and not an actual mirror. That is, his "looking-glass" shows White Christian Americans exactly as they are because it accurately reflects how they see others and, in turn, makes them look at themselves in the same way—by seeing only surface skin color and not inner character. Moreover, by looking at their own skin instead of others', they will also see—or at least be able to reflect on—how thin human skin is. If Apes's White readers were to actually pause to look at their own skin after reading these lines, they would readily see its thinness.

Query 14 of Jefferson's *Notes* gives Apes's metaphor for the shallowness of Whites' principles particular depth. It is there that Jefferson specifically notes the greater visibility of blood vessels in white skin as a significant asset. In Jefferson's logic, white skin becomes the perfect medium for registering aesthetically appealing blushes, particularly when compared to black skin. "Are not the fine mixtures of red and white, the expressions of every passion by greater or less suffusions of color in the one, preferable to that eternal monotony, which reigns in the countenances, that immoveable veil of black which covers all the emotions of the other race?" he asks (205). Apes, by asking White people to look at their own skin, either actually or imaginatively, compels them to reflect on how physically insubstantial all skin is—and especially so in White Americans' case, given both Jefferson's and their own observations—to serve as the basis of all civil and religious rights, much less full membership in the human race.

This recognition, in turn, requires Apes's audience to realize how insubstantial one's principles must be to discriminate against someone with a different skin color instead of following the basic Christian principle of loving them as Christ would. When White Christian Americans come to see themselves as they see others, Apes reasons, they should be able to recognize just how little they resemble not only Christ but also "a [Daniel] Webster, an [Edward] Everett, and a [William] Wirt, and many others who are distinguished characters" whom he offers up as model White Christians who "advocate our cause daily" (60).[28] With this conclusion, Apes draws once more on the mirror's connection to the *imitatio* principle, suggesting that White Americans must reform themselves in the image not only of Christ but also of their own White contemporaries whose advocacy on behalf of Indigenous and Black people reflects that their principles are truly Christian and egalitarian, and not just skin deep.

By contrast, most White Christian Americans' treatment of Indigenous Americans demonstrates that they fail to act on either Christ's ideal of loving one another or a commonly held principle that originated with another "distinguished character" that Apes notes among them, but without explicitly naming him—Thomas Jefferson. Whereas Walker directly engages with and contradicts Jefferson and his racial claims in *Notes*, Apes's allusions to both Jefferson and his influential *Notes* register on a much lower frequency throughout the essay, as we have seen above with respect to Apes's discussion of white skin's whiteness and thinness. Even so, Jefferson's natural philosophical claims about racial difference bear significant weight in the main argument of his "Looking-Glass," thereby argumentatively and politically distancing Apes from Walker.

More precisely, Apes invokes Jefferson's theory of the greater proximity of White and Indigenous people to each other than either race's proximity to people of African descent in a rhetorically roundabout way. As part of anticipating, like his predecessors Walker and Stewart had, that "this kind of talk" in his confrontational essay "will seem surprising and horrible" to many White readers, Apes adopts and adapts the rhetorical structure of the Golden Rule and, at the same time, indirectly alludes to Jefferson's *Notes* by declaring that "(the whites) say they think as much of us as they do of themselves." "This," Apes explains, "I have heard repeatedly, from the most respectable gentlemen and ladies" (55).

Both this crucial principle of Indigenous and White equality and how Apes presents it mark a significant argumentative shift within his

"Looking-Glass." At the start of his essay, Apes presents Indigenous and White equality as a matter of divine creation and judgment alone. He praises God as "the maker and preserver of both the white man and the Indian, whose abilities are the same, and who are to be judged by one God, who will show no favor to outward appearances, but will judge righteousness" (53). When he asserts this equality the second time in the essay, as we saw above, he emphasizes how it has been widely accepted as true by prominent Americans. By referring to "the most respectable gentlemen and ladies," he surely has in mind Jefferson, with his *Notes*, as the most influential author and proponent of this theory in the early United States. As we saw in Chapter 1, Walker cites Jefferson and his arguments formally as part of modeling his adherence to conventions of learned Enlightenment discourse and, thereby, establishing himself as Jefferson's intellectual peer. By contrast, Apes finds much more power in how Jefferson's natural philosophical theory of the races has become established fact and more widely diffused and, thus, commonplace in the nineteenth-century United States by way of other influential and "respectable gentlemen and ladies." Thus, Apes is able to scold, without citing chapter and verse from *Notes*, "and having heard so much precept, I should now wish to see the example" (55). This extremely subtle and complicated invocation of Jefferson's racial theories in *Notes* as both established scientific facts and commonplace popular ideas would have registered only with his White readers who were the most invested in inflecting the racial debates of the early United States with Enlightenment natural and political philosophy—that is, Jefferson's intellectual and political heirs. What Apes makes clear to all of his readers is that, as an Indigenous man, a minister, and a skilled close reader of the Bible, secular American print, and American culture, he is uniquely positioned to see that most White American Christians do not practice either the foundational sacred or secular principles they preach.

To recall the wider context of what occasioned Jefferson's comparative assessments of White Americans' and Indigenous Americans' abilities that Apes significantly implies, I return briefly to query 6 of *Notes*, on "Productions Mineral, Vegetable, and Animal." Again, it is here that Jefferson engages European Enlightenment thinkers' hypotheses about climate and evolution—specifically George-Louis Leclerc, comte de Buffon's "theory of the tendency of nature to belittle her productions on this side of the Atlantic," as Jefferson puts it (97).[29] Buffon influentially had theorized that plants and animals evolved or devolved in relation to the climate in which they lived and proposed North America as a site of such devolution. Jefferson was acutely sensitive to applications of this theory to humans, which meant that White Americans would rank below White Europeans in Buffon's hierarchy of humankind. As evidence against devolution in Virginia, Jefferson presents the "Indian of North America," whom he and other natural philosopher peers have observed to be "neither more defective in ardor, nor more impotent with his female, than the white reduced to the same diet and exercise" (88). He further deems Indigenous men to be brave for "meet[ing] death with more deliberation, and endur[ing] tortures with a firmness unknown almost to religious enthusiasm with us," "affectionate to [their] children," and "strong and faithful" in their friendships (90). He also specifically praises Indigenous men's "keen" sensibility and their "vivacity and activity of mind," which he declares "equal to ours in the same situation"—meaning the minds of people of European descent in the American climate (91).

These, then, are the specific passages that Apes very subtly "takes" in the Methodist sense—and "steals" in Brunson's sense—from Jefferson's *Notes* and combines with the Golden Rule to ground his moral and political argument in his "Looking-Glass." As Christians, Apes reasons, Whites should do unto Indians as they would have Indians do unto them. And as Americans who believe in both the political principles and the scientific theories of their Founding Father Thomas Jefferson—which, again, Apes understood as originating with God, the ultimate author—they should know better than to discriminate against people who were created as equal with them but with a different skin color, he scolds. That is, if the givens are the Golden Rule and Jefferson's conclusion in his influential *Notes* that White and Indigenous Americans' "abilities are the same," as Apes puts it, then he is able to "ask if degradation has not been heaped long enough upon the Indians?" "Is it right to hold and promote prejudices?" and "Could there be a more efficient way to distress and murder them by inches than the way they [whites] have taken?" (53–54).

It is with this logic that Apes most significantly departs from Walker, by accepting Jefferson's racial theories as established fact, rather than debunking them as the product of subjective bias, to make his case. But even as he is doing so, he continues to borrow Walker's language. In the last question, Apes includes a phrase that Walker uses three times in the third edition of the *Appeal*. We remember that Walker describes Whites' incremental but ultimately lethal abuse of Black men, women, and children as taking their lives "by the inches." Significantly, the first instance comes as part of Walker's mocking rebuttal to the recently deceased Jefferson in article 1 of his *Appeal*: "Here let me ask Mr. Jefferson, (but he is gone to answer at the bar of God, for the deeds done in his body while living,) I therefore ask the whole American people, had I not rather die, or be put to death, than to be a slave to any tyrant, who takes not only my own, but my wife and children's lives by the inches?" (17).[30] As we have seen, Walker further explains: "Mr. Jefferson's very severe remarks on us have been so extensively argued upon by men whose attainments in literature, I shall never be able to reach, that I would not have meddled with it, were it not to solicit each of my brethren" to acquire a copy of Jefferson's *Notes* and refute it themselves. Apes much more subtly shows us in his "Looking-Glass" that he has followed Walker's advice and acquired a copy of *Notes*, but instead adopted some of Mr. Jefferson's most admiring remarks about Indigenous Americans and based half of his argument for better treatment on Jefferson's resulting theory of Indigenous equality with Whites of European descent.

Again, the "very severe remarks" to which Walker alludes come in query 14 of *Notes*, where Jefferson compares Black to White Americans. As in query 6, where Jefferson includes the celebrated speech by Logan of the Cayuga and Mingo people as proof of Indigenous Americans' "vivacity and activity of mind," linguistic ability serves again in query 14 as a key indicator of the races' different intellectual and creative capacities. Indians will "astonish you with strokes of the most sublime oratory; such as prove their reason and sentiment strong, their imagination glowing and elevated," Jefferson reasserts in query 14 to further degrade people of African descent in America (207). For these abilities, he reaffirms that Indigenous Americans are equal to White people of European descent, emphasizing that they must be such orators naturally, in that Indians have not enjoyed the "advantages" of education or exposure to the arts and sciences that Blacks have been afforded in their proximity to Whites as slaves in America.

By contrast, Jefferson says he has yet to "find a black that had uttered a thought above the level of plain narration" (207)—the claim that we have seen Walker engage in his article 4. Looking beyond Virginia's borders, and switching from oratory to print, Jefferson considers the examples of Boston's Phillis Wheatley and England's Ignatius Sancho, both of whom other prominent White European intellectuals and activists had offered up as specimens of the literary potential of the Black race realized. Jefferson, though, famously finds Wheatley unexceptional to his pronouncement that he had discovered misery—"often the parent of the most affecting touches in poetry"—but "no poetry" among Blacks and summarily dismisses the imitative "compositions published under [Wheatley's] name" as "below the dignity of criticism" (208). And while he deems Sancho to be "nearer to merit in composition," he qualifies his literary achievements as "do[ing] more honor to the heart than the head" and criticizes his imagination as "wild and extravagant, escap[ing] incessantly from every restraint of reason and taste" (208). Black authors, as Jefferson sees them through the lens of other late-Enlightenment, early-Romantic arguments about race, are unworthy of the designation because they are incapable of imaginatively generating an original story or poem or of writing a well-reasoned and affectively tasteful essay. These literary critical assessments are particularly significant to his natural philosophical ranking of people of African descent at the bottom and Indigenous Americans sometimes nearer, and sometimes at, the top of the hierarchy of humans in Jefferson's Virginia.[31]

While Jefferson had dismissed Ignatius Sancho for writing too emotionally, Walker clearly recognized the role that Jefferson's own emotions played in such supposedly objective scientific and literary critical observations, notably with respect to Jefferson's deeply subjective examination of authorship and his exceptionally aggressive dismissal of Phillis Wheatley. Thus, Walker culminates his highly rational indictment of Jefferson and his arguments with his own emotional fury and fervor to demonstrate that a Black author is capable of writing from both head and heart. As we saw in Chapter 1, one of the ways in which he does this is by transforming Jefferson's natural philosophical inquiry into a rhetorical question that typographically provides its own emphatic affirmative answer: "Are we MEN!!—I ask you, O my brethren! are we MEN?" (19). Given Jefferson's influential assertions in *Notes* that Indigenous people are no less men than White people, and perhaps even superior, Apes has no need to ask this question of his Indigenous brethren in his "Looking-Glass." Instead, he is able to insist on White Americans' self-contradiction, asking them why they treat Indigenous Americans as if they are lesser when they have accepted Jefferson's racial theories that they are equal as men as fact.

It is important to note that Apes does not include Jefferson's damning observations about people of African descent or his ranking of them below both White and Indigenous Americans. But he certainly had read them, given their proximity to Jefferson's observations about Indigenous people, and recognized the importance of literary ability to Jefferson's distinctions among the three races. Apes's strategy, then, of publishing an essay that so closely resembles Walker's *Appeal* in its language and rhetorical style is surprising given Jefferson's tenacious theories of the different races' literary capacities. Like Garrison and Stewart, Apes sought to build on the significant attention that Walker's *Appeal* had attracted and sustained by echoing aspects of Walker's words and rhetoric to advance a related cause. But in light of Jefferson's lasting influence, Apes's strategic imitation of aspects of Walker's text, even as he argumentatively sets himself apart from Walker, would have carried a different risk than it did for either Garrison or Stewart. White readers who were both well-versed in the ethnological debates of the period and hostile to Apes's scathing indictment of White Americans' unchristian and undemocratic treatment of Indigenous Americans could easily have pointed to Apes's rhetorical debt to Walker and contrasted it with Logan's purportedly sui generis speech in Jefferson's *Notes*. That is to say, for an Indigenous man to manifest an intellectual debt to a Black man—and for him to do so audaciously while confronting White people with their political hypocrisy as Americans and moral failings as Christians—was to risk provoking a defensive and dismissive response from readers who were even more committed to White supremacy than Jefferson had been.[32] With a charge of mere imitation, in both letters and reasoning, Apes could have been demoted to the status of Wheatley and Sancho by Jefferson's White intellectual heirs, and Indigenous Americans to being equal with Blacks instead of Whites.[33]

But Apes's readers were more likely White Methodist Bostonians than White supremacist ethnologists, given his choice to publish what is, in part, an engagement with ethnology within a didactic essay appended to a religious tract. Thus, the most likely risk that associating his "Looking-Glass" with Walker's *Appeal* carried was these readers refusing to read it, or rejecting his argument out of hand, as too politically radical. As I have suggested, Apes published his politically polemical and didactic essay under the unsuspicious cover of a religious tract of conversion narratives to increase the chances that potentially sympathetic White readers *would* read it and focus on the Christian and American principles at its core and take them to heart. If it had fallen into the hands of any White supremacist ethnologists looking for evidence of Indigenous unoriginality and, thus, inferiority to Whites, Apes—if given a chance to defend himself—could have invoked standard Methodist textual practices of borrowing freely from other texts to evangelize throughout the United States. When we take such a complex view of these different strategies of textual engagement and for negotiating textual authority—a view that considers not just the Enlightenment's intellectual textual debates about race and Romantic expectations of creative originality, but also contemporary religious evangelical engagements in and deployments of print—we are better able to understand why and how Apes drew on and hybridized these sacred and secular principles and texts and their authority to ground his bold indictment of White Christian Americans and their sinful and undemocratic treatment of Indigenous people.

* * *

After discreetly publishing his confrontational "Looking-Glass," Apes became an even more public and committed political activist, taking up the Mashpee people's struggle with the Commonwealth of Massachusetts for sovereignty over their land on Cape Cod. Apes ministered to them, urging them to assert their religious and civil rights and to adopt him into their tribe. For making their fight his own, Apes was arrested, jailed, charged with several other Mashpee members with "riot, assault, and trespass," sentenced to thirty days in jail, and fined one hundred dollars.[34] The so-called Mashpee Revolt attracted national attention, with local and national newspapers invoking southern political discourse about secession to accuse the Mashpee of attempting to secede from the United States, and to charge Apes with having incited them to violent rebellion. As when these same charges were made against Walker and his *Appeal*, we see White supremacists ultimately exerting significant rhetorical and physical force against Apes for his interventions in order to maintain the fiction that the oppressed, rather than the oppressors, were the initiators of destabilizing violence.

In December 1833, after serving his sentence as a political prisoner, Apes wrote and published "An Indian's Appeal to the White Men of Massachusetts" in regional newspapers. With this explicit adaptation of the title of Walker's pamphlet to make another appeal to White Americans as an Indigenous American, we see that Apes's encounter with the racially biased U.S. legal system only added fuel to the fire of his rhetoric and print-based activism. Unlike Walker, he lived to meet with real, positive results: the Massachusetts General Court "granted their request for the incorporation as the Marshpee District with the right to govern themselves like any other Massachusetts community."[35] He subsequently published an overtly political pamphlet, *Indian Nullification of the Unconstitutional Laws of Massachusetts Relative to the Mashpee Tribe; or, The Present Riot Explained*, in 1835—a controversial and now landmark text in the history of American Indian political dissent and a lasting contribution to Indigenous political theory.

It would diminish these and Apes's numerous significant political and authorial accomplishments to characterize them all as effects of Walker's *Appeal*. Instead, it is more just to Apes to recognize just how much he made of what we might consider to be his intellectual and political apprenticeship under Walker's powerful example and from "stealing" Walker's text, to become one of the fiercest, most controversial, and eventually most respected advocates for racial justice for Indigenous people in all of American history, literature, science, and political theory.

CHAPTER 4

Taking Walker's *Appeal* West

Reverend William Paul Quinn's *The Origin, Horrors, and Results of Slavery*

In 1834 William Paul Quinn, an itinerant minister, aid to fugitive enslaved people, and eventual bishop in the African Methodist Episcopal Church (AME), published the twenty-four page tract *The Origin, Horrors, and Results of Slavery* in Pittsburgh.[1] In the introduction, Quinn informs his readers, "I have faithfully given you a few of my thoughts on Slavery, and have endeavored in a few pages to give you, from the pen of a most faithful witness, a description of Slavery as it has existed in various parts and ages of the world" (iii–iv). Yet, as several scholars beginning with Dorothy Porter have noticed, the thoughts in Quinn's "few pages" and the pen that recorded them are not just his but also David Walker's.[2] The majority of Quinn's tract's third section, "A Hint to the Congress of the United States," is copied nearly verbatim from the last four pages of the third article of Walker's third and last edition of his *Appeal*.

Quinn was not the only the only antislavery pamphleteer to have copied significant portions of his text directly from Walker's *Appeal* without any attribution to Walker. We will see another in Paola Brown's 1851 *Address on the Subject of Slavery* in Chapter 6. Quinn's and Brown's reasons for, and the circumstances of, their using Walker's text differ significantly. In what follows, I focus on Quinn's tract as a case of what Eric Gardner calls African American literature in "unexpected places"—specifically, of Walker's *Appeal* circulating both under a different cover and in the early antebellum near West just four years after Walker's last edition and his death.[3] Both nineteenth-century readers and later scholars of the *Appeal* have focused primarily on its circulation across the Mason-Dixon Line on a north-south axis.[4] Quinn's *The Origin, Horrors, and Results of Slavery* offers an important opportunity to think about Walker's *Appeal* going west, and doing so in an unexpected way: with a good chunk of Walker's words and argument discreetly inserted into a hybrid religious tract and political pamphlet that the AME minister William Paul Quinn wrote, assembled, had printed, and likely personally circulated as he preached in and founded numerous churches in Western Pennsylvania, Ohio, Indiana, Illinois, Kentucky, Missouri, and Iowa.[5]

In this chapter, I also present the first extended reading of Quinn's text, analyzing it as a compositional and generic hybrid—partly his own writing and partly Walker's (and also Thomas Branagan's), and at once a religious tract and political pamphlet—written, published, and circulated as an effect of Walker's *Appeal* by a man with a complicated identity. In these ways, I respond to Gardner's call to consider African American literature produced in the West and other neglected places, to "broaden even further the list of authors and texts that we study," and to expand our "sense of genre and the literary" in the works by Black authors that we study (9). While Quinn identifies himself as "of African Descent" on the title page, most of his biographers suggest that he was born in India, the Caribbean, or Central America and arrived in Pennsylvania by way of England, where he had converted to Quakerism before converting to Methodism after coming to the United States in the first decade of the nineteenth century.[6] His profound dedication to the African Methodist Episcopalian Church as a traveling minister and eventual bishop makes it clear that he considered himself to be one of the "coloured citizens of the world" to whom Walker appealed. This identification extends into Quinn's text as he addresses his primary audience—free Black Christian American readers—as his "dearly beloved fellow countrymen" and urges them to identify sympathetically with and work on behalf of "no less than two and a half millions of Africans, who are in a state of servitude, suffering, and degradation truly lamentable!" (iii). In attempting to "awaken" free Black Americans to a broadened and engaged idea of Black identity, Quinn also challenges our ideas about Black identity as well, so that we further expand our ideas about Black-authored texts and authorship in ways that move us from the more narrow scholarly definitions that Gardner and others have challenged toward the more capacious ways of thinking about identity and textuality that Quinn and Walker held in common (iii).

More specifically, I examine how Quinn, like Stewart and Apes, revised and extended Walker's original *Appeal* shortly after its publication for new audiences—primarily to address free Black Americans in what was considered the West in 1834, urging their dedication to the causes of both antislavery and racial uplift through adherence to Christian principles. He also specifically appealed to White Americans in elected office to use their lawmaking power to change Black lives for the better. This dual aim gives Quinn's text its generic hybridity as both a religious tract and a political pamphlet. As the former, it offers an unusual opportunity to consider a specifically African Methodist Episcopalian take not just on Walker's *Appeal* but also on the religious tracts that were circulating by the hundreds of thousands throughout the nation, of which only a few were aimed specifically at Black readers and all of which avoided the topic of slavery.[7] As we have seen, in article 4 of all three editions of his *Appeal*, Walker pays his sublime emotional tribute to the AME Church founder, Bishop Richard Allen: "Richard Allen! O my God!! The bare recollection of the labours of this man, and his ministers among his deplorably wretched brethren, (rendered so by the whites) to bring them to a knowledge of the God of Heaven, fills my soul with all those very high emotions which would take the pen of an Addison to portray" (65). Walker's passionate praise surely drew Allen's and other AME ministers' notice, including Quinn's. In recognizing Quinn's *The Origin, Horrors, and Results of Slavery* as a response not only to this praise but also and especially to Walker's evangelical appeal to "Men of color, who are also of sense" to "cast [their] eyes upon the wretchedness of [their] brethren, and to do [their] utmost to enlighten them—*go to work and enlighten your brethren!*" we recognize how the effects of Walker's *Appeal* extend into both the print and larger histories of the major Black church in the United States (33).[8]

I also read the text as a political pamphlet in which Quinn carefully and strategically enhanced Walker's appeals to White readers, specifically targeting South Carolina legislators and members of the U.S. Congress to condemn legislation that was passed after, and partly in response to, Walker's *Appeal*. Quinn sought to enlighten the former about their misguided legislation against Black literacy and education and the latter to use their power to put "a period" to slavery (15). In speaking to powerful White Americans, Quinn, like Walker, recognized the need for his rhetoric and reasoning to surprise and impress readers, who expected little or nothing of writers of African descent. As such, Quinn's *The Origin, Horrors, and Results of Slavery* reads as an important textual effect of Walker's *Appeal*, written to reach unexpected audiences—free Black Americans in the antebellum near West and powerful White state and national legislators—thereby extending Walker's reach to the unexpected places of the AME Church's ministries on the American frontier and into the very halls of power where lawmakers had sought to censor Walker's pamphlet and other confrontational publications like it.

I open the chapter with some biographical details about Quinn's mysterious origins, his extensive missionary work for the early AME Church, and Black activism in 1830s Pittsburgh to shed some light on how Quinn might have encountered and extended the reach of Walker's *Appeal* as part of his remarkable, even hemispheric, commitment to religious, political, and social reform.

Quinn's Origins and Results

Nineteenth- and twentieth-century biographical accounts of Quinn present competing stories of his origins and coming into the AME Church, with some deliberate mystery sustained by church elders and historians due to the complicated questions that his national origin and racial identity raise for the history of the Black church, especially given Quinn's centrality in its early history and growth.[9] Both Daniel Alexander Payne's 1891 official history of the AME Church and Charles Spencer Smith's 1922 supplement to it omit any mention of Quinn's birthplace or racial identity, focusing instead on his tireless work for the early church. Other biographers suggest that he may have been born in Chester County, Pennsylvania, Honduras, or Calcutta, India—possibilities that I will consider below.[10] Smith recognizes him as "the first and the only person to be chosen by a General Conference of the African Methodist Episcopal Church to do general missionary work" and his resounding success in this work for having "established 47 churches with 2,000 members" as well as "7 traveling elders, 20 traveling preachers and 27 local preachers, 50 Sunday schools with 200 teachers, and 2,000 scholars; 40 temperance societies" and "17 camp meetings" in Indiana and Illinois between 1840 and 1844 (16).[11] If anything, these impressive numbers underrepresent the scale of Quinn's expansion of the church as a missionary throughout the antebellum near West and, beginning in 1844, as a bishop; during his tenure, he established hundreds of churches, Sunday schools, and camp meetings throughout the West, including in the slaveholding states of Missouri and Kentucky.[12] Smith's commentary on Quinn's achievements represents them even more dramatically, specifically by foregrounding the militancy required to establish and defend the faith in his outposts: "He was matchless in heroism, superb in courage, and relentless in his attacks on the foes of his people. He was a militant soldier of the Cross. He was a giant in his day.... Only a super-man could have borne the brunt of the battle as he did and gloriously triumphed" (17). As both the statistics and the rhetoric in Smith's account make clear, Quinn's commitment to the Black church and its members was certain, even if his national origin and racial identity were not.

An 1868 biography of Quinn by Henry Highland Garnet—the subject of the next chapter—emphasizes even more Quinn's battles as not just spiritual but also necessarily physical. Garnet observes that, "in the early part of the Bishop's ministry in western Pennsylvania, bad men had a habit of breaking up religious meetings of the Methodists, both of the whites and the colored people" by way of introducing a story about Quinn meeting this violence with counterviolence in the era of Garrisonian nonviolent resistance. In response to a gang of White supremacists menacing an 1838 camp meeting, Quinn

> arose without speaking a word, and seizing an ample green stick ... he walked out among the rioters, who received him with a storm of jeers and derisive shouts. But the tables were speedily turned. Right and left the undaunted Quinn swept his ponderous weapon, and right and left ruffians fell like wheat before the reaper's scythe. Piercing cries for mercy began to be heard, instead of oaths and obscene epithets. On and on brother Quinn went through the band of villains, just precisely as though he was threshing corn.... Astonished at the boldness of a single man, and intensely pained by his blows, the ranks of the enemy were broken, and they fled like chaff before a tempest.... *Then that church in the wilderness had rest.* I must not omit to state that during the entire transaction, which I have briefly described, the Rev. gentleman did not speak a single word, and when the work was finished, he calmly took his seat on the stand, and since that time Methodist camp meetings have never been disturbed in Allegheny county.[13]

While Garnet's account of the incident parallels Smith's characterization of Quinn as a "super-man," Garnet grounds his representation of Quinn's heroic resistance in personal and familial knowledge of the actual man. At the beginning of the biography, he notes that he first encountered Quinn "in New York City in the year 1828" when Quinn was the pastor of a church across the street from the African Free School that Garnet attended after escaping from slavery with his family. The school, opened by the New York Manumission Society in 1787, was dedicated to educating formerly enslaved and free Black children. As Leslie M. Harris has noted of its critical contribution to Black abolitionism, "many black leaders of the radical abolitionist movement of the 1830s and 1840s obtained their early education at the African Free Schools in the 1820s and 1830s" including Garnet.[14] The schools also had a direct connection to early African American print culture, as Jacqueline Bacon has documented. The editors of *Freedom's Journal* gave free copies to the African Free School's library; notices and editorials about the schools frequently appeared in its pages, promoting the value of education and encouraging parents to send their children; and the school was one of its advertisers. We recall that Walker was Boston's *Freedom's Journal* agent and his only other published work—his 1828 speech before the Massachusetts General Colored Association on the importance of self-improvement to racial solidarity—was printed in the paper.[15]

As part of this community of activism, self-protection, and self-improvement through education and print in New York City, Quinn and his wife testified on behalf of Garnet's sister Eliza, who was captured and tried in New York in 1829 as a fugitive, with the Quinns' testimony saving her from being sent back into slavery. On the basis of speaking with Quinn later in life, likely to prepare his biography, Garnet emphasizes that the man's eloquence equals his physical might: "The Bishop's manner of narrating his trials and multifarious experiences is marvelously interesting and captivating. The quiet dignity, and the ease, and beauty of his language that characterize his conversation, are seldom surpassed or equaled. His words seem literally to flow in eloquent streams from his mouth" (33).

Garnet's biography offers an important way into Quinn's 1834 *Origin, Horrors, and Results of Slavery*, shedding some indirect light on the circumstances of the tract's composition, publication, and reception, which are nearly as obscure as Quinn's origins.[16] While Garnet does not mention the tract in the biography, his locating Quinn in New York in 1829—the year Walker published the first edition of his *Appeal*—suggests a possible city and community in which Quinn might have encountered Walker's pamphlet.[17] Moreover, Garnet's dual emphasis on Quinn's eloquence and physical might, and his willingness to use both, are mirrored in Quinn's text, its arguments—including those borrowed from Walker's *Appeal*—and its generic hybridity as a didactic religious tract and a political pamphlet.

A brief glance at the African American community in early 1830s Pittsburgh and in the AME Church's Western Conference sheds more direct light on the circumstances of the composition, publication, and circulation of Quinn's text. In mid-1833 AME Church leaders transferred Quinn from his post in the New York Conference to the recently organized Western Conference. He was based in Pittsburgh, serving in the 306-member Pittsburgh Circuit as both its head and one of its itinerant ministers. Pittsburgh was the largest circuit in the church's 1,194-member Western Conference.[18] Robert S. Levine has described how Pittsburgh in the early 1830s was "a city that included among its burgeoning population approximately 450 African Americans," out of which emerged an effective group of activists who "made significant progress in organizing mutual aid societies, churches, and schools," and an antislavery society. Martin R. Delany joined their ranks in mid-1831 and soon after began studying with Quinn's fellow minister Reverend Lewis Woodson at the Bethel AME Church and helped found the city's African Education Society.[19] It was in this new and rich context of western Black activism and education that Quinn prepared, published, and circulated *The Origin, Horrors, and Results of Slavery*, likely extending its reach beyond Pittsburgh and more deeply into the church's Western Conference, either personally or by way of his fellow circuit riders.

As noted above, Quinn's hybrid tract/pamphlet is a slim 24 pages. Originally, it would have circulated in the paper wrappers that were typical of both religious tracts and political pamphlets, including all the texts featured in this book.[20] Its relative brevity puts it in closer company with Maria Stewart's *Religion and the Pure Principles of Morality* (a slender tract of 12 pages) than the explicitly political pamphlets, including Walker's *Appeal* (88 pages in its third edition and 96 pages in Garnet's 1848 edition including Garnet's additions), and Paola Brown's 64-page *Address on the Subject of Slavery*. Like religious tracts, then, it would have been more cheaply printed and easily carried in numbers than a political pamphlet like the *Appeal*, allowing for even broader circulation.

As for the text, its bookends—that is, the introduction and especially the conclusion and closing hymn—are the parts that read most like a religious tract. These are the sections in which Quinn directly addresses his Black readers, designates his pamphlet as a "tract" (iii), establishes why slavery is a religious issue, and sermonizes to his "much esteemed reader" (20). In the introduction, he also makes it clear that he specifically seeks to enlist free Black people in the "cause of liberty." Already, "millions of philanthropists and patriots in many nations are diffusing to the South, North, East, and West the grand and glorious principles of civil and religious liberty," Quinn claims, exaggerating to a significant degree the number of White antislavery activists at the time to motivate all free Black Americans to join—if not take back—the cause. To his readers who may have felt removed from it due to their location on the western frontier, he declares, "It is equally our duty as our dignity, our privilege as our happiness, and our safety as our interest, to stir ourselves from our lethargy, embark in the cause of freedom—to rank ourselves on the Lord's side, and fight the good fight of faith." For Quinn, fellow feeling activates all of this work: "We should cherish and manifest a spirit of sympathy for every brother and sister in slavery," he instructs (iii). Through "a careful perusal of these pages," he promises, all of his readers will "acquire a greater measure of the spirit of unfeigned patriotism, or love to those who are our kinsmen according to the flesh" (iv).

Quinn was clearly an experienced and effective preacher who also recognized the power of print and individual reading to draw those who were uninterested, reluctant, and even hostile into the flock. He addresses this power explicitly at the end of his introduction when he declares his ultimate aim: "My object in thus addressing you by the press, is to excite you to watch and pray daily, at God's throne, until the spirit of light, love and liberty shall be poured down on every soul of the eight hundred millions that people our globe" (iv). With this, Quinn places what is also a didactic tract among the hundreds of thousands of religious publications—including Stewart's and Apes's—that were circulating throughout the United States at the time.[21] While Apes's and Quinn's tracts were self-published and Stewart's was published by Garrison, rather than issued under the auspices of one of the religious tract societies publishing and circulating tracts on an unprecedented scale, all three contribute to the extensive Christian print culture that proliferated in the United States following the model of the Religious Tract Society of London.

An "Address to Christians Recommending the Distribution of Religious Tracts," first issued by the London society and reprinted by the American Tract Society in 1824, offers an influential articulation of the printed tract's particular usefulness with which Quinn was likely familiar:

> It is *not so likely to give offence* as some other methods of doing good. When we speak to a neighbour or a stranger on divine things, he is apt to consider us as assuming the place of a master, and setting up

for his superior in knowledge and goodness. Pride instantly takes the alarm. He scorns to be dictated, as he conceives it. His heart is steeled against counsel, and a tart answer, expressive of disdain, is all the fruit of our labour. But when a little Tract is put into his hand, the teacher is not the giver of the book; but a third person, an absent *lettered sage*. It is read apart from him who gave it. The idea of inferiority, which was so mortifying, is removed. There is not that enmity against paper and print, which was raised by the presence and living voice of the instructer [sic]; and he listens with greater candor and patience. This method has more the appearance of a person's teaching himself, than when he is spoken to by another, and is on that account more agreeable to his feelings, and the truth is more readily received. Some are accessible in no other way.[22]

In that Quinn's tract indicates him as the author, the dynamic of a reader being addressed by an anonymous and absent sage is not precisely the same as with an anonymously authored tract published by one of the religious tract societies, as is described here. Nevertheless, the printedness of Quinn's tract alone would have produced a similar effect, allowing Quinn's readers to receive his—and Walker's—messages more readily than if he were preaching to them in person.

Moreover, as a circuit rider throughout the West, Quinn was particularly well positioned to distribute his tracts widely to readers who otherwise would not have been reached by either a preacher or a tract they could peruse on their own. The tract societies' "Address to Christians" specifically discusses how to reach such readers, narrating different scenarios in which an "intimate and respected friend" does so successfully:

If he sees a person walking along the road, who is likely to listen to instruction, he reaches him a Tract. At every turnpike he hands the gate keeper one; and wishes him God's blessing with it. When he comes to an inn, he puts a Tract into the hands of the waiter, the servant-maid, the hostler; the driver never fails to have two or three. If he saunter about the town, he looks into the habitations of the poor, and talks kindly to them, and gives the parents or the children one or two of his little books, with an affectionate wish that God may bless them. When he stops at a friend's house, he presents them to the children and servants. Besides these personal distributions, he sends parcels of his Tracts to ministers of his acquaintance, and other friends in the country, for them to distribute in a similar manner. (15)

It is likely that Quinn distributed *The Origin, Horrors, and Results of Slavery* using these same methods during his travels throughout the western states—that is, if he was able to afford a large enough edition to circulate them widely and freely. At the time, the AME Church had a limited publishing operation, only publishing its first hymn book in an edition of a thousand in 1835. At the May 1836 General Conference, members including Quinn passed resolutions "in order that the book concern might be benefited and its usefulness enlarged," authorizing the general book steward to "publish such religious books, tracts and pamphlets as may be deemed best for the interests of the Connection."[23] As Mitch Kachun has noted, "before the 1840s the operations of the Book Concern remained those of a routing agency, and its influence in the denomination was negligible."[24] Thus, Quinn's 1834 tract was almost surely a self-funded publication by an itinerant minister of limited means.

These circumstances would have limited the number of copies he had printed, especially when compared to the scale of the religious tract societies' publishing efforts. The small size of the edition seems confirmed by the existence of only one known copy that had been housed at Howard's Moorland-Spingarn Library, but that has gone missing and is now only available in the form of a photocopied surrogate. Yet self-publication also afforded Quinn some of the liberties he took in departing from the primary characteristic of the genre: that is, its focus on spiritual, and not earthly, matters. In listing the "qualities [that] should be sought for and united in a good Tract," the tract societies' "Address to Christians" begins with "*Pure truth*":

> This, flowing from the sacred fountain of the Bible, should run from beginning to end, uncontaminated with error, undisturbed with human systems; clear as crystal, like the river of life. There should be nothing in it of the *shibboleth* of a sect; nothing to recommend one denomination, or to throw odium on another; nothing of the acrimony of contending parties against those that differ from them; but pure, good-natured Christianity, in which all the followers of the Lamb, who are looking for the mercy of the Lord Jesus Christ unto eternal life, can unite with pleasure, as in one great common cause.

Nor should any worldly scheme be interwoven with the truth; nor attempted to be concealed under its folds. Here should not be seen the slightest vestige of any carnal end, in any form or for any purpose, however laudable some may think it. (18–19)

Quinn clearly violated this advice by concealing his political arguments against slavery under the folds of what reads in the beginning and the end as a didactic religious tract. The result is a hybrid text with the generic characteristics of both a religious tract and a political pamphlet, produced for what Quinn clearly saw as not just the laudable but also the urgent purpose of ending slavery and enlisting free Black Americans in the near West and powerful lawmakers in both the South and Congress to the cause.

Quinn's (and Walker's and Branagan's) Political Pamphlet

The three body text sections of *The Origin, Horrors, and Results of Slavery* constitute the political essay within the tract and include the section that Quinn copied from Walker as well as another copied from Thomas Branagan. The first section, "On the Irrationality of Slavery," reads immediately as a revision of Walker's approach to the topic in his article 1. Whereas Walker's text starts from the physical and mental effects of slavery on the enslaved—twice declaring, in the preamble and the beginning of article 1, "we, (coloured people of these United States of America,) are the *most wretched, degraded,* and *abject* set of beings that *ever lived* since the world began" and adding the italics in the second iteration (3)—Quinn instead makes slavery the subject and agent of this suffering: "SLAVERY originates, diversifies, augments, and perpetuates the greatest physical and mental sufferings, with the provision of the fewest and feeblest consolations to sustain the mind under them." With respect to both the scale of and reasons for this suffering, Quinn is at once much more specific and more rhetorically and rationally elaborate than Walker:

> Where human suffering of the most aggravated and appalling nature exists, on a scale of no less magnitude than between two and three millions of our dark-complexioned fellow-brethren of mankind, without being counteracted or counterbalanced by an opposite scale of felicities, or joyful considerations of an equal or superior magnitude,

then it is a system possessing a dreadfully preponderating power in annihilating all good, and of creating evil and misery of every form, and of every degree, and as such is most justly worthy of the supreme and universal abhorrence of the population of the whole world, and should be regarded as a system most equitably doomed to everlasting extinction. (5)

Here, we can see Quinn's language flowing "in eloquent streams," as Garnet put it, to establish his main argument: because slavery offers only suffering and no form of consolation, it is irrational and, therefore, an abhorrent evil that should be banished from the earth and replaced by "the real Church of Christ," which "might adopt the apocalyptic strains of the angel respecting Babylon, and apply them to her cause" of redemption. As Quinn theologically and politically reasons his case, Christianity is the only rational alternative to the moral evil of slavery because it offers love and salvation in return for earthly woes and, therefore, is the only "true, complete, and invincible anti-slavery society" (5).

While Quinn devotes a good portion of this first section to the economic and moral irrationality of slavery, his specific occasion for writing and publishing his tract/pamphlet—and for revising Walker's *Appeal*—becomes clearer near the end of the section. There, he declares that "slavery, by legislative enactments, will not allow the ministers of the gospel to go among her two millions and a half of mourning captives, and proclaim liberty, joy, and salvation!" nor will it allow enslaved people the "mighty, strong, abundant, and all-sufficient" consolations of the Holy Bible (10). With these complaints, Quinn introduces his next section, "An Address to the Legislators of South Carolina," written directly in response to an act passed in 1834 that legally prohibited any person from teaching any enslaved person to read or write, and that specifically forbade free Black people opening schools to teach reading and writing to both enslaved and free Black people in the state.[25]

Payne's history of the AME Church offers a significant clue about why Quinn might have felt compelled to weigh in from western Pennsylvania on this legislation passed in South Carolina. At the 1833 meeting of the Western Conference in Pittsburgh, attendees led by Quinn introduced two resolutions that focused on education: "*Resolved*, As the sense of this Conference, that common Schools, Sunday-schools, and temperance societies are of the highest importance to all people; but more especially to us as a people," and "*Resolved*, That it shall be the duty of every member of this

Conference to do all in his power to promote and establish these useful institutions among our people." Of the profound significance of these resolutions to the history of the wider AME Church, Payne declares that they "constitute a new era in the history of our Church, because they are the first of the kind on record. Seventeen years had passed away from the founding of the African Methodist Episcopal Church before a word was said in its Conferences on the important subject of education; and it remained for this, the youngest and least of our four Conferences, to give the first utterance on a subject so vital to the interests of the colored race in these United States. . . . In this case the order of light seems to have been reversed. We always look for its rising in the east, but in this instance its dawning was in the west!" (98). Given Quinn's ministry in and eventual leadership of the AME Church's Western Conference, these resolutions represent what he saw as a priority for Black people not just in the West but also nationwide, just as Walker did in devoting article 2 of his *Appeal* to education and its central role in racial uplift. That South Carolina had so severely restricted education for both enslaved and free Black people just a year after the western AME churches' resolutions on the importance of education surely caught Quinn's attention and moved his pen.

Quinn also undoubtedly recognized how Walker's *Appeal* had played no small part in South Carolina's statute and numerous others like it being introduced and passed in southern legislatures from late 1830 through 1834, as southerners regularly invoked and yoked together the *Appeal*, Garrison's *Liberator*, and the 1831 Southampton uprising as evidence of the dire threats posed by Black literacy. I want to suggest that we can see Quinn's acknowledgment of this censorship in how he narrows from Walker's appeal to all White Christian Americans to address specifically and directly the White men in power whose legislation and votes affected Black people most directly. Quinn represents these men and their actions, not those of antislavery activists, as sensational and irrational. He begins, "Your conduct, in the recent legislative enactments, I can assure you, have excited astonishment and consternation from one end of the Federal Union to the other. Daring step! The period is not distant, at which, I am confident, your own consciences will reprobate your conduct with greater severity than I am either able or willing to do it." Even so, and before that self-reprobation happens, the minister "cannot be altogether silent" and takes it upon himself to try to understand what caused these men to pass the law. "Were you in the full exercise of your judgment and recollection, when you passed the execrable act?" Quinn directly asks them. "Bodies of men, as well as individuals, have their moments of infatuation, and insanity; I do not say ebriety [intemperance]," he acknowledges, giving legislators the benefit of the doubt of temporarily impaired judgment, at least rhetorically and for the moment (11).

Even though Quinn's irony and patronizing tone here are just as apparent and confrontational as Walker's—rhetorically, if not visually—his primary mode of engaging these powerful southern White men is careful and eloquent reasoning over his own visibly expressed emotion (excepting the lone exclamation point after characterizing their actions as daring). This is not at all to suggest that Walker was less reasonable, or that Quinn viewed him or his *Appeal* as such, but rather to read Quinn's consistent foregrounding and display of rationality over emotion in his tract/pamphlet as a bit of cautious overcompensation for the stronger feelings that underwrite Walker's reasoning—feelings that Quinn saw as having excited not just southerners' strongest feelings but also their most severe censorship of and restrictions on hundreds of thousands of Black people. At the same time, Quinn depends on Walker's affective precedent and its effects on southerners' emotions; with Walker already having spoken more broadly and scathingly to all Christian Americans, Quinn is able to target the most powerful White people more specifically and attempt to reason with them. Thus, we see him addressing South Carolina's legislators and offering that their "detested act" might be "a sin of ignorance" rather than of infatuation or insanity—that is, that they have written and voted on laws against Black literacy and education out of ignorance, not impaired rationality. In case that is so, Quinn proceeds to enlighten these lawmakers about what they do not know about slavery, or what they do know but have forgotten or suppressed: that now "wretched" enslaved people had been "contented and happy . . . while they were in their own country" before they "were forced, and dragged from it, as if they had been horses or hogs" by usurpers of God's authority. Then he insists to the legislators, "Show your authority, if any authority you can pretend" (11). From here, Quinn introduces the ridicule to which these men have exposed themselves by everyone who recognizes how a law against literacy and education as well as the legality of slavery contradict freedom and equality as the basic principles of the American Revolution, the Founding, and God's creation of man.

Although Quinn progresses through his points logically and quickly, with his tone growing more pitched as he does, his punctuation is noticeably restrained throughout, especially when compared to Walker's. He places only single exclamation points at the end of both individual sentences and sequential sentences with augmenting affect, as we see here: "Slavery in a free state! Are not freedom and slavery diametrically opposite! Americans! talk no more of Asiatic or European despotism and tyranny; talk no more of the freedom of America. A country free, while a considerable part of its inhabitants are in a state of the most humiliating and abject slavery! What a burlesque! What an insult to common sense!" (12). In this passage, which resembles some of the *Appeal*'s more rhetorically heated moments, Quinn's text is more visually and aurally muted than Walker's. And whereas Walker had emphasized the natural right and Christian duty of the enslaved to resist their masters violently, Quinn disavows this as his aim, at least rhetorically. He does so in a way that both resonates with how Garrison and Stewart each suggested and disavowed their incitement to revolt: "To occasion, or encourage insurrection or sedition, is infinitely remote from my intention. Every thing of the kind, all good men detest, and, to the utmost of their power, suppress," he announces (14). Even so, he also notes, "What human nature is, we all know; and what effect oppression necessarily has upon it, we know," and emphasizes "the fate of St. Domingo" as "fresh" in Black Americans' minds before declaring, "That the tragical, the bloody scene which has recently been acted in that unhappy island, should ever be re-acted among us, God forbid!" (14).

Whereas Walker refers his Black audience to "the history particularly of Hayti" to learn what drove enslaved Haitians to revolt, Quinn assumes that Black Americans, the South Carolinian legislators, and his White audience more broadly, are immediately familiar with this history.[26] Even as he includes this fearsome reminder, Quinn distinguishes himself from Walker's jeremiadic style and the most prophetic moments of the *Appeal* by specifying, "I do not prophecy; I caution and warn; nay, I studiously avoid both the oriental stile of antiquity, and the prophetical language of divinity" (14). But, again, the disavowal is merely rhetorical; he has conjured the history and, like Garrison and Stewart, the possibility of Black violent resistance nonetheless. This rhetorical opening up of some distance between himself and such prophets of revolt further suggests Quinn's assumption that his White audience was aware of Walker's "incendiary" pamphlet and its prophecies.[27] Copies of the *Appeal* reached Charleston in late March of 1830 via a White sailor from Boston who was arrested for distributing copies to Black longshoremen there; vigorous suppression and enforcement of existing laws limiting Black people's movement and gatherings followed.[28]

As a result of these seeming modulations of Walker's visual and argumentative approaches, Quinn's *The Origin, Horrors, and Results of Slavery* is less obviously directly confrontational than Walker's *Appeal*. To put it metaphorically, Quinn places his jabs carefully rather than punching with both fists as Walker does. But it is important to recognize that he was likely able to do so thanks to Walker having significantly softened up his opponents just three years earlier.[29] The impact of Quinn's rhetorical strategy is difficult to determine, though, since I have not been able to locate any discussion of Quinn's text in any newspapers at the time. What is apparent in Quinn's text is that he had carefully read Walker's *Appeal* and registered both its textual and cultural effects and decided to adapt his approach accordingly, confronting powerful White lawmakers specifically and trying to reason with them carefully about the consequences of their actions and the proper uses of their authority, even as he borrowed from Walker's suppressed pamphlet to do so.[30]

We see Quinn's strategy of carefully placing his punches most clearly in his tract/pamphlet's third section, "A Hint to the Congress of the United States." After opening it with a plea for his Black readers' indulgence as he "suggest[s] a hint, and only a hint, to the Congress of the United States," Quinn elaborates this "hint" in two long paragraphs of his own words. "Congress, may, without delay, take this subject" of slavery, Quinn prods more than hints to its members, "into their most serious consideration, and adopt such judicious measures, as to them shall appear the most proper and eligible, for meliorating the condition of the poor slaves, and putting a period, with all convenient speed, to slavery in their territories" (15). He also suggests that rebellion will be the consequence of Congress's failure to do so, asking, "Is not liberty a most desirable thing, and the yoke of bondage galling, to every human being? Do not our slaves consider themselves as oppressed most cruelly, as well as unjustly oppressed? Do they not meditate revenge? For wishing, for attempting, by just measures, to regain their liberty, who can blame them?" (16). Following these strategically rhetorical questions—and, thereby, his hints at, rather assertions of, inevitable and just resistance—Quinn reminds members of Congress that their duty is to "provide for the general safety of the nation," and that Congress should "take warning from the fate of others," invoking "Hispaniola in general, and St. Domingo in particular" as places that "will long continue to be remembered." Having again conjured up the specter of the Haitian Revolution in both his Black readers' and White Congressmembers' minds, Quinn offers the latter words of encouragement: "That a period is approaching, in which liberty, peace and religion, will universally flourish, is truly a consolatory consideration." His consolation, however, is brief: "But the Most High fulfils his designs, and accomplishes his promises," Quinn cautions, "by the intervention and agency of instruments and means." Only Congress has the power to act before God does, he reminds them: "Happy would it be for themselves, and for the world, if Christian powers would advert to what is competent for them, and incumbent upon them, for the happiness of mankind, and the honor of that great Being, who is the common friend and father of all men, black as well as white." He concludes the portion written in his own words with a final hint that also takes the form of a rhetorical question: "Shall I not entertain the fond, the pleasing hope, that Congress will, at their ensuing session, enter on the consideration of this truly important subject, and begin to make arrangements for the effectual relief of the oppressed, exiled sons and daughters of Africa?" (16).

It is immediately after this question that Quinn inserted Walker's text as a new paragraph, noting it as an "ADDITION" to his hint to Congress without attributing it to Walker. He even borrowed the word *addition*, as we notice upon locating the passage as drawn from the end of article 3 of the third edition of the *Appeal*.[31] When we read what he borrowed from Walker, it is initially unclear why he would have added it to a section explicitly addressed to the U.S. Congress. In the *Appeal*, Walker is instead specifically addressing "the preachers and people of the United States [who] form societies against Free Masonry and Intemperance, and write against Sabbath breaking, Sabbath mails, Infidelity, &c. &c."—that is, clergy and reform society members, not elected officials.[32] I read Quinn as having kept without altering this first sentence of Walker's addition, even though it risked attenuating the borrowed text's connection to his own, because it leads to a claim that he shares with Walker: that "Slavery and oppression" are "the fountain head" of all of America's "evils" in need of reform, as Walker puts it (46). The last paragraph of the borrowed section also includes some of the most striking typography and dire warnings in Walker's *Appeal*. As Quinn reproduced it, he maintained both Walker's typographical emphasis and his growing incredulity and outrage—written in the first person—at Americans' hypocrisy with respect to both their Christian and founding principles of equality and freedom. Thus, both Walker and Quinn appeal, "O Americans! Americans!! I call

God—I call angels—I call men, to witness, that your DESTRUCTION *is at hand, and will be speedily consummated unless you* REPENT."[33]

Here, again, there is argumentative continuity with Quinn's preceding text, as he has already offered a similar warning to Congress about imminent divine intervention unless they act first. But he made this point in his own words, and more subtly—why use Walker's words to make it not only again, but also more forcefully, and at some risk of them being recognized as Walker's? That is, if we take Quinn at his word that he was actually, and not just rhetorically, addressing South Carolina's legislators and the U.S. Congress in this section, why would he have risked provoking from them the same legislative and violent responses to his tract as to Walker's *Appeal*, in that these would have been precisely the readers who were most likely to recognize that it was circulating in their midst once again, under Quinn's cover?

I believe that an important clue about why Quinn took these chances—even if they were only rhetorical, given the tract/pamphlet's publication and circulation in the West—can be detected in Walker's passing mention of Dutch slavery within the section that Quinn borrows. Of Walker's text, the sentence referring to Dutch slavery is the only part that Quinn did not copy verbatim. Walker claims that the White Christians of the United States of America "have and do now treat us more cruel than any people have treated another, on this earth since it came from the hands of its Creator (with the exceptions of the French and the Dutch, they treat us nearly as bad as the Americans of the United States)" (46). Quinn's rendering reads, "they [White Americans] have and do now treat us more cruel than any people (with the exception of the French and Dutch) have treated another on this earth since it came from the hands of its Creator" (17). As we see here, Quinn's revision changes Walker's claim significantly, making it the French and the Dutch who treat their enslaved people more cruelly than the Americans. That this was a deliberate rewriting becomes even clearer when we see that Quinn devoted the entirety of his culminating political section to the "Treatment of Slaves in the Dutch Settlements." Though scholars have not noticed it, it is also borrowed—from Thomas Branagan's 1804 pamphlet *A Preliminary Essay on the Oppression of the Exiled Sons of Africa*, a sensational early antislavery text published in Philadelphia, as well as one of the most significant engagements with and critiques of Jefferson's claims about slavery and racial difference in *Notes on the State of Virginia*.[34]

Quinn appropriated the entirety of Branagan's fourth chapter, which opens with a claim that is close to Quinn's revision of Walker's claim about who treats their enslaved people worse in the previous section: "The Dutch mode of treating the slaves in their colonies coincides, in many particulars, with that of the English. It is not more mild; but, alas, still more sanguinary and cruel."[35] (Quinn changed Branagan's "that of the English" to "that of others" to include the United States in the claim.[36]) Branagan dedicates the rest of his chapter to substantiating this claim through graphic descriptions of the treatment of enslaved people in the "principle settlements in the West-Indies"—descriptions that he has based on his own eye witnessing. As he announces at the outset of the chapter, he has "visited, and therefore can speak with certainty" about slavery in the Dutch West Indies (87). In his copying from Branagan, Quinn maintained Branagan's first-person *I*, just as he did in what he took from Walker. In doing so here, Branagan's eyewitness authority becomes Quinn's. Given Quinn's mysterious national origins, this may not just be a rhetorical sleight of hand.

While most of Quinn's biographers have suggested that he was born in India, Payne—the AME historian and Quinn's twenty-year colleague—claimed that Quinn was born in Honduras.[37] Perhaps the long-standing confusion about Quinn's birthplace, then, is the same as Christopher Columbus's confusion upon arriving in the New World: Quinn may well have been born in the West Indies, not India. Thousands of enslaved people in the Dutch, British, and French Caribbean islands were sent to South America to work, or as punishment for rebelling; consequently, Honduras and other Central and South American colonies and countries on the Caribbean Sea were considered part of the West Indies in the nineteenth century.[38] The possibility that Quinn was originally West Indian rather than South Asian Indian would help explain not just his self-identification as "of African descent" but also his seemingly slight but actually major revision of Walker's text and its main argument—to claim that Dutch, and not American, racial slavery was the worst in the history of the world—as deeply personal, even though he borrowed this section and its first-person observations from Branagan. Beyond this biographical connection, Quinn's introduction of Branagan's text into his tract/pamphlet discursively connects free Black people in the near-western United States with their fellow Black women, men, and children suffering in slavery not just in the United States but also in the Caribbean. Recognizing Branagan's text in Quinn's, then, helps us recognize his Pittsburgh-published hybrid tract/pamphlet as unexpectedly hemispheric.

As Quinn's tract/pamphlet, his AME biographers, and Walker's *Appeal to the Coloured Citizens of the World* all make clear, one's geographic origins or current home ultimately mattered less than a conscious identification with and a commitment to enslaved and free Black people throughout the world. In *The Origin, Horrors, and Results of Slavery*, Quinn leverages this issue of identification to make it not just a matter of free Black people sympathizing with enslaved people and their suffering but the very crux of abolition— slavery will end only when free Black people, and not just "white people, and nations of white people, are exerting themselves in behalf of our African people," he asserts in his conclusion (22). "Does it become us to do nothing to convince the government, congress, and people of this country, that we are worthy of our freedom and that society, so far from being injured by our liberty, is greatly benefitted thereby?" Quinn demands (23). As he recognized and made clear here for his free Black readers, whether or not they identified with and acted on behalf of their enslaved brothers and sisters, White people certainly considered them to be one and the same, and only nominally free, because of their shared skin color. Thus, Quinn—like most Black activists at the time, including Walker and Stewart—advised his readers on the great importance of their propriety to enslaved people's liberty by way of proving their equality: "Be good citizens, be industrious, be sober, be good husbands, and be good wives, and be good brothers and sisters, be good parents and children, and be good and honest hearted christians [sic]." If they did so, then they could justly ask of God, "Come thou Great Deliverer, once more awake thine almighty arm, and set thy African captives free, and let them experimentally feel and fully and eternally enjoy the glorious liberty of the children of God" (23).

Good Citizenship in the Republic of Print Versus Spiritual and Political Exigency and Methodist Textual Practice

But what about Quinn's propriety as a good citizen in the republic of print? His unattributed borrowings from two authors and, most significantly, his representation of not just their words and arguments but also their observations and feelings as his own by including passages written in the first person certainly went farther than Apes's ministerial "taking" of Walker's and Jefferson's texts, considered in the previous chapter as an extension of the common Methodist preaching practice of "taking the text." Here, again, it is important to consider Methodist textual practices, including copying without attribution and rewriting others' texts to fit one's own arguments, that can be traced back to the church founder John Wesley. As Henry Abelove has explained of the centrality of these practices in early Methodist preaching and publishing, "in every case" of the "written material Wesley gave his flock," Wesley "rewrote or abridged or pirated or plagiarized. To this general rule there are no exceptions. Not once did Wesley reprint anything by any other author without either redoing it or removing the author's name from the title page. Often he did both." "Wesley stuck to this rewriting, pirating and plagiarizing," Abelove notes, "even though he got into serious trouble doing so." In 1745 the printer Robert Dodsley requested that a chancery bill be issued against Wesley for violating his copyright to both Edward Young's *Night Thoughts* and the works of Elizabeth Rowe; Wesley settled with Dodsley out of court and promised "never to plagiarize those particular authors again." A separate plagiarism scandal arose with the discovery that Wesley had republished Samuel Johnson's *Taxation No Tyranny* as his own work with the title *A Calm Address to Our American Colonies*, and many newspapers reprinted it with attribution to Wesley.[39] Despite these exposures, Wesley "kept to his custom of processing everything he republished," doing so, Abelove argues, because it "guaranteed that the reading material the Methodists bought at the society-rooms and from the helpers would always bear his own imprint. It would come from him. . . . What was important, what was essential, was that the Methodists should continue to look just to him."[40]

Similarly, Quinn's printing of his name on *The Origin, Horrors, and Results of Slavery* as its author ensured that his readers would know it came from him. Yet, in noting this in the context of Wesley's history of appropriating texts as his own, I do not mean to suggest that Quinn was strictly following Wesley's model of textual practices, authorship, or authority. Rather, I mean to foreground the centrality of unconventional (that is, non-Romantic) textual practices (including the unattributed and sometimes illegal copying of texts) in the histories of both the Methodist and African Methodist Episcopal Churches and acknowledge these practices as significant to understanding Quinn's incorporation of others' texts into his own. Recognizing this profoundly different concept of authorship as it was practiced in religious—and specifically Methodist—writing helps us recognize it as another dimension of the important but neglected alternative to the idea of generatively original authorship that was being promoted in Romantic literature—and weaponized in natural science, as we see in Jefferson's *Notes* in his dismissal of Phillis Wheatley—with dire consequences for people of African descent.

Here, I mean to suggest the case of Quinn's tract/pamphlet and the Methodist and AME practices of generatively unoriginal authorship as complementary to both Lara Langer Cohen's and Geoffrey Sanborn's considerations of the challenges posed to Romantic conceptions of literary authorship by African American writers, particularly by William Wells Brown.[41] Brown and his unattributed incorporations of significant and numerous passages from a range of other texts feature in both Cohen's and Sanborn's analyses, with Sanborn concluding that they "point us toward a still-unfamiliar way of reading early African American writing, one in which form does not equal containment, subjectivity does not equal freedom, and aesthetics is not reducible to politics" (919). When we look beyond Brown and the genres of the slave narrative and the early African American novel to Quinn and his hybrid religious and political essay published in tract/pamphlet form, we see that the aesthetics of what Sanborn calls plagiarism and Cohen calls "generative unoriginality" are not reducible to the traditionally literary either, and that such intertextuality was a more common, if still controversial, textual practice in religious writing and publishing. Further consideration of such important intersections of religious and literary publishing necessarily changes our understanding of print-related laws and customs, recovers other important alternatives to the Romantic imperative of originality in textual production, and illustrates the inter-influence of literary and religious forms in African American print and print history more broadly, as we will see further in the example of Paola Brown in Chapter 6.

Given Quinn's text's hybridity as a religious tract and a political pamphlet, it is equally important to recognize the history of unattributed copying endemic to political pamphlets in Britain and Europe as well as in colonial America and the early United States. As Padhraig Higgins succinctly explains, "Like all forms of print culture in the eighteenth century, political pamphlets were reprinted, extracted, summarized, reviewed, and plagiarized in a variety of different media, making them more widely available than is often assumed."[42] In the American context, Thomas Paine's *Common Sense* is the best-known political pamphlet to have been subjected to such treatment, by both French Enlightenment philosophers borrowing portions of his text without attribution and printers throughout the colonies reprinting the pamphlet without Paine's authorization.[43] With respect to the broader "culture of reprinting" in the United States between 1834 (the year of Quinn's tract/pamphlet) and 1853, Meredith McGill has called important attention to "a host of miscellanies, pamphlets, magazines and newspapers that relied on uncopyrighted [foreign and domestically published] texts for much of their material" and how this reprinted material circulated alongside original American writing in the same print formats and literary genres.[44]

Quinn wrote and assembled his tract/pamphlet within these religious, political, literary, and commercial cultures of reprinting. Even so, there is a significant difference between the legal statuses of Walker's and Branagan's texts that complicates Quinn's borrowing. As we have seen, Walker did not copyright his text; in place of a copyright notice, we find his prominent notice to readers that foregrounds the widest possible circulation of its message. By contrast, the 1804 Philadelphia printing of Branagan's text was copyrighted; its printer, John W. Scott, included a prominent notice of its protection under law on the verso of the title page. (See Figure 9.) Yet the simplicity of this notice belies the intricacies of this particular case of copyright that further complicate Quinn's seemingly simple instance of copying from Branagan with both personal and institutional motives.

To unpack this complexity, I turn briefly to Thomas Branagan's own knotty biography. Like Quinn, he also came to Philadelphia from the Caribbean and converted to Methodism soon after arriving. Whereas Quinn may have been enslaved in the West Indies, the Irish-born Branagan traveled there by working on a ship that was transporting enslaved people from West Africa. Gary B. Nash details how Branagan also served on a "British privateer that preyed on the ships carrying French planters and their slaves" from Haiti to American ports, worked as an overseer on a plantation in Antigua, and finally arrived in Philadelphia around 1798, becoming a devout Methodist who was preaching the gospel throughout the city by 1801. According to Nash, Branagan wrote his *Preliminary Essay* as his attempt to expiate "his guilt through identification with those he had formerly oppressed" (178). Significantly, Richard Allen was among those who financially supported Branagan's publication of the pamphlet; Allen, and his fellow Black Philadelphian activists Absalom Jones and James Forten also sponsored Branagan's 1805 antislavery epic poem *Avenia*. In the same year, Branagan published a second political pamphlet, *Serious Remonstrances, Addressed to the Citizens of the Northern States*, in which he advocated for the colonization of freed Black people by depicting enslaved people who had come to Philadelphia after being emancipated in the South as "pests to society, being sunk into the lowest

A

Preliminary Essay,

ON THE

OPPRESSION OF THE

EXILED SONS OF AFRICA.

CONSISTING OF

ANIMADVERSIONS ON THE IMPOLICY AND BARBA-
RITY OF THE DELETERIOUS COMMERCE AND
SUBSEQUENT SLAVERY OF THE

HUMAN SPECIES;

TO WHICH IS ADDED,

A DESULTORY LETTER WRITTEN TO

NAPOLEON BONAPARTE,

ANNO DOMINI, 1801.

By THOMAS BRANAGAN,

Late Slave-trader from Africa, and Planter from Antigua; who, from conscientious motives, relinquished a lucrative situation in that island; and now from a deep sense of duty, publishes to the world the tragical scenes, of which he was a daily spectator, and in which he was unhappily concerned.

PHILADELPHIA:
PRINTED FOR THE AUTHOR, BY JOHN W. SCOTT,
NO. 27, BANK-STREET.
1804.

Figure 9. Title page and copyright notice on verso of Thomas Branagan's *A Preliminary Essay on the Oppression of the Exiled Sons of Africa* (Philadelphia: John W. Scott, 1804), RB 268919, The Huntington Library, San Marino, California.

state of debasement" and White citizens of the North as forced "to provide for, and support them, with all their vices upon them."[45] To make his argument sensationally, he raised the specter of interracial sexual relationships and White unemployment as dreaded consequences of the influx of Black people in the North. In response to the latter pamphlet, Allen, Jones, and Forten publicly broke with Branagan, and legislation was introduced in Pennsylvania to restrict Black migration and civil liberties.[46]

As part of a recent literary historical consideration of Branagan's *Avenia*, Christopher N. Phillips points to a footnote in an endnote to the poem that reveals who, surprisingly, held the copyright to Brangan's *Preliminary Essay*. In this unexpected place, Branagan declares, "I offered the first edition of my 'Preliminary Essay' to Richard Allen, on consideration of his paying the printer's bill."[47] Allen may have made good on this copyright granted by Branagan; the copy of *Preliminary Essay* held by the University of California at Los Angeles does not include the copyright notice (the New York Public Library's copy does), and instead has the table of contents printed on the verso of the title page, suggesting that it may have been printed as part of another edition of the pamphlet.[48] Whether Allen was directly responsible for this edition or not, it seems quite likely that Quinn would have been aware of both Allen's sponsorship of and break with Branagan, in that Quinn had worked very closely with Allen since the earliest days of the AME Church, and given the publicity of Allen's dissociation from Branagan.[49] Keeping in mind both Quinn's significant interest in free Black people's propriety and his familiarity with Branagan as a writer, I think it is fair to speculate that he would have read *Avenia* himself and noted the telling footnote about Allen's holding copyright to *Preliminary Essay*.

Given these intriguing possibilities, then, I want to suggest that we might consider Quinn's apparent violation of Branagan's copyright as Quinn implicitly reclaiming the right that Branagan had granted Allen for his sponsorship, making good on that right as a minister in Allen's church and also Allen's proxy in 1834 after his death in 1831. Quinn may also have reappropriated Branagan's text both to contradict Branagan's focus on free Black people's vices in Philadelphia in his *Serious Remonstrances* pamphlet and to activate Black people's virtuous potential across Pennsylvania in Pittsburgh— and beyond. Thus, while removing Branagan's name as author and replacing it with his own might initially seem unvirtuous of Quinn as a citizen of the republic of letters, when we understand the complicated politicized print context in which he did so, we can see that he may have been separating

Branagan's text from its author in order to preserve an important firsthand exposé of slavery's cruelties from the racism of its author and his subsequent pamphlet. Moreover, in that the father of the AME Church had held copyright to the text from which Quinn copied, we can think of Quinn as having followed both the letter of the law and the abolitionist spirit of both of the texts he had appropriated and published under his name. And that Quinn might have done all of this without naming names—specifically Branagan's— further works to point up the critical purpose with which Walker *does* name names, including Jefferson's, Henry Clay's, and numerous other White politicians and public figures whom he specifically indicates to indict for their dual hypocrisy as Christians and Americans.

Ultimately, I read Quinn's unauthorized reprinting of Branagan's chapter on the physical torture of enslaved people in the West Indies, then, as working in combination with his unattributed borrowings from Walker's *Appeal* to do three things. First, borrowing Walker's addition and Branagan's chapter adds significant force to Quinn's own rehearsals of the sins of which White people are capable, and to his urgings of White people with political power in the United States to right these grave wrongs. Second, Branagan's words and arguments combine powerfully with Quinn's and Walker's to awaken free Black people in the U.S. near West to the urgent need to dedicate themselves to freeing their enslaved brothers and sisters and, thereby, unite the race nationwide to gain divine deliverance. And the third effect combines both of the previous two: by drawing on Walker and Branagan, Quinn places his *Origin, Horrors, and Results of Slavery* within an extensive hemispheric, and even Atlantic World, print network of antislavery writing, whether or not his Black or White readers recognized Walker's or Branagan's contributions to Quinn's pamphlet or knew anything about the tangled provenance of the Branagan text.

In these ways, Quinn's tract/pamphlet, like all the other texts examined in this book, is at once an effect of Walker's *Appeal* and a text with significant effects of its own. We understand the essay and its arguments even more fully when we consider it within a geographically extensive network of antislavery and race-related print. Given the richness of both Quinn's life and text, I suspect that the interpretive possibilities I have suggested and connections I have made with respect to people, places, and texts in this chapter only hint at part of a much broader and denser network of texts and set of textual practices about which there is much more to discover and understand.[50] At the very least, I hope that unpacking these complications of

Quinn's life and tract/pamphlet and sketching the Venn diagram of the print cultures in which he produced it help us understand how Walker's *Appeal* circulated in unexpected ways and places—including in both the antebellum western frontier and the history of the AME Church—and also to understand *The Origin, Horrors, and Results of Slavery* as a surprisingly elaborate response to Walker's arguments, tone, and visual text in several neglected contexts.

CHAPTER 5

"As Being Bound with You"

Henry Highland Garnet's 1848 Edition of Walker's *Appeal*

While William Paul Quinn's *The Origin, Horrors, and Results of Slavery* adapted and extended Walker's confrontational rhetoric and arguments to the American West in 1834, Walker's pamphlet had gone out of print in Boston in 1830 with the third and last edition that Walker published shortly before his death. In 1848 Henry Highland Garnet brought the *Appeal* back into print and circulation by reprinting Walker's second edition in New York City.[1] With it, he included two prefaces, a brief biography of Walker, and his own "Address to the Slaves of the United States of America"—the first published version of a speech he originally delivered at the 1843 National Convention of Colored Citizens in Buffalo, New York, and delivered again at the 1847 National Convention of Colored People in his hometown of Troy, New York.[2]

Garnet's reasons for bringing Walker's *Appeal* back into print and his "Address" into print for the first time when and as he did are quite personally, politically, and historically complicated. To engage with and understand these complications, this chapter takes the central rhetorical conceit of Garnet's address—where he says to his audience of enslaved people, "We therefore write to you as being bound with you"—literally as well as figuratively (90). That is, I use the content of Garnet's "Address" to understand the material form he eventually gave his reprinting of Walker's *Appeal* bound with his address in 1848.

When considering the two texts' relationship to each other, scholars have tended to think of Garnet's published "Address" as an appendix or addendum to Walker's *Appeal* in the 1848 pamphlet. Lori Leavell, in her close attention to Garnet's pamphlet, reverses this hierarchy by positioning Walker's text "as a kind of long preface introducing Garnet's text" that authorizes the radicalism of Garnet's "Address."[3] This chapter builds on Leavell's careful reading of the pamphlet's materiality, Garnet's "role as compiler," and "the volume's role in the circulation of Walker's and Garnet's text" to reorient us from readings that consider the relationship of Walker's *Appeal* and Garnet's "Address" in the 1848 pamphlet as hierarchical rather than mutual.[4] I examine and read the pamphlet instead as Garnet's material instantiation of his address's rhetorical conceit of being "bound with," showing how Garnet understood and positioned the two texts as being bound together—rhetorically, argumentatively, politically, and especially racially and tactically—both when he originally wrote and delivered the "Address" in 1843 and when he published it with the *Appeal* in 1848.

To insist on Garnet's "Address" as a direct effect of Walker's *Appeal* is to go against the grain of the two major readings of the "Address" that situate it in a broader context. Stanley Harrold, in *The Rise of Aggressive Abolitionism*, collects and reads the addresses to enslaved people that Gerrit Smith, William Lloyd Garrison, and Garnet wrote and delivered in conversation with each other in 1842 and 1843 as "captur[ing] an American antislavery movement in tension between its peaceful past and violent future—between agitation and civil war."[5] While he notes the important precedent of Walker's *Appeal*, Harrold also claims that Smith's address "originate[d] the legitimization of contacting slaves" (20). Derrick R. Spires takes a broader view in a recent essay, arguing that, while Garnet's "Address" "represented a radical departure from the typical antislavery tropes of the enslaved as powerless victims, it was in keeping with a tradition of Black political theory" that includes Walker's *Appeal* as well as with "rhetoric coming out of white-led organizations, and the way free Black citizens had begun addressing each other."[6]

By refocusing our attention on how Walker's *Appeal* and Garnet's "Address" are bound together in both form and content in Garnet's 1848 pamphlet—and how White antislavery activists' addresses to enslaved people and the 1843 and 1848 versions of Garnet's "Address" are necessarily bound up with Walker's *Appeal*—this chapter reaffirms the enduring effects of Walker's *Appeal* on Black and White antislavery activists' most significant attempts to communicate with enslaved people in the 1840s. Specifically, I establish how Garnet wrote, delivered, sought to have published, and eventually self-published his "Address to the Slaves" to resume a conversation between free and enslaved Black people that he recognized Walker as having initiated in 1829 and 1830 with three editions of his *Appeal*. As Garnet saw it, White abolitionists had interrupted and overtaken vital intraracial communications with their Great Postal Campaign of 1835, subsequently prohibiting all attempts from the North to communicate with enslaved people after the southern backlash to their campaign only for White abolitionists to reclaim this right for themselves to advise the enslaved, beginning in 1842.

Spires richly rereads Garnet's "Address to the Slaves" in the contexts of the broader Colored Conventions movement and, more specifically, newspaper responses to the "Address" and the 1843 convention debates. He also foregrounds the significant work that women—including Maria Stewart and Garnet's wife, Julia Williams Garnet—indirectly and directly contributed to the "Address," the conventions, print conversations about them, and Black political theory. His essay thus offers a multidimensional and important correction to both contemporary and subsequent scholarly understandings of the "Address" and the 1843 Colored Convention, as part of a significant body of scholarship that foregrounds the significant cultural work of the Colored Conventions movement.[7] In doing so, Spires points out that readings that focus "on Garnet individually rather than on the convention as a whole" effectively "turn the event into a battle of wills and character," thereby "reduc[ing] the convention's political stakes to a narrowly defined abolitionism."[8] I heed Spires's critique even as I reassert Walker's *Appeal* as the primary lens for understanding the print precedents to Garnet's "Address" and Garnet's motivation for writing, defending, and publishing it as he did. That is, while I primarily refer to Garnet as the sole author of the "Address to the Slaves" and consider his individual motivations, and also foreground Walker's agency and arguments throughout this chapter, I present this first extended consideration of how they and their works are bound together—intellectually, politically, textually, and, in the 1848 pamphlet, materially—to productively complicate our dominant focus on individual author as well as the alternative of anonymous corporate authorship that Spires posits in his essay as emerging from the Colored Conventions.

As Spires also makes clear, to focus on Walker's influence and Garnet's motivations is to focus narrowly on men's agency and male-authored works. In this chapter, I ground my arguments in available textual evidence; therefore, I do not attend to the less visible ways in which Black women were intimately bound up in the production of these texts, beyond noting Garnet's indication that he had secured permission from Walker's widow, Eliza Dewson, to reprint the *Appeal*. Given this approach, I specifically want to foreground Spires's well-founded and productive speculation about the ways in which Maria Stewart and Julia Williams Garnet likely contributed significantly to Garnet's "Address" and affirm with him that these and other women's significant contributions to these debates and texts should not be obscured by Walker's more obvious influence, even if they are not recoverable through print.[9]

I begin with brief readings of Smith's and Garrison's respective 1842 and 1843 addresses that preceded Garnet's 1843 "Address to the Slaves," revisiting them for how these leading White abolitionists claimed the right to communicate directly with enslaved people before Garnet but after Walker. I also recover signs of Walker's *Appeal*'s continuing influence on William Lloyd Garrison, reading the most *Appeal*-like aspects of the rhetoric and arguments in his address to the enslaved, and how he puts Walker's style in service of advising enslaved people not to resist forcefully. I dedicate the sections that follow to close readings of an 1842 Liberty Party meeting speech by Garnet, the 1848 printed version of his "Address to the Slaves," and the 1843 Buffalo convention's minutes for the debates about the version he delivered at the convention. I examine how Garnet responded critically and repeatedly to White abolitionists' sudden interest in addressing enslaved people, and specifically to Smith's and Garrison's addresses for how they both sought to proscribe the agency of both their enslaved addressees and free Black activists in the antislavery movement. These readings establish how Garnet recognized, and rhetorically and materially responded to, White abolitionists having significantly changed both the terms and the stakes of a conversation and relationship between "brethren" that he understood David Walker to have initiated with his *Appeal*. With the 1848 publication of Walker's *Appeal* and his "Address to the Slaves," Garnet restored this bond between enslaved and free Black Americans, and materialized the bond between Walker and himself—bonds that he understood and asserted as biological, political, and textual, in spite of the significant legal, geographical, and educational distance between enslaved and free Black Americans, and the temporal and ontological distance between the deceased Walker and himself.

Communicating with Enslaved People

During the 1830s, in the wake of Walker's *Appeal* and violent southern responses to it, Garrison's *Liberator* and the manifold publications of the American Anti-Slavery Society (AASS) univocally insisted on nonviolence as the only acceptable means of resisting and ending slavery. They did so even as they adopted Walker's demand for immediate abolition and, as we have seen, publicized slavery's violence and its likely consequence of further violence with similarly graphic rhetoric and typography, thereby broadcasting a noticeably mixed message. Consequently, legislators and the press in the South saw little reason to distinguish among Walker's *Appeal*, Garrison's *Liberator*, and the AASS's periodicals and pamphlets, despite their opposite positions on enslaved people's right to violent resistance, branding them all "incendiary" publications, enforcing their legal and extralegal censorship, and placing bounties on their printers' and publishers' heads for attempting to foment "servile insurrection." This insistence on the immediate danger posed by antislavery print *did* incite violence, but from slavery's supporters, not enslaved people, as proslavery rioters seized and burned shipments of AASS publications in southern post offices and arrested and whipped Black and White people who were found with these publications in their possession during the society's Great Postal Campaign of 1835.[10]

In response to these accusations and violent acts of censorship, on September 3, 1835, the AASS issued a renewed "declaration of [its] principles and objects" written by Judge William Jay, one of the society's leaders.[11] Half of the twelve principles variously defend the freedom of the press, reassert that the society deprecates violent resistance and deplores servile insurrection, and deny that the contents of their publications encourage slave revolts. Principle 8 specifically declares, "These publications are not intended for the slaves, and were they able to read them, they would find in them no encouragement to insurrection."[12] Both southerners' accusations and the AASS's denials in its 1835 declaration show how, even though Walker's *Appeal* had been out of print since 1830, and had been vigorously censored, confiscated, and destroyed—as well as significantly outnumbered by the AASS's steam-printed antislavery publications that the organization had prioritized since its founding in 1833—the southern response to Walker's "incendiary pamphlet" continued to set the terms for the proslavery response to all antislavery print, regardless of what the content of such print actually said with respect to violent resistance.[13] Accordingly, slavery supporters' and moral suasion abolitionists' vigorous condemnations of Walker's *Appeal* also set the terms for the AASS's response to this backlash, with the society's leaders capitulating to proslavery alarmism by insisting on the key differences between their publications and Walker's pamphlet. In contrast to Walker's *Appeal to the Coloured Citizens of the World*, they insisted that the only intended audiences for their publications were literate White northerners and southern masters—not enslaved or free Black people in the South—and their message, accordingly, was strictly emancipation, not insurrection.[14]

By 1839 Gerrit Smith was one of the antislavery movement's major sponsors and, in the 1840s, a leader of both the newly formed Liberty Party and a smaller faction of "abolitionists who advocated and carried out interactions with slaves in the South."[15] Smith and his White and Black adherents had grown impatient with Garrison's and the AASS's limited strategies for abolition and helped organize the Liberty Party with its platform of politically abolishing slavery. On January 19, 1842, Smith delivered an "Address of the Anti-Slavery Convention of the State of New-York to the Slaves in the United States of America." Though addressed to his "AFFLICTED BRETHREN," as Smith nominates his purported enslaved audience, he begins by speaking to his fellow White abolitionists—those at the New York convention and beyond—about their right to address enslaved people: "The doctrine obtains almost universally, that the friends of the slave have no right to communicate with him—no right to counsel and comfort him. We have, ourselves, partially at least, acquiesced in this time-hallowed delusion: and now, that God has opened our eyes to our great and guilty error, we feel impelled to make public confession of it; to vindicate publicly our duty to be your advisers, comforters and helpers; and to enter upon the discharge of that duty without delay."[16] Despite this pledge of immediacy, Smith delays advising, comforting, and helping the enslaved in his speech in favor of further "vindicat[ing] the right of [White] abolitionists to address" them and condemning abolitionists for having ceded this right (22). "Why do abolitionists concede," Smith asks, "that their labors for the slave must be expended directly upon his master . . . ? Is it not because they are not yet entirely disabused of the fallacy, that slavery is a legitimate institution? that it has rights? that it creates rights in the slaveholder, and destroys rights in the slave?" (21).

Smith subsequently argues that, in order to remedy this misplaced and unjust extension of rights to the slaveholder at the cost of abolitionists' freedom of speech, abolitionists must "fully and solemnly utter the doctrine, that they are *bound* to enter into and maintain all practicable communications with the slave" (21, emphasis added). He most optimistically imagines that, after hearing these figuratively duty-bound White abolitionists address enslaved people, "the candid and intelligent will not only respond to it, but, ere they are aware, they will have been carried along by its train of consequences and influences to the conviction, that the abolitionist has a perfect moral right to go into the South, and use his intelligence to promote the escape of ignorant and imbruted slaves from their prison-house." Of this logic Smith explains, "The motto of the abolitionists, as well as of our Commonwealth, should be 'HIGHER'; and they should feel, that unless they are continually rising higher and higher in their bold and righteous claims, all the past attainments of their cause are left unsure" (21–22). As Harrold has concluded of the speech, "even if no slave read it, Smith thought his Address could encourage northern abolitionists to take aggressive action against slavery" (19).

That Garnet—a prominent Black activist and an ardent Liberty Party member (but not present at the New York convention where Smith gave his address)—figuratively heard and responded to Smith's call to duty, and sought to elevate his claims even higher, is evident not just in his own 1843 "Address to the Slaves" at the Buffalo Convention of Colored Citizens but also in a speech he delivered on February 16, 1842—less than a month after Smith's address—at a Massachusetts Liberty Party meeting in Boston. Harrold notes of the relationship between Smith's and Garnet's speeches, "It is clear in the remarks Garnet made . . . that the two men exchanged ideas" (29). Specifically, Garnet, like Smith, uses the language of bondage to heighten both White and Black abolitionists' obligation to those who are enslaved. Yet Garnet forges this bond out of embodied identification and sympathy, more than moral duty or racial identity, by alluding to Hebrews 13:3: "Remember them that are in bonds as bound with them; [and] them which suffer adversity as being yourselves also in the body." To the members of the Massachusetts Liberty Party in attendance Garnet declared, "To accomplish the object in view we must feel for the slaves 'as bound with them,' we must place ourselves, so far as we can in their position, and go forward with the fixed consequences that we are *free* or *enslaved* with them."[17] Whereas Smith's address makes clear that enslaved people's bond with White abolitionists is contingent and can be broken—"It is on the condition that you shall not stain it with blood, that you will be entitled to expect that we shall continue to advocate your cause unitedly and hopefully," Smith stipulates to his enslaved audience (22)—Garnet's bond is attenuated only by the limits of his Black and White audience members' capacity for fellow feeling with enslaved people—"We must place ourselves, so far as we can in their position" (206).

Having forged this more empathetic bond, Garnet strategically introduces both the possibility and justice of enslaved people's violent resistance to their oppression in contrast to Smith's absolute rejection of it. Speaking to an audience of White and free Black Liberty Party activists instead of the enslaved,

Garnet declares, "Do you ask, were I them, trampled under foot by these traders in the souls of men, what would I do? I can't say precisely what I should do—but, sir, in the language of Shakspeare [sic] I will say, All that man dares to do, I would do." With this, Garnet, who had been enslaved as a child, couches the possibility and justice of enslaved people's violent resistance "in the language of Shak[e]speare." He further qualifies it by adding, "I cannot harbor the thought for a moment that their deliverance will be brought about by violence. No, our country will not be so deaf to the cries of the oppressed; so regardless of the commands of God, and her highest interests. No, the time for a last stern struggle has not come (may it never be necessary). The finger of the Almighty will hold back the trigger, and his all powerful arm will sheathe the sword till the oppressor's cup is full" (207). Thus, unwilling to rule out either the possibility or the necessity of a violent end to slavery, Garnet will assure his audience only that he does not desire this end, even as a Black man who is deeply sympathetic to his brethren's suffering. An article about the meeting and the speech in the *Emancipator and Free American* notes that his audience responded positively, even though—or perhaps because—the message was mixed, by adding an affirmative "(Hear, hear)" immediately after Garnet's words (207).

William Lloyd Garrison was no more willing to have the rival and growing Liberty Party set the terms either for abolitionists' conversations with enslaved people or for enslaved people's resistance than he was for Walker's *Appeal* to dominate the conversation and set the terms for ending slavery. Harrold notes that "some of Garrison's closest associates denounced Smith's Address [to the Slaves] as a dangerous violation of the long-standing abolitionist commitment to nonviolent and legal means" (22). Just over a year after Smith's speech, Garrison delivered his own "Address to the Slaves of the United States of America" at the New England Anti-Slavery Convention in Boston on May 31, 1843. Multiple rhetorical elements of the print version of his speech suggest that he was addressing not just the enslaved but also dissenters from the AASS who had formed the American and Foreign Anti-Slavery Society and the Liberty Party—and also, once again, Walker's *Appeal*. Whereas Smith had addressed his enslaved audience as "Afflicted Brethren," Garrison addresses them as "Brethren and Fellow Countrymen," thereby extending the basis of abolitionists' right to address enslaved people beyond the idea of a common brotherhood to their shared nationality.[18] Even so, he stops short of both the affective bond and the political citizenship that Walker had recognized in enslaved people by explicitly addressing them as his "*dearly beloved Brethren and Fellow Citizens*" (3, emphasis in the original). Again, as Spires has succinctly and significantly argued, by addressing his audience as citizens, Walker was "speaking 'colored citizens' into being, making a claim about their relationship to traditionally recognized citizens, and calling on them to assume the rights and subjectivity of citizenship"—a claim that Garnet clearly registered.[19]

Whereas Smith's mode of addressing enslaved people is procedural and simplistic as well as paternalistic—"We will very briefly enumerate some of the things, which [the abolitionists] are doing for you, and also some of the things which you should do, and some of the things which you should not do, for yourselves"—Garrison's mode of address is both more rhetorically complicated and much closer to Walker's in its effective and affective blend of Christian and political rhetoric, didacticism, and solicitude.[20] "We wish you to know who you are," Garrison begins, "—by whom and for what purpose you were created—who are your oppressors, and what they profess to receive as self-evident truths, in regard to the rights of man—who are your friends, and in what manner they stand ready to aid you—what has been effected in your cause within the last ten years in the United States—and what is the prospect of your emancipation from chains and servitude." With respect to the first point, he assures his enslaved audience, "You are men—created in the same divine image as all other men—as good, as noble, as free, by birth and destiny, as your masters—as much entitled to 'life, liberty, and the pursuit of happiness,' as those who cruelly enslave you—made but a little lower than the angels of heaven, and destined to an immortal state of existence—equal members of the great human family. These truths you must believe and understand, if you desire to have your chains broken, and your oppression come to a speedy end."[21] Through these assurances—followed by a demand that enslaved people accept and believe in them—Garrison insists on Black people's humanity even as he limits their agency. In his assurance "You are men," we hear the faint echo of Walker's interrogatory affirmation, "Are we MEN!!—I ask you, O my brethren! are we MEN?" (19). Walker's much stronger rhetorical and typographic emphasis doubly amplifies the passivity that Garrison ultimately enforces in his address with his suggestion that enslaved people only desire to have their chains broken, instead of acting to break them themselves, as Walker's type itself explicitly encourages by rising up on the page, as I have argued.

The rest of Garrison's address leans even more obviously and heavily on Walker's *Appeal*. We see this most clearly in Garrison's insistence to enslaved people, "Your masters have no more right to enslave you, than you have to enslave them," and in the Walker-like reciprocal logic and didactic rhetoric of this important rights-based claim. The *Appeal*'s lasting influence is further visible—and audible—in Garrison's allusion to Jefferson's self-contradiction between the Declaration of Independence and *Notes on the State of Virginia*, using Jefferson's own words against both the Founding Father and fellow liberty-loving defenders of slavery in the passage quoted above, much like Walker does. And following Walker's example in the fourth article of his *Appeal*, Garrison also condemns colonization as a condition of emancipation elsewhere in his address.

With these similarities, Garrison was not just borrowing from Walker's *Appeal* with his address to enslaved people but also effectively rewriting it. In his "Address to the Slaves," we can see Garrison putting Walker's rhetoric and reasoning to the purpose of contradicting the *Appeal*'s most controversial moments—its arguments for enslaved people's equal right to violent self-defense and its prideful celebrations of Black people as formidable revolutionary foes—and instead insisting that the only just actions enslaved people can take are running away and patiently awaiting divine deliverance, which Garrison promises will be rewarded imminently. "Take courage! Be filled with hope and comfort! Your redemption draws nigh, for the Lord is mightily at work in your behalf," Garrison imperatively encourages and promises enslaved people. As signs of God's work, he offers them the "many friends—warm, faithful, sympathizing, devoted friends—who will never abandon your cause; who are pledged to do all in their power to break your chains; who are laboring to effect your emancipation without delay, in a peaceable manner, without the shedding of blood" (89).

As the ultimate proof of abolitionists' unwavering commitment to them, Garrison presents a Walker-like catalog of physical abuses—but violence that White abolitionists, not enslaved Black people, have suffered "for [enslaved people's] sakes, and because they are [enslaved people's] friends": "Some of them have been beaten with stripes; others have been stripped, and covered with tar and feathers, others have had their property taken from them, and burnt in the streets; others have had large rewards offered by your masters for their seizure; others have been cast into jails and penitentiaries; others have been mobbed and lynched with great violence; others have lost their reputation, and have been ruined in their business; others have lost their lives" (89). While Garrison arguably could have intended this catalog of suffering to make White abolitionists relatable to his enslaved Black audience (again imagining that he actually, and not just rhetorically, meant to address enslaved people, as Harrold argues that he, Smith, and Garnet did), it effectively displaces enslaved people's bodies and the tortures they suffer in favor of foregrounding the harm done to White abolitionists' bodies by slavery. While Garrison limits enslaved people's actions to enduring this suffering, hopefully and courageously waiting for deliverance, and running away—and we should note that this last option exposes only Black enslaved people's bodies, and not their White masters' or White abolitionists', to likely harm—he is nearly unlimited in the adjectives and verbs he uses to describe White abolitionists' agency and character. White abolitionists, by voluntarily subjecting their bodies to pain, Garrison argues, "have proved themselves to be truly courageous, insensible to danger, superior to adversity, strong in principle, invincible in argument, animated by the spirit of impartial benevolence, unwearied in devising ways and means for [enslaved people's] deliverance, the best friends of the whole country, and the noblest champions of the human race" (89).

As we will see in what follows, Garnet reading Garrison's address to enslaved people in light of Smith's—and particularly Walker's *Appeal*—saw clearly that White abolitionists had reclaimed abolitionists' right to address them only to reassert White agency—from bravely suffering and cleverly devising ways to liberate enslaved people, to refusing proslavery's limits on White people's rights and freedoms, including speech—at the cost of Black agency and available actions for resisting.[22] I want to suggest that such assertions of freedom for White abolitionists gained at the expense of the enslaved people's rights and agency thus confirmed for Garnet that fellow Black people were best suited to address and advise those who were enslaved about the full extent of their humanity, agency, and capacity, including their sole fitness to decide for themselves how best to resist their masters. Realizing as much also compelled Garnet to reckon with how free Black activists had limited themselves and their enslaved brethren by aligning with Garrisonians and, thereby, against the deceased Walker and his out-of-print *Appeal*.

I dedicate the next section of this chapter to reading Garnet's 1848 "Address to the Slaves," in the context of his delivery of the first version of it in 1843, for how he seized the opportunity of Black activists meeting together for the first time since 1835 to restore the rhetorical and affective bond between free and enslaved Black people, joining them in racial solidarity as Walker first had with his *Appeal*, so that they all could free themselves of all the limitations White people had placed on them since the *Appeal*'s publication.

Garnet's 1848 "Address"

Garnet began his "Address to the Slaves" by addressing his enslaved audience as "Brethren and Fellow Citizens," just as Walker had. More accurately, this is how Garnet addressed them in 1848. Because we do not have a print version of what he delivered in 1843, we cannot be certain that he used the same terms of address in Buffalo (which also necessarily would have included those hearing his speech at the convention). As Spires reminds us, neither the 1848 printed version of the "Address" nor the Buffalo convention's minutes give us "direct access to what Garnet read or to his performance in 1843. They instead point to an absence, a black hole; we know it happened, and we have a sense of its shape because of how the surrounding discourse responded to its gravity, but we cannot *see* it."[23] Even so, in that Garnet notes in the 1848 preface to his "Address" that he has "retain[ed] . . . all of its original doctrine," I argue that we should understand his designation of enslaved people as "Fellow Citizens" as an essential and, therefore, original part of this doctrine, which Garnet makes even more explicit later in the speech: "Forget not that you are native-born American citizens, and as such, you are fully entitled to all the rights that are granted to the freest" (94).[24]

Following this address, Garnet begins by admitting to his enslaved audience—and scolding the more immediate audiences he had at the 1843 and 1847 conventions—that Black activists, including himself, have been too passive up to this point and, as a result, they bear no small degree of blame for their enslaved brethren's continued bondage and suffering: "Your brethren of the north, east, and west have been accustomed to meet together in National Conventions, to sympathize with each other, and to weep over your unhappy condition. In these meetings we have addressed all classes of the free, but we have never until this time, sent a word of consolation and advice to you. We have been contented in sitting still and mourning over your sorrows, earnestly hoping that before this day, your sacred liberties would have been restored. But, we have hoped in vain" (90).[25] To move free and enslaved Black Americans alike from these passive and insufficient actions, Garnet returns to Hebrews 13:3. This time, though, he significantly pivots from suggesting that sympathy binds free and enslaved Black people together to asserting a bond that is not just a simile but an actuality: "We therefore write to you as being bound with you," he declares. As Garnet has come to see it—after Walker's *Appeal* and Smith's and Garrison's "Addresses to the Slaves"—free Black activists and enslaved Black people share an exclusive bond—one that is not merely rhetorical and affective, but real and immediate, and both voluntary and involuntary—a bond forged by genealogy, their shared experiences of race-based oppression, and genuine love.[26] As such, Garnet asserts, this bond is strong enough to overcome the "deep gulf" that slavery has "fixed" between the enslaved and free Black people, thus giving the latter the unique ability—and thus the exclusive right—to address and advise the enslaved (90).[27]

Again, we cannot know that Garnet spoke precisely these words at the convention. In fact, it is likely that he said, "We therefore speak to you," rather than "write to you," given that the latter makes more sense in print. But in addition to how integral the idea of being bound together is both to the arguments in his address and to his eventual physical binding of it together with Walker's *Appeal*, Garnet's use of the same allusion to Hebrews 13:3 the year before in his Liberty Party address, and a newspaper account of Garnet's address at the 1843 convention that describes Garnet as having "fairly enchained the audience," make it reasonable to assume that he organized the convention version of his address around this same conceit and language of positive bondage.[28]

While Garnet most directly derives this conceit from Hebrews 13:3, he also draws here on a now-familiar moment in article 2 of Walker's *Appeal* to articulate the interdependent fates of free and enslaved Black people. Although Walker does not use the language of bondage to represent this relationship—and perhaps even deliberately avoids it—he addresses at length how nominal Black freedom and slavery are interdependent as part of castigating his free Black readers for forgetting the enslaved and thinking themselves truly free in what is ultimately a White supremacist society:

> Do any of you say that you and your family are free and happy, and what have you to do with the wretched slaves and other people? . . . Look into our freedom and happiness, and see of what kind they are composed!! They are of the very lowest kind—they are the very *dregs!*—they are the most servile and abject kind, that ever a people

was in possession of! If any of you wish to know how FREE you are, let one of you start and go through the southern and western States of this country, and unless you travel as a slave to a white man (a servant is a *slave* to the man whom he serves) or have your free papers, (which if you are not careful they will get from you) if they do not take you up and put you in jail, and if you cannot give good evidence of your freedom, sell you into eternal slavery, I am not a living man: or any man of colour, immaterial who he is, or where he came from, if he is not *the fourth from the negro race!!* (as we are called) the White Christians of America will serve him the same they will sink him into wretchedness and degradation for ever while he lives. And yet some of you have the hardihood to say that you are free and happy! May God have mercy on your freedom and happiness!! (33–34)

Again, of free Black Americans' resulting obligation to use what freedoms they have to work to free not just those who are enslaved, but also all oppressed people of color, including themselves, Walker concludes this argument by declaring,

I advance it therefore to you, not as a *problematical*, but as an unshaken and for ever immovable *fact*, that your full glory and happiness, as well as all other coloured people under Heaven, shall never be fully consummated, but with the *entire emancipation of your enslaved brethren all over the world*. You may therefore, go to work and do what you can to rescue, or join in with tyrants to oppress them and yourselves, until the Lord shall come upon you all like a thief in the night. (34)

Whereas, here, Walker directly addresses all of his free Black readers with the threat of divine punishment for neglecting enslaved and oppressed people of color worldwide, Garnet culminates his opening assertion of Black people being bound together with tenderness: "As such we most affectionately address you" (90). Eddie S. Glaude Jr. offers an important elucidation of this idea of racial solidarity in Garnet's "Address" as based on experience and affect, rather than the ethnological understanding of race that was being asserted by White people at the time, describing Garnet's idea of Blackness as an identity "grounded in the experience of a violent, racist culture, not in any deep (and disturbing) ontological commitment to 'the race.'" As such, Garnet's idea of being bound together makes possible "a sense of self-respect repeatedly denied in antebellum America," Glaude argues, and thus provides "a ballast for African Americans' sense of their own moral and national identity: the sense of being a person and a community of a particular kind, who lives and exists by some values rather than others."[29]

It is on the basis of these connections and the specific values they engender that Garnet powerfully declares to his enslaved addressees, "TO SUCH DEGRADATION IT IS SINFUL IN THE EXTREME FOR YOU TO MAKE VOLUNTARY SUBMISSION" (92, emphasis in the original). I read this declaration, emphasized typographically in the 1848 printing after Walker's example, as the rhetorical and moral pivot point in the address, where Garnet turns to present a plan of actions that the enslaved can and must take to cast off both slavery and sin. Glaude provides the crucial insight that this shift "from the sinful character of slavery and its proponents to the sinful aspect of the slave's submission" works to expose "the moral reform movement and immediate abolition's strengths as weaknesses, for their boisterous faith in the moral capacities of individuals fell silent when confronted with the agency of people of color" (154). With his enslaved audience's obligation thus established, Garnet emphasizes their agency and their need to activate it by beginning with emphasizing that they are best suited to pleading the cause of emancipation: "Brethren, the time has come when you must act for yourselves. It is an old and true saying, that 'if hereditary bondmen would be free, they must themselves strike the blow.' You can plead your own cause, and do the work of emancipation better than any others," he affirms, paraphrasing a key line in George Byron's *Childe Harold* (93). He subsequently catalogs the forms of exploitation and torture suffered by enslaved people's family members, recalls the "undying glory that hangs around the ancient name of Africa," affirms their rights as "native-born American citizens," and asserts that their tears and blood have enriched the land that they work without pay. While this litany would seem to be intended to agitate enslaved people to do the work of emancipation—that is, to resist the violence of slavery with force—Garnet instead advises them to meditate on all of these things, "and then go to your lordly enslavers, and tell them plainly, that YOU ARE DETERMINED TO BE FREE" (94, emphasis in the original).

He then details what reasoning they should use to plead their own cause, and what they should demand in exercising this freedom and power of speech:

> Appeal to their sense of justice, and tell them that they have no more right to oppress you, than you to have to enslave them. Entreat them to remove the grievous burdens which they have imposed upon you, and to remunerate you for your labor. Promise them renewed diligence in the cultivation of the soil, if they will render to you an equivalent for your services. Point them to the increase of happiness and prosperity in the British West Indies, since the act of Emancipation. Tell them in language which they cannot misunderstand, of the exceeding sinfulness of slavery, and of a future judgment, and of the righteous retributions of an indignant God. Inform them all that you desire, is FREEDOM, and that nothing else will suffice. (94)

In this, we immediately notice that these are all arguments and forms of reasoning that abolitionists—more specifically Garrisonians—had been using to address slaveholders to persuade them to emancipate. But the crucial difference here is that Garnet has enslaved people directly verbally confronting and reasoning with their masters, instead of abolitionists doing so on their behalf through print issued from the North. By thus asserting enslaved people's God-given ability, right, and obligation to take direct action, specifically by pleading their own cause, Garnet obviates the mediation of anyone else (White people in particular) or anything else (including print) speaking for them from a distance.

Garnet makes enslaved people's direct verbal confrontation of their masters the precondition of their subsequent direct action: a strike. Tell them all of the above, he urges his enslaved addressees, "and for ever after cease to toil for the heartless tyrants, who give you no other reward but stripes and abuse" (94). With this, Garnet not only borrows a tactic from the burgeoning labor movement but also binds enslaved people's resistance to slavery to labor rights and actions.[30] He powerfully reasons that enslaved people are no different from any other kind of worker whose wages are being stolen, and asserts their equality by emphasizing their common ability to voice the theft, deny their labor to those stealing it, and demand their just wages from their bosses despite their legal status as enslaved.

Verbal confrontation, reasoned argumentation, and refusal to work for unpaid labor are all crucial, yet underappreciated direct acts of resistance to slavery that Garnet advocates in his "Address to the Slaves." I see their importance not just to Garnet's plan of action for enslaved people but also to his assertion of their equal rights and abilities with all humans, as having been overshadowed by a historical pattern of foregrounding the suggestions of violence in Garnet's address at the expense of its other powerful advice. While his plan of actions for gaining freedom logically culminates in violence, as his opponents at the convention recognized and insisted, it is important to emphasize that, in Garnet's logic here, it is a counterviolent response rather than the instigation of violence—that is, as enslaved people instinctively and rightfully defend themselves and their families against their masters responding to their rightful strike with force.[31] "If they [the masters] then commence the work of death" rather than presenting a counterargument to enslaved people's reasoned and just claims, Garnet asserts, "they, and not you, will be responsible for the consequences" (94).

With this, we can infer that Garnet theorized all resistance to slavery as counterviolence against the instigating and indefensible, tyrannical violence of slavery, and all violent defenses of slavery as unreasonable. Thus, he subsequently advises, "You had far better all die—*die immediately*, than live slaves, and entail your wretchedness upon your posterity" (emphasis in the original). And he acknowledges that bloodshed is the likeliest outcome of the plan of resistant actions he has outlined: "However much you and all of us may desire it, there is not much hope of Redemption without the shedding of blood." Accordingly, he concludes, "if you must bleed, let it all come at once—rather, *die freemen, than live to be slaves*" (94, emphasis in the original). With its immediatism, the multifaceted radicalism of Garnet's provocation to his audiences comes through: both enslaved and free Black people must be willing to take any and all necessary actions and suffer all the possible consequences to become truly free people in what is a White supremacist, rather than egalitarian United States.

With this close, step-by-step reading of Garnet's articulations of enslaved and free Black people's multiple forms of agency in his "Address," I want to underscore how violent resistance is the ultimate act—the last in a series of actions, and not the desired final aim of these actions—that Garnet, like Walker, recognized Black people to be capable of as fully fledged human beings, and to be as justified in using as American citizens dutifully overthrowing tyranny as Whites were in the American Revolution. I argue that, even if both the resistant direct actions that Garnet urges of enslaved people and the logic and rhetorical fervor of his "Address," that is, both of their free exercises of speech, culminate in defenses of violent self-defense—just as Walker's arguments frequently do in his *Appeal*—we should locate this violence at the extreme end of the full spectrum of actions that Garnet, like

Walker, affirmed as rightful for both enslaved and free Black people to take, without necessarily desiring them to take it, as U.S. citizens and full human beings. In fact, in the 1848 version of the address he specifically declares, "We do not advise you to attempt a revolution with the sword, because it would be INEXPEDIENT. Your numbers are too small" (96).[32]

The final confirmation that Garnet's sole purpose was less to incite violent resistance than to make it available as a rightfully and, thus, equally available form of resistant action to be taken by oppressed people comes with his address's conclusion: "Let your motto be RESISTANCE! RESISTANCE! RESISTANCE!—No oppressed people have ever secured their liberty without resistance." With this last claim, Garnet implies not only the precedent and justification of the American (and French) Revolution but also the Haitian Revolution, which Walker also invokes in his *Appeal*. Yet Garnet is careful to clarify that he is not urging *only* violent resistance with this motto, and that he specifically respects the capacity of enslaved people to determine for themselves what is the most appropriate form of resistant action to take in their specific circumstances: "What kind of resistance you had better make, you must decide by the circumstances that surround you, and according to the suggestion of expediency," he concludes (96).

With this culminating advice, Garnet crucially asserts that only enslaved people can—and must—determine their proper circumstances and options for resistance, decide on what is the best action for them to take, and then take deliberate action. In thus foregrounding what I ultimately read as Garnet's argument for enslaved people's absolutely equal right to and capacity for self-determination, I mean to suggest that readings of Garnet's "Address," like readings of Walker's *Appeal*, that have focused on its arguments for violent action above all else have critically obscured how Walker's and Garnet's most radical and important arguments were for the full rights and freedoms of all Black people. Thus, I ultimately contend that it is less violence than their shared insistence on Black people's citizenship, rationality, Christian duty, and, thus, full humanity that binds these two texts most closely together and makes them even more radical.

Debating Garnet's 1843 "Address" and Its Publication

Some of Garnet's fellow participants in the 1843 Buffalo convention were the first to focus on its suggestion of violence at the expense of all else that Garnet wanted his "Address" to do for enslaved and free Black Americans. The convention's official published minutes record the former *Colored American* newspaper editor Charles B. Ray as the first to raise concerns about its potentially "objectionable" points and emphasize the risks of the convention printing and circulating it under its auspices, either as a stand-alone pamphlet or in its minutes, as written.[33] In explaining his motion, Ray offered to make Garnet chair of a committee charged with revising it with the assurance that he would receive "the usual credit due to chairmen of committees presenting documents to public bodies" (13). But Garnet understood that Ray's motion was meant to strip his address of its most radical advice to enslaved people—that they resist their masters by using any and all means they deemed necessary when they determined that the time was right—and, moreover, to ensure that the "Address" as he had written it would never reach his intended audience directly. Instead, Ray's motion would embed a significantly revised and moderated version of the address within the convention's printed proceedings and thus be directed to a free rather than an enslaved audience.

The minutes record Garnet's response: "H. H. Garnit [sic] arose to oppose the motion of reference, and anticipating more than was contemplated by the mover, and fearing the fate of the address, if the motion prevailed, proceeded to give his reasons why the motion should not prevail, why the address should be adopted by the Convention, and sent out with its sanction" (13). What we can infer here is that Garnet wanted the convention to publish his "Address" as its own pamphlet—just as Walker's *Appeal* had been, but at Walker's own expense—and, thereby, to endorse his arguments and "sanction" their circulation to those who were enslaved.[34] Moreover, he wanted the address's advice to enslaved people to take direct action on their own behalf to reach them directly, without either White abolitionists' or the National Convention of Colored Citizens' minutes mediating that message. Here, I read the minutes as reflecting Garnet's understanding that only as its own separately published pamphlet would his "Address to the Slaves" work to restore the unattenuated bond between free and enslaved Black people that Walker had first forged with his *Appeal*.

In fiercely opposing Ray's motion, Garnet "went into the whole merits of the case," the minutes note, both redelivering and amplifying the main points of his "Address." He was allowed to speak for "nearly one hour and a half," during which he "reviewed the abominable system of slavery" and "what had been done to move the slaveholders to let go their grasp, and asked what more could be done—if we have not waited long enough—if it were not time to speak louder and longer—to take higher ground and other steps." The minutes describe it as "a masterly effort" and note that the "whole Convention, full as it was, was literally infused with tears" as Garnet "concluded amidst great applause" (13). This response must have reaffirmed for Garnet the power of speaking "louder and longer" and only added to his commitment to doing so to the enslaved via print, like Walker before him had in his oratory-influenced *Appeal*.[35]

Frederick Douglass, who was among the convention's Garrisonian delegation, also recognized this power and sought to contain it by renewing his and his fellow conventioneers' commitment to resisting slavery without violence—including in speech and print that sought to incite it. Speaking immediately after Garnet, Douglass defended Ray's motion to revise and suppress Garnet's "Address," arguing "that there was too much physical force, both in the address and the remarks of the speaker last up" (13). The minutes note that Douglass was "for trying the moral means a little longer" and was concerned "that the address, could it reach the slaves, and the advice, either of the address or the gentleman, be followed, while it might not lead the slaves to rise in insurrection for liberty, would, nevertheless, and necessarily be the occasion of an insurrection; and that was what he wished in no way to have any agency in bringing about, and what we were called upon to avoid" (13). With this objection, Douglass made it clear that he recognized the negative potential of the bond that Garnet sought to reforge between enslaved and free Black people through print; he anticipated that if Black abolitionists at the convention were to help put Garnet's "Address" into the hands of enslaved people, as Walker had his *Appeal*, free Black activists would have the blood of both slaveholders and their enslaved brethren on their hands. But as the minutes record Douglass's concerns, what is less clear is who—or what—would be the agent responsible for inciting such insurrection, with Douglass distinguishing among Garnet's "Address" as a material text (that is, the object that would "reach the slaves," as either a stand-alone pamphlet or published within the convention minutes); its contents (the advice of the "Address"); and Garnet's defense of his "Address" at the convention (which is to say, the even stronger advice for enslaved people to resist that Garnet presented as part of his lengthy and passionate defense of the "Address").

By thus parsing Douglass's remarks as they were recorded, I read them as evincing his concern that if Garnet's "Address" were to become its own pamphlet—like Walker's *Appeal*, a pamphlet that was not only addressed to but also circulated among enslaved people—then that material text would be as potentially dangerous to Black people who encountered it as its message urging them to resist heavily armed, legally protected, and extremely motivated White southerners. Again, Douglass knew from his own experiences in the Auld household that enslaved people's literacy was tightly controlled by both law and custom—itself an effect of Walker's *Appeal*, as I argue in the introduction—and that print had the power to move both White and Black people to action. This double awareness surely informed his distinction between Garnet's argument "lead[ing] the slaves to rise in insurrection" and the pamphlet itself "necessarily be[ing] the occasion of an insurrection for liberty." On the basis of the precedent of southerners' responses to Walker's *Appeal*, and further confirmed by their no less violent reactions to the *Liberator* and the AASS's publication campaign, Douglass was most concerned about White southerners' agency. Consequently, even though Douglass had physically resisted his overseer—the "turning-point in [his] career as a slave" that he would dramatize in his *Narrative of the Life*, published two years after the Buffalo convention—he argued against the convention sanctioning and printing Garnet's "Address to the Slaves" so that he and the rest of the conventioneers "would in no way have any agency in bringing about" what he foresaw as the enslaved people's certain violent defeat even before they had a chance to rise up.³⁶

In responding to Douglass's concerns during the heated debate, Garnet not only reiterated but also amplified the most controversial advice in his address. In doing so, he again insisted on and foregrounded enslaved people's agency over the agency of both their masters and free Black people. According to the minutes, Garnet "said that the most the address said in sentiment, with what the gentleman [Douglass] excepted to, was, that it advised the slaves to go to their masters and tell them they wanted their liberty and had come to ask for it; and if the master refused it, to tell them, then we shall take it" (13). Again, in the 1848 print version of this advice, Garnet declares, "Go to your lordly enslavers, and tell them plainly, that YOU ARE DETERMINED TO BE FREE.... Do this, and for ever after cease to toil for the heartless tyrants, who give you no other reward but stripes and abuse. If they then commence the work of death, they, and not you, will be responsible for the consequences" (94). If these imperatives represent the "original doctrine" of the 1843 speech that Garnet says he retained in the printed version, then we can see that the intense debates about his address at the convention made Garnet somewhat less cagey in defending enslaved people's right to use violence in the moment of defending his "Address" than he was in the eventual 1848 print version. Against Douglass's objections at the 1843 convention—and speaking off the cuff instead of from a script and more like Walker in his *Appeal*'s more emotionally heated moments—Garnet boldly asserted that the enslaved people were justified in striking first, forcefully taking their freedom when the slaveholders inevitably refused to grant their request for it—"let the consequence be what it may," the minutes record him concluding (13). In responding to Garnet, Douglass again emphasized that however justified enslaved people might be in attempting to take their freedom by force, even as a last resort, their masters' response would be even more violent and ultimately devastating: enslaved people telling their masters they want their liberty "would lead to an insurrection, and we were called upon to avoid such a catastrophy [sic]" (13).

The convention's attendees heeded Douglass's cautions and voted to send Garnet's "Address to the Slaves" back to a committee still chaired by Garnet, but now also including Douglass.[37] The established Garnet apparently had more allies on the committee than the relative newcomer Douglass did, as they made only "some very slight alterations" and reintroduced the "Address" with the resolution "that each member of this Convention who is friendly to the sentiments contained in this address, come forward and sign it in the name of the ever living God, and that measures be taken to print 1000 copies for circulation" (17).

With this, we can see that Garnet changed his strategy from urging the convention to issue his "Address to the Slaves" with its sanction as a corporate body, to calling on individuals at the convention who supported the "sentiments" of his address to step forward one by one and sign it, like the signers of the Declaration of Independence. As Spires has argued, the "Address" "was never meant to be 'Henry Highland Garnet's 'Address to the Slaves,'" but rather issued as "a corporate public assertion of the convention's intentions."[38] Yet, in this request for individual signatures, we see an important shift in Garnet's strategy, from seeking the corporate authorship that Spires notes as typical of convention-issued documents to strategically enacting a form of multiple, collective authorship on the model of the Declaration of Independence. Thus, in shifting from institutional and anonymous authorship to multiple authors who were individually designated by their signatures, Garnet urged his fellow freemen to exercise their independence as individuals by separating from the corporate identity of the convention and equally standing alongside him as a group of discrete, aligned individuals all under God—the only higher authority, he argued, that should govern them. Douglass's and others' resistance to his "Address," I argue, had revealed to Garnet what he wanted his potential cosigners to understand as well: that the convention's democratic, yet corporate structure—like that of the U.S. government after independence—toned down its politics, with a more moderate or even conservative majority effectively working to suppress the most radical positions on rights by emphasizing stability and safety over the Revolutionary War–era ideals of freedom, rebellion, and interdependent independence that Walker had extended into the nineteenth century and made equally available to Black Americans.

Convention members' fears of White power and its potential to harm not just enslaved but also free Black people who lived in the border states, prevailed in the end as all of Garnet's strategies for publication were voted down.[39] Those who voted against Garnet's "Address" confirmed his argument that neither free nor enslaved Black people can act freely and fully in a White supremacist society enforced by overwhelming violence and its constant threat. But as Garnet recognized in both his address and his defense of it, for nominally free Black people to submit to this domination and, worse, to keep each other down as Black agents of White power was worse than the Garrisonian passivity of merely meeting, sympathizing, sitting still, mourning, and hoping that slavery would end and "sacred liberties" would be "restored."[40] Like Walker argues in article 2 of the *Appeal*, Garnet understands that free Black men have shackled themselves and, worse, strengthened the chains worn for so long by the enslaved instead of voluntarily binding together to claim their fullest freedoms.[41]

In 1847 Garnet once again delivered his "eloquent and impressive address to the Slaves of the United States," at the National Convention of Colored People assembled in Garnet's home city of Troy, New York.[42] At this gathering, he devoted his energy and political capital to convincing the attendees to move forward with funding not just the national newspaper they had voted in 1843 to establish but also an entirely Black-controlled, national printing press—that is, to make good on realizing their bond with the enslaved and other free Black people through print, and at a greater scale than Walker or any of the Black-published newspapers had.[43] According to the convention proceedings, Garnet, as he had in Buffalo, insisted anew that "some method hitherto untried, needed to be resorted to," but this time argued "that the most successful means which can be used for the overthrow of Slavery and

Caste in this country, would be found in an able and well-conducted Press, solely under the control of the people of color" (6). Here, again, and no less than in his "Address," Garnet understood the power of the word—both spoken and printed—as fear-inspiring direct action, arguing that the "establishment of a National Printing Press would send terror into the ranks of our enemies" (6). But he also newly acknowledged the risk of alienating antislavery White allies and offers that a national press would not just inspire terror but also "encourage all our friends, whose friendship is greater than their selfishness" (6). Despite these kinder words and this imagined interracial bond with White activists fostered by the press, Garnet met once more with strong resistance for speaking so boldly from Douglass, who "was in favor of a Press" but "was satisfied" that a national press "could not be well sustained" and who founded the *North Star* only two months after the Troy convention (6–7). In response, Garnet the minister turned to seeking only God's support instead of his fellow activists', ending his argument by declaring that "with or without the sanction of the Convention, a Press would be established, by the help of God" (6).

Douglass, in turn, helped draft an "Address to the Slaveholders" as a member of the 1847 convention's Committee on Abolition. In pointed contrast to Garnet's "Address to the Slaves" in both its audience and argument, the committee's "Address to the Slaveholders" declared it "impossible . . . to contemplate any appeal to the slave to take vengence [sic] on his guilty master" and "the perfection of folly, suicidal in the extreme, and abominably wicked" to argue "in favor insurrection and bloodshed, however well intended" (31). Whereas Garnet concluded his "Address to the Slaves" with, "Let your motto be RESISTANCE! RESISTANCE! RESISTANCE!" (96), the Abolition Committee's report specifically revised this motto and redirected it to Black abolitionists: "We will do all that we can to *agitate*! AGITATE!! AGITATE!!!," they declare with Walker-style augmenting italicization, capitalization, and punctuation that increases to suggest a vocal crescendo (32).

Following his peers' effective repudiation of both his and Walker's radicalism in late 1847, and with the revolutions in Europe beginning in early 1848, Garnet renewed his commitment to resistance and his determination to harness the power of the press—but now to print his "Address to the Slaves" and reprint Walker's *Appeal*. With this new strategy, Garnet made explicit the implicit influence that Walker and his *Appeal* had maintained on him, and on Black and White abolitionism in the 1840s, despite the South's vigorous suppression of the pamphlet, Garrison's and other White abolitionists' disavowal of Walker directly addressing enslaved people and justifying their violent resistance, and the pamphlet having been out of print since early 1830. By bringing Walker's *Appeal* back into print and circulation along with his own "Address to the Slaves," Garnet bound together not just their two texts but also U.S. abolitionism and global struggles for freedom.[44]

Garnet's 1848 Pamphlet

On May 5, 1848, the *North Star*—the newspaper Douglass had founded just weeks after arguing against establishing a corporate national Black newspaper at the Troy convention—carried an advertisement announcing "NEW PUBLICATIONS. WILL BE READY IN A FEW DAYS, WALKER'S APPEAL, with a brief sketch of his life by Henry Highland Garnet. Also, GARNET'S *Address to the Slaves of the United States.*"[45] That Garnet paid his convention opponent Douglass to place this ad in his *North Star* reminds us that these activists were necessarily bound together, to some degree—particularly in print—even when they were politically and ideologically at odds and seemingly acting independently of each other in their efforts to end slavery.[46] The *North Star* offered Garnet a chance to reach several of his target audiences—Douglass's free Black subscribers, White and Black Garrisonians, and slavery supporters keeping an eye on the opposition—with news that the most "incendiary" abolitionist pamphlet ever published was being reissued, and that his own controversial "Address to the Slaves" was coming with it at a time when reports of political upheaval and popular uprisings abroad were increasing.

Just a week earlier, the *North Star*'s March 24 Foreign News column contained "very unexpected intelligence" received via steamer from France about another revolution that was underway there.[47] The same column in the April 14 issue featured an article headed "Continued Excitement in Europe" that announced, "Every arrival from Europe brings intelligence of further commotion and *revolution*," followed by summaries of political upheaval and revolutionary violence in France, Prussia, Bavaria, and Russia."[48] And on April 28, Douglass printed a letter from Garnet that included an excerpted article from the Troy *Daily Post* directly connecting an attempt to transport seventy-seven enslaved people to freedom in the North aboard the schooner *Pearl* to the revolution underway in France. The *Daily Post* article begins with the suggestion that, "A result of the grand sympathy meeting, got up in

Washington, to glory in the success of Republicanism in France, with the fine speeches at them, in favor of the rights of man, appears to have been, to lead a number of slaves, who were probably listeners, to think that they too were to share in the glorious boon of freedom. On Monday, from 60 to 70 slaves started for the free States, but were pursued and overtaken, and will probably be sold to Louisiana and Mississippi traders, doomed, members of Christian churches though they probably mostly are, to the perfect horrors of slavery." Commenting on this hypocrisy, Garnet editorializes, "Louis Philippe laughs at this—Metternich opens his eyes, and Nicholas shrugs his shoulders and says: that this is rascality among rascals, and intolerable hypocrisy among hypocrits [sic]."[49] With this, we can clearly see how Garnet recognized in the regular and growing news of uprisings abroad his opportunity to convert the extended delay in publishing his "Address to the Slaves" into an incredible advantage: he could bind together not only his and Walker's appeals to enslaved people to resist their masters but also enslaved people's resistance in the United States with the revolutions in Europe.[50]

Garnet forges the latter bond most explicitly in the section of the printed "Address" where he announces that "the time has come" for the enslaved to act for themselves: "You can plead your own cause, and do the work of emancipation better than any others," he encourages. He follows this advice with a reassuring sentence that I suggest he likely added in April 1848 while preparing the address for publication: "The nations of the old world are moving in the great cause of universal freedom, and some of them at least, will ere long, do you justice" (93). With this, Garnet positions enslaved Black Americans' and Europe's underclasses as sharing in the cause of universal freedom while also seeming to suggest the former may soon gain allies from abroad in their fight. Again, in the preface to his address, Garnet describes the modifications he made to the 1843 version in preparing it for publication as slight. But this insertion is quite significant for what it adds to his "original doctrine" of the right and duty of enslaved people in the United States to resist their masters, making that right and duty not just American but universal and this movement as underway instead of imminent (89). Garnet recognized that he was publishing his pamphlet in a historical moment and that, by doing so, he was also writing U.S. enslaved people's resistance into that history.

With respect to the specifically book historical implications of the 1848 pamphlet, although Garnet had vehemently argued at the 1843 convention that his address to the enslaved should be issued as its own pamphlet, it would not have had as much heft, either argumentatively or materially, as it does when bound together with Walker's *Appeal* and the paratexts that Garnet added.⁵¹ Garnet's "Address" on its own likely would have made only a thin eight-page pamphlet; its physical vulnerability as such necessarily would have limited its circulation even among readers in the North and given it little chance of surviving the surreptitious means by which it would have had to be transported to reach the enslaved.⁵² By combining it with the second edition of Walker's much lengthier *Appeal* (the edition that Garnet likely personally owned)—as well as with a biography of Walker, prefaces to the *Appeal* and the "Address," and a frontispiece illustration depicting a robed Black figure being divinely delivered a paper reading *Libertas* and *Justitia*—Garnet was able to make a much more substantial "little book" that he prayed might "be borne on the four winds of heaven, until the principles it contains shall be understood and adopted by every slave in the Union" in his preface to his address (89).⁵³

I read these materials in response to Beth A. McCoy's call for "more work exploring race and paratextuality [that] needs to be done," and in light of Lori Leavell's specific consideration of the 1848 pamphlet's contents and argument that Garnet "sought to regenerate Walker's influence" by "reprinting the *Appeal*."⁵⁴ I argue that Garnet—acting as editor, author, and publisher— uses the pamphlet's paratexts—its preface to the *Appeal* and the biography of Walker—to represent him as a specifically literary—that is, an original, imaginative, and aesthetically and technically accomplished—author who has been inadequately recognized and unjustly forgotten, rather than disqualified, as such. In his preface to Walker's *Appeal*, Garnet presents his reprinting of Walker's text as an act of historical preservation rather than of history making, announcing, "Such is the very high esteem which is entertained for the memory of DAVID WALKER, and so general is the desire to preserve his 'Appeal,' that the subscriber has undertaken, and performed the task of re-publication, with a brief notice of his life" (iv). Significantly, Garnet also dutifully notes that he "procured permission from his widow, Mrs. Dewson," to do so (vii). As I have established in Chapter 1, Walker prioritized the circulation of his *Appeal* over his copyright, placing his notice to Black readers to circulate it among those who could read and read it to those who could not in place of a copyright notice. With this again in mind, I want to suggest that Garnet's extension of Walker's *droit d'auteur* to

Walker's widow is more than a courtesy here—we should read his making specific note of it as an important part of his deliberate canonization of Walker as an original, belletristic author with his reprinting and renewed circulation of the *Appeal*.

In the preface's second paragraph, Garnet establishes the value of Walker's *Appeal* by recognizing it in the vanguard of what had become, by the late 1840s, a well-established national antislavery movement with a prolific press. "The work is valuable," Garnet argues, "because it was among the first, and was actually the boldest and most direct appeal in behalf of freedom, which was made in the early part of the Anti-Slavery Reformation" (iv). With this valuation and placement, Garnet canonizes Walker and his *Appeal* as the fountainhead of the major works of antislavery literature and, moreover, as a great author and work of American literature for the *Appeal*'s bold and direct appeal for freedom.

Beyond these belletristic justifications for bringing Walker's *Appeal* back into print, Garnet also knew that to reissue this exceptionally bold and direct appeal was also to reactivate it after nearly two decades of dormancy—as his purported financial sponsor for the pamphlet's publication John Brown also understood.[55] By focusing on abolition's literary history more than on the present, and on Walker's historical achievement as a writer more than as revolutionary, I contend, Garnet's preface strategically works both to canonize Walker as a great author and to strategically obscure—to a degree—his and perhaps his unacknowledged sponsor's potentially history-making revolutionary motive for publication.

The three-page "Brief Sketch of the Life and Character of David Walker" that also precedes Garnet's reprinting of the *Appeal* further works to expand the public memory of Walker and his text beyond southerners' and White abolitionists' narrow focus on violence by further emphasizing Walker as an established author and his *Appeal* as an influential work of literature. McCoy has encouraged us to attend carefully to how paratexts "have functioned centrally as a zone transacting ever-changing modes of white domination and of resistance to that domination" (156). With this in mind, we can see how Garnet's paratextual canonization of Walker and his *Appeal* also implicitly contradicts Jefferson's enduringly influential argument that people of African descent were intellectually incapable of producing literature and, thereby, adds additional evidentiary support to Walker's own argument and evidence against these claims in the *Appeal*. Significantly, McCoy also engages Jefferson's scientific racist denigrations of Black literary capacity.

Paratexts written by "white prefacers and editors" for slave narratives, she argues, reduce "fugitive author to fugitive reporter, a construction that accommodates Thomas Jefferson's distasteful declaration that 'never yet could I find a black had uttered a thought above the level of plain narration.'" By "serving neither the text nor its author" in these cases, she posits, "the paratext [in slave narratives] serves something else: an indirect white supremacy, different from the brutality against which white abolitionists fought but one that interferes with the fugitive writer's authorial primacy nonetheless" (157). McCoy's final claim here makes clear how Garnet, as a Black prefacer and editor, intended for the paratexts in his pamphlet to have the opposite effect: his preface to the *Appeal* and biography of Walker repeatedly insist on Walker's authorial primacy.[56]

In explaining that he has written the biography to satisfy "the desire of the reader of any intellectual production, to know something of the character and life of the author," Garnet presents Walker as no different from any other celebrity author whose work has caught the public's attention and inspired its curiosity about the man behind the words.[57] But because the author is literally dead in the case of Walker, the writings make the man: Garnet asserts that Walker's character "is indicated in his writings" and that the "few materials [that] can be gathered" about him stand as "proof" of his friends' opinion "that he possessed a noble and courageous spirit, and that he was ardently attached to the cause of liberty" (v).[58] The story that Garnet tells of Walker's life in Boston after leaving home in North Carolina for the North specifically emphasizes how Walker "applied himself to study, and soon learned to read and write, in order that he might contribute something to the cause of humanity." While he notes that Walker also became a prosperous businessman who devoted all of his profits to reform, he pronounces him "emphatically a self-made man" who "spent all his leisure moments in the cultivation of his mind" (vi). By thus foregrounding Walker's intellectual self-cultivation over his entrepreneurial success, Garnet subtly adds to his arguments against Jefferson's and other scientific racists' claims about Black people's limited intellectual aspirations and authorial deficiencies. More specifically, Garnet's portrait of Walker also contradicts charges made in the wake of the *Appeal*'s publication that Walker could not have been its author. As we have seen, the March 22, 1830, *Boston Courier* mocked both the southern reaction to Walker's pamphlet and Walker as its author. "Is it possible," the writer asks, "that the people of those states, whose representatives and political writers talk so loudly of their physical as well as political power, can really be frightened by a pamphlet, written (or said to be written) by an uneducated African?" The writer claimed to have sought Walker out personally and determined that the pamphlet "is not, cannot have been, the work of that man."[59] Garnet counters all such charges of forgery by emphasizing the intense, extended period of study that Walker undertook before writing his *Appeal*, just as Garrison did in defending Walker's authorship in the *Liberator*. Here, this defense works to further cement Walker's canonical status as a great American author who had deservedly achieved this status by embodying the great American principle of self-reliance through his necessary autodidacticism, given the racial inequities in formal education that Walker attacks in the second article of his *Appeal*.

Walker's impressive intellectual efforts, in combination with his "overflowing heart," resulted in what Garnet describes as the "little book" that "produced more commotion among slaveholders than any volume of its size that was ever issued from an American press." As Garnet presents them, Walker is David, the South is Goliath, and his *Appeal* the stone, invoking this biblical precedent for Walker's feat: "It was merely a smooth stone which this David took up, yet it terrified a host of Goliaths." This analogy also works to argue that in the world of letters—and the age of the novel—size does not matter to a work's significance and, therefore, to it and its author's canonization. "When the fame of this book reached the South," Garnet writes, "the poor, cowardly, pusillanimous tyrants" not only "grew pale behind their cotton bags, and armed themselves to the teeth" but also appealed to northern authorities to censor Walker as an author (vi).

Garnet follows this claim with his version of southern efforts to censor and suppress Walker's pamphlet: "The Governor of GEORGIA wrote to Hon. Harrison Gray Otis, the Mayor of Boston, requesting him to suppress the Appeal. His Honor replied to the Southern Censor, that he had no power nor disposition to hinder Mr. Walker from pursuing a lawful course in the utterance of his thoughts" (vi). With this, Garnet underscores how Walker's powerful little book also provoked an outsized challenge to constitutional freedom of speech—a challenge that should excite White Americans to reassert this right as Garnet had for himself and Black Americans, both at the 1843 and 1848 conventions and in his "Address."

Of the significance of censorship to the history of authorship, Michel Foucault has observed that "texts, books, and discourses really began to have authors" in the early modern period, "to the extent that authors became subject to punishment, that is, to the extent that discourses can be transgressive"

(108).⁶⁰ In the biography of Walker, we see Garnet as asserting, *avant* Foucault, how southern authorities' attempts to subject Walker to state punishment for his transgressive writing confirm his authorial bona fides. And we see how Garnet—with an eye always toward citizenship in the republic, not just the republic of letters—also understands here that any White northern defense against White southerners' attempt to contradict the Bill of Rights must extend to offering Black people equal protection under law.

In subsequently narrating how extrajudicial bounties were put on Walker's head and the extreme lengths to which slavery's defenders went to thwart him, Garnet insists on representing Walker as "the youthful author" rather than the fanatic and incendiary that the press insistently had designated him as, thus making clear that Walker's pursuers were the actual fanatics and incendiaries (vii). At the same time, Garnet characterizes Walker's dedication to his *Appeal* and the work of abolition as romantically heroic, at once self-sacrificing and defiant, as we see when he imagines Walker declaring that he would stay in Boston because "he had nothing to fear from such a pack of coward blood-hounds" and that "if he did go, he would hurl back such thunder across the great lakes, that would cause them to tremble in their strong holds" (vii). Taking some literary creative license here, Garnet has Walker envisioning Canada as a country of even freer speech than the United States—and, militaristically, as a strategic base of operations where he would be able to generate even more fearful words and arguments to "hurl" south into the whole of the United States. Yet Walker "did not leave the country, but was soon laid in the grave," Garnet laments, not because he was unable or unwilling to leave, but because he was fatally censored—"hurried out of life by poison," according to "the opinion of many"—before he could write something even more powerful than his *Appeal* (vii).⁶¹

While this conclusion invites Garnet's readers to see Walker as an author who was assassinated for what he wrote—and to imagine what more great works he might have produced had he lived a full life—the bulk of the biographical sketch focuses on the significance of what Walker accomplished in the time he had. We recall that in the preface he had already described Walker's *Appeal* as "among the first" appeals "made in the early part of the Anti-Slavery Reformation" (iv). In the sketch he proclaims Walker to be the first antislavery activist: "Before the Anti-Slavery Reformation had assumed a form, he was ardently engaged in the work" (vi). I read Garnet making this claim of Walker's priority to theorize Walker as the author of not just his *Appeal* but also the northern antislavery movement and resistance by enslaved people in the South, including Nat Turner's 1831 uprising. To put it in Foucauldian terms, Garnet's biography of Walker positions him as a "founder of discursivity" for having produced "the possibilities and the rules for the formation of other texts" and "an endless possibility of discourse" through both his activism and his *Appeal* (114). This is to say that, in the paratexts of his pamphlet, we see Garnet theorizing an idea of authorship which encompasses social practice, especially in the biographical sketch that not only praises Walker for his historical achievements but ultimately theorizes him as having authored the ideas of and conditions for real actions the enslaved could take to end their bondage. To put it typographically, Garnet represents Walker as a capital-*A* Author for how he engaged in the work before anyone else, translated his actions into the words of his *Appeal*, and, through it, produced both "the possibilities and the rules for the formation of other texts" and "an endless possibility of discourse," including Garnet's own "Address to the Slaves."[62]

Delegates at the State Convention of the Colored Citizens of Ohio in January 1849 fully embraced the powerful possibilities that Walker and Garnet presented together in the "little book" that Garnet published in 1848. The convention's official minutes include their resolution "That we still adhere to the doctrine of urging the slave to leave immediately with his hoe on his shoulder, for a land of liberty, and would accordingly recommend that five hundred copies of Walker's Appeal, and Henry H. Garnet's Address to the Slaves, be obtained in the name of the Convention, and gratuitously circulated."[63] In 1843 Ohio's delegates at the Buffalo convention had voted against the publication of Garnet's address out of fear that it would bring violence to them and their fellow free Black people living in the border states. But in just five years' time, Black Ohioan activists themselves had come to calling for their enslaved Black neighbors to stop working for their masters and liberate themselves. Gathered together in early 1849, they agreed that buying and circulating copies of Walker's *Appeal* and Garnet's "Address," as Garnet had bound them together in one pamphlet, would be the most effective way to reach and activate their enslaved brothers and sisters over the border with this powerful advice.

By gathering at the convention, debating a course of action, and resolving to urge enslaved people to liberate themselves and to buy and freely circulate copies of Garnet's pamphlet, these Black activists figuratively and voluntarily bound themselves as free Ohioans with their enslaved brothers and sisters just across the Mason-Dixon Line. By taking these actions, they were also making good on their own call in another resolution to "colored inhabitants throughout this State" to take "immediate and energetic action on their part, in aiding our brothers and sisters in fleeing from the prison-house of bondage to the land of freedom." Going even farther, the convention's delegates also activated print's ability to prompt and to punish, as punishment for those "who would not aid our brothers and sisters in this most glorious cause" by resolving that these persons' names "should by every community be published to the world as a bitter enemy to the cause of justice and humanity" (18).

These resolutions at the 1849 Ohio convention were not mere words but rather the discursive possibilities produced by Walker, furthered by Garnet, and put into powerful practice by Black activists. As the United States retrenched by strengthening protections for slaveholders and increasing punishment for those who aided self-liberating people in their flight to freedom in moving toward the Fugitive Slave Law in 1850, Black Ohioans instead absorbed and activated the lessons of both Walker's *Appeal* and Garnet's "Address to the Slaves," buying and circulating them as Garnet had bound them together, in recognition of the powerful bond that they shared not only with their enslaved Black brothers and sisters across the Ohio River but also with the rest of the world, which was actively rising up in favor of justice and humanity.

CHAPTER 6

The Northern Exposure of Walker's *Appeal*

Producing and Reproducing African American Antislavery Literature and Authorship in Canada

In 1851 Paola Brown, a free Black Pennsylvanian who had emigrated to Canada in the 1820s, published the pamphlet *Address on the Subject of Slavery* in Hamilton, Ontario.[1] Compared to Walker, most of the other writers featured here, and those who fled slavery and wrote and published their narratives in Canada, Brown's life and writings are more obscure. Nineteenth-century newspapers reveal that Brown was an ardent activist in the fledgling communities of Black emigrants from the United States, and that he petitioned the Canadian government on several issues including the return of a self-liberated enslaved person back to the United States. In the *Liberator* in 1832, William Lloyd Garrison published Brown's "Circular Address to the Free People of Color Throughout the United States," along with one of his Canadian petitions.[2] And it seems that Brown was the town crier in Hamilton, Ontario, until the town passed a bylaw silencing his bell and his reportedly booming voice as unwelcome nuisances.[3] Brown was well-enough known and respected in Hamilton—despite having been silenced as town crier and accused in 1833 of fraudulent fundraising for the Colbornesburg settlement, where he had previously lived—that 210 citizens invited him to lecture at City Hall. But as the full title of his pamphlet—*Address Intended to Be Delivered in the City Hall, Hamilton, February, 7, 1851, on the Subject of Slavery*—indicates, he never actually delivered his invited address. During his introductory remarks, someone apparently turned off the gas to the building, leaving Brown and his audience in darkness and preventing him from giving his full address.[4]

Brown was determined to have his voice heard, or at least read, and had his address printed as a pamphlet sometime before July 1851.[5] With this move from oratory into print, we can positively identify one of Brown's adversaries: Thomas Smallwood, a formerly enslaved man who became active in the Underground Railroad in the mid-Atlantic states and emigrated to Canada under pressure for his activism. Smallwood wrote and published what we would now call his slave narrative, *A Narrative of Thomas Smallwood*, in or soon after July 1851.[6] In its preface, he accuses Brown of passing his *Address* off as his own work and not the "copy" of David Walker's *Appeal* that Smallwood recognized it to be from having read Garnet's 1848 reprint edition of Walker's text. Of his own *Narrative*, Smallwood pointedly emphasizes, "This little work, with the exception of the quotations and a portion of the matter in the preface is wholly original" (viii-ix). Smallwood explains that he is "led to make these remarks from the fact that I have seen a book for sale in this city purporting to be a production of Mr. Paola Brown, of Hamilton; but the fact is, it is a copy, almost verbatim, of a book known as 'Walker's Appeal,' written by a coloured man of that name" (ix).

From here, Smallwood's indictment turns searing: "In order to shew the reader more plainly the diabolical attempt of Mr. P. Brown to rob the memory of an estimable man, of one of the boldest productions against slavery ever written and published in America, I will give the preface to a brief sketch of the life and character of DAVID WALKER; together with the sketch itself, written by Henry Highland Garnet, and published with the second edition of the book referred to in 1848. Hence it will be seen that Mr. Brown is not honest in putting forth a work like the one in question in his name and as his own production" (ix). With this, Smallwood makes it clear that he did not consider Brown to be an author—that is, the originator and owner of the words and ideas in a printed text to which one rightfully attaches one's name—but a fraud (for passing Walker's writing off as his own) and a thief (for profiting from another's labors and, more criminally, for diabolically "rob[bing]" all African Americans of "the memory" of one of their greatest writers and activists). That Smallwood stopped short of explicitly charging Brown with plagiarism foregrounds how the relationship between authorship and ownership of intellectual property in international law was actively and unevenly evolving in theory and practice, across national and provincial borders, and with many kinds of authors and publishers working in very different circumstances.[7] Smallwood's case against Brown also stands as an important instance of the moral, legal, political, and economic questions raised in copyright debates between the United States and Britain in the 1850s directly intersecting with the moral, legal, political, and economic questions in the ongoing slavery debate that the 1850 Fugitive Slave Act put new pressure on as thousands of people fled north.[8] British Canada was caught in the middle of both debates, sharing a long border with the United States across which people and print moved and were subject to very different laws regarding their status as alienable property. Brown's and Smallwood's works manifest the conflicts in law and custom that such circulation occasioned.

Put another way, Brown's pamphlet offers an unusual opportunity for a case study in what we might think of as the print culture of the Fugitive Slave Act. Literature written in response to the law's passage and its significant effects on people's lives—most prominently, Harriet Beecher Stowe's *Uncle Tom's Cabin*—has received substantial and sustained attention. Publications by self-liberated and relocated enslaved and free Black people—in this case, Smallwood and Brown—who turned to print to make sense of their and others' experiences of moving from the United States with its slavery and racism to Canada are only beginning to receive more scholarly attention.[9] Thus, Brown's *Address* and Smallwood's preface offer unusual insights into some of the legal freedoms and practical complications that living in a British province brought to Black individuals, their fledgling communities, and their White neighbors. More surprisingly, they also reveal the international reach of Walker's *Appeal* and the neglected role it played in Black American emigrants negotiating their shared citizenship not only with White Canadians but also with each other in the small communities of people and print in Canada during the era of the Fugitive Slave Act.

With specific respect to the print cultural and personal stakes of Smallwood's charges against Brown violating Walker's rights as an author, we see that they were complexly motivated. Smallwood exposing Brown's unauthorized copying of Walker's text positioned Brown as a foil to Smallwood, the original and respectable author, thereby authenticating and authorizing Smallwood and his slave narrative at the cost of both Brown's and his political pamphlet's reputations. Smallwood's moral indictment of Brown and his own emphatic propriety also served as assertions of a fledgling Black Canadian community's understanding and strict enforcement of intellectual property rights at a time when both the spirit and the letter of the laws respecting them were still open to interpretation and exploitation. Plagiarism, piracy, and other forms of unattributed borrowing were widely practiced and often tolerated in the antebellum United States in what Meredith McGill has termed the period's "culture of reprinting," as we have seen in the example of William Paul Quinn's appropriation of Walker's *Appeal* in Chapter 4. By contrast, Smallwood made it clear that such immoral, if not actually illegal, acts would not be countenanced among a group of writers who were more likely to be dismissed as frauds than acknowledged as authors because of their race, as much by White Canadians as by White Americans. By making his case in the preface to his slave narrative, Smallwood turned to the court of public opinion to restore the words in Brown's *Address* to their rightful owner (David Walker) and, thereby, to Black (and also to White) people the memory of one of their boldest writers and most estimable men, regardless of national borders or the status of copyright law in and between the United States and the British Empire.

But should we understand Brown's pamphlet primarily on Smallwood's terms? Recent scholarship has begun to suggest some compelling alternatives as part of rethinking the slave narrative, possessive individualism, generative originality, and proprietary authorship as the dominant frameworks for understanding of African American literature and print. Ongoing studies of a broader range of writings are enabling us to recognize varieties of identities and degrees of artistic and political agency and labor for Black authors who wrote different kinds of texts and who were not circumscribed by "a possessive individualist relation to text(s)," as Lloyd Pratt succinctly puts it.[10] The best of this scholarship also considers the significance of genre and print format to a text's production and reception within and across racial and national borders, and recovers the influence of American chattel slavery on many aspects of publishing practices and laws including copyright.[11]

This chapter builds on these efforts, and on this book's fourth chapter, by taking Smallwood's accusation and Brown's *Address* equally seriously, and by positioning both in relation to Walker's interest in maintaining some degree of authorial control over his work even as he prioritized the wide circulation and reading of his pamphlet and encouraged various translations of its messages into action. I begin by analyzing more closely Smallwood's charges against Brown and the degree to which Brown did, in fact, copy Walker's *Appeal* but also edited and added to it in important ways that Smallwood discounts. Doing so allows for a more complex understanding of the many forms of labor, several laborers, and evolving international laws involved in textual production than either the strict legal concept of plagiarism or the Romantic and racialist concepts of the proprietary author and the original genius permit, especially as the latter has been overprivileged in our focus on the slave narrative in historicizing African American literature.[12] Next, I analyze Brown's *Address* as a particularly rich example of the "creative unoriginality" that literature scholars have begun to recognize and reevaluate as "a cultural dominant of early African American print culture" in contrast to the exception that Smallwood positions Brown's pamphlet as.[13]

More specifically, I argue that we should acknowledge that Brown's *Address* is an instance of unacknowledged copying and illicit profiteering on Smallwood's terms. We also should read it as a legitimate, if idiosyncratic, response to Walker's *Appeal* on Walker's terms. And, ultimately, we should understand it as an important updating of Walker's *Appeal* in the context of post–Fugitive Slave Act Canada. Here, again, it is important to recall Walker's notice to readers in place of a copyright notice on the verso of the third and final edition of his pamphlet's title page. As I have argued, by adding this notice, Walker conspicuously prioritized the dissemination and reading of his message, and community formation via these acts, over the protection of his individual ownership of his ideas and words by either law or custom. Bearing this in mind here, specifically in the context of international debates about copyright and enslaved fugitives, we can and should consider Brown's *Address* as an unexpected, but effective response to Walker's aims. Brown, I argue, both borrows and further extends the reach of Walker's powerful words and arguments to freeborn and self-liberated Black Americans who had settled in Canada in search of greater freedom and equality, while also actively adapting and revising them to address the rapidly and significantly changing circumstances of racism and slavery in the United States in the time since Walker's three editions and Garnet's recent reprint.

While Walker described the "coloured people of [the] United States" as the "most degraded, wretched, and abject set of beings that ever lived since the world began" (3), Brown recognized how the Fugitive Slave Act becoming law in late 1850 and its subsequent and aggressive enforcement occasioned what the historian Steven Lubet describes as "near panic in African-American communities throughout the North" and the same for White Canadian communities dealing with the influx of African American emigrants that resulted.[14] According to the *Pennsylvania Freeman*, 40 percent of Boston's Black residents fled to Canada in response to the law taking effect; freeborn and self-liberated Black people throughout the North added significantly to these numbers.[15] As Lubet explains, "free blacks could hope to fare only slightly better than escapees, because the new law provided them scant opportunity to prove their freeborn or manumitted status" (50).

In this dynamic and international social and political context, I closely read Brown's *Address* to recover how Brown carefully adapted and revised the text of Walker's *Appeal* specifically to address Black and White Canadians and Americans as they were affected by the Fugitive Slave Act. As we will see, Brown's strategic adaptation and, thereby, renewal of Walker's *Appeal* to these new circumstances is most clearly visible in his moderations of Walker's hostile tone and his most dire predictions and threats. Based on this reading, I argue that understanding Brown's *Address* solely as an unauthorized copy of Walker's *Appeal* misses the subtle, yet very important diplomatic work that Brown intended his pamphlet to do in easing tensions between Black and White people during a time of tremendous migration and adaptation.

My comparative close reading of Walker's and Brown's pamphlets further reveals that Brown also drew text from other political and religious pamphlets and tracts to compile and complete his *Address*. For Brown, as for Quinn, these borrowings as well as his adoption of several of the generic and rhetorical conventions of such pamphlets and tracts are important components of what was ultimately Brown's multipronged strategy to complete a publishable text that would reach local, national, international, and interracial audiences affected by the Fugitive Slave Act.

Put most simply, the reading that follows begins by recovering the motives behind Smallwood's charge, confirming Brown's misdeeds on Smallwood's terms, and analyzing their perpetration with respect to conventions of authorship, publishing, and citizenship in the United States and Canada in the early 1850s. Ultimately, in this chapter I look beyond the framework of property to recognize and understand alternative ideas and practices of authorship and textual production when reaching the broadest possible audience by any means necessary remained the priority under rapidly changing, and significantly worsening, legal and social circumstances since Walker's 1829 and 1830 publication of his *Appeal* and even Garnet's recent republication of it in 1848.

The High Stakes of Authorship in Black Canadian Settlements

As we have long recognized and seen in action in previous chapters, Thomas Jefferson's supposedly scientific assessments of Black writers' creative and intellectual limitations—claims that built on and extended the influence of other Enlightenment thinkers' dismissals of Black writers as unoriginal "parrots," and that nineteenth-century ethnologists in turn elaborated and extended as part of the multidisciplinary defense of slavery—continued to burden Black authors in the nineteenth century.[16] Scholars have been particularly attentive to the extra scrutiny faced by formerly enslaved writers whose literacy, much less their literariness, cast doubt on the authenticity of their writings, as well as to the layers of documentation that were typically written and signed by prominent White people and added to their narratives to certify their veracity and publication.[17] With respect to these conventions of the slave narrative specifically, Thomas Smallwood's is both no exception and exceptional. For example, writings by prominent White authors presented in his book's preface work to validate his own, much like in Frederick Douglass's 1845 *Narrative*. But instead of presenting a series of letters and statements like those in Douglass's book that verify the details of his life as told in the narrative and the writing as the author's own, Smallwood weaves his own literary philosophical commentary on slavery into a tissue of *Moby-Dick*–like extracts from canonical British literature, many of which address slavery and all of which are cited with reference to either their author (Milton, Cowper, and Byron, among others) or title (*The Revolt of Islam*, *Cymbeline*). Here, again, I turn to Beth McCoy's important call for scholars to attend to just such paratextual materials in African American literature, and her argument that "its marginal spaces and places have functioned centrally as a zone transacting ever-changing modes of white domination and resistance to that domination."[18] With this argument in mind, I read the prefatorial quotations and citations in Smallwood's narrative as Smallwood modeling proper citizenship in both the republic of letters and his new nation. By thus establishing his authorial bona fides, Smallwood turns to charge a fellow Black emigrant writer with not just literary impropriety for reproducing another author's work without proper attribution but also intellectual theft for selling the work of a great author—established as such by Garnet in his 1848 pamphlet—as his own.

That this accusation immediately follows Smallwood's treasury of great White authors on slavery highlights by comparison just how contingent, relational, and dynamic Smallwood's, Brown's, and Walker's statuses as Black authors were. As we have seen, Garnet's authorship-focused preface to his edition of the *Appeal* and his biographical sketch of Walker—both of which Smallwood includes in his *Narrative*'s front matter after his indictment of Brown—foreground how even a highly esteemed Black author could be forgotten or erased from the canon. In their small and vulnerable community of Black authors and publishers, the actions of individual writers inevitably affected others, even across national borders. Smallwood and Brown faced additional scrutiny as part of an influx of strangers who were met with citizenship but also suspicion until they proved themselves to be honorable community members. In the 1830s, Brown was accused in both the Canadian and American press of fraudulently raising funds for a settlement of free Black emigrants in Canada.[19] And in the Hamilton *Weekly Spectator* article about Brown's lecture, the reporter mocks both Brown's self-designation as an esquire and his performance during what he was able to deliver as obviously affected and, thus, ridiculous for a Black man, noting "the peculiar manner in which the lecturer rolled his tongue through his mouth, rendering the language rather thick and confused."[20] While it is unclear whether the 1830 charges were legitimate, and even though the *Weekly Spectator* reporter's commentary alludes to the ridiculousness of both Brown's character and race, these public perceptions of Brown clearly informed Smallwood's indictment of him for fraudulently profiting off of Walker's labors.

Tilar J. Mazzeo, in a nuanced study of plagiarism and literary Romanticism, distinguishes between the two forms of plagiarism that writers were commonly charged with in the era: culpable and poetical. "Only culpable plagiarism represented a moral indictment of an author, and it was almost impossible to demonstrate conclusively during the period," according to Mazzeo. The difficulty of substantiating a charge of culpable plagiarism was due to having to establish that borrowings "were *simultaneously* unacknowledged, unimproved, unfamiliar, and conscious. In the absence of any one of these elements, culpable plagiarism could not be said to have occurred." Poetical plagiarism, on the other hand, "could be persuasively charged ... if borrowings were simply unacknowledged and unimproved." The violation in such cases was aesthetic rather than moral—a transgression "of the conventional norms by which 'literature' was evaluated as distinct from other forms of expression, and authors found guilty of poetical plagiarisms were simultaneously guilty of writing badly." As Mazzeo very helpfully establishes, plagiarism in this sense "signaled a failure to achieve the minimum aesthetic objectives that constituted a successful work of Romantic-period literature.[21]

As Smallwood presents the case for his charge of plagiarism, Brown's pamphlet is both immoral and criminal, published for nothing more than his personal gain of both money and status—thus, he has committed a version of culpable plagiarism in Smallwood's eyes. Brown wrongs Walker by robbing not just an author but a deceased and defenseless one of his own words; moreover, Brown deprives all people of African descent of the memory of one of their greatest authors—one whose words Smallwood implies as being equal to those of the British greats in his preface, thereby further burnishing Walker's reputation beyond Garnet's efforts. More personally, Brown robs Walker's widow, Eliza, of any support that her late husband's work might have provided her. While Smallwood does not mention her in his indictment of Brown, Garnet specifically notes in his preface to his 1848 edition of the *Appeal* that he has republished Walker's work only after "having procured permission from his widow, Mrs. Dewson."[22] But, as I suggested in the previous chapter, because Walker did not copyright his pamphlet, securing Eliza (Walker) Dewson's official permission was unnecessary. That Garnet sought it nonetheless suggests that he respected both Walker's surviving family and the spirit, and not just the letter, of the Copyright Act of February 3, 1831, which granted a widow(er) or child/children of a deceased author a fourteen-year copyright renewal if the author died before the expiration of his or her copyright.[23]

Following this indictment of Brown, Smallwood dedicates the remainder of his preface to reprinting Garnet's preface to Walker's *Appeal* and his biographical sketch of Walker—both duly attributed to Garnet and enclosed within quotation marks—as part of restoring and further solidifying David Walker's reputation before beginning the story of his own life. To sharpen the contrast between Brown the ignominious copyist and himself, Walker, and also Garnet as original authors, Smallwood follows Garnet's biographical sketch of Walker with a concluding declaration of his own motives for writing and publishing and his significant labor as an author: "Let no one suppose that I have written this for the sake of pecuniary gain, such is not the case; but to defend myself against those who are not just enough to 'render unto Cesar the things which are Cesar's.' I have labored night and day at my calling, therefore I have no need of charity at the hands of anyone. And from the proceeds of honest toil I have given away many pounds. Six pounds would not refund what I have given to fugitives during the last fall and winter;—this I am prepared to prove" (xii). With this, Smallwood offers up an example of his charity—specifically, of monetarily assisting Fugitive Slave Act refugees, just as David Walker had sponsored self-liberating people prior to the act—as a final, if implicit, rebuke of Brown's attempt to profit both from Walker's similarly intense labors as a scholar and author and from the slavery issue instead of writing his own book and otherwise laboring for the cause. Once again, though, Smallwood's words and labors are not selfless; sales of his *Narrative* will go toward "refund[ing]" the money he has given to fugitives (without completely reimbursing him). By thus positioning his publishing venture as explicitly not for profit, Smallwood sought to gain in cultural capital in direct proportion to what he lost in economic capital, and to what Brown would lose by being exposed as a mere copyist and con artist.[24] And although Smallwood had aided fugitives in Canada and the United States at significant risk and expense to himself and his family, his understanding of authorship ultimately rested on property rights—which were, of course, the same basis as slave catchers' enforcement of and personal profit from the Fugitive Slave Act. Without overdrawing this parallel, we can see how Smallwood, by zealously restoring the words of Walker's *Appeal* to their rightful owner after they had been separated from him upon their crossing of the border into Canada (and doing so with significant benefits to himself as an author), prioritized the protection of individual authorial property rights over Walker's demand for the widest possible dissemination and reading of his message, even in the context of the Fugitive Slave Act.[25]

By pointing up Smallwood's motives in exposing Brown's moral, though not legally criminal, violation of Walker's rights as an author, and how property rights underwrite both the Fugitive Slave Act and Smallwood's understanding of the relationship of author to text, I do not mean to turn the tables and condemn Smallwood instead of Brown, or to exculpate Brown. Rather, I want to call attention to how the concepts of both proprietary authorship and possessive individualism oversimplify the multidimensional complexities of all of these authors and their writings as they were involved in intricate legal, political, social, cultural, and geographical contexts. At the same time, to cast aside these concepts as they apply to and were applied, and rejected, by these authors would also be both to neglect important dimensions of these people, works, and their contexts and to ignore these writers' and thinkers' individual, and communal, investments in proprietary authorship and possessive individualism, particularly in response to slavery. A closer look at Brown's *Address* reveals Brown to have been at once, and at the very least, an appropriator of the majority of Walker's text who tried to disguise his borrowing and gain credit for Walker's work as his own (that is, a culpable plagiarist to a degree), but also Walker's proxy in spreading his word beyond the United States and mobilizing an international community against slavery. At the same time, we will see that Brown was also a proprietary author in his own right—not just with respect to the parts of the essay that he wrote himself but also and specifically as a political pamphleteer subject to punishment for his transgressive publication. Finally, working from Mazzeo's definition of a poetical plagiarist, I argue that we should recognize Brown as an editor who laboriously synthesized what is actually an array of source texts along with his own writing into a generatively unoriginal submission to international antislavery print.

Looking at the title page of Brown's *Address*, we can clearly see that the only author named is "Paola Brown, Esq." (See Figure 10.) It announces the text printed within as "by" Brown, and the postnominal *esquire* is meant to add to the author's respectability and authority.[26] When we confirm that Brown does not acknowledge David Walker within the pamphlet in any way and that the majority of its contents were taken from Walker's *Appeal*, it becomes clear that Brown was "not honest in putting forth" his *Address* "in his name and as his own production," as Smallwood rightly charges (ix). But when we keep genre in mind, we recognize that Brown's claim of authorship of a controversial political pamphlet is more than a moral and economic matter: by replacing Walker's name with his own on what was still an incendiary text in 1851, even in Canada, Brown transferred not only praise and profit from Walker to himself but also legal liability for the text's political content and its effects.

Michel Foucault's history and theory of authorship's emergence in relation to political speech and punishment in "What Is An Author?" is relevant again to Brown's case. "Texts, books, and discourses really began to have authors" in the early modern period, Foucault observes, "to the extent that authors became subject to punishment, that is, to the extent that discourses can be transgressive" (108).[27] As southern governors' appeals to Boston's mayor Harrison Gray Otis for the arrest of Walker and authorities' suppression of his pamphlet make clear, an author of a transgressive political text in the nineteenth-century United States was no less subject to legal and extralegal persecution than an early modern English author would have been. While the First Amendment of the U.S. Constitution prevented, or at least discouraged, Walker's and other authors' legal prosecution for publishing

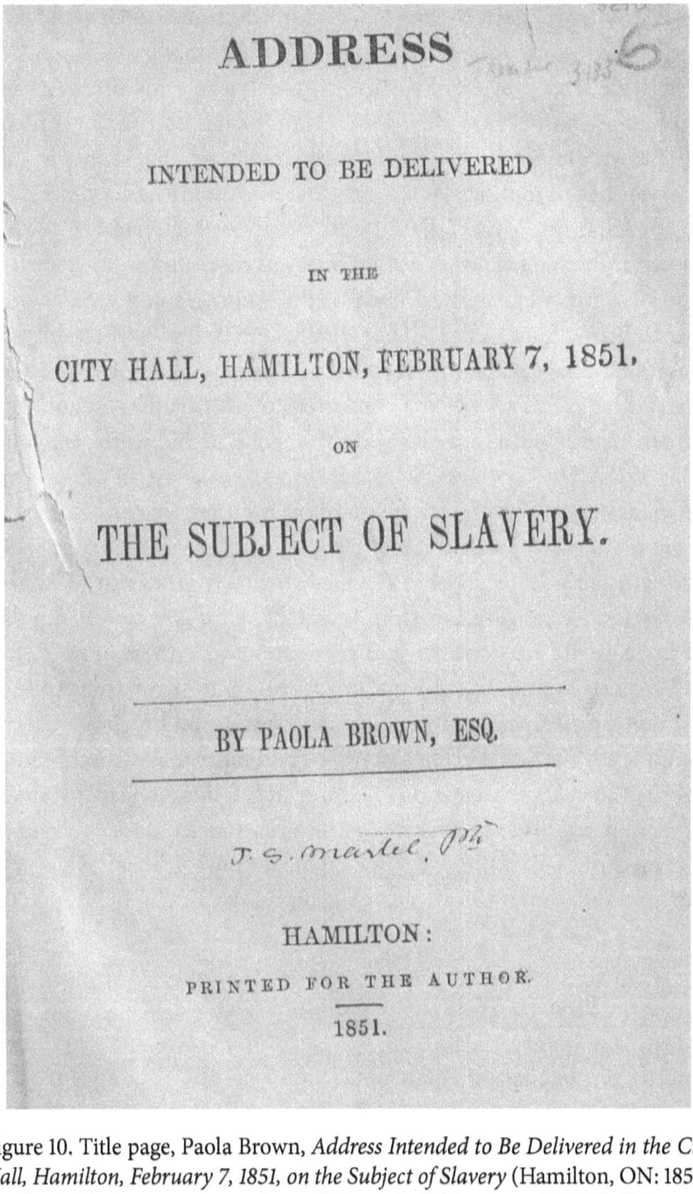

ADDRESS

INTENDED TO BE DELIVERED

IN THE

CITY HALL, HAMILTON, FEBRUARY 7, 1851,

ON

THE SUBJECT OF SLAVERY.

BY PAOLA BROWN, ESQ.

HAMILTON:

PRINTED FOR THE AUTHOR.

1851.

Figure 10. Title page, Paola Brown, *Address Intended to Be Delivered in the City Hall, Hamilton, February 7, 1851, on the Subject of Slavery* (Hamilton, ON: 1851), Lande Collection, Rare Books and Special Collections, McGill University Library.

politically controversial texts, in Canada freedom of speech was respected by English common law rather than constitutionally guaranteed. And whether those who prevented Brown from delivering his intended address may have done so because they were aware of its incendiary contents, or even if Brown staged his own silencing as a publicity stunt, we can be sure—given his pamphlet's title—that he published the pamphlet to further the popular impression that his "intended" speech had been censored. Thus, even if Brown's claim of authorship was dishonest with respect to the question of who had generated most of the *Address*'s contents, it was also made with Brown's awareness of the legal and extralegal vulnerabilities that came with publicly claiming responsibility for politically transgressive speech. As the *Weekly Spectator*'s reporter notes, "certain persons" came to the lecture "armed with serpents and fire-crackers" and were guilty of "diabolical conduct" toward Brown for daring to speak.[28] And as Smallwood's charge makes clear, Brown also made himself vulnerable as a citizen of the republic of letters, by custom if not by settled international copyright law, by borrowing so heavily from Walker's *Appeal* without acknowledging his source. When we read rather than scorn Brown's *Address* as Smallwood would have us do, it becomes more apparent that these were risks that Brown recognized and was willing to run in his urgency to adapt and revise Walker's powerful arguments against slavery and racism so that they would apply to the new world created by the Fugitive Slave Act. And as we will see in the comparative close reading that follows, even if respect and profit were among Brown's motives—and even if they were primary—they do not cancel out either his real labor on behalf of the causes of slavery, citizenship, and religion or the sincerity of this work.[29]

Finding Walker's *Appeal* in Brown's *Address*

Brown's *Address* begins with an introduction whereas Walker's *Appeal* opens with a preamble, perhaps because Brown hoped this simple substitution would obscure his significant debt to Walker's text. It is also possible that he decided that Walker's obvious allusion to the U.S. Constitution was inappropriate in Canada, even if the subject of his *Address* is also American slavery, and titled his introduction less specifically.[30] The first words of Walker's preamble and Brown's introduction also differ, not because Brown begins in his own voice before switching to Walker's, but because he starts his copying from the fifth paragraph of Walker's preamble instead of from the beginning. (See Figures 11 and 12.) With this, we confirm that Smallwood was right: Brown was, indeed, copying almost verbatim from Walker's *Appeal*. But as Smallwood's qualification of his charge indicates—that Brown's *Address* is an *"almost* verbatim" copy of Walker's *Appeal* (emphasis added)—the text of the *Address* that Brown borrows from Walker exhibits both repetition and important differences, much like we saw in Quinn's text.

A wide-angle look at the two pamphlets shows that Brown appropriated much more of the text of Walker's *Appeal* than Quinn did in his tract/pamphlet. Brown incorporated all but the first five paragraphs of the *Appeal*'s preamble into his introduction, and he borrowed the majority of article 1 and significant portions of article 2. The third and last article of Brown's pamphlet represents his most significant departure from Walker's text and his most substantial editorial and authorial labors. (Interestingly, Brown kept Walker's Constitution-like roman-numbered articles even though he titled his preamble as an introduction.) In Brown's article 3, he abridged and combined Walker's articles 3 and 4 and added to them a good deal of his own writing as well as material he had gathered and adapted from other texts on slavery, American Methodism, and U.S. history. Walker's article 4—"Our Wretchedness in Consequence of the Colonizing Plan"—is the lengthiest of the *Appeal*. As we saw in Chapter 1, Walker argues vehemently against what he calls the "colonizing trick" of the American Colonization Society and its supporters who seek to colonize Black Americans outside of the United States not in the interest of freedom but rather from a racist desire to rid the country of their presence (76).[31] Brown—who had sought and found greater liberty in Canada than in the United States, and who was addressing fellow Black and White Canadians with his pamphlet—clearly recognized how Walker's anti-emigration argument conflicted with their situation and, therefore, excluded these portions of Walker's *Appeal* from his *Address*.

Such editing is not the only evidence of Brown's departures from some of Walker's arguments despite his significant dependence on Walker's text, nor is Brown's *Address* the first instance of him engaging with and offering an alternative to aspects of the *Appeal*. In 1832, less than two years after the publication of the third and last edition of Walker's pamphlet, Brown submitted his "Circular Address to the Free People of Color Throughout the United States" to the *Liberator*. Its title's resemblance to Walker's *Appeal to the Coloured Citizens of the World*, its temporal proximity to Walker's

INTRODUCTION.

THE sources from which our miseries are derived, and on which I shall comment, I shall not combine in one, but shall put them under distinct heads, and expose them in turn. In doing which, keeping truth on my side, and not departing from the strictest rules of morality, I shall endeavor to penetrate, search out, and lay open, for your inspection. If you cannot or will not profit from them, I shall have done my duty to you, my country, and my God.

And as the inhuman system of Slavery is the source from which most of our miseries proceed, I shall begin with that curse to nations which has spread terror and devastation through so many nations of antiquity, and which is raging to such a pitch at the present day in Spain and Portugal. It had one tug in England and France, and in the United States of America, yet the inhabitants thereof do not learn wisdom and erase it entirely from their dwellings, and from all with whom they have to do. The fact is, the labor of slaves comes so cheap to avaricious usurpers, and is, as they think, of such great utility to the country where it exists, that those who are actuated by sordid avarice only, overlook the evils which will, as sure as the Lord lives, follow after the good. In fact, they are so happy to keep in ignorance and degradation, and to receive the homage and labor of the slaves, they forget that God rules in the armies of Heaven and among the inhabitants of the earth, having his ears continually open to the cries, tears, and groans of his oppressed people; and being a just and holy Being will, at one day, appear fully in behalf of the oppressed, and arrest the progress of the avaricious oppressors. For although the destruction of the oppressors, God may not

Figure 11. The beginning of Brown's introduction to his *Address*, borrowed from Walker's preamble (Figure 12), unnumbered p. iii, Lande Collection, Rare Books and Special Collections, McGill University Library.

the breasts of my afflicted, degraded and slumbering brethren, a spirit of inquiry and investigation respecting our miseries and wretchedness in this *Republican Land of Liberty!!!!!!*

The sources from which our miseries are derived, and on which I shall comment, I shall not combine in one, but shall put them under distinct heads and expose them in their turn; in doing which, keeping truth on my side, and not departing from the strictest rules of morality, I shall endeavour to penetrate, search out, and lay them open for your inspection. If you cannot or will not profit by them, I shall have done *my* duty to you, my country and my God.

And as the inhuman system of *slavery,* is the *source* from which most of our miseries proceed, I shall begin with that *curse to nations,* which has spread terror and devastation through so many nations of antiquity, and which is raging to such a pitch at the present day in Spain and in Portugal. It had one tug in England, in France, and in the United States of America; yet the inhabitants thereof, do not learn wisdom, and erase it entirely from their dwellings and from all with whom they have to do. The fact is, the labour of slaves comes so cheap to the avaricious usurpers, and is (as they think) of such great utility to the country where it exists, that those who are actuated by sordid avarice only, overlook the evils, which will as sure as the Lord lives, follow after the good. In fact, they are so happy to keep in ignorance and degradation, and to receive the homage and the labour of the slaves, they forget that God rules in the armies of heaven and among the inhabitants of the earth, having his ears continually open to the cries, tears and groans of his oppressed people; and being a just and holy Being will at one day appear fully in behalf of the oppressed, and arrest the progress of the avaricious oppressors; for although the destruction of the oppressors God may not effect by the oppressed, yet the Lord our God will bring other destructions upon them—for not

Figure 12. Walker, *Appeal*, 3rd ed., p. 5, showing where Brown began drawing from Walker's preamble for his introduction.

pamphlet, and its first words' emphasis on the degradation that Blacks have suffered in the United States clearly announced it to the *Liberator*'s readers as being in dialogue with Walker, even as it offered an alternative proposal—for Black Americans to find true equality and citizenship in Canada. As we have seen, William Lloyd Garrison had published several articles on Walker's *Appeal* beginning in 1831, and one of the longest of these agreed with and added to Walker's vehement condemnation of colonization. *Liberator* readers thus would have recognized Brown's "Circular Address" not just as a response to Walker's *Appeal* but also specifically as a refutation of Walker's and Garrison's anti-colonization arguments made in the form of an invitation to join Brown by resettling in Canada.[32]

In this earlier address, Brown describes how Black residents of Ohio, Illinois, and "several other States" who "were driven from their homes, and thrust forth as wanderers upon the face of the earth . . . were cordially received, protected, and admitted at once to all the rights of citizenship" in Canada. "Here they found the theoretical maxim of the American Constitution, that 'All men are born *equal*, and endowed by their Creator with certain inalienable rights,' practically in existence—here no distinction of color, race, language, or religion, prevails to deprive a single individual of his civil and religious rights in the amplest sense," Brown recounts (1). In misattributing the Declaration of Independence's statement of equality to the Constitution in his argument for its fulfillment in Canada, it seems that Brown not only confused the two founding U.S. texts but also wrote his "Circular Address" without Walker's *Appeal* at hand. As we have seen, Walker, in concluding article 4, quotes the opening two paragraphs of what he clearly designates as the Declaration of Independence, then immediately after demands, "See your Declaration Americans!!! Do you understand your own language?" (85).

It is entirely possible that Brown had not obtained a copy of Walker's *Appeal* by 1833 and was only able to read accounts of it such as those that had been published in the *Liberator*, for which he had worked as a subscription agent in Canada.[33] Thus, he may well have based his response to Walker's anti-emigration arguments in his "Circular Address" only on what he had seen reprinted and debated in the pages of the *Liberator*.[34] But by 1851, when he published his *Address on Slavery*, Brown had obtained copies of both Walker's 1830 third edition and Henry Highland Garnet's 1848 reprinting of Walker's second edition. Close comparative textual analysis reveals that he drew from and combined both in the manuscript he gave his printer.[35] That he would have worked from two versions of the text shows that Brown did much more work to create his text than Smallwood's charges of robbery and dishonesty recognize—and than would seem to be necessary if Brown was motivated to publish something on the slavery issue solely for personal profit. Moreover, by working with these two versions of the *Appeal*, Brown was responding not just to Walker but also to Garnet's reprinting of Walker and his "Address to the Slaves of the United States of America" that Garnet bound with Walker's *Appeal*, just as Smallwood was. As Brown uses them, the textual differences between the two editions of the *Appeal* are less significant than Garnet having bound his text with Walker's with the aim of updating Walker's message for 1848. A closer reading of Brown's *Address* reveals how he chose to adapt, edit, and supplement Walker's words and arguments instead of faithfully reprinting and appending his own argument after Garnet's example. Using a strategy that is closer to William Paul Quinn's allowed Brown to appeal to both a Canadian and an American audience by using a powerful, if controversial, source that he strategically edited to address Black emigration to Canada and the opportunities and tensions that resulted.

At first glance, many of the changes Brown made to Walker's text so that it would appeal to Black and White Canadian audiences in 1851 appear to be relatively minor. That they are mostly some words and dates changed or added to bring the text into Brown's present time and place belies the significant argumentative impact of these changes. For example, where Walker declares it "really so amusing to hear the Southerners and Westerners of this country talk about *barbarity*, that it is positively, enough to make a man *smile*" (15), Brown's text finds it amusing "to hear the Southern Slave-holders of that country"—meaning the United States—talk about the same (13).[36] Such slight but consistent modifications signal that Brown's text's perspective is located outside of the United States. More significantly, Brown's edits confine slavery to the U.S. South, even though the Compromise of 1850 was needed to address slavery's expansion into the West. Similarly, whereas Walker directly and repeatedly addresses "Americans," "Christian Americans"—to emphasize the double and reflexive hypocrisy of both—and, less frequently, "whites," Brown repeatedly inserted or added "slaveholding" to each of these designations to qualify them and, thereby, restrict Walker's indictment to White Christian American slaveholders. A noticeable example comes at the end of both Walker's and Brown's second articles. Whereas Walker concludes his with a vehement and exasperated prayer, "*Oh! my God, have mercy on Christian Americans!!!*" (39), Brown's text less emotionally and more narrowly states, "I pray that my God will have mercy on the slaveholders" (38). In article 1, another of Brown's simple insertions of "slaveholders" is even more significant, effectively scaling back Walker's indictment of the entire White race for all of human history so that it only applies to White slaveowners. In Walker's *Appeal*, "The whites have always been an unjust, jealous, unmerciful, avaricious and blood-thirsty set of beings, always seeking after power and authority" (20), but in Brown's *Address* it is only "white slaveholders" who have been so (17). And whereas Walker concluded his overview of the history of slavery with the warning that "'Every dog must have its day,' the American's [sic] is coming to an end" (18), Brown changed it to "The American Slaveholders [sic] is coming to an end," then added the more specific, yet still dire, prediction that "when God Almighty shall commence his battle in the slaveholding States on account of Slavery; tyrants will wish they never were born" (15).

I read all such instances of Brown's subtle modifications of Walker's text—and there are many—as conscious and meaningful acts of authorship. Brown's deliberate choices of words and modes of address consistently manifest his sensitivity to White Christian Canadian readers who likely were reluctant to imagine the entire White population of the United States as deserving either condemnation or mercy. In this new context, Brown adapted Walker's militant rhetoric so that it would not position White Canadian readers as having to choose between the text's arguments against racism and slavery and racial solidarity with their White U.S. neighbors. By limiting his text's searing condemnations and dire predictions to slaveholders in the U.S. South, Brown encouraged his White Canadian readers to see their new Black neighbors from the United States as free of racism and, thereby, to be so themselves.

Brown's frequent insertions of the word *slaveholders* into Walker's text also suggest that he recognized the cross-border transit of both people and texts and likely hoped that some White readers in the United States might receive his *Address* more warmly than they had Walker's *Appeal* given that Brown limits his indictment to slaveholders only.[37] Brown paid close attention to the antislavery press in the United States; we recall that he was a subscription agent for the *Liberator* in Colbornesburg in 1832 and that his actions in the settlement were under scrutiny in its pages. Thus, he also was well aware of how some of Walker's arguments had alienated powerful abolitionist advocates—Garrison in particular. By 1851 Brown doubtless was also aware of how many northern White Americans who, previously, had not been particularly sympathetic to or even interested in the antislavery movement now resented the Fugitive Slave Act for extending slavery's reach above the Mason-Dixon line and drafting them into service as slave catchers. Which is to say that, even as Brown borrowed much of Walker's text and maintained the thrust of its main arguments, he also learned from what he likely saw from his vantage point, after the passage of the Fugitive Slave Act, as Walker's tactical mistake of making slavery a racial and national crime rather than the regionally specific one of slaveholding. Thus, he not only replaced Walker's name with his own and changed his title but also modified Walker's text to narrow its indictment from all White Americans to only White slaveholders in the interest of giving its still-important antiracist and antislavery arguments a new chance with all other White Americans and Canadians. In doing so, Brown thus recognized and addressed different classes of White readers more than Walker had in his original *Appeal* to solicit potential White allies across international borders.

Moderating Walker's Militancy

Some of Brown's most substantive modifications of *Walker's Appeal* significantly altered Walker's justifications and promises of Black people's violent resistance to White violence and domination. Again, we have seen how Walker himself was well aware of the aggressiveness of both his rhetoric and his arguments, acknowledging that his "language, perhaps is too harsh for the American's [sic] delicate ears" (45). Brown understood that White Canadians, having had no part in U.S. racial slavery, would be even more sensitive to Walker's repeated prophecies of an inevitable race war. Accordingly, Brown revised Walker's original text to offer White Canadians important reassurances that they had nothing to fear from Black emigrants when everyone enjoys equality. He also wanted the same message to resonate with White people in the northern United States; therefore, his text more narrowly acknowledges that its "language perhaps is too harsh for the American slaveholders' delicate ears" (44).

Brown's article 2 contains some of most significant evidence of his moderating editorial work. In it, he chooses to omit Walker's reprinting of the 1829 newspaper article about the thwarted uprising of enslaved people in Ohio. We remember that the report of the incident occasions some of

Walker's most incendiary statements in the *Appeal* about violence and the potential for militant Black resistance:

> I give it as a fact, let twelve black men get well armed for battle, and they will kill and put to flight fifty whites.—The reason is, the blacks, once you get them started, they glory in death. The whites have had us under them for more than three centuries, murdering, and treating us like brutes; and, as Mr. Jefferson wisely said, they have never *found us out*—they do not know, indeed, that there is an unconquerable disposition in the breasts of the blacks, which, when it is fully awakened and put into motion, will be subdued, only with the destruction of the animal existence. Get the blacks started, and if you do not have a gang of tigers and lions to deal with, I am a deceiver of the blacks and of the whites. (29)

Brown did not include any of this in his *Address*. Nor did he include Walker's strongest caution about, and justification of, violent resistance that follows immediately after: "If you commence, make sure work—do not trifle, for they will not trifle with you—they want us for their slaves, and think nothing of murdering us in order to subject us to that wretched condition—therefore, if there is an *attempt* made by us, kill or be killed ... it is no more harm for you to kill a man, who is trying to kill you, than it is for you to take a drink of water when thirsty" (29–30). Again, these are the passages that specifically provoked condemnation from both southern lawmakers fearful of slave revolts and northern abolitionists who advocated moral suasion as the only acceptable means of ending slavery. As we saw in Chapter 2, Garrison's coverage of Walker's *Appeal* in the first issues of the *Liberator* included his repeated denouncements of it for these passages as well as negative responses from other abolitionists and articles about southern legal efforts to limit its circulation and Black people's literacy.[38] As an agent for the *Liberator*, Brown very likely read these responses with significant interest and remembered them when crafting his version of Walker's text.

Where Brown's text does address Black people's militant potential, he relocated and significantly revised a lengthy discursive footnote in Walker's article 4 and incorporated it into his article 2 to reassure his White Canadian readers that their Black emigrant neighbors were friends, not foes. In this footnote, Walker addresses the disproportionate population of White and enslaved people in Georgia, South Carolina, Virginia, and Jamaica most of all, where Walker excitedly calculates and bets on—with notably striking typography—the odds of Black success in the race war dreaded by Jefferson in *Notes on the State of Virginia* and realized in Haiti. Walker concludes the note by declaring that "Blacks, would almost take the whole of South America, because where they go as soldiers to fight death follows in their train" (72). In smoothing Walker's threats, Brown's editing is somewhat rough: "I have said much about our ignorance, but take the blacks as soldiers, to fight death follows in their train" (27–28). He further moderated this claim by once again extending Walker's text from the United States in 1830 to Canada later in the decade: "Oh! I shall never forget 1836 and 1837: every colored man, as soon as he heard the Canadas were to be invaded, fled to arms under their brave leader Sir Allan McNab, and other officers. Therefore, I say to our Canadian friends, fear not, we can work and make good soldiers too, in times of troubles or war" (28). (See Figures 13 and 14.)

Having offered such reassurances of Black emigrant-citizens' fidelity to Canada to the death, Brown presents his version of Walker's militant footnote: "For instance, in the two States of Georgia and South Carolina, there are perhaps not much short of seven or eight hundred thousand persons of color; and if I were a gambling character, I would not be afraid to stake down upon the board five cents against ten that there are in the single State of Virginia, six or seven hundred thousand colored persons; five hundred and sixty thousand of whom (let them be well equipped for war,) I would put against every State on the whole continent of America" (28). Brown's version increases Walker's 1830 estimates of the populations of enslaved people in the states listed by one hundred thousand each to represent their exponential expansion in the twenty years that had passed since the publication of the third edition of Walker's *Appeal*. Because these numbers—and particularly the last sentence, which, logically, includes Canada as one of the nation-states on the continent, as signaled by Brown's capital-*S* "State"—would likely not have been comforting to White Canadian readers, Brown specifically stopped short of threatening the total race war that Walker had. "I would put [450,000 blacks] against every white person on the whole continent of America," Walker boldly and proudly claims. "Why?" he anticipates readers asking; he answers, "because I know that the Blacks, once they get involved in a war, had rather die than to live, they either kill or be killed.) The whites know this too, which makes them quake and tremble" (71). Brown specifically revised Walker's language to limit the imagined scenario to only enslaved Black people fighting for their freedom rather than all Black people fighting against are too servile to assert our rights as men—or they would not fool with us as they do. Would they fool with any other people as they do with us? No, they know too well, that they would get themselves ruined. Why do they not bring the inhabitants of Asia to be body servants to them? They know they would get their bodies rent and torn from head to foot. Why do they not get the Aborigines of this country to be slaves to them and their children, to work their farms and dig their mines? They know well that the Aborigines of this country, or (Indians) would tear them from the earth. The Indians would not rest day or night, they would be up all times of night, cutting their cruel throats. But my colour, (some, not all,) are willing to stand still and be murdered by the cruel whites. In some of the West-India Islands, and over a large part of South America, there are six or eight coloured persons for one white.* Why do they not take possession of those

---

* For instance in the two States of Georgia, and South Carolina, there are, perhaps, not much short of six or seven hundred thousand persons of colour; and if I was a gambling character, I would not be afraid to stake down upon the board FIVE CENTS against TEN, that there are in the single State of Virginia, five or six hundred thousand Coloured persons. Four hundred and fifty thousand of whom (let them be well equipt for war) I would put against every white person on the whole continent of America. (Why? why because I know that the Blacks, once they get involved in a war, had rather die than to live, they either kill or be killed.) The whites know this too, which make them quake and tremble. To show the world further, how servile the coloured people are, I will only hold up to view, the one Island of Jamaica, as a specimen of our meanness.

In that Island, there are three hundred and fifty thousand souls —of whom fifteen thousand are whites, the remainder, three hundred and thirty-five thousand are coloured people! and this Island is ruled by the white people!!!!!!!!! (15,000) ruling and tyranizing over 335,000 persons!!!!!!!!—O! coloured men!! O! coloured men!!! O! coloured men!!!! Look!! look!!! at this!!!! and, tell me if we are not abject and servile enough, how long, O! how long my colour shall we be dupes and dogs to the cruel whites?—I only passed Jamaica, and its inhabitants, in review as a specimen to show the world, the condition of the Blacks at this time, now coloured people of the whole world, I beg you to look at the

places? Who hinders them? It is not the avaricious whites—for they are too busily engaged in laying up money—derived from the blood and tears of the blacks. The fact is, they are too servile, they love to have Masters too well!! Some of our brethren, too, who seeking more after self aggrandisement, than the glory of God, and the welfare of their brethren, join in with our oppressors, to ridicule and say all manner of evils falsely against our Bishop. They think, that they are doing great things, when they can get in company with the whites, to ridicule and make sport of those who are labouring for their good. Poor ignorant creatures, they do not know that the sole aim and object of the whites, are only to make fools and slaves of them, and put the whip to them, and make them work to support them and their families. But I do say, that no man, can well be a despiser of Bishop Allen, for his public labours among us, unless he is a despiser of God and of Righteousness. Thus, we see, my brethren, the two very opposite positions of those great men, who have written respecting this "Colonizing Plan." (Mr. Clay and his slave-holding party,) men who are resolved to keep us in eternal wretchedness, are also bent upon sending us to Liberia. While the Reverend Bishop Allen, and his party, men who have the fear of God, and the wellfare of their brethren at heart. The Bishop, in particular, whose labours for the salvation of his brethren, are well known to a large part of those, who dwell in the United States, are completely opposed to the plan—and advise us to stay where we are.

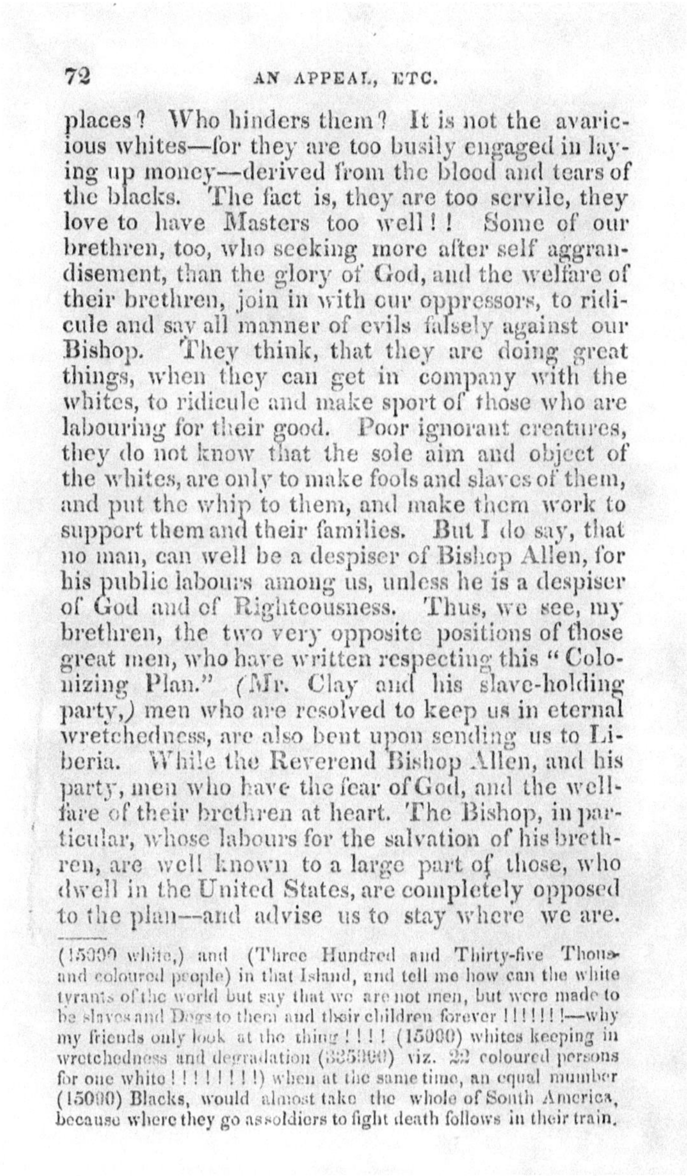

(15000 white,) and (Three Hundred and Thirty-five Thousand coloured people) in that Island, and tell me how can the white tyrants of the world but say that we are not men, but were made to be slaves and Dogs to them and their children forever!!!!!!!—why my friends only look at the thing!!!! (15000) whites keeping in wretchedness and degradation (335000) viz. 22 coloured persons for one white!!!!!!!!) when at the same time, an equal number (15000) Blacks, would almost take the whole of South America, because where they go as soldiers to fight death follows in their train.

Figure 13. Footnote added to Walker's *Appeal*, 3rd ed., pp. 71 and 72.

their folly, they will be irretrievably lost for ever, while in time ! It is a notorious fact that the major part of the white Americans have, ever since we have been among them, tried to keep us ignorant, and make us believe that God made us and our children to be slaves to them and theirs. Oh ! my God, have mercy on Christian Americans ! The word "Nigger," is a word derived from the Latin, which was used by the old Romans to designate inanimate beings, which were black—such as soot, pot, wood, house, &c., also, animals which they considered inferior to the human species, as a black horse, cow, hog, bird, dog, &c.; the white American slaveholders have applied this term to us Africans, by way of reproach for our color, to aggravate and heighten our miseries, because they have their feet on our throats, and we cannot help ourselves. How many millions of souls of the human family, have the blacks beat nearly to death, to keep them from learning to read the word of God, and from writing, and telling lies about them, by holding them up to the world as a tribe of talking Apes, void of intellect, incapable of learning, &c.; and still hold us up with indignity as being incapable of acquiring knowledge ! See the inconsistency of the assertions of those wretches. They beat us inhumanly, sometimes to death, for attempting to inform ourselves by reading the word of our Maker, and at the same time tell us that we are beings void of intellect ! How admirably their practices agree with their professions in this case. Let me cry shame upon you American slaveholders for such outrages upon human nature ! If it were possible for the whites always to keep us ignorant and miserable, and make us work to enrich them and their children, and insult our feelings by representing us as talking Apes, what would they do ? But glory, honor and praise to Heaven's king, that the sons and daughters of Africa will, in spite of all the opposition of their enemies, stand forth in all the dignity and glory that is granted by the Lord to his creature man. I have said much about our ignorance, but take the blacks as soldiers, to fight death follows in

[28]

their train. Oh! I shall never forget 1836 and 1837: every colored man, as soon as he heard the Canadas were to be invaded, fled to arms under their brave leader Sir Allan McNab, and other officers. Therefore, I say to our Canadian friends, fear not, we can work and make good soldiers too, in times of troubles or war. For instance, in the two States of Georgia and South Carolina, there are perhaps not much short of seven or eight hundred thousand persons of color ; and if I were a gambling character, I would not be afraid to stake down upon the board five cents against ten that there are in the single State of Virginia, six or seven hundred thousand colored persons ; five hundred and sixty thousand of whom (let them be well equipped for war,) I would put against every State on the whole continent of America. Why, if you tell them they are a fighting for freedom, why, because I know that the blacks, once they get involved in a war, had rather die than to live, they either kill or be killed ; the white slaveholders know this too, which make them quake and tremble.

Upon this head, read the lesson of St. Domingo, when the blacks there rose upon their masters, the proportion between the two was as 500,000 to 50,000 ; the whites were driven from the country with horrible cruelties, the natural revenge of a servile and oppressed race. Powerful armies were sent against these revolted slaves, millions upon millions were spent for their subjugation, but in vain. Now the slaveholders say that slavery is a sin and an evil. Now what does Paul say, he says, (and as some affirm that we say) " Let us do evil that good may come, whose damnation is just." (Romans, 3rd chap. 8th v.) Peter says, when speaking of selling men, women and children, he says, " And many shall follow their pernicious ways, by reason of whom the way of truth shall be evil spoken of, and through covetousness shall they with feigned words make merchandize of you ; whose judgment now of a long time lingereth not, and their damnation slumbereth not." (The second Epistle of Peter, 2nd chap. 2nd and 3rd vs.)

Figure 14. Brown's substantial editing of Walker's footnote (Figure 13) on pp. 27 and 28 of his *Address*, Lande Collection, Rare Books and Special Collections, McGill University Library.

all White people in the ultimate apocalyptic race war: "Why, if you tell them they are a [sic] fighting for freedom, why, because I know that the blacks, once they get involved in a war, had rather die than to live, they either kill or be killed; the white slaveholders know this too, which make them quake and tremble" (28). Here, again, Brown significantly edited Walker's text to reassure his White Canadian readers as well as potentially sympathetic White readers in the northern United States that only slaveholders in the southern U.S. states had something to fear from Black people. Unlike Walker's *Appeal*, Brown's *Address* assures its White audiences—both Canadian and American—that he and his fellow Black emigrants from the United States do not see all White people as their enemies.

In one of Brown's most substantive additions to his version of Walker's article 2, he introduces Walker's key White interlocutor—Thomas Jefferson. In doing so, Brown added his own paraphrased version of Jefferson's anticipation of Judgment Day with which query 18 of *Notes on the State of Virginia* concludes, but that Walker notably omitted from his *Appeal*: "Mr. Jefferson, in his notes on Virginia, says,—'Oh! you Virginians, Oh! you Virginians, I tremble, I tremble, for my country when I reflect that God is just; that his justice cannot sleep for ever: a revolution in the wheel of fortune will take place one day, and God has no attributes of mercy to take sides with us in such a contest" (29). To this, Brown added an important reflection on his status as an American Canadian, an acknowledgment of the threat that he likely poses as such to some White Canadians, and a guarantee: "I say I love my country where I was born; I always have loved it; but for this cause shall I cruelly treat one of another country? God forbid. I am a citizen of the world, a subject of Great Britain, having taken the oath of allegiance many years ago. I am a candidate for heaven, where, I am confident, whoever, by obedient walking, is so happy as to arrive, will never be interrogated in respect to his nation, color, or profession; for God is no respector [sic] of persons" (29). By thus offering himself as an example of a friend instead of a foe, Brown further attempts to allay any concern that White Canadians might have had about the Black emigrants to whom they had extended citizenship choosing race over nation if the race war that Jefferson anticipated were to transpire. To do so, he not only reaffirms the loyalty he pledged in exchange for the citizenship he was granted by Great Britain (and denied by the United States) but also asserts that this loyalty is ensured by his desire for the ultimate form of citizenship in God's kingdom. With these assurances, Brown presents the model emigrant's understanding of the order of allegiances: God comes before country and race; this understanding, in turn, guarantees that he will not dishonor his secular oath of national allegiance.

As we have seen, in one of the most emotional and self-referential moments of his *Appeal*, Walker contemplates becoming the target of violence for his justification of its rightful use to resist slavery. The passage comes as part of Walker's introduction of the newspaper article about the thwarted uprising of enslaved people, when he confronts and condemns a lack of racial solidarity: "Some of my brethren [are] in league with tyrants, selling their own brethren into *hell upon earth*, not dissimilar to the exhibitions in Africa, but in a more secret, servile and abject manner." As we remember, that anyone Black would treat other Black people so is what gives Walker significant pause: "Oh Heaven! I am full!!! I can hardly move my pen!!!" he exclaims (25). We recall as well how he presses on nevertheless and the sentence continues: "and as I expect some will try to put me to death, to strike terror into others, and to obliterate from their minds the notion of freedom, so as to keep my brethren the more secure in wretchedness. . . . I shall give the world a development of facts, which are already witnessed in the courts of heaven" (25–26).

In borrowing from Walker's *Appeal*, Brown was willing to make not just Walker's words but also his feelings his own—if to a lesser degree. After reproducing Walker's contemplation of intraracial betrayal, Brown, too, declares, "Oh, heaven! I am full! I can hardly move my pen!" (22). In addition to reducing the intensity of the emotions with the decrease in the number of exclamation points, Brown also edited out Walker's acknowledgment of how he is made vulnerable by what he writes. Rather than anticipating that he will be put to death and that his text will occasion further oppression, Brown turns in the text to God for support in forging ahead with his writing. To do so, he borrowed nearly verbatim another of Walker's first-person moments from a few pages later in article 2: "I aver that when I look over these ["those" in Brown] United States of America, and the world, and see the ignorant deceptions and consequent wretchedness of my brethren, I am brought oftimes solemnly to a stand, and in the midst of my reflections, I exclaim to my God, 'Lord, didst thou make us to be slaves to our brethren the whites?'"[39] Here, again, Brown emphasizes interracial brotherhood over the violent opposition of the races. In his version of Walker's *Appeal*, the first-person *I* becomes not just Brown, who feels overwhelmed as he surveys the United States and the world from his vantage point geographically north in Canada but also any Black woman or man contemplating inequality. In this position, I suggest, Brown also rhetorically becomes the equivalent of the figure of the supplicant kneeling slave in the well-known Wedgwood icon who asks, "Am I not a Man, and a Brother?" instead of the threatening race warrior suggested by Walker's *I*.[40]

Brown, in His Own Words (Mostly)

Brown's reaffirmation of his loyalty to his adopted country and allaying of his White Canadian readers' anxieties also work to license one of the lengthiest sections of the pamphlet that is mostly Brown's own writing. In the last ten pages of Brown's article 2, he presents an extended commentary on the state of his former country from the perspective of a "judicious foreigner" (29). While his tone echoes Walker's, the flow of his language is noticeably choppier. Brown writes:

> With what a smile of contempt must the judicious foreigner view, on the floor of the Capitol at Washington, an American slaveholder expiating on the cause of liberty, virtue, and patriotism, especially when he reflects that the main tenant, or, as it were the corner stone (may I not rather say the whole fabric?) of the religion he professes, is simply the divine command already mentioned; and when he looks back to the time that tried men's souls, as they said it did, when a price of three cents was put upon a pound of tea, what is it that is trying our souls? I say, Slavery and the Fugitive Slave Law. When they could resolve, that 'we will neither import, nor purchase any slaves imported, after the 1st day of December next, (1775) . . . ;' and, in their solemn, unequivocal, positive, and pointed Declaration of Independence, they say—'We hold these truths to be self-evident, that all men are created equal . . .'—when the foreigner views this disclaimer in the cause of liberty, &c; when he views the public prints, or newspapers, offering human beings for sale, (and frequently inserted for no fault;) when, after a lapse of 60 or 70 years he sees the 13 or 31 stripes stoop so low in such a base and ignoble traffic, . . . with what disgust must he turn away from such a hypocritical people, and exclaim, with one of their modern writers, 'I tremble for my country when I reflect that God is just; that his justice cannot sleep forever;' for surely, indeed, we cannot form to ourselves an idea of an object more ridiculous than an American slaveholder or patriot, signing declarations of

independence with one hand, and with the other brandishing his bloody whip over his affrighted slave. For the truth of the Declaration of Independence, let the reader refer to St. Paul, ch. xvii. to the Romans, vs. 22 to 30. (29–30)

As this lengthy excerpt shows, Brown was unsteady on his own legs as a writer. The ideas come in a torrent of words, conjuring up associations that frequently interrupt their logical progression along a historical timeline spanning from the American Revolution through the Compromise of 1850 to the present moment of writing in 1851. In sorting them out, we can see that his perspective here is not only Canadian but also godlike, with Brown looking down from above on the United States and specifically the floor of Congress and seeing the hypocrisy of a White Christian slaveholding congressman from the South holding forth on America's founding principles and Christian virtues. From here, he observes the contradiction between an early national willingness to end the slave trade and the effective national expansion of southern slavery with the passage of the Fugitive Slave Act in 1850. In surveying what Brown calls the "public prints" of the United States and discovering that the broadsides and newspapers that once carried the Declaration of Independence instead feature ads for "human beings for sale," he—now a "foreigner"—"turn[s] away from such a hypocritical people" with both "disgust" and fear that God's punishment for such sinful hypocrisy is imminent. But whereas Jefferson trembles for his entire country suffering judgment for slavery, Brown sees only the "American slaveholder or patriot" as damned. In this view, only those like Jefferson, who espouse—and, in Jefferson's case, author—principles of equality while practicing slavery need to fear God's wrath.

Yet even Jefferson may not be beyond salvation, as Brown sees him. He looks beyond Jefferson's *Notes* to "1816 or 1817, directly after the war with Great Britain, [when] Mr. Jefferson, seeing the evils of slavery, desired the Ministers of the Gospel of Jesus Christ to preach against the great evils of slavery, which they did openly" (30). For Brown, foregrounding Jefferson's conversion to preaching abolition (but not to fully emancipating the people he enslaved) serves as a transition to a lengthy discussion of the Methodist Episcopal Church in the United States, written mostly in Brown's own words but also paraphrased from an unspecified source or sources.

In this section of Brown's article 2, what has been a political pamphlet effectively becomes a bureaucratic one, containing statistics about the church's hierarchy and membership numbers as of June 1844, detailing (via paraphrase) a May 1844 Methodist conference in Baltimore, and reprinting a resolution passed on a White Methodist bishop's slaveholding. The abrupt and awkward shift seems to be due to Brown modeling his second article after Walker's reprinting of a newspaper article about the thwarted uprising of enslaved people in his article 2, as is suggested by the similarity of the two authors' first-person emotional responses to the different news they present. Like Walker finding it hard to write through his despair at recognizing Black people's willingness to betray each other, Brown is affectively overcome by the situation in which the Methodist Church finds itself with respect to its participation in slavery: "I stop here to get breath, and say, O! my, God, here is a reverend Divine, a Bishop, contrary to the rules of the book of discipline and the laws of God, holding his fellow beings in that cruel condition of slavery. Oh! Jesus! Master! have mercy upon the slaveholders, for they know not what they do" (32–33). Like Walker's emotional pause—"Oh Heaven! I am full!!! I can hardly move my pen!!!"—Brown's is also only rhetorical and he continues on for several pages addressing the hypocrisy of a slaveholding Methodist Church (25). His investment in offering quite so many specifics of this situation becomes clear when he finally declares, "I am a Methodist. I love the Methodist Church: I love her doctrine and discipline, and love her people, too" (36). But once again, lest he alienate any readers with this affiliation—even if he has lost them in the details of the workings of the American Methodist Episcopal Church—Brown adds, "I love all churches that names [sic] the name of Christ. I believe that God has a people in all his churches; and may my God preserve us all to His heavenly kingdom" (36).[41]

After a final page and a half drawn from an unattributed newspaper article about the 1850 U.S. Census report of the growth of the enslaved population in the previous ten years and congressional apportionment, Brown closes his article 2 with his own words and ideas, sounding like Walker at his most ministerial:

> Now my dearly beloved brethren, I have strove to show you how Slavery has managed to keep together, and has lasted so long: it is done by Congressional men, and I am sorry to say it. It is kept so strong by the ministers of the Gospel of my blessed Lord and Master, Jesus Christ.
>
> Clear the churches of slaveholders, and slavery will cease. If a slaveholder have a vote upon every five slaves, the Northern men, or the

men of the non-slaveholding states, should have a vote upon every five horses or every five cows or sheep they own. The poor slaves are cattle, and what is more than another animal? I pray that my God will have mercy on the slaveholders. (37–38)

Brown's concluding proposal in this section—that livestock should count toward congressional apportionment in the U.S. North if enslaved people are so counted in the South—comes after significant negotiations of his own to reconcile several kinds of texts into a union. Acting as both editor and author to complete article 2 of his *Address*, and addressing American readers as a Canadian citizen, Brown concludes with a meditation on another dual identity—that of the slave in the United States, countable by the census but ineligible for citizenship given her or his legal status as property, not as a person. For Brown, who was never enslaved but also not a U.S. citizen because of his race, emigrating to Canada made possible multiple new identities: citizen, activist, lecturer, author. Publishing his pamphlet made these identities all the more real, even if he adopted them unconventionally.

Thus, when we read, rather than discount Brown's *Address* as a mere copy of Walker's *Appeal*, as Smallwood did, what becomes clearly discernible is Brown's legitimate interest in and efforts toward making an important contribution to interracial and cross-border relations in the wake of the Fugitive Slave Act. As with Quinn's borrowing from Walker, Brown respected the lasting power of Walker's rhetoric, many of his arguments about racism and slavery, and his prioritization of circulating his pamphlet as widely as possible more than he (Brown) respected conventions of authors' literary property rights that Garnet and Smallwood embraced. With this in mind, it is more just to both Walker and Brown to read the latter's *Address* as a legitimate, if unconventional, response to Walker's notice to readers. The reward that Walker promises his readers for fulfilling his expectation that they will read it carefully and circulate it widely is nothing less than redemption: "and the day of our redemption from abject wretchedness draweth near, when we shall be enabled, in the most extended sense of the word, to stretch forth our hands to the LORD our GOD, but there must be a willingness on our part" (title page verso). Recalling this, we can recognize Walker's *Appeal* as having enabled Brown—"in the most extended sense of the word"—to stretch his hand as an author and editor, and Brown's *Address* as the material manifestation of the "willingness on [his] part" to risk being accused of violating Walker's *droit d'auteur* and illicitly profiting from Walker's labors. We have seen how he did so in the interest of spreading a modified version of Walker's still-powerful gospel in a Canada that was deeply affected politically, socially, legally, economically, and culturally by U.S. racial slavery. In this sense, Brown made good on Walker's title and his aims for a global audience by extending his *Appeal*, via his *Address*, to Black Canadians as among the "coloured citizens of the world."

By doing so, Paola Brown joins Maria Stewart, William Apes, William Paul Quinn, and Henry Highland Garnet in answering Walker's original appeal by extending its powerful antiracist arguments to an even greater number of audiences within the "coloured citizens of the world"—Black women, Indigenous Americans, free Black people living on the U.S. western frontier, enslaved people in the U.S. South in the context of the Revolutions of 1848 in Europe, and Black Canadian refugees from the United States and its Fugitive Slave Law, among others. To reach these audiences, each of their pamphlets necessarily challenged the dominant ideas of authorship, readerships, citizenship, personhood, agency, and authority—ideas that White people in power both explicitly and implicitly developed to ensure their hold on power, and that many Black people adopted and adapted as well. These material texts and their complex engagements with creativity, imitation, compilation, revision, printedness, literary property, circulation, and censorship represent just some of the many textual effects of David Walker's *Appeal*—effects that we will continue to discover as we deepen our understanding of the cultures of print and people in the nineteenth century and loosen the hold of White supremacy on our own culture and all of its laws and customs.

CONCLUSION

Walker's Ideal Reader

W. E. B. Du Bois

Reprinted by Henry Highland Garnet, repurposed by Maria Stewart, William Apes, William Paul Quinn, and Paola Brown, and preserved in its original editions by supporters as well as some opponents, David Walker's *Appeal* endured well beyond what it should have. It was vulnerable not only materially—as a seventy-six to eighty-eight page pamphlet that was bound in its different editions only in a paper wrapper and frequently circulated hand to hand—but also because of its exceptionally bold and controversial content. As Walker noted in an addition to his third edition, slavery made both Black bodies and books vulnerable to abuse and destruction, especially when they were found together: "If they find us with a book of any description in our hand, they will beat us nearly to death—they are so afraid we will learn to read, and enlighten our dark and benighted minds" (73). By this last edition, Walker had learned just how subject a book like his—for circulating in the South and directly appealing to free and enslaved Black people to recognize and assert their freedom and equality—as well as its author, possessors, and readers were to violent suppression. We have seen how he facetiously asks in an added note, "Why do the Slave-holders or Tyrants of America and their advocates fight so hard to keep my brethren from receiving and reading my Book of Appeal to them?—Is it because they treat us so well? . . . But why are the Americans so very fearfully terrified respecting my Book?—Why do they search vessels, &c. when entering the harbours of tyrannical States, to see if any of my Books can be found, for fear that my brethren will get them to read" (82). Making a signature rhetorical move of the *Appeal* here, Walker quickly turns his book's and Black people's physical vulnerability into White people's moral and mortal peril for betraying their democratic and Christian ideals.

He insists that "the Americans . . . see the fearful terror they labor under for fear that my brethren will get my Book and read it—and tell [him] if their declaration is true—viz. if the United States of America is a Republican Government?—Is this not the most tyrannical, unmerciful, and cruel government under Heaven[?]" (82). We also recall that near the end of the same note, he speculates that "perhaps the Americans do their very best to keep my Brethren from receiving and reading my 'Appeal' for fear they will find in it an extract which I made from their Declaration of Independence" (82). With this, Walker implies that his "Brethren," by reading the Declaration as he has reprinted it, will recognize immediately their rights to freedom and equality and demand them just as "the Americans" had in the revolution.

In this book, I have resisted the tendency to reduce radical resistance by Black and Indigenous people to physical violence in favor of recognizing a range of verbal and textual acts—talking back, studying, debating, writing, transporting and distributing pamphlets, reading to oneself and to others, annotating, reprinting, and editing—as important but often overlooked physical, intellectual, active, and effective forms of resistance in themselves. W. E. B. Du Bois was also interested in reconstructing a fuller range of actions that Black Americans could and did take to oppose slavery and racism and, in his significant efforts to do so, he several times invoked Walker's *Appeal*.[1] The pamphlet serves as a touchstone in his 1940 book *Dusk of Dawn: An Essay Toward an Autobiography of A Race Concept*, where Du Bois describes how "historically, beginning with their thought in the eighteenth century and coming down to the twentieth, Negroes have tended to . . . emphasize two lines of action" (192).[2] He designates Walker's *Appeal*— "that tremendous indictment of slavery by a colored man published in 1829, and resulting very possibly in the murder of the author"—as the exemplar of the first line of action: a "program of organized opposition to the action and attitude of the dominant white group, includ[ing] ceaseless agitation and insistent demand for equality: the equal right to work, civic and political equality, and social equality" (192–193).[3] Significantly, Du Bois specifies that the active resistance exemplified by the *Appeal* "involves the use of force of every sort: moral suasion, propaganda and where possible even physical resistance" (193). Following Walker, like Garnet, Du Bois insists on the full spectrum of actions as rightfully available to Black people in their resistance and, in doing so, both claims and qualifies physical resistance as the last but still just resort; moral suasion and propaganda, by contrast, require no such qualification. And even though he was writing about the past, Du Bois's discussion of physical resistance as a historically available option in Black resistance implicitly renewed that option for Black Americans living in the age of Jim Crow segregation.

In this conclusion, I foreground the kinds of actions that Du Bois took as a reader of Walker's *Appeal* over the violent actions that the writings of either of them justified as a legitimate and necessary form of resistance. While scholars have recognized Walker's presence in and influence on Du Bois's writings and thoughts, only recently has it become possible for us to see firsthand what Du Bois did as a reader with an actual copy of Walker's *Appeal*. In spring 2016, Emory University acquired Du Bois's personal first-edition copy of the pamphlet through a private collector.[4] Only six copies from Walker's first edition were previously known to be extant, and this seventh—stamped, signed, and annotated by Du Bois—is especially significant for what it allows us to recover about how one of Walker's most ideal, and influential, Black readers physically and intellectually interacted with the text, marking it up as a reader and as a writer in his own right.[5]

Because Du Bois's copy was trimmed when bound in boards, the width of the pamphlet's already narrow margins was reduced. As a result, his annotations are light, mostly confined to long pencil bracketings of particular passages in the margins, with different degrees of interest and/or importance indicated by double long brackets. Even so, much can be made of the passages that Du Bois bracketed and their influence on Du Bois's thoughts and arguments about racial discrimination and Black resistance in the twentieth century. They tend to focus on Walker's confrontations of White Americans with their religious and political hypocrisy, the historically and globally unprecedented barbarity of U.S. racial slavery, and Walker's invocations of the Haitian Revolution and claims of Black people's physical advantages over Whites when it comes to violent confrontation.[6] What I want to focus on by way of concluding is the only instance of handwriting in Du Bois's copy beyond his signature on the pamphlet's front free endpaper and his marginal long brackets: his manual corrections of the typesetter's errors that Walker indicates in the errata list he squeezed onto the last page of the first edition. (See Figures 15 and 16.)

In the section of article 2, "Our Wretchedness in Consequence of Ignorance," where Walker recounts his interrogation of a bootblack with respect to his limited goals for his son's education, the text in what Leon Jackson refers to as State A (that is, likely the first version of the first edition) reads: "Said I, did your son learn, while he was at school, the widt [*sic*] hand depth

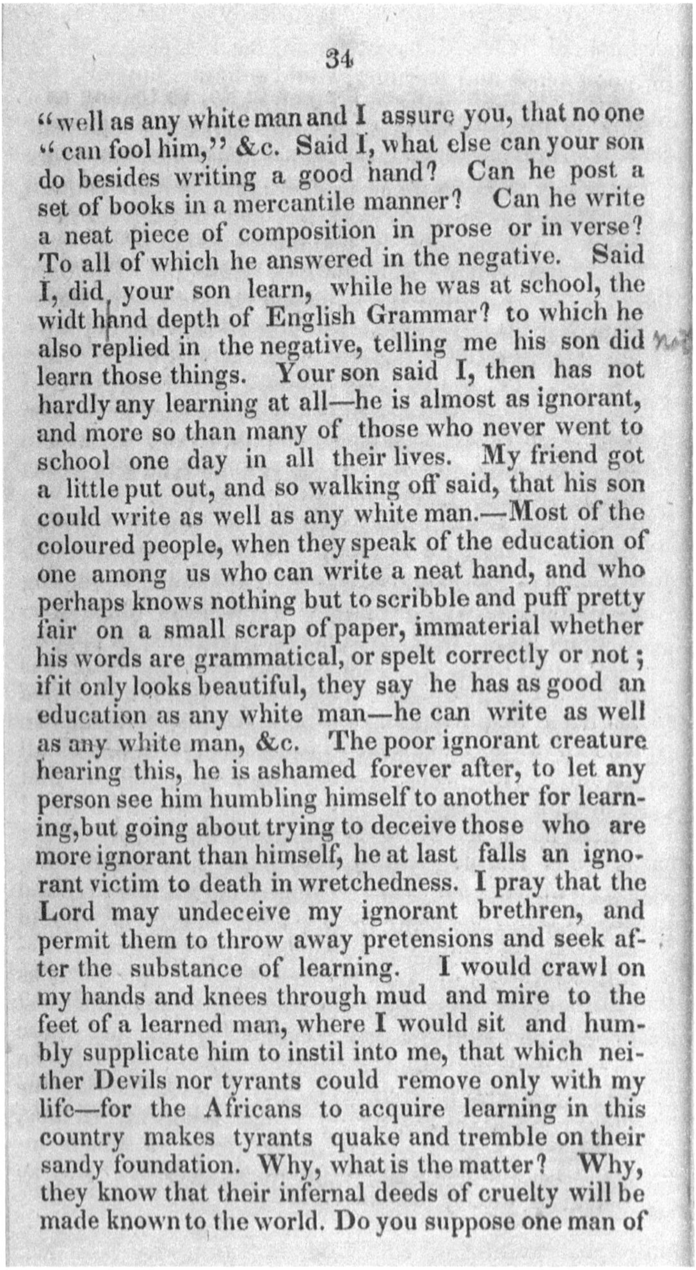

34

"well as any white man and I assure you, that no one "can fool him," &c. Said I, what else can your son do besides writing a good hand? Can he post a set of books in a mercantile manner? Can he write a neat piece of composition in prose or in verse? To all of which he answered in the negative. Said I, did your son learn, while he was at school, the widt h[a]nd depth of English Grammar? to which he also replied in the negative, telling me his son did *not* learn those things. Your son said I, then has not hardly any learning at all—he is almost as ignorant, and more so than many of those who never went to school one day in all their lives. My friend got a little put out, and so walking off said, that his son could write as well as any white man.—Most of the coloured people, when they speak of the education of one among us who can write a neat hand, and who perhaps knows nothing but to scribble and puff pretty fair on a small scrap of paper, immaterial whether his words are grammatical, or spelt correctly or not; if it only looks beautiful, they say he has as good an education as any white man—he can write as well as any white man, &c. The poor ignorant creature hearing this, he is ashamed forever after, to let any person see him humbling himself to another for learning, but going about trying to deceive those who are more ignorant than himself, he at last falls an ignorant victim to death in wretchedness. I pray that the Lord may undeceive my ignorant brethren, and permit them to throw away pretensions and seek after the substance of learning. I would crawl on my hands and knees through mud and mire to the feet of a learned man, where I would sit and humbly supplicate him to instil into me, that which neither Devils nor tyrants could remove only with my life—for the Africans to acquire learning in this country makes tyrants quake and tremble on their sandy foundation. Why, what is the matter? Why, they know that their infernal deeds of cruelty will be made known to the world. Do you suppose one man of

Figure 15. Detail of W. E. B. Du Bois's hand corrections to his copy of the first edition of Walker's *Appeal* (1829), p. 34. Courtesy of Stuart A. Rose Manuscript, Archives, and Rare Book Library, Emory University.

76

  The innocent and poor at once
   To rifle and destroy.
9 Not lions, couching in their dens,
   Surprise their heedless prey
  With greater cunning, or express
   More savage rage than they.
10 Sometimes they act the harmless man,
   And modest looks they wear ;
  That so deceiv'd, the poor may less
   Their sudden onset fear.

PART II.

11 For God they think, no notice takes
   Of their unrighteous deeds
  He never minds the suff'ring poor,
   Nor their oppression heeds.
12 But thou, O Lord, at length arise,
   Stretch forth thy mighty arm ;
  And by the greatness of thy pow'r
   Defend the poor from harm.
13 No longer let the wicked vaunt,
   And, proudly boasting, say,
  "Tush, God regards not what we do ;
  " He never will repay."—*Common Prayer Book.*

---

1 Shall I for fear of feeble man,
  The Spirits course in me restrain ?
  Or, undismay'd in deed and word,
  Be a true witness of my Lord.
2 Aw'd by mortal's frown, shall I
  Conceal the word of God Most High!
  How then before thee shall I dare
  To stand, or how thine anger bare ?
6 Shall I to sooth th' unholy throng,
  Soften the truth, or smooth my tongue,
  To gain earth's gilded toys or flee
  The cross endur'd, my Lord, by thee ?
7 What then is he whose scorn I dread ?
  Whose wrath or hate makes me afraid,
  A man ! an heir of death ! a slave
  To sin ! a bubble on the wave !
8 Yea, let men rage : since thou wilt spread
  Thy shadowing wings around my head :
  Since in all pain thy tender love
  Will still my sure refreshment prove.

       Wesley's Collection.

ERRATA.—Page 34, 9th line from the top, read his son did not learn instead, of did learn. Also, same page, 8th line from the top, in the word width there is a small typographical error.

Figure 16. Errata list at the end of W. E. B. Du Bois's copy of Walker's *Appeal*, 1st ed. (1829), p. 76. Courtesy of Stuart A. Rose Manuscript, Archives, and Rare Book Library, Emory University.

of English Grammar?" (34). In his copy, Du Bois penciled in a "not" after "did" and inserted a line to separate the *h* from *and* in "hand" so that the text correctly reads "did not your son learn, while he was at school, the width and depth of English grammar." Here, we can see Du Bois's hand correcting the *Appeal*'s typesetter's, so that the text accords with proper spelling and sense and, thereby, Walker's goal to produce a document that irrefutably proves the Black intellectual capacity he so vigorously argues for in its pages. As Walker and Du Bois equally understood, what would be an ordinary printer's error in any other text was much more significant in a Black-authored text, carrying the potential to make both the entire text and the Black race vulnerable. There was no room for error in any Black argument for equality, and especially not in one that argued for it so confidently. But what the conventions of print confined Walker to correcting in an errata list Du Bois was better able to remedy as a reader with a pencil. Thus, what otherwise would have been an instance of a reader catching and correcting a printing error we can read as a simple but significant action that Du Bois took as an activist to realize Walker's wish for Black people to cultivate orthographic and grammatical correctness on the page itself. That he did so becomes all the more meaningful when we recognize that this error was made in precisely the part of article 2 where Walker stresses proper spelling and grammar as essential steps toward full liberation and equality. Du Bois—a similarly outspoken proponent of formal education as the key to racial uplift—doubtless understood that the printed form that Walker's argument about education took on the page held the potential to undermine that argument if left uncorrected on the page itself; an errata list would be a belated and weak defense against a hostile reader's eye and biased mind. What, I want to suggest, was likely an errata list insisted upon by Walker served for Du Bois as a prompt to the man who was in many respects Walker's ideal reader to intervene manually in the body of the text to resolve the contradiction, even if the correction—grammatical, orthographical, and visual—could only be made in pencil and, thus, without the full authority of print, and for his eyes only.

Walker and Du Bois also equally understood that racist White people were not the only ones who denied Black people the kind of education that would allow them to realize their intellectual capacities as human beings. It is farther down on the same page with the typesetting error where Walker critically observes that "most of the coloured people, when they speak of the education of one among us who can write a neat hand, and who perhaps knows nothing but to scribble and puff pretty fair on a small scrap of paper, immaterial whether his words are grammatical, or spelt correctly or not; if it only looks beautiful, they say he has as good an education as any white man—he can write as well as any white man, &c." (1st ed., 34). Here, as we saw in Chapter 1, Walker distinguishes between the appearance of being educated and the substance of an actual formal education. To undereducated men such as the "elderly coloured man" with whom Walker "promiscuously fell in conversation"—who claimed to have provided a good education for his son at great expense—neat handwriting may look learned, but as Walker points out, handwriting is not the same as orthography and neither adds up to the art of composition, which requires broad and continuous learning and repeated practice (33). Again, Walker meant his *Appeal* itself to serve as a powerful demonstration of this argument—but it could only do that if "his words [were] grammatical" and "spelt correctly." Thus, in light of Walker's arguments about education in article 2, and of Du Bois's 1903 essay "The Talented Tenth," Du Bois's manual corrections become legible as important actions taken by a genuinely educated man and deeply sympathetic reader to save Walker's text from error and their shared argument about the significance of education to the race from self-contradiction. Before citing Walker's *Appeal* as a "Voice crying in the Wilderness" in "The Talented Tenth" (38), Du Bois opens the essay with the controversial claim that "the Negro race, like all races, is going to be saved by its exceptional men. The problem of education, then, among Negroes must first of all deal with the Talented Tenth; it is the problem of developing the Best of this race that they may guide the Mass away from the contamination and death of the Worst, in their own and other races" (33). While he later revisited and revised this idea to the "Guiding Hundredth," he maintained his sense of the need for an educated leadership even in a broadened effort.[7] That Du Bois made no other editorial insertions in or annotations of Walker's text with his own words suggests Du Bois's deep respect for Walker as an early exemplar of the best of the race, and for his *Appeal* as an exceptional document that was otherwise fully capable of speaking for both itself and the entire race.

As we have seen, Walker and Du Bois shared this abiding faith in formal education and a willingness to speak out against Black people who disagreed; neither was willing to compromise on this point in favor of other means of achieving racial solidarity. And both made good on their own educations by using speaking, writing, and publishing to educate both Black and White people in the United States and the world about history, the problems of the past and present, and the available paths to a more just future that could realize the full potential of both races and the nation. These beliefs and actions made both men radically dangerous in the eyes of powerful White Americans and the state policed them as such. While Du Bois suggests in *Dusk of Dawn* that Walker may have been murdered for having dared to resist in the form of writing, publishing, and circulating his *Appeal*, we now know that tuberculosis and not a bounty hunter prematurely ended Walker's life soon after the publication of the last edition in 1830. By contrast, Du Bois lived to be over ninety-five years old—a lifetime that spanned from the end of the Civil War to just before the twentieth century civil rights movement's march on Washington. He died in Ghana where he had gone to work on his *Encyclopedia Africana*. The U.S. State Department took this last massive scholarly undertaking of Du Bois's career as an opportunity to exile him from the country that he critiqued so incisively and insistently, refusing to renew his passport so that he could return to the United States. This effective revocation of his citizenship was the culmination of several decades of U.S. governmental suspicion of and accusation against Du Bois for his affiliations with the Socialist and Communist parties, his outspoken pacifism during the two world wars, and for a life publicly dedicated to pursuing equal rights for Black Americans and relentlessly critiquing America for contradicting its founding ideals.

While Du Bois took much of his personal library with him to Ghana, his copy of Walker's *Appeal* either stayed in the United States or returned stateside.[8] It is now held by a Georgia university that was named after a slaveholding Marylander and that formerly employed, but apparently did not own, enslaved people to work on its grounds.[9] Thus, its fate partially fulfills, if belatedly, one of Walker's most important aims for his *Appeal*: that copies would make their way into the South and the hands of not just enslaved people and a few sympathetic antislavery readers but also of slaveholders and others who tolerated and benefited—and continued to benefit—from slavery otherwise. We know that Walker sent at least sixty copies of the *Appeal* into Georgia and that their discovery by authorities occasioned significant alarm and some of the most restrictive legislation with respect to enslaved people's literacy and mobility and the circulation of controversial print.[10] Whereas Southern officials confiscated and destroyed these copies in the nineteenth century, Emory University purchased Du Bois's copy of Walker's *Appeal* in the twenty-first century for an undisclosed but surely substantial sum and promotes it as "one of the most important documents in African American history," "a cornerstone" of its research and teaching programs, and a resource that is available to all who are able to visit its Stuart A. Rose Manuscript, Archives, and Rare Book Library.[11]

Emory University's investment in Du Bois's copy of Walker's *Appeal* reflects the canonical status that both men have achieved as major American writers and intellectuals. Even so, a United States that continues systematically to undereducate, incarcerate, and murder Black Americans cannot be said to have heeded, in any broadly consequential ways, Walker's repeated dire warnings to alter its course. All of these inequities present significant barriers for many who would find Walker's *Appeal* to be most relevant and resonant today and well into our future. The educational and social barriers to accessing Du Bois's copy in a special collections library at a prestigious university are high. And a very real digital divide restricts access to the high-quality scans of several original copies of the *Appeal* that are now freely available on archive.org and elsewhere online. Thus, a "candid and careful perusal" of Walker's still-relevant text remains out of reach for far too many, now because of structural and institutional racism more than overt censorship and suppression (Walker, title page verso).

How many textual effects might Walker's *Appeal* and Stewart's, Apes's, Quinn's, Garnet's, and Brown's pamphlets produce in our times if they could finally reach all citizens of the world, and especially those of color, without any barriers? Those of us with any degree of power and privilege must unite, to heed their still-urgent appeals and act to remove these barriers as best we can. I offer this book, then, as one more effect of the powerful textual effects of Walker's *Appeal*, and as one of my contributions to this crucial work of making the United States finally make good on what Walker deeply believed was not only necessary but actually possible: fully equal rights and possibilities for all.

NOTES

Introduction

1. David W. Blight, *Frederick Douglass: Prophet of Freedom* (New York: Simon and Schuster, 2018), 39.

2. Frederick Douglass, *Narrative of the Life of Frederick Douglass, An American Slave* (Boston, MA: American Anti-Slavery Society, 1845), 33.

3. "G." [William Lloyd Garrison], "Singular Panic," *Genius of Universal Emancipation*, January 15, 1830, 147.

4. Lori Leavell's essay "'Not Intended Exclusively for the Slave States': Antebellum Recirculation of David Walker's *Appeal*" (*Callaloo* 38, no. 3 [Summer 2015]: 679–695) is a crucial study of the "pamphlet's broader movement" and its "after-life" by focusing on "the role of periodicals in circulating the *Appeal* beyond Boston and the South" (679). On southern print and legislative responses to Walker's *Appeal*, see chapter 5 of Peter P. Hinks, *To Awaken My Afflicted Brethren: David Walker and the Problem of Antebellum Slave Resistance* (University Park, PA: Pennsylvania University Press, 1997), 116–172; chapter 5 of Herbert Aptheker, *One Continual Cry: David Walker's Appeal to the Colored Citizens of the World (1829-1830): Its Setting and Meaning* (New York: Humanities Press, 1965), 45–53; Clement Eaton, "A Dangerous Pamphlet in the Old South," *Journal of Southern History* 2, no. 3 (August 1936): 323–334; and Hasan Crockett, "The Incendiary Pamphlet: David Walker's *Appeal* in Georgia," *Journal of Negro History* 86, no. 3 (2001): 305–318.

With respect to my capitalization of *Black* and *White* throughout the manuscript, I do so to signal the cultural constructions and histories of both racial identities, as we see in all the texts featured in this book. For a prominent argument that both should be capitalized, see Kwame Anthony Appiah, "The Case for Capitalizing the *B* in Black," *Atlantic*, June 18, 2020, https://www.theatlantic.com/ideas/archive/2020/06/time-to-capitalize-blackand-white/613159/.

5. E. Jennifer Monaghan situates Walker's *Appeal* within her discussion of slavery and literacy, specifically addressing the two stages of legal responses to the pamphlet—prohibiting supposedly dangerous print and preventing Black people from learning how to read—and their effects in *Reading for the Enslaved, Writing for the Free: Reflections on Liberty and Literacy* (Worcester, MA: American Antiquarian Society, 2000), esp. 334–341. Interestingly, she does not make the connection between Walker's *Appeal* and Auld's halt to Douglass's reading lessons. For more on the Walker-Douglass connection, see my essay "David Walker and Frederick Douglass," in *Nineteenth-Century American Literature in Transition*, vol. 2, ed. Justine S. Murison (Cambridge: Cambridge University Press, forthcoming 2022).

6. Again, for an important consideration of the consequences of laws and practices related to Walker's *Appeal* (and other antislavery print) on Douglass, see Monaghan, *Reading for the Enslaved*, esp. 339–341, as well as my "David Walker and Frederick Douglass."

7. The most recent edition of the *Norton Anthology of African American Literature* follows in the tradition of 1960s African American activist, Black nationalist, and Black Power scholarship with its headnote to its excerpt from Walker's *Appeal*, which asserts that "the most militant voice among the early African American protest writers belonged to David Walker, whose call to violent resistance against slavery so alarmed authorities in the South that they were reputed to have put a price on his head" ("David Walker," in *Norton Anthology of African American Literature*, ed. Henry Louis Gates Jr. and Valerie Smith, 3rd ed. [New York: W. W. Norton, 2014], 1:159). The note does distinguish between White and Black readers' responses to the pamphlet by emphasizing that "Most black readers found the *Appeal* an inspiring articulation of African American pride and a fearless call to radical action in the name of those principles of justice to which Americans, white as well as black, were supposed to be dedicated" (159). Updated editions of the Heath and Norton anthologies of American literature have also introduced more multidimensional readings of Walker's pamphlet and its effects. In the former, Paul Lauter draws attention to the continuing double standard for Black violent resistance and revolution in the concluding paragraph of his author page entry for David Walker for the *Heath Anthology of American Literature*: "Still, it is one of the ironies of our history that Patrick Henry's cry—'Give me liberty or give me death'—evokes intense sentiments of patriotism; whereas, David Walker's assertion—'Yea, I would meet death with avidity far! far!! in preference to such *servile submission*'—has evoked primarily fear" ("David Walker," *Heath Anthology of American Literature*, http://college.cengage.com/english/lauter/heath/5e/resources/author_pages/early_nineteenth/walker_da.html). And in the most recent *Norton Anthology of American Literature*, the headnote leads by positioning it as "central to the development of African American writing of the antebellum period" and such writing's characteristic "willingness to critique national ideologies and practices," before noting that the pamphlet "became notorious for its militant assertion that blacks, when faced with possible enslavement, should 'kill or be killed'" (*Norton Anthology of American Literature*, 9th ed., vol. B, ed. Amy Hungerford et al. [New York: W. W. Norton, 2017], 773–774).

8. Elizabeth McHenry, *Forgotten Readers: Recovering the Lost History of African American Literary Societies* (Durham, NC: Duke University Press, 2002), 27. In similarly suggesting the need to broaden our readings of Walker's *Appeal*, Douglas A. Jones Jr. asserts that "the point is not so much to establish that the *Appeal* directly caused bloody acts of black resistance; rather, it is to note how the text marked the boundaries of the performative field of black oppositionality and ideology in the period" (*The Captive Stage: Performance and the Proslavery Imagination of the Antebellum North* [Ann Arbor: University of Michigan Press, 2014], 62).

9. Manisha Sinha offers the most significant recent historical consideration of Walker's *Appeal* in chapter 8 of her monumental book *The Slave's Cause: A History of Abolition* (New Haven, CT: Yale University Press, 2016), 228–265. With respect to Walker's significance in African American historiography, see John Ernest, *Liberation Historiography: African American Writers and the Challenge of History, 1794–1861* (Chapel Hill: University of North Carolina Press, 2004). In rhetoric studies, see Jeremy Engels, "Friend or Foe? Naming the Enemy," *Rhetoric and Public Affairs* 12, no. 1 (2009): 37–64. In theater/performance studies, see Alex W. Black, "Abolitionism's Resonant Bodies: The Realization of African American Per-

formance," *American Quarterly* 63, no. 3 (2011): 619–639; Sarah Jane Cervenak, "Gender, Class, and the Performance of Black (Anti) Enlightenment: Resistances of David Walker and Sojourner Truth," *Palimpsest* 1, no. 1 (2012): 68–86; and D. Jones, *Captive Stage*. In political history and theory, see Sandra M. Gustafson, *Imagining Deliberative Democracy in the Early American Republic* (Chicago: University of Chicago Press, 2011), 137–142; and Melvin L. Rogers, "David Walker and the Political Power of the Appeal," *Political Theory* 43, no. 2 (April 2015): 208–233. In religious studies, see Eddie S. Glaude Jr., *Exodus! Religion, Race, and Nation in Early Nineteenth-Century Black America* (Chicago: University of Chicago Press, 2000); and Chernoh M. Sesay, "The Dialectic of Representation: Black Freemasonry, the Black Public, and Black Historiography," *Journal of African American Studies* 17, no. 3 (2013): 380–398. At the intersection of African American studies and the history of science, see Ian Finseth, "David Walker, Nature's Nation, and Early African-American Separatism," *Mississippi Quarterly* 54, no. 3 (Summer 2001): 337–362; and Britt Rusert, *Fugitive Science: Empiricism and Freedom in Early African American Culture* (New York: New York University Press, 2017), esp. 41–44. In American studies, see Celeste-Marie Bernier, "'Iron Arguments': Spectacle, Rhetoric and the Slave Body in New England and British Antislavery Oratory," *European Journal of American Culture* 26, no. 1 (2007): 57–78; Elizabeth J. West, "From David Walker to President Obama: Tropes of the Founding Fathers in African American Discourses of Democracy, or The Legacy of Ishmael," *American Studies Journal*, no. 56 (2012), https://doi.org/10.18422/56-06. The following represents some of the most significant and extensive work on Walker's *Appeal* in literary studies after McHenry: Marcy J. Dinius, "'Look!! look!!! at this!!!!': The Radical Typography of David Walker's *Appeal*," *PMLA* 126, no. 1 (January 2011): 55–72; Gene Andrew Jarrett, *Representing the Race: A New Political History of African American Literature* (New York: New York University Press, 2011); Benjamin Shearer Beck, *David Walker's "Appeal" and Everyday Abolition* (master's thesis, University of Colorado Boulder, 2011); Lori A. Leavell's "Poe's Steadfast Servant in the Aftermath of Walker's *Appeal*," *Mississippi Quarterly* 66, no. 4 (2013): 539–564; Stefan M. Wheelock, *Barbaric Culture and Black Critique: Black Antislavery Writers, Religion, and the Slaveholding Atlantic* (Charlottesville: University of Virginia Press, 2016); chapter 1 of Kevin Pelletier's *Apocalyptic Sentimentalism: Love and Fear in U.S. Antebellum Literature* (Athens: University of Georgia Press, 2015), 35–58; chapter 8 of Christopher C. Apap's *The Genius of Place: The Geographic Imagination in the Early Republic* (Durham: University of New Hampshire Press, 2016), 185–206; Tara Bynum, "Why I Heart David Walker," *J19* 4, no. 1 (Spring 2016): 11–17; Carrie Hyde, *Civic Longing: The Speculative Origins of U.S. Citizenship* (Cambridge, MA: Harvard University Press, 2018), esp. 62–66; and Derrick R. Spires, *The Practice of Citizenship: Black Politics and Print Culture in the Early United States* (Philadelphia: University of Pennsylvania Press, 2019). In book history/print culture studies, see esp. Leon Jackson's essay "The Talking Book and the Talking Book Historian: African American Cultures of Print—The State of the Discipline," *Book History* 13 (2010): 251–308; and his unpublished conference paper "David Walker in the Archive" (presented at the American Literature Association Annual Conference, Boston, MA, May 25, 2019). Jackson is currently at work on an article and a book that will present crucial new information about the writing, printing, and circulation of the *Appeal*; I thank him for sharing his work in progress with me as well as for his enthusiasm for and encouragement with this book. Also in book history/print culture studies, see Leavell's important essays "'Not Intended Exclusively for the Slave States'" and "Recirculating Black Militancy in Word and Image: Henry Highland Garnet's 'Volume of Fire,'" *Book History* 20 (2017): 150–187.

10. Cheryl A. Wall offers an important analysis of how "even as state and local governments moved quickly to censor Walker's *Appeal*, its influence on black orators and writers could not be suppressed," as part of her broad examination of the underappreciated significance of the essay as a major genre in African American literature; see *On Freedom and the Will to Adorn: The Art of the African American Essay* (Chapel Hill: University of North Carolina Press, 2018), 53. Wall focuses on Walker's influence on Stewart and Garnet, the subjects of my second and fifth chapters. Among most twentieth-century historians, Aptheker is a notable exception in noting that Walker's *Appeal* is "a document of historic import . . . not only because of the direct and considerable impact it had upon its own day . . . [but] also because it projects most of the arguments and questions that were to be used and raised in the next generation of decisive struggle against slavery" (*One Continual Cry*, 59). Even so, he only considers Garnet's 1848 reprinting of the *Appeal* and his "Address to the Slaves." More recently and extensively, Hinks considers a broader array of the pamphlet's effects, yet he only briefly mentions Stewart, Garnet, Douglass, and Du Bois (as well as Amos G. Beman) as figures "in the mainstream of antebellum black activism" and beyond who "gave Walker credit for being a central influence on their lives" near the end of chapter 4 of *To Awaken* (113). A major reading of Walker's *Appeal* with respect to literary and print history comes in chapter 2 of Robert S. Levine's *Dislocating Race and Nation: Episodes in Nineteenth-Century American Literary Nationalism* (Chapel Hill: University of North Carolina Press: 2008), 67–117. There, Levine similarly notes that "Walker has gained a reputation for militancy, even though much of the *Appeal* is concerned with countering white racial prejudice and developing strategies for black empowerment in the United States" (70). For previous scholarly considerations of Walker's connection specifically to Stewart, Apes, Quinn, Garnet, and Brown individually, see the concluding section of this introduction as well as notes in the chapters that follow. With respect to the *Appeal*'s place not just in African American literary history but also its significant work in defining the field, see chapter 1 of Jarrett's *Representing the Race*, 21–48. After McHenry's call for us to move beyond reading Walker's *Appeal* in relation to the question of violence, several scholars have attended to how many prominent, and mostly White-authored, nineteenth-century publications were inspired by Walker's text, including William Lloyd Garrison's *Liberator*, the antiliteracy and antimobility legislation that was debated and published in several southern states between 1829 and 1832, countless newspaper articles dedicated to tracking Walker's *Appeal* during the same period, Robert Montgomery Bird's 1836 novel *Sheppard Lee*, and Edgar Allan Poe's story "The Gold Bug." On Walker's influence on Garrison's founding of the *Liberator*, see Donald M. Jacobs, "David Walker and William Lloyd Garrison: Racial Cooperation and the Shaping of Boston Abolition," in *Courage and Conscience: Black and White Abolitionists in Boston*, ed. Jacobs (Bloomington: Indiana University Press, 1993), 1–20. On the *Appeal* in periodical publications and Bird's novel *Sheppard Lee*, see Leavell's essay "'Not Intended Exclusively for the Slave States,'" and on the *Appeal* and "The Gold Bug," see also her "Poe's Steadfast Servant."

11. With "hemispheric," I mean to signal the multinational and diasporic experiences and thinking of these writers—or *cosmopolitans*, as Ifeoma Kiddoe Nwankwo terms them—not to make an imperialistic claim that a project that is mostly focused on U.S. writers and publications represents the literary and/or print history of the hemisphere. See Nwankwo's *Black Cosmopolitans: Racial Consciousness and Transnational Identity in the Nineteenth Century Americas* (Philadelphia: University of Pennsylvania Press, 2005). And by "literary," I mean not simply fiction and poetry, but what Carrie Hyde calls the "highly speculative

traditions—political philosophy, Christian theology, natural law, literature, and didactic writing" through which early American conceptions of citizenship, rights, the human, the social, art, and the political were both theorized and practiced (*Civic Longing*, 8). I also heed Wall's emphasis on other genres—the essay most of all—as vitally important but neglected traditions within the more traditional concept of the literary in *On Freedom*.

12. Joanna Brooks, "The Unfortunates: What the Life Spans of Early Black Books Tell Us About Book History," in *Early African American Print Culture*, ed. Lara Langer Cohen and Jordan Alexander Stein (Philadelphia: University of Pennsylvania Press, 2012), 40–52; Joseph Rezek, "The Print Atlantic: Phillis Wheatley, Ignatius Sancho, and the Cultural Significance of the Book," in *Early African American Print Culture*, 19–39; Wall, *On Freedom*, 1.

13. As of June 2019, the Moorland-Spingarn Research Center was the only institution known to have a copy of Quinn's *The Origin, Horrors, and Results of Slavery*, which librarians there were unable to locate except in photocopy facsimile. Efforts to locate the original continue.

14. L. Jackson, "Talking Book," 290.

15. Zakiyyah Iman Jackson, *Becoming Human: Matter and Meaning in an Antiblack World* (New York: New York University Press, 2020), 1.

16. Carla L. Peterson, *"Doers of the Word": African-American Women Speakers and Writers in the North (1830–1880)* (Oxford: Oxford University Press, 1995), 14.

17. See my "'Look!! look!!! at this!!!!'"

18. The *Oxford English Dictionary* defines *effects*, in this sense, as "a reproduction of a musical sound, created by a synthesizer; an alteration of the sound of a musical instrument (or sometimes a voice) in recording or performance, created by an electronic device (frequently *attributive*, denoting such a device). Chiefly in *plural*" ("effect, n. 4d," *OED Online*, Oxford University Press, December 2018, https://www.oed.com/view/Entry/59664).

19. Henry Louis Gates Jr., *The Signifying Monkey: A Theory of African-American Literary Criticism* (New York: Oxford University Press, 1988), xxii.

20. John Bryant, *The Fluid Text: A Theory of Revision and Editing for Book and Screen* (Ann Arbor: University of Michigan Press, 2002), 1.

21. Walter Johnson, "On Agency," in *Journal of Social History* 37, no. 1 (2003): 113–124.

22. Judith Butler, *The Force of Nonviolence* (London: Verso, 2020), 12–13.

23. Kellie Carter Jackson, *Force and Freedom: Black Abolitionists and the Politics of Violence* (Philadelphia: University of Pennsylvania Press, 2019), 2.

24. Leavell, "Recirculating Black Militancy," 152.

25. Chapter 2 of Michael Warner's *Publics and Counterpublics* (Brooklyn, NY: Zone, 2002), 65–124, offers several defining characteristics of what he terms *counterpublics* that certainly apply to the group of texts here. But his concluding thoughts about what happens to "alternative publics" when they become social movements—"they acquire agency in relation to the state" and "enter the temporality of politics and adapt themselves to the performatives of rational-critical discourse," and, thereby, "cede the original hope of transforming not just policy but the space of public life itself"—make me wary of the designation for the authors and pamphlets under study here, as they draw no such distinction between rational-critical discourse and transforming policy and public life (124). As Joanna Brooks has noted of such complications, "Contradictions between public sphere ideals and sociopolitical practices in early America and the cultural forms emergent from these contradictions—including the forms of the black counterpublic—constitute a rich field yet to be fully imagined and resolved." See her

essay "The Early American Public Sphere and the Emergence of a Black Print Counterpublic," *William and Mary Quarterly* 62, no. 1 (2005): 71n6. In relation to the binary opposition suggested by using the term *counter-archive* and the many reading, writing/recording, storage, and assemblage processes that complicate a strict opposition, see Wendy W. Walters's introduction to *Archives of the Black Atlantic: Reading Between Literature and History* (Oxfordshire: Routledge, 2013), 1–9.

26. Eric Slauter dedicates part of *The State as a Work of Art: The Cultural Origins of the Constitution* (Chicago: University of Chicago Press, 2009) to showing how "the modern interpretive divide between those who see the Constitution as a static document and those who see it as a living organism was present in the revolutionary era" (19). On historical and modern concepts of the Constitution as a living text, see David A. Strauss, *The Living Constitution* (Oxford: Oxford University Press, 2010). In specific light of the evangelical rhetoric of Walker's *Appeal*, see John W. Compton's *The Evangelical Origins of the Living Constitution* (Cambridge, MA: Harvard University Press, 2014). For previous studies of Walker's and other radical abolitionists' attitudes toward and uses of the Constitution, see chapter 4 of Elizabeth Beaumont's *The Civic Constitution: Civic Visions and Struggles in the Path Toward Constitutional Democracy* (Oxford: Oxford University Press, 2014), 119–162. I thank my former undergraduate student and research assistant Ryan Ziencina for his research on this topic.

27. Hinks suggests that David Hooton and Mathew Teprell were likely Walker's printers, given the proximity of their shop to Walker's and Walker's debt to them in probate records (*To Awaken*, 116). My research and Leon Jackson's suggest the same; Jackson's research is ongoing. Jackson has also determined that there were at least two different versions, or more technically, states, of the pamphlet's first edition and notes that the first state of the first edition is characterized by what he describes as "shoddy composition" ("David Walker in the Archive," 5–6).

28. David Walker, *Walker's Appeal to the Coloured Citizens of the World*, 3rd ed. (Boston, MA: 1830), 23. Unless otherwise noted, all of the text quoted from the *Appeal* throughout this book comes from the third edition and will be cited in the text.

29. William Lloyd Garrison, "Walker's Pamphlet," *Liberator*, January 1, 1831, 1.

30. Henry Highland Garnet, "An Address to the Slaves of the United States of America," in *Walker's "Appeal," with a Brief Sketch of His Life by Henry Highland Garnet and Also Garnet's "Address to the Slaves of the United States of America*," by David Walker and Henry Highland Garnet (New York: J. H. Tobitt, 1848), 90.

31. On the subjective biases, vulnerabilities, and incompleteness specifically in the Americas and the Atlantic World, see Diana Taylor, *The Archive and the Repertoire: Performing Cultural Memory in the Americas* (Durham, NC: Duke University Press, 2003); Saidiya Hartman, "Venus in Two Acts," *Small Axe* 12, no. 2 (2008): 1–14; Ann Laura Stoler, ed., *Along the Archival Grain: Epistemic Anxieties and the Colonial Common Sense* (Princeton, NJ: Princeton University Press, 2009); Marisa J. Fuentes, *Dispossessed Lives: Enslaved Women, Violence, and the Archive* (Philadelphia: University of Pennsylvania Press, 2016); and Laura Helton, Justin Leroy, Max A. Mishler, Samantha Seeley, and Shauna Sweeney, "The Question of Recovery: An Introduction," *Social Text* 33, no. 4 (2015): 1–18. For a recent essay collection on best practices for assembling and maintaining physical and digital archives of materials related to vulnerable and dispersed populations, see David C. Sutton and Ann Livingstone, eds., *The Future of Literary Archives: Diasporic and Dispersed Collections at Risk* (York, UK: Arc Humanities Press, 2018).

32. Other candidates for extended consideration include David Ruggles's 1835 *Appeal to the Colored Citizens of New York and Elsewhere in Behalf of the Press* and Hosea Easton's 1837 *Treatise on the Intellectual Character, and Civil and Political Condition of the Colored People of the United States*. While Ruggles's *Appeal* is noticeably close to Walker's in its verbal (and visual) emphasis on the contradiction of slavery in the "Land of Liberty" and its insistence "that our [blacks'] contest is for *freedom* and that the PRESS is the weapon which we wield in behalf of our rights," Ruggles published it in six parts in the *Emancipator* newspaper rather than as a stand-alone pamphlet. His choice of a different venue for publication does not disqualify his *Appeal* for consideration but rather necessitates distinct and further attention to the differences that this choice of medium makes to its message, particularly given its embeddedness within a polyvocal newspaper, even if it was a cause-based one. Easton, who worked closely with Walker as a fellow activist and member of the Massachusetts General Colored Association in Boston, published his *Treatise* as a pamphlet, yet he took care to distinguish it genre- and tone-wise from Walker's fiery polemical political appeal, presenting it instead as a more formal and even more traditionally scholarly social treatise. That said, it warrants close comparison with Walker's *Appeal* as one of its most proximate textual effects. But borrowing from the note that Easton's printer Isaac Knapp likely added at the end of Easton's *Treatise* (regarding the sermon promised on its title page but missing from the text), I have "omitted [Easton's *Treatise* from this book] on the account that it would swell the work far beyond our calculation" and hope to return to it, either in my own work or others', as we continue the conversation about Walker's *Appeal*. See David Ruggles, *Appeal to the Colored Citizens of New-York and Elsewhere in Behalf of the Press*, Emancipator, (January 13, 20, 27, and February 3, 10, and 17, 1835), unnumbered p. 3 for first three and final installments, and unnumbered p. 2 for nos. 4. and 5. The quotation comes from no. 1, unnumbered p. 3. See also Hosea Easton, *A Treatise on the Intellectual Character, and Civil and Political Condition of the Colored People of the United States* (Boston, MA: Isaac Knapp, 1837), unnumbered p. 55.

33. Again, on southern responses to Walker's pamphlet, see chapter 5 of Hinks, *To Awaken* as well as Eaton, "Dangerous Pamphlet," 323–334; and Crockett, "Incendiary Pamphlet."

34. The headnote to the most recent (third) edition of the *Norton Anthology of African American Literature* decidedly foregrounds the pamphlet's militancy and situates it in relation to the uprising led by Nat Turner in 1831. It opens with the declaration that Walker's was the "most militant voice among early African American protest writers" and concludes by implying a cause-and-effect relationship between Walker's *Appeal* and Nat Turner's Rebellion: "Walker did not live to see Nat Turner's insurrection in Southampton County, Virginia, in August 1831, only fourteen months after the publication of the last edition of the *Appeal*." The note also positions the *Appeal* as an "enabling text and a touchstone by which its successors— from Garnet's own 'Call to Rebellion' speech in 1843, through Eldridge Cleaver's *Soul on Ice* (1967), to the nationalist-infused hip-hop expression of artists such as Public Enemy, Sister Souljah, and Dead Prez—can be measured, valued, and preserved in a tradition," but without noting any of the other more immediate—and less militant—texts that the pamphlet enabled beyond Garnet's (159–160). With respect to presentations of Walker's *Appeal* in anthologies of American literature, see Paul Lauter's previously noted conclusion to his author entry on Walker as well as the headnote to the *Appeal* in the ninth edition of the *Norton Anthology of American Literature*, which does the most to position it within a tradition of African American critiques of "national ideologies and practices," recasting Walker's primary intention as arguing for "blacks' rights to U.S. citizenship" rather than "push[ing] blacks into a race war,"

while acknowledging its militant arguments, Whites' fearful responses, and influence on Garnet's "Address to the Slaves" (773–774). While this note sensitively balances Walker's political philosophical engagements with the pamphlet's moments of militancy and White readers' focus on these aspects at the time, introducing students to a more complex idea of the *Appeal*, it also neglects Walker's significant influence on his contemporaries beyond Garnet.

35. With respect to book historical methodologies and histories of the book and print in early America, the second and third volumes of *A History of the Book in America* (Chapel Hill: University of North Carolina Press, 2010 and 2007, respectively) have been indispensable to my work, particularly the essays by James N. Green on "The Rise of Book Publishing," Meredith L. McGill on copyright in both volumes, Michael Winship on "Manufacturing and Book Publishing" and "Distribution and the Trade," and David Paul Nord on "Benevolent Books: Printing, Religion, and Reform." Winship's *'The Greatest Book of Its Kind': A Publishing History of 'Uncle Tom's Cabin'* (Worcester, MA: American Antiquarian Society, 2002) has been useful to my broader thinking about the intricacies and intersections of race, slavery, and book publication using empirical bibliographical research. McGill's essay "Format" (*Early American Studies* 16, no. 4 [2018]: 671–677) has also been valuable to my thinking about the pamphlet as both a print format and literary genre. In trying to think multidimensionally about the "physical properties of texts—their visual appearance, tactile feel, and oral performance"— and their importance not just to early American communities, but also African American communities with wide-ranging visual and verbal capacities and attitudes toward books and other visual and material objects, Matthew P. Brown's *The Pilgrim and the Bee: Reading Rituals and Book Culture in Early New England* (Philadelphia: University of Pennsylvania Press, 2007) has been an important guide. With respect to book historical approaches to early African American texts, see also Brooks's "Early American Public Sphere and the Emergence of a Black Print Counterpublic"; Cohen's and Stein's introductory essay to *Early African American Print Culture* (1–16) and all the essays in that collection; Leavell's essays; and Leon Jackson's "Talking Book."

36. Jesse McCarthy, "On Afropessimism," *Los Angeles Review of Books*, July 20, 2020, https://lareviewofbooks.org/article/on-afropessimism/.

37. Dorothy Porter, ed., *Early Negro Writing: 1760–1837* (1971; repr., Baltimore: Black Classic Press, 1995); Marilyn Richardson, ed., *Maria W. Stewart, America's First Black Woman Political Writer* (Bloomington: Indiana University Press, 1987); Peterson, *"Doers of the Word"*; Hinks, *To Awaken*; Peter P. Hinks, ed., *David Walker's "Appeal"* (University Park, PA: Pennsylvania State University Press, 2000); McHenry, *Forgotten Readers*; Frances Smith Foster, "A Narrative of the Interesting Origins and (Somewhat) Surprising Developments of African-American Print Culture," *American Literary History* 17, no. 4 (2005): 714–740; Hillary E. Wyss, *Writing Indians: Literacy, Christianity, and Native Community in Early America* (Amherst: University of Massachusetts Press, 2000); Finseth, "David Walker, Nature's Nation, and Early African-American Separatism"; Maureen Konkle, *Writing Indian Nations: Native Intellectuals and the Politics of Historiography, 1827–1863* (Chapel Hill: University of North Carolina Press, 2004); Phillip H. Round, *Removable Type: Histories of the Book in Indian Country, 1663–1880* (Chapel Hill: University of North Carolina Press, 2010); Jarrett, *Representing the Race*; Leavell's three essays, "Poe's Steadfast Servant," "'Not Intended Exclusively for the Slave States,'" and "Recirculating Black Militancy"; Beck, *David Walker's "Appeal"*; Eric Gardner, *Unexpected Places: Relocating Nineteenth-Century African American Literature* (Jackson: University of Mississippi Press, 2009), and *Black Print Unbound: The*

"Christian Recorder," *African American Literature, and Periodical Culture* (Oxford: Oxford University Press, 2015); Leon Jackson, "Talking Book" and "David Walker in the Archive"; Lara Langer Cohen, with Jordan Alexander Stein, introduction to *Early African American Print Culture* (1–16), her chapter "Notes from the State of San Domingue: The Practice of Citation in *Clotel*" (160–177) in the same collection, and chapter 3 of *The Fabrication of American Literature: Fraudulence and Antebellum Print Culture* (Philadelphia: University of Pennsylvania Press, 2012), 101–132; Christopher Hager, *Word by Word: Emancipation and the Act of Writing* (Cambridge, MA: Harvard University Press, 2013); Benjamin Fagan, *The Black Newspaper and the Chosen Nation* (Athens: University of Georgia Press, 2016); Bynum, "Why I Heart David Walker"; Wall, *On Freedom*; and Spires, *Practice of Citizenship*. Of course, I am solely responsible for any shortcomings in my attempts to do justice to Walker's, Stewart's, Quinn's, Garnet's, and Brown's works, and for falling short of any of the model scholarship that I cite here and throughout.

38. Sean Wilentz, ed., *David Walker's "Appeal"* (New York: Hill and Wang, 1995).

39. *Documenting the American South* website, https://docsouth.unc.edu. My deep thanks to Chris Hager for first pointing me to the *Documenting the American South* archive for Brown's pamphlet and its borrowings from Walker.

40. For a prominent articulation of the necessary complementarity of research in digital and physical archives, see, for example, G. Sayeed Choudhury and David Seaman, "The Virtual Library," in *A Companion to Digital Literary Studies*, ed. Ray Siemens and Susan Schreibman (Oxford: Blackwell, 2008), http://www.digitalhumanities.org/companionDLS/.

41. L. Jackson, "Talking Book," 288.

Chapter 1

1. Marcy J. Dinius, "'Look!! look!!! at this!!!!': The Radical Typography of David Walker's *Appeal*," *PMLA* 126, no. 1 (2011): 55–72.

2. Elizabeth McHenry, *Forgotten Readers: Recovering the Lost History of African American Literary Societies* (Durham, NC: Duke University Press, 2002), 41–49.

3. Tara Bynum, "Why I Heart David Walker," *J19* 4, no. 1 (2016): 15–16.

4. Peter P. Hinks's major book *To Awaken My Afflicted Brethren: David Walker and the Problem of Antebellum Slave Resistance* (University Park: Pennsylvania State University Press, 1997) marks the beginning of intense scholarly study of Walker's *Appeal*. His chapters 6 through 8 (173–258) offer substantial readings of Walker's strategies for addressing and activating readers, and of the intellectual, oratorical, and print precedents on which Walker draws to do so. See also McHenry, *Forgotten Readers*, esp. 41–49; Douglas A. Jones, Jr., *The Captive Stage: Performance and the Proslavery Imagination of the Antebellum North* (Ann Arbor: University of Michigan Press, 2014), 62–64; Kevin Pelletier, *Apocalyptic Sentimentalism: Love and Fear in U.S. Antebellum Literature* (Athens: University of Georgia Press, 2016), esp. chap. 1 (35–58); Bynum, "Why I Heart David Walker"; and Cheryl A. Wall, *On Freedom and the Will to Adorn: The Art of the African American Essay* (Chapel Hill: University of North Carolina Press, 2018), 41–53.

5. Jarrett offers the most thorough close comparison of Jefferson's *Notes* and Walker's *Appeal* to date; see chapter 1 of *Representing the Race: A New Political History of African American Literature* (New York: New York University Press, 2011), 21–48, quote on 38.

6. Ian Finseth, "David Walker, Nature's Nation, and Early African-American Separatism," *Mississippi Quarterly* 54, no. 3 (Summer 2001): 337–362. See also Britt Rusert, *Fugitive Science:*

Empiricism and Freedom in Early African American Culture (New York: New York University Press, 2017), 41–44; and Wall, *On Freedom*, 43–53.

7. Thomas Jefferson, *Notes on the State of Virginia*, 8th American ed. (Boston, MA: David Carlisle, 1801).

8. Dustin Gish and Daniel Klinghard recently have observed that "perhaps the greatest obstacle to understanding Jefferson's political ambitions for [*Notes*] is a common tendency to view the book as lacking any coherent literary structure or unifying political purpose.... There is a widespread sense among scholars that the evident idiosyncrasies and minutiae that comprise the textual surface of the book exhaust its substantive depth; which is to say, it is held by most to be merely a compilation of disconnected, if erudite, reflections, observations, and eccentric details, which together convey an attentive mind or perhaps a spirit, but not a coherent thesis" (*Thomas Jefferson and the Science of Republican Government: A Political Biography of "Notes on the State of Virginia"* [Cambridge: Cambridge University Press, 2017], 4).

9. Stephen W. Brown, "Encyclopedias and the Essay," in *Encyclopedia of the Essay*, ed. Tracy Chevalier (London: Fitzroy Dearborn, 1997), 254–255.

10. Daniel Brewer, *The Discourse of Enlightenment in Eighteenth-Century France: Diderot and the Art of Philosophizing* (Cambridge: Cambridge University Press, 1993), 13.

11. As Keith Thomson explains, "Although much of Jefferson's style of scientific thinking centered on his reading of English natural philosophy from his days at William and Mary College, much came also from two French sources. One was Denis Diderot's *Encyclopédie* and its successor, the *Encyclopédie Méthodique*, by Diderot and Jean le Ronde d'Alembert, which summarized for the first time a vast range of human knowledge and introduced Jefferson to such subjects as ancient civilizations and modern technology. He recommended these works to all his friends and, when in Paris, arranged subscriptions for them. The second work, just as large in scope, was Buffon's *Histoire Naturelle, Générale et Particulière*" (*Jefferson's Shadow: The Story of His Science* [New Haven, CT: Yale University Press, 2012], 46–47). I also thank James N. Green for sharing his unpublished essay "Memory, Reason, Imagination: Subject Classification in the 1789 Catalogue of the Library Company of Philadelphia," in which he confirms that Jefferson "arrange[d] for the Virginia legislature to buy an unbound copy of the second folio edition" of the *Encyclopédie*, "which had somehow turned up in the hands of an obscure merchant in Alexandria Virginia," and that Jefferson seems to have "appropriated it for his own use" rather than sharing it with all Virginians as a publicly-held text (4).

12. Charles Monaghan and E. Jennifer Monaghan, "Schoolbooks," pt. 3 of sec. 3, "Educating the Citizenry," in *A History of the Book in America*, vol. 2, *An Extensive Republic: Print, Culture, and Society in the New Nation, 1790–1840*, ed. Robert A. Gross and Mary Kelley (Chapel Hill: University of North Carolina Press, 2010), 309.

13. Lindley Murray, *English Grammar, Adapted to the Different Classes of Learners* (Boston, MA: T. Bedlington, 1825), Internet Archive.

14. Hugh Blair, quoted in Murray, *English Grammar*, 6.

15. In the pamphlet's first edition, the printer(s) used Arabic instead of roman numerals for the chapter/article headings. In the second and third editions, they are printed as roman numerals. On David Walker's and other radical abolitionists' attitudes toward and uses of the Constitution, see esp. chapter 4 of Elizabeth Beaumont's *The Civic Constitution: Civic Visions and Struggles in the Path Toward Constitutional Democracy* (Oxford: Oxford University Press, 2014), 119–162, and McHenry, *Forgotten Readers*, 29–30. With respect to early American

Constitutional debates about slavery and the nation's formation, see David Waldstreicher, *Slavery's Constitution: From Revolution to Ratification* (New York: Hill and Wang, 2009).

16. I address Walker's unusual level of involvement with his printer(s)/typesetter(s) in "'Look!!,'" esp. 59 and 68n5.

17. Wall is a notable exception. In her reading of the *Appeal* and Walker's strategies for reaching his different readers, she notes, "Its instructions were particularly germane to those who read the text aloud to their peers" (*On Freedom*, 44).

18. David Walker, letter to Thomas Lewis, December 8, 1829, slide 6 in "David Walker's *Appeal*: Anti-Slavery Literature in the Executive Communications," The Uncommonwealth: Voices from the Library of Virginia, February 9, 2011, https://uncommonwealth.virginiamemory.com/blog/2011/02/09/david-walkers-appeal-anti-slavery-literature-in-the-executive-communications/. I thank Jordan Stein for calling my attention to this letter through a recent Twitter post, especially because the portion of the letter that Hinks reproduces in *To Awaken* specifically excludes Walker's terms for circulation (135–136).

19. See especially the long footnote Walker added to page 82 of the third edition of the pamphlet, which I quote and discuss in the last section of this chapter.

20. For a concise overview of debates about authors' "final intentions" in literary criticism and editorial theory from the mid- through the late twentieth century, see chapter 4 of Steven Mailloux, *Interpretive Conventions: The Reader in the Study of American Fiction* (Ithaca, NY: Cornell University Press, 1982), 93–125, esp. 94–99.

21. I believe there is an error in this note either as Walker wrote it or as it was printed, omitting the "do not" before "mean," so that it should read as "I do not mean to convey the idea, that there will be no more Books of this Third Edition printed." That is, I read Walker as having meant to suggest (1) that his pamphlet could be reprinted from its third edition, and (2) that the text was no longer dynamically evolving but rather stable with no more additions or notes to be added to future printings. This makes it particularly interesting, then, that Garnet reprinted Walker's second edition in his 1848 edition of the *Appeal*. While the third edition would have been more complete and represented Walker's fullest statement of his case, I imagine that Garnet worked with what he had, given the pamphlet's limited availability, and given both thorough efforts to suppress it and Walker's death.

22. The claim that Walker circulated copies of his pamphlet by secreting them inside used clothes that he sold to sailors from his Boston shop has been one of the most compelling stories of Walker's efforts. The claim circulated most prominently in Sean Wilentz's 1995 introduction to the Hill and Wang edition of the *Appeal*. He posits, "But historians have suggested that Walker also took more elaborate smuggling measures. At his shop near the docks, sailors looked for cheap clothing (so-called slop goods) for their upcoming voyages; and Walker supplied them with used items, many of them obtained from other sailors, who had sold them for ready cash. It was a simple matter to collect batches of printed material, sew them into the linings of the clothing, and have them carried off undetected by sympathetic sailors bound for Wilmington, Charleston, Savannah, and New Orleans. Within days, copies of antislavery literature could be sent all across the South, spreading out from the ports along river routes to literate blacks who could relay the message to slaves at large" (introduction to *David Walker's "Appeal"* [New York: Hill and Wang, 1995], xv). From indefatigable archival research, Leon Jackson compellingly argues, "We need to let go of the idea that Walker smuggled copies of the *Appeal* into the South by hiding them in the linings of the clothes he sold to sailors. Awesome though this idea is, it's completely without merit.... There is not a shred of evidence,

published or unpublished, to corroborate the idea. Indeed, the bulky dimensions of the *Appeal* alone militate against the idea" (Leon Jackson, "David Walker in the Archive," paper presented at the American Literature Association Annual Conference, Boston, MA, May 25, 2019, 7–8).

23. Wall also offers a similar close reading of Walker's chief claim, foregrounding Walker's repetition of it as "a strategy that is crucial to the power of the *Appeal*," working "to convey the prophetic warning that God will avenge the oppression of his people; the day of reckoning is close at hand." She also offers an important three-part analysis of the rhetorical purposes of its "extremity": "The first is simply to intensify the call for amelioration," the "second is comparative," situating the "condition of enslaved blacks in the United states" in relation to "enslaved populations throughout history," with Walker "driv[ing] home the point that slavery in Christian America is worse than in so-called heathen nations," and the third "is to heighten the contradiction between the nation's democratic principles and its material realities" (*On Freedom*, 46–47).

24. *Boston Daily Evening Transcript*, September 28, 1830, quoted in McHenry, *Forgotten Readers*, 35–36. Walker published the third edition of his *Appeal* in late March of 1830 (L. Jackson, "David Walker in the Archive," 6).

25. Of the evolving legislation that eventuated in now-familiar copyright notices and their placement, Meredith L. McGill explains that the Copyright Act of 1802 added to existing copyright law in the United States "the requirement that the copyright record be inscribed on the work itself." "In the case of books," she writes, "it required that the author or proprietor 'give information by causing the copy of the record, which . . . he is required to publish in one or more of the newspapers to be inserted at full length in the title page' or, in its now-familiar position, on the page immediately following." See her essay "Copyright," in *A History of the Book in America*, ed. Robert A. Gross and Mary Kelley (Chapel Hill: American Antiquarian Society and University of North Carolina Press, 2010), 2:203. Joanna Brooks notes that Absalom Jones and Richard Allen were "the first African Americans to take advantage of federal copyright law" for their 1794 pamphlet *Narrative of the Proceedings of Black People During the Late Epidemic in Philadelphia* ("The Early American Public Sphere and the Emergence of a Black Print Counterpublic," *William and Mary Quarterly*, 62, no. 1 [2005]: 84).

26. Henry Highland Garnet emphasizes Walker's generosity in his brief biography of Walker that he included in his 1848 edition of the *Appeal*: "His hands were always open to contribute to the wants of the fugitive. His house was the shelter and the home of the poor and needy" ("A Brief Sketch of the Life and Character of David Walker," in *Walker's Appeal, with a Brief Sketch of His Life by Henry Highland Garnet and also Garnet's Address to the Slaves of the United States of America* [New York: J. H. Tobitt, 1848], vi).

27. Of Walker's title, Derrick R. Spires notes, "When David Walker addressed his *Appeal* (1829) to the 'colored citizens of the world, but in particular, and very expressly, to those of the United States of America,' he was similarly "speaking 'colored citizens' into being," as Absalom Jones had in a 1799 petition, "making a claim about their relationship to traditionally recognized citizens, and calling on them to assume the rights and subjectivity of citizenship" (*The Practice of Citizenship: Black Politics and Print Culture in the Early United States* [Philadelphia: University of Pennsylvania Press, 2019], 5).

28. I understand these changes between the first and two subsequent editions as suggesting Walker carefully hand-edited a print copy from the first edition which he gave to his printer(s) to use to set the second edition, so they understood his use of capitalization was not

only intentional but also essential to the text, and that they should closely follow his guidance about how to set the text's type. On the possible identity of Walker's printers, see note 27 in the introduction to this book.

29. Dinius, "'Look!!,'" 56–57.

30. As Kellie Carter Jackson notes of this passage, "This gendered appeal stands in stark contrast to the nonthreatening abolitionist slogan, 'Am I not a Brother?' portraying a shackled black man pleading for his liberation. Walker called for white Americans to see black humanity as a form of manliness and for the enslaved to be motivated by manliness as a justification for self-defense" (*Force and Freedom: Black Abolitionists and the Politics of Violence* [Philadelphia: University of Pennsylvania Press, 2019], 18).

31. See especially the *Boston Courier* article titled "The 'Incendiary Pamphlet,'" which reproduces a letter from Virginia's governor William B. Giles to Boston's mayor Harrison Gray Otis which characterizes Walker twice as a "sanguinary fanatic" (*Boston Courier*, March 4, 1830, 2). Another Boston-published article on legislation introduced in North Carolina in response to discoveries of Walker's pamphlet circulating there quotes a story in the *Raleigh (NC) Register* that refers to the "diabolical pamphlet written by Walker of Boston" (quoted in "North Carolina Legislature," *Boston Weekly Messenger*, December 23, 1830, 1). On legislative responses to the *Appeal*, see chapter 5 of Hinks, *To Awaken*, 116–172; Hasan Crockett, "The Incendiary Pamphlet: David Walker's *Appeal* in Georgia," *Journal of Negro History* 86, no. 3 (2001): 305–318; and Lori Leavell, "Poe's Steadfast Servant in the Aftermath of Walker's *Appeal*," *Mississippi Quarterly* 66, no. 4 (2013): 539–564.

32. Walker cites the article that he reprints in article 2 as drawn from Boston's *Columbian Centinel* (September 9, 1829). The title pages of all three editions of the *Appeal* state that it was "Written in Boston, [in the] State of Massachusetts, Sept[ember] 28, 1829."

33. Peter Otto, "Sublime," in *An Oxford Companion to the Romantic Age: British Culture 1776–1832*, ed. Iain McCalman et al. (Oxford: Oxford University Press, 1999), 723.

For my previous reading of this passage, see "'Look!!,'" 60. I thank Derrick Spires for encouraging me to reconsider this reading.

34. Quoted in Walker, *Appeal*, 3rd ed., 26.

35. The language in the newspaper story that Walker reprints is somewhat unclear about the racial identity of the owner and driver of the group of enslaved people—describing him as a "negro driver, by the name of Gordon, who had purchased in Ma[r]yland about sixty negroes" (quoted in 3rd ed., 26). But a February 5, 1831, letter to the *Liberator* specifically notes that "Gordon is a colored man who purchased in Maryland about sixty slaves, and drove them in handcuffs and chains to the Mississippi, to work his new farm" (J. I. W. to William Lloyd Garrison, *Liberator*, February 5, 1831, 22). A reply to this letter by "Leo" in the February 19 *Liberator* notes that "Leo has some acquaintance with Gordon" (Leo to Garrison, *Liberator*, February 19, 1831, 30).

36. Notably, Murray comments on the didactic force of the negative example in the introduction to *English Grammar*: "From the sentiment generally admitted, that a proper selection of faulty composition is more instructive to the young grammarian, than any rules and examples of propriety that can be given, the Compiler has been induced to pay peculiar attention to this part of the subject, and though the instances of false grammar, under the rules of Syntax, are numerous, it is hoped they will not be found too many, when their variety and usefulness are considered" (4–5).

37. David Walker, "Address. Delivered Before the General Colored Association of Massachusetts, by David Walker," *Freedom's Journal*, December 20, 1828, 295–96.

38. See especially Jefferson's contradictions of George-Louis Leclerc, comte de Buffon and Abbé Guillaume-Thomas Raynal in *Notes*, 97–101. Both Jarrett and Finseth focus on Walker's self-insertion into this conversation as an intellectual peer, considering how Walker reasons like, but against Jefferson and his European Enlightenment peers, without attending to how Walker also writes like Jefferson's *Notes*, at times mockingly, but mostly as faithfully following its example of textual engagement and intellectual debate.

39. For Jefferson's comparison of European and American Whites, see *Notes*, 96–100.

40. Wall reads Walker's analogy of Jefferson's conclusions about the Black and White races as "a parable that illustrates" their "respective situation" (*On Freedom*, 49). For a rich analysis of numerous African Americans' responses to Jefferson's *Notes* in the print public sphere, see chapter 1 of Rusert, *Fugitive Science*, 33–64.

41. Elias B. Caldwell speech, quoted in Walker, *Appeal*, 58.

42. John Randolph speech, quoted in Walker, *Appeal*, 61.

43. I have inserted an asterisk in Walker's "niger" to suggest the spelling of this epithet as it is typically rendered today.

44. The only definition that Sheridan offers for *negro* is "a blackamore" (*A Complete Dictionary of the English Dictionary*, 2nd ed. (London: Charles Dilly, 1789), s.v. "Negro."

45. On the historical and cultural significance of *Freedom's Journal*, see Jacqueline Bacon, *"Freedom's Journal": The First African American Newspaper* (Lanham, MD: Lexington Books, 2007).

46. Richard Allen, letter to *Freedom's Journal*, quoted in Walker, *Appeal*, 65.

47. Otto, "Sublime," 723.

48. Leo to William Lloyd Garrison, *Liberator*, January 29, 1831, 17.

49. William Lloyd Garrison, "Walker's Pamphlet," *Liberator*, January 1, 1831, 1.

50. Garrison, response to Leo, in "Walker's Appeal," *Liberator*, January 29, 1831, 17.

51. J. I. W. to William Lloyd Garrison, *Liberator*, February 5, 1831, 22.

52. Wall reads these anecdotes in somewhat different terms, noting that Walker "records conversations with people he has met, including the colored bootblack who has announced himself content in his situation, and thereby becomes a prime example of the degradation of black people's spirit. By combining a personalized witness with traditions of oral performance," Wall argues, "Walker lays the ground for the development of a distinctly 'African American' essay" (*On Freedom*, 42).

53. On Walker's occupation as a used clothing dealer and his work, social, and activist contexts in Boston, see chapter 3 of Hinks, *To Awaken*, 63–90. Leon Jackson has important research and writing on Walker's trade in progress; I look forward to how his findings will shift our understanding of Walker, the *Appeal*, and African American activist and trade networks in the early nineteenth century.

54. Untitled article, *Boston Courier*, March 22, 1830, 3.

55. This passage bears a strong resemblance to a well-known passage in Edmund Burke's *Reflections on the Revolution in France* in which Burke argues against working-class revolution: "The occupation of a hair-dresser, or of a working tallow-chandler, cannot be a matter of honour to any person—to say nothing of a number of other more servile employments. Such descriptions of men ought not to suffer oppression from the state; but the state suffers oppression, if such as they, either individually or collectively, are permitted to rule. In this you think you are combatting prejudice, but you are at war with nature.*" Significantly, Burke's footnote is Ecclesiasticus 38:24–25: "'The wisdom of a learned man cometh by opportunity of leisure: and

that he hath little business shall become wise.'—'How can he get wisdom that holdeth the plough, and that glorieth in the good; that driveth oxen; and is occupied in their labours; and whose talk is of bullocks?'" Given the relevance of both texts to Walker's argument in article 2, it seems likely that he read Burke—either in an edition of Burke's writing, or quoted elsewhere—and is implicitly responding to his argument and invocation of scripture here. It is possible that this edition would have been available to him: Edmund Burke, *Reflections on the Revolution in France*, in *The Works of the Right Honourable Edmund Burke*, 1st American ed. (Boston, MA: John West and O. C. Greenleaf, 1807), 3:66.

56. Jefferson, *Notes*, 207.

57. Finseth notes that "Walker does not rebut the essential core" of Jefferson's position "that racial difference and conflict are part of the natural order. One implication is that the *Appeal*, no less than *Notes on the State of Virginia*, raises the question of whether whites and blacks can peacefully coexist" (354).

58. Pelletier, in chapter 1 of his *Apocalyptic Sentimentalism*, 33–58, offers an important extended reading of how Walker's *Appeal* "aspires not merely to hasten the destruction of white America but to fundamentally reimagine racial relations in the antebellum period," focusing on how the text "seeks to establish a form of sympathetic connection between his white audience and slaves, one that might catalyze a change in or even a dismantling of the slave system" by addressing "his readers' hearts" (39).

59. On Walker's *Appeal* and the jeremiadic tradition, see Dolan Hubbard, "David Walker's *Appeal* and the American Puritan Jeremiadic Tradition," *Centennial Review* 30, no. 3 (1986): 331–346; Eddie S. Glaude Jr., *Exodus! Religion, Race, and Nation in Early Nineteenth-Century Black America* (Chicago: University of Chicago Press, 2000), 42–43; Willie J. Harrel, "A Call to Consciousness and Action: Mapping the African-American Jeremiad," *Canadian Review of American Studies* 36, no. 2 (2006): 149–180; and Wall, *On Freedom*, 45–46. Rufus Burrow Jr. offers a much broader and important reading of the *Appeal* in the biblical tradition of prophecy in *God and Human Responsibility: David Walker and Ethical Prophecy* (Macon, GA: Mercer University Press, 2003).

60. *The Bible*, Authorized King James Version (New York: Oxford University Press, 1998).

61. On Walker's and other Black abolitionists' specific rhetorical appeal to the Declaration of Independence as the founding document of their equality with whites and their right to freedom, see Jacqueline Bacon, "'Do You Understand Your Own Language?' Revolutionary *Topoi* in the Rhetoric of African-American Abolitionists," *Rhetoric Society Quarterly* 28, no. 2 (1998): 55–75. Arthur Riss explores the opposite use to which the Declaration was put in the nineteenth century in *Race, Slavery, and Liberalism in Nineteenth-Century American Literature* (Cambridge: Cambridge University Press, 2006).

62. The slight exception is the third edition, in which the middle exclamation point after "See your Declaration Americans" and the first after "ALL MEN ARE CREATED EQUAL" are slightly lower than the others; this apparently unintentional printing variation only visually heightens the emphasis and outrage suggested by the multiple exclamation points. Theodor Adorno, in his essay "Punctuation Marks," notes that an "exclamation point looks like an index finger raised in warning." See Adorno, "Punctuation Marks," trans. Shierry Weber Nicholsen, *Antioch Review* 48, no. 3 (1990): 300.

63. Jay Fliegelman has argued that the Declaration itself "was written to be read aloud" and that this fact "becomes a crucial clue to elements of its meaning." See *Declaring Independence: Jefferson, Natural Language, and the Culture of Performance* (Stanford, CA: Stanford

University Press, 1993), 4 and throughout. Neither Walker nor his printer(s) were the first to emphasize typographically the statement of equality in the Declaration. For example, in the *Genius of Universal Emancipation*, Benjamin Lundy includes an article on the occasion of July 4 that typographically emphasizes in several places the important principles of the Declaration of Independence; for example, "'ALL MEN WERE CREATED EQUAL;' and, of course, that every human being has a perfect right to 'LIBERTY and the pursuit of happiness'" ("Fourth of July," *Genius of Universal Emancipation and Baltimore Courier*, July 8, 1826, 357–358). The article appears close enough to the publication of the first edition of Walker's *Appeal* that it may have been seen by Walker and/or his printer(s); clearly, though, the typography and thus the emphasis differ from that of the *Appeal*. And, of course, Jefferson himself used typography to emphasize his differences with the official text of the Declaration in his autobiography. There, he explains, "As the sentiments of men are known not only by what they receive, but what they reject also, I will state the form of the Declaration as originally reported. The parts struck out by Congress shall be distinguished by a black line drawn under them; and those inserted by them shall be placed in the margin, or in a concurrent column" (Thomas Jefferson, *Autobiography*, in *The Writings of Thomas Jefferson*, ed. H. A. Washington [Washington, DC: Taylor and Maury, 1853], 1:19).

64. Declaration of Independence, quoted in Walker, *Appeal*, 85.

65. On the literary canonization of Walker's *Appeal* as the representative text of early Black militancy and nationalism, see note 7 in the introduction to this book.

66. Robert S. Levine, *Dislocating Race and Nation: Episodes in Nineteenth-Century American Literary Nationalism* (Chapel Hill: University of North Carolina Press, 2008), 103.

Chapter 2

1. On Walker's powerful influence on Garrison's political positions on colonization, racial intermarriage, Black self-elevation, and racial unity and Walker's foundational role in Boston's radical abolitionist movement, see Donald M. Jacobs, "David Walker and William Lloyd Garrison: Racial Cooperation and the Shaping of Boston Abolition," in *Courage and Conscience: Black and White Abolitionists in Boston*, ed. Jacobs (Bloomington: Indiana University Press, 1993), 1–20. Martha S. Jones describes Stewart's pamphlet *Religion and the Pure Principles of Morality* as "a collaboration born out of radical abolitionism's early cross-racial alliances" in *All Bound Up Together: The Woman Question in African American Public Culture* (Chapel Hill: University of North Carolina Press, 2007), 24. Erica Ball links Stewart and Walker with respect to the "tendency to imbue self-improvement with religious and even revolutionary significance" in *To Live an Antislavery Life: Personal Politics and the Antebellum Black Middle Class* (Athens: University of Georgia Press, 2012), 33.

2. On the southern reaction to the *Liberator*, see Archibald H. Grimké, *William Lloyd Garrison, the Abolitionist* (New York: Funk and Wagnalls, 1891), esp. 122–132.

3. For Garrison's dependence on Black subscribers to, financial supporters of, and contributors to the *Liberator* in its early years, see Donald M. Jacobs, "William Lloyd Garrison's *Liberator* and Boston's Blacks, 1830–1865," *New England Quarterly* 44, no. 2 (1971): 259–277.

4. Garrison recalled his introduction to Stewart in an April 1879 letter to her: "Soon after I started publication of The Liberator, you made yourself known to me by coming into my office and putting into my hands, for criticism and friendly advice, the manuscript embodying your devotional thoughts and aspirations, and also various essays pertaining to the condition of the class with which you were complexionally identified.... You will recollect, if not the

surprise, at least the satisfaction I expressed on examining what you had written—far more remarkable in those early days than it would be now, where there are so many educated persons of color who are able to write with ability. I not only gave you words of encouragement, but in my printing office put your manuscript into type, an edition of which was struck off in tract form, subject to your order. I was impressed by your intelligence and excellence of character" (quoted in Elizabeth McHenry, *Forgotten Readers: Recovering the Lost History of African American Literary Societies* [Durham, NC: Duke University Press, 2002], 75). It is also likely that Garrison's *An Address, Delivered before the Free People of Color, in Philadelphia, New-York, and Other Cities* (Boston, MA: Stephen Foster, 1831), which he gave as a lecture in June 1831 and published as a pamphlet in July, also encouraged Stewart to reach out to Garrison with her writings and interest in publishing.

5. Cheryl A. Wall, *On Freedom and the Will to Adorn: The Art of the African American Essay* (Chapel Hill: University of North Carolina Press, 2018), 53.

6. Kristin Waters and Carol B. Conaway, introduction to *Black Women's Intellectual Traditions: Speaking Their Minds*, ed. Waters and Conaway (Burlington: University of Vermont Press, 2007), 5. Following Marilyn Richardson's 1987 edition of Stewart's 1830s writings, Lora Romero offered the first substantial analysis of Stewart's "politicized version of domesticity to license her intrusion into [the] male-dominated arena" of Black nationalism as well as the masculinist and womanist politics that conspired to exile Stewart "from the African American nationalist memory," up to that point, in *Home Fronts: Domesticity and Its Critics in the Antebellum United States* (Durham, NC: Duke University Press, 1997), 54.

7. Carla L. Peterson, *"Doers of the Word": African-American Women Speakers and Writers in the North (1830–1880)* (Oxford: Oxford University Press, 1995), 66.

8. In his biography of William Lloyd Garrison, Wendell Phillips Garrison estimates "from internal evidence [that] it appears that the third edition of the 'Appeal' was published shortly after March 6, 1830" (*William Lloyd Garrison, 1805–1879* [New York: Century, 1885], 1:161n). Peter Hinks is more tentative, offering that Walker published the last edition "probably sometime in the spring of 1830" ("Editor's Note: The Three Editions of the *Appeal*," in his edition of *David Walker's "Appeal"* [University Park: Pennsylvania State University Press, 2000], xlv).

9. Jacobs cites Lundy's proposal to relocate the *Genius of Universal Emancipation* to Washington, D.C., as motivating Garrison's decision to base the *Liberator* in Boston instead (Jacobs, "William Lloyd Garrison's *Liberator*," 259). In the introduction to his edition of *Walker's "Appeal*,*"* Peter P. Hinks argues, "While many thinkers and forces influenced Garrison's transformation, the role of Walker was unquestionably paramount" (Hinks, introduction to *David Walker's "Appeal*,*"* xi–xlix, xliii).

10. For a detailed history of the earliest Black newspapers, see Jacqueline Bacon, *Freedom's Journal: The First African-American Newspaper* (Lanham, MD: Lexington Books, 2007). See also Robert Fanuzzi, "Frederick Douglass's 'Colored Newspaper': Identity Politics in Black and White," in *The Black Press: New Literary and Historical Essays*, ed. Todd Vogel (New Brunswick, NJ: Rutgers University Press, 2001), 55–70. Significantly, David Walker was a subscription agent for *Freedom's Journal* in Boston.

11. William Lloyd Garrison, "To the Public," *Liberator*, January 1, 1831, 1.

12. [William Lloyd Garrison], "Walker's Pamphlet," *Liberator*, January 1, 1831, 3.

13. Garrison's previous condemnation of Walker's *Appeal* was similarly partial. To a *Genius of Universal Emancipation* article reprinting reports of legislative responses to the discovery of Walker's *Appeal* in Virginia and Georgia, Garrison added, "We have had this

pamphlet on our table for some time past, and are not surprised at its effects upon our sensitive southern brethren. It is written by a colored Bostonian, and breathes the most impassioned and determined spirit. We deprecate its circulation, though we cannot but wonder at the bravery and intelligence of its author" ("G.," "Singular Panic," *Genius of Universal Emancipation*, January 15, 1830, 147.

14. Garrison, "Walker's Appeal. No. 1.," *Liberator*, January 8, 1831, 6. And while he publicly deprecated the *Appeal*'s circulation, he circulated it himself privately, giving a copy of the third edition as a gift to Samuel J. May—"from his friend and admirer," as we see in Garrison's inscription on the first page of Walker's preamble—now held by Cornell University's Special Collections in the Samuel J. May Antislavery Collection. For more on this gift, see Benjamin Shearer Beck, *David Walker's "Appeal" and Everyday Abolition* (master's thesis, University of Colorado Boulder, 2011), 21–26.

15. On Garrison's strategies as a provocateur and specifically his exchanges with other newspapers, see Rodger Streitmatter, *Mightier than the Sword: How the News Media Have Shaped American History* (Boulder, CO: Westview Press, 2016) 21.

16. By the January 29, 1831, number of the *Liberator*, some editors had had time to respond. Garrison printed a selection of responses from proslavery editors of northern newspapers next to an editorial response to Walker's *Appeal* that he reprinted from the *Greensborough (NC) Patriot*. For both, see *Liberator*, January 29, 1831, 61.

17. Garrison, "Three Curiosities!!!," *Liberator*, October 22, 1831, 171. Garrison quotes an untitled January 4, 1831, Charleston *Mercury* article.

18. On the challenges to civil liberties occasioned by the turn to radical abolitionism, see Russel B. Nye, *Fettered Freedom: Civil Liberties and the Slavery Controversy, 1830–1860* (East Lansing: Michigan State College Press, 1949), and chapter 11 of Brian Gabrial, *The Press and Slavery in America, 1791–1851: The Melancholy Effect of Popular Excitement* (Columbia: University of South Carolina Press, 2016), 149–159.

19. Augusta Rohrbach, "'Truth Stronger and Stranger Than Fiction': Reexamining William Lloyd Garrison's *Liberator*," *American Literature* 73, no. 4 (2001): 731. See also my "'Look!! look!!! at this!!!!': The Radical Typography of David Walker's *Appeal*," *PMLA* 126, no. 1 (2011): 55–72.

20. In his article "David Walker and William Lloyd Garrison," Jacobs focuses on Walker's influence on several of Garrison's political positions and notes instances of Garrison "echoing the sentiments, if not the language, expressed the year before by Walker," but without considering Walker's typographic and rhetorical influence on Garrison (13).

21. Clement Eaton's article "A Dangerous Pamphlet in the Old South" remains the authoritative study of the southern legal response to Walker's *Appeal*, while Peter Hinks offers important additions and corrections to Eaton's study in chapter 5 of *To Awaken My Afflicted Brethren: David Walker and the Problem of Antebellum Slave Resistance* (University Park, PA: Pennsylvania University Press, 1997), 116–172.

22. Grimké, *William Lloyd Garrison*, 127; Hinks, *To Awaken*, 237–240.

23. Quoted in Grimké, *William Lloyd Garrison*, 127–128.

24. Garrison, "To the Public," *Liberator*, January 1, 1831, 1.

25. Hinks argues for Garrison's direct debt to both Walker and northern Black readers' awareness and respect for him: "Garrison clearly recognized the depth of allegiance blacks in Boston and in the North felt for Walker, that he was 'regarded among his people as a man inspired'—as one of the *Liberator*'s early white commentators described him" (*To Awaken*, 112). I want to suggest instead a visual and rhetorical debt to the style of Walker's *Appeal* while

leaving more room for different readerships of and relationships to Walker's pamphlet within the numerous and diverse Black communities of Boston and the North.

26. See also Jacobs, "William Lloyd Garrison's *Liberator.*"

27. An example of one such contributor is the prominent Black Philadelphian James Forten's daughter Sarah, who sent Garrison a poem after reading the first number of the *Liberator*. Garrison published it and several other contributions under her pseudonym "Ada" before learning her identity. See Julie Winch, *A Gentleman of Color: The Life of James Forten* (Oxford: Oxford University Press, 2002), 264.

28. Louis Ruchames, ed., *The Letters of William Lloyd Garrison*, vol. 2, *A House Dividing Against Itself, 1836–1840* (Cambridge, MA: Harvard University Press, 1971), xxix.

29. Garrison to Samuel J. May, February 14, 1831, in *Letters of William Lloyd Garrison*, vol. 1, *I Will Be Heard, 1822–1835*, ed. Walter M. Merrill (Cambridge, MA: Harvard University Press, 1971), 114. It is unknown when Garrison gave the copy to May. While Garrison may have sent it in the 1830s, it is also possible that he contributed it to the archive of antislavery materials that May donated to Cornell University in the 1870s, where it is now housed. The dedication can be viewed digitally here: http://reader.library.cornell.edu/docviewer/digital?id=may814905#page/3/mode/1up. And more information about May's collection and Garrison's and others' contributions to it can be found here: https://rmc.library.cornell.edu/mayantislaverycoll/. I thank Derrick Spires for a timely reminder about this copy and dedication.

30. The only other publications Garrison advertises as being printed and sold at the *Liberator*'s office before Stewart's are his *Address Delivered before the Free People of Color* and Thomas Day's 1776 *Fragment of an Original Letter on the Slavery of Negroes*. See *Liberator*, July 9, 1831, 111, and *Liberator*, August 20, 1831, 136.

31. Garrison, "Incendiary Publications," *Liberator*, October 8, 1831, 1.

32. Letter quoted in Garrison, "Incendiary Publications."

33. Jacobs emphasizes how Garrison's public denouncement of his procolonization position and his vigorous condemnation of the colonization movement also strategically factored in Garrison's efforts to attract and sustain Black support ("David Walker and William Lloyd Garrison," 12).

34. Advertisement, *Liberator*, October 8, 1831, 3. Garrison dedicated the entire front page and part of the second page of the next number of *Liberator* (October 15, 1831) to his letter to the editors of the *National Intelligencer*, indicting both the letter writer and the *Intelligencer*'s editors for their incendiary remarks. On the second page, he boldly declares, "I NEVER WILL DESERT THE CAUSE" (Garrison, "To the Editors of the National Intelligencer," *Liberator*, October 15, 1831, 165–166).

35. For an important history of the outpouring of religious print in the early nineteenth century and its influence on print culture more broadly, see David Paul Nord, "Benevolent Books: Printing, Religion, and Reform," in *A History of the Book in America*, vol. 2, *An Extensive Republic: Print, Culture, and Society in the New Nation, 1790–1840*, ed. Robert A. Gross and Mary Kelley (Chapel Hill: University of North Carolina Press, 2010), 221–246.

36. Noah Webster, *An American Dictionary of the English Language* (1828), s.v. "production."

37. Phillis Wheatley, *Poems on Various Subjects Religious and Moral* (London: A. Bell, 1773). Of the significance of the *Poems* as a book and its frontispiece portrait of Wheatley, Megan Walsh argues that they "played a vital part not only in the history of black American

writing, but also in how Americans came to conceive of illustrated writing as an important signifier of authorial, commercial, and cultural achievement" (*The Portrait and the Book: Illustration and Literary Culture in Early America* [Iowa City: University of Iowa Press, 2017], 67).

38. It is also interesting to note that Garrison misspells Stewart's surname just as Jefferson misspells Wheatley's (master's) surname as *Whately*. Cheryl A. Wall notes that "Stewart worked for years as a domestic in a minister's parsonage before mounting the podium in the cause of citizenship rights for free blacks" (*On Freedom*, 40).

39. I will return to Jefferson's claims about Blacks' limited intellectual capacity and imitation as well as Walker's counterarguments at greater length in the next chapter.

40. Maria W. Stewart, *Religion and the Pure Principles of Morality: The Sure Foundation upon Which We Must Build* (Boston, MA: Garrison and Knapp, 1831), 2, 10–11.

41. In her brief analysis of Stewart's writings, Martha Jones describes her as a "skilled rhetorician" who "crafted her message such that her provocations were muted by reassurances" (*All Bound Up*, 24). Christina Henderson analyzes Stewart's "juxtaposition of Christian mercy and retributive violence" at length in her article "Sympathetic Violence: Maria Stewart's Antebellum Vision of African American Resistance," *MELUS* 38, no. 4 (2013): 52–75, 52.

42. It is important to note that, while Stewart's essay incorporates generic elements of the spiritual autobiography/conversion narrative, autobiographical details are scant and limited to the introduction. As Joycelyn Moody has observed, "Stewart opted against writing 'personal' narratives, apparently in the belief that her causes and the communities they influenced would be better served by a communal rather than an individualistic discourse" (*Sentimental Confessions: Spiritual Narratives of Nineteenth-Century African American Women* [Athens: University of Georgia Press, 2001], 28).

43. Garrison, "Threats to Assassinate," *Liberator*, September 10, 1831, 145.

44. In *We Are Coming: The Persuasive Discourse of Nineteenth-Century Black Women* (Carbondale: Southern Illinois University Press, 1999), Shirley Wilson Logan considers Stewart's insistence on the "prophecy that God would help them only if they helped themselves" as "her version of Ethiopianism activism" and analyzes how Stewart "employed African and Western discursive practices syncretically to create community with her Boston audiences" (43).

45. Stewart, quoted in Peterson, *"Doers of the Word,"* 59. Peterson focuses more on the conditions under which Stewart published *Meditations* than on the conditions under which the works collected in *Meditations*—including *Religion and the Pure Principles of Morality*—were originally published in the 1830s. For readings of the indebtedness of Stewart's rhetoric to the jeremiad, see chapter 1 of Joycelyn Moody's *Sentimental Confessions*, 26–50; Lena Ampadu, "Maria W. Stewart and the Rhetoric of Black Preaching: Perspectives on Womanism and Black Nationalism," in *Black Women's Intellectual Traditions*, 38–54; Willie J. Harrel Jr., "A Call to Political and Social Activism: The Jeremiadic Discourse of Maria Miller Stewart, 1831–1833," *Journal of International Women's Studies* 9, no. 3 (2008): 300–319; and chapter 6 of Cedrick May's *Evangelism and Resistance in the Black Atlantic, 1760–1835* (Athens: University of Georgia Press, 2008), 116–125.

46. It is also possible that Garrison, as Stewart's editor and possibly the compositor of the pamphlet, made these decisions about punctuation. But given Garrison's tendency toward Walker-like graphic typography as well as Stewart's preference for rhetorical over typographical impact, it seems likely that the choice was Stewart's.

47. Peterson argues that Stewart's "invectives directed *primarily* against her own people rather than her people's oppressors . . . allowed Stewart to focus more specifically on the question of agency, in particular on the agency of black women. As a result, Stewart was able, in a way that Walker was not, to clarify the movement from means to ends, from sin to redemption, from the present condition of black degradation to a future state of social equality, thereby rewriting the genre of the jeremiad." She further posits, "Stewart's thinking the gap between promise and fulfillment registers as a primarily female space sustained by women's work and women's culture" (*"Doers of the Word,"* 66). While I agree that Stewart shifts to focus on the agency of Black women and their essential role in fulfilling Black promise, I read Stewart as arguing that women's work is essential to activating God's favor—that is, women's agency encourages a watchful and approving God's all-powerful agency that promises to fulfill Black potential.

48. William Huntting Howell, *Against Self-Reliance: The Arts of Dependence in the Early United States* (Philadelphia: University of Pennsylvania Press, 2015), 23. For a broader study of the principle of imitatio Christi, see Maximilian von Habsburg, *Catholic and Protestant Translations of the "Imitatio Christi," 1425–1650: From Late Medieval Classic to Early Modern Bestseller* (Surrey: Ashgate, 2011).

49. On Stewart's intense conversion experience following her husband's death in late 1829 and her various associations with Methodist, Baptist, and Episcopalian churches, see Marilyn Richardson, *Maria W. Stewart, America's First Black Woman Political Writer* (Bloomington: Indiana University Press, 1987), 8–9. For a discussion of the significance of the principles of Christian imitation and perfection to early American Methodism, see Jeffrey Williams, *Religion and Violence in Early American Methodism* (Bloomington: Indiana University Press, 2010).

50. See esp. chapter 2 of Hazel V. Carby's *Reconstructing Womanhood: The Emergence of the Afro-American Woman Novelist* (Oxford: Oxford University Press, 1987), 20–39. For an important study of Black women and girls' ongoing rejections of the long-standing requirement to imitate White standards of womanhood and dominant respectability discourse, see also Stephanie D. Sears, *Imagining Black Womanhood: The Negotiation of Power and Identity Within the Girls Empowerment Project* (Albany: SUNY Press, 2010).

51. For the foundational study of how religion was cast as belonging to White American women by "divine right" in the cult of true womanhood, see Barbara Welter's essay "The Cult of True Womanhood, 1820–1860," reprinted in *Locating American Studies: The Evolution of a Discipline*, ed. Lucy Maddox (Baltimore: Johns Hopkins University Press, 1999), 43–70.

52. Untitled notice, *Liberator*, November 12, 1831, 183.

53. "Mrs. Steward's [sic] Essays," *Liberator*, January 7, 1832, 2–3.

54. Richardson was the first to discover that Stewart had published a new edition of her collected works in 1879 after receiving the first payment of the pension she was due as a widow of a veteran of the War of 1812 (*Maria W. Stewart*, 79).

55. "Constitution of the Afric-Amercan Female Intelligence Society of Boston," *Liberator*, November 12, 1831, 2.

56. Stewart, "An Address Delivered Before the Afric-American Female Intelligence Society," *Liberator*, April 28, 1832, 66–67.

57. Quoted in McHenry, *Forgotten Readers*, 77. Though McHenry doesn't cite it, she borrows the quote from Alexander Crummell, in a letter from Boston dated May 28, 1879, printed

in Stewart's pamphlet *Meditations from the Pen of Mrs. Maria W. Stewart* (Washington, DC: Enterprise Publishing Company, 1879), 10.

Chapter 3

1. In this chapter, I spell Apes's surname as he spells it throughout the pamphlet *The Experiences of Five Christian Indians of the Pequod Tribe* (Boston, MA: published by author, 1833), in which he first published "An Indian's Looking-Glass for the White Man." Apes spelled his name this way for the majority of his published works, only spelling it as *Apess* in his last published work, the second edition of his *Eulogy on King Philip* (1837). Scholars since Barry O'Connell's *On Our Own Ground: The Complete Writings of William Apess, a Pequot* (Amherst: University of Massachusetts Press, 1992) have followed O'Connell's spelling, despite O'Connell's note that the "spelling of his name cannot itself be definitively given" (xivn2). I also occasionally follow Apes's use of the word *Indian* to designate the peoples who now identify as American Indian, Indigenous, and Indigenous people, to indicate how he identified himself. Walker's preferred word is *Aborigines* [sic] in his brief discussion of them in the *Appeal*: "Why do they [White Americans] not get the Aborigines of this country to be slaves to them and their children, to work their farms and dig their mines? They know well that the Aborigines of this country, or (Indians) would tear them from the earth. The Indians would not rest day or night, they would be up all times of night, cutting their cruel throats" (71). As we now know, Walker was wrong about American Indians not having been enslaved by Whites; see Alan Gallay, *The Indian Slave Trade: The Rise of the English Empire in the American South, 1670–1717* (New Haven, CT: Yale University Press, 2002). Some also enslaved Blacks; see Christina Snyder, *Slavery in Indian Country: The Changing Face of Captivity in Early America* (Cambridge, MA: Harvard University Press, 2010).

2. For a legal history of the Indian Removal Act and these cases, see Jill Norgren, *The Cherokee Cases: Two Landmark Federal Decisions in the Fight for Sovereignty* (Norman: University of Oklahoma Press, 2004).

3. William Apes, "An Indian's Looking-Glass for the White Man," in *Experiences of Five Christian Indians*, 53.

4. Scholarship that has linked and compared Walker and Apes to varying degrees includes Joanna Brooks, *American Lazarus: Religion and the Rise of African American and Native American Literatures* (Oxford: Oxford University Press, 2003); Andy Doolen, *Fugitive Empire: Locating Early American Imperialism* (Minneapolis: University of Minnesota Press, 2005); Philip F. Gura, *The Life of William Apess, Pequot* (Chapel Hill: University of North Carolina Press, 2015); Sandra Gustafson, *Imagining Deliberative Democracy in the Early Republic* (Chicago: University of Chicago Press, 2011); David Kazanjian, "Colonial," in *Keywords for American Cultural Studies*, 2nd ed., ed. Bruce Burgett and Glenn Hendler (New York: New York University Press, 2014), 48–53; Maureen Konkle, *Writing Indian Nations: Native Intellectuals and the Politics of Historiography, 1827–1863* (Chapel Hill: University of North Carolina Press, 2004); O'Connell, *On Our Own Ground*; Barry O'Connell, "'Once More Let Us Consider': William Apess in the Writing of New England Native American History," in *After King Philip's War: Presence and Persistence in Indian New England*, ed. Colin G. Calloway (Hanover, NH: University Press of New England, 1997), 162–177; Jean M. O'Brien, *Firsting and Lasting: Writing Indians Out of Existence in New England* (Minneapolis: University of Minnesota Press, 2010); Phillip H. Round, *Removable Type: Histories of the Book in Indian Country, 1663–1880* (Chapel Hill: University of North Carolina Press, 2010); Jace Weaver, *That*

the People Might Live: Native American Literatures and Native American Community (Oxford: Oxford University Press, 1997); and Karen A. Weyler, *Empowering Words: Outsiders and Authorship in Early America* (Athens: University of Georgia Press, 2013).

5. Apes, "Looking-Glass," 54.

6. Thomas Jefferson, *Notes on the State of Virginia*, 8th American ed. (Boston, MA: David Carlisle, 1801), 207. As noted in Chapter 1, this is the edition that Walker read and that also would have been available to Apes in Boston.

7. For a collection of studies of various representations of Indigenous people throughout American history and culture, see the essays in Gretchen M. Bataille, ed., *Native American Representations: First Encounters, Distorted Images, and Literary Appropriations* (Lincoln: University of Nebraska Press, 2001).

8. Apes was denied a license to be an exhorter (in Providence in the mid-1820s) and an official preacher in 1827 by authorities in the church. By the time of the second refusal, he had been licensed as an exhorter and the Albany conference of Methodists offered to renew this lesser license as consolation for not promoting him to preacher. Believing racism was the reason for this refusal, he left the Methodist Episcopal Church to join the splinter Methodist Society, based in New York, which granted him a preaching license in 1829. For more on Apes's baptism and ensuing struggles with ordination, see Gura, *Life of William Apess*, 33–43.

9. John H. Wigger, *Taking Heaven by Storm: Methodism and the Rise of Popular Christianity in America* (Oxford: Oxford University Press, 1998), 29.

10. Alfred Brunson, *A Western Pioneer; or, Incidents of the Life and Times of Rev. Alfred Brunson, A.M., D.D.* [. . .], vol. 1 (Cincinnati, OH: Hitchcock and Walden, 1872), 89.

11. Karim M. Tiro, "Denominated 'SAVAGE': Methodism, Writing, and Identity in the Works of William Apess, a Pequot," *American Quarterly* 48, no. 4 (1996): 653–679, 654.

12. For more on the outpouring of religious print in the first half of the nineteenth century, see David Paul Nord, "Benevolent Books: Printing, Religion, and Reform," in *A History of the Book in America*, vol. 2, *An Extensive Republic: Print, Culture, and Society in the New Nation, 1790–1840*, ed. Robert A. Gross and Mary Kelley (Chapel Hill: University of North Carolina Press, 2010): 221–246.

13. William Apes, "The Experience of the Missionary," in *The Experiences of Five Christian Indians of the Pequod Tribe*, 3.

14. Garrison's brief notice about Walker's *Appeal* in the first number of the *Liberator* is titled "Walker's Pamphlet" (*Liberator*, January 1, 1831, 3). On the origins of the word *pamphlet*, its formation as both a format and a genre, and pamphlets becoming "closely associated with slander or scurrility," see chapter 1 of Joad Raymond's *Pamphlets and Pamphleteering in Early Modern Britain* (Cambridge: Cambridge University Press, 2003), 4–26, 8.

15. Of the relationship of the spiritual autobiographies to "Looking-Glass," Gura suggests that "these accounts were prefatory to what in the Puritan era would have been termed the 'application' of Apess's texts, specifically, how they served as 'looking-glasses' or mirrors for white people to see themselves as they were" (70). As I have begun to suggest and will show further, Apes's own Methodist era is the more accurate lens through which to read these texts and their relationship to each other, and to Walker's *Appeal* and Jefferson's *Notes*.

16. Herbert Grabes, *The Mutable Glass: Mirror-Imagery in Titles and Texts of the Middle Ages and English Renaissance* (Cambridge: Cambridge University Press, 1982), 60.

17. See Maximilian von Habsburg, *Catholic and Protestant Translations of the "Imitatio Christi," 1425–1650* (Surrey: Ashgate, 2011).

18. See Elias Smith, *The Clergyman's Looking Glass* (Portsmouth, NH: n.p., 1803); John Dodge, *A Mirror, or Looking Glass for the Rising Generation and Young Convert* (New York: n.p., 1804); and Mason Locke Weems, *The Drunkard's Looking Glass*, 3rd ed. (n.p.: n.p., 1814).

19. Maureen Konkle also considers Apes's "use of the figure of the looking-glass to represent the necessity of looking carefully at one's own moral failings" in relation to contemporary examples and notes that his "use of the metaphor go[es] somewhat further" by providing "the means of unmasking the motivations of the white man's knowledge. What the white man sees in the mirror are ultimately his own moral feelings, but more immediately the political implications of his misrepresentation of Native peoples" (*Writing Indian Nations*, 117–118). Other scholars who have considered the figure of the mirror in relation to Apes's rhetorical and argumentative strategies of reversal include O'Connell, *On Our Own Ground* (xxii–xxiii); Gary Ashwill, "Savagism and Its Discontents: James Fenimore Cooper and His Native American Contemporaries," *ATQ* 8, no. 3 (1994): 211–227; Renée L. Bergland, *The National Uncanny: Indian Ghosts and American Subjects* (Hanover, NH: published by the University Press of New England for Dartmouth College, 2000), 121–139; Carolyn Haynes, "'A Mark for Them All to . . . Hiss at': The Formation of Methodist and Pequot Identity in the Conversion Narrative of William Apess," *Early American Literature* 31, no. 1 (1996): 25–44; Scott Michaelsen, *The Limits of Multiculturalism: Interrogating the Origins of American Anthropology* (Minneapolis: University of Minnesota Press, 1999), 63; Bernd C. Peyer, *The Tutor'd Mind: Indian Missionary-Writers in Antebellum America* (Amherst: University of Massachusetts Press, 1997), 154–155; and Gordon M. Sayre, "Defying Assimilation, Confounding Authenticity: The Case of William Apess., *A/B* 11, no. 1 (1996): 1–18.

20. Sabine Melchior-Bonnet's *The Mirror: A History*, trans. Katharine H. Jewett (London: Routledge, 2001) considers ideas of the mirror's capacity to reveal aspects of the self in popular culture and fiction.

21. Sacavan Bercovitch, *The American Jeremiad* (Madison: University of Wisconsin Press, 2012), xii. E. Brooks Holifield summarizes Methodist theology's contrast with the Calvinist idea of predestination as faith that "men and women had a natural ability to choose the good . . . they located sin in the moral exrcise of the will rather than in a fallen human nature lying behind all our exercises" (*Theology in America: Christian Thought from the Age of the Puritans to the Civil War* [New Haven, CT: Yale University Press, 2003], 264).

22. On the political functions of Walker's deployment of the jeremiad, see Melvin L. Rogers, "David Walker and the Political Power of the Appeal," *Political Theory* 43, no. 2 (2015): 208–233. On the specific connection between Walker's confrontation of Jefferson and Walker's use of the jeremiad, see Wilson Jeremiah Moses, *Black Messiahs and Uncle Toms: Social and Literary Manipulations of a Religious Myth*, rev. ed. (University Park: Pennsylvania State University Press, 1993), 38–46; Dolan Hubbard, "David Walker's 'Appeal' and the American Puritan Jeremiadic Tradition," *Centennial Review* 30, no. 3 (1986): 331–346; and Gene Andrew Jarrett, *Representing the Race: A New Political History of African American Literature* (New York: New York University Press, 2011), 24.

23. Walker, *Appeal*, 47.

24. Jefferson quoted in Walker, *Appeal*, 18; Walker's emphasis.

25. For the history of the incorporation of this biblical story into American racial slavery, see chapter 13 of David M. Goldenberg, *The Curse of Ham: Race and Slavery in Early Judaism, Christianity, and Islam* (Princeton, NJ: Princeton University Press, 2003), 178–182.

26. As Leon Jackson has pointed out, the "body-as-book trope" is a "very old trope made new" and "African Americans rendered it explicitly and literally." Though it was published twelve years after Apes's "Looking-Glass," William Grimes's autobiography contains an instance particularly relevant to Apes's idea of human skin as parchment: "If it were not for the stripes on my back which were made while I was a slave, I would in my will leave my skin as a legacy to the government, desiring that it might be taken off and made into parchment, and then bind the constitution of glorious, happy, and *free* America. Let the skin of a slave bind the charter of American liberty!" (*Life of William Grimes, the Runaway Slave*, quoted in Leon Jackson, "The Talking Book and the Talking Book Historian: African American Cultures of Print—The State of the Discipline," *Book History* 13 [2010]: 265).

27. This idea of authorship brings to mind Emily Dickinson's later work, specifically poem 709/788, "Publication—Is the Auction." On the significance of the contexts of slavery and abolition to Dickinson's ideas of both authorship and auctions in this poem, see Benjamin Friedlander, "Auctions of the Mind: Emily Dickinson and Abolition," *Arizona Quarterly* 54, no. 1 (1998): 1–26.

28. The Cherokee Nation hired William Wirt, former U.S. attorney general, to represent them before the Supreme Court in *Cherokee Nation v. Georgia* (Norgren, *Cherokee Cases*, 53).

29. Much as only a limited audience would have recognized how Apes implicitly calls on Jefferson and his *Notes*, portions of Jefferson's *Notes* are "meant for an audience of one, George Louis Leclerc, comte de Buffon, the Leading French scientist of the day," as Robert A. Ferguson notes in his essay "'Mysterious Obligation': Jefferson's *Notes on the State of Virginia*," *American Literature* 52, no. 3 (1980): 381–406, 384.

30. The other two instances of this phrase occur in an addition to the third edition—"But do slave-holders think that we thank them for keeping us in miseries, and taking our lives by the inches?" (63)—and near the end of the *Appeal* when Walker asserts that Whites "think that we do not feel for our brethren, whom they are murdering by the inches" because "some" Americans (implying Jefferson) "have represented us [blacks] to be [brutes]" (77–78).

31. For a rich description of the global Enlightenment context in which Jefferson came to these conclusions, drawing on the racial philosophy of David Hume and Immanuel Kant, see Simon Gikandi, *Slavery and the Culture of Taste* (Princeton, NJ: Princeton University Press, 2011), esp. 99–109. On Jefferson's literary criticism and racial science more specifically, see William Huntting Howell, *Against Self-Reliance: The Arts of Dependence in the Early United States* (Philadelphia: University of Pennsylvania Press, 2015), chapter 2, 46–81, and Mark Alan Mattes, "Penman's Devil: The Chirographic and Typographic Urgency of Race in the *Letters of the Late Ignatius Sancho, an African*," *Early American Literature* 48, no. 3 (2013): 577–612.

32. For a crucial study of nineteenth-century efforts to empirically verify Jefferson's racial theories, see Ann Fabian, *The Skull Collectors: Race, Science, and America's Unburied Dead* (Chicago: University of Chicago Press, 2010).

33. Scholars now recognize Apes's "Looking-Glass" as a major Indigenous contribution to the ethnological debates of the eighteenth and nineteenth centuries. Michaelsen, in an important reading of the essay, argues that it is "fundamentally anthropological in its attempt to thematize the question of color" (63). Interestingly, he also suggests that "one might usefully compare this text's nearly unique strategies to Wallace (W. D.) Fard and Elijah Muhammad in the construction of Black Muslim theology," missing Walker as Apes's more immediate and direct Black interlocutor (65). He does invoke Jefferson's *Notes* as "the crucial text for

understanding" the ideas that Apes draws from scientific racism, suggesting that "Apes's text works precisely in this territory" (66). Michaelsen also posits that "Apess's crossing of the color line—showing that bad people can manifest white skin, for example—potentially turns the text into parody of scientific racism" (68). But because he does not recognize Walker's *Appeal* as Apes's most direct model, he does not discern that Apes is specifically engaging with Jefferson's claims through Walker in what is otherwise a very perceptive reading of "Looking-Glass."

34. Quoted in Gura, *Life of William Apess*, 85.

35. Gura, *Life of William Apess*, 96. Gura gives a thorough account of Apes's activism with the Mashpee, the tribe's agitation for sovereignty, and hostile newspaper coverage of the effort and events on tribal land in chapter 5 of *The Life of William Apess*, 77–99.

Chapter 4

1. W[illiam] Paul Quinn, *The Origin, Horrors, and Results of Slavery* (Pittsburgh, PA: published by author, 1834), reprinted in *Early Negro Writing, 1760–1837*, ed. Dorothy Porter (Baltimore: Black Classic Press, 1995), 614–636. All citations refer to the 1834 printing. Quinn refers to his publication as a "tract"—and also as a "little book"—in his introduction (iii, iv).

2. Porter was the first scholar to bring attention to Quinn's pamphlet in her *Early Negro Writing*, which also includes Walker's *Appeal*. Peter P. Hinks makes the connection between the texts in *To Awaken My Afflicted Brethren: David Walker and the Problem of Antebellum Slave Resistance* (University Park, PA: Pennsylvania University Press, 1997), 115n50, as does John Ernest in *Liberation Historiography: African American Writers and the Challenge of History, 1794–1861* (Chapel Hill: University of North Carolina Press, 2004), 351n2. Lori Leavell offers Quinn's pamphlet as an example of "excerpts and reprints [that] would appear throughout the century in the US and beyond" in her essay "'Not Intended Exclusively for the Slave States': Antebellum Recirculation of David Walker's *Appeal*," *Callaloo* 38, no. 3 (Summer 2015): 692n2. While catching Quinn's borrowing from Walker, scholars up to this point have not noted that he also copied the section in his tract that follows the Walker addition—"Treatment of Slaves in the Dutch Settlements"—from another source: Thomas Branagan's pamphlet *A Preliminary Essay on the Oppression of the Exiled Sons of Africa* (Philadelphia: John W. Scott, 1804).

3. Eric Gardner, *Unexpected Places: Relocating Nineteenth-Century African American Literature* (Jackson: University Press of Mississippi, 2009).

4. Hinks's *To Awaken* both captures and replicates this north-south axis by depending on newspaper accounts of responses to the *Appeal* circulating in the South. Hinks notes, "David Walker was especially interested in disseminating the *Appeal* in the South, where he believed its message of resistance and divine concern was most needed. Yet the work also moved in the North, and with relatively greater ease" (151), and concludes his survey with the claim, "Thus Walker's *Appeal* made appearances in the United States from New Orleans to Boston" (152). As Leavell rightly notes, Hinks's "narrative of Boston-to-the South, however, obscures the pamphlet's broader movement, in part by failing to recognize its after-life." She limits her focus, though, to responses to the *Appeal* in the *Philadelphia Inquirer* and the *New York Evening Post* and, thus, to "call[ing] attention to the role of periodicals in circulating the *Appeal* beyond Boston and the South" (679).

5. Porter notes that, by 1832, Quinn was a deacon in the church and traveled to these states to preach and establish churches (*Early Negro Writing*, 517). For Quinn's locations and missionary accomplishments from 1832 through 1844, see also Daniel Alexander Payne,

History of the African Methodist Episcopal Church (Nashville: AME Sunday School Union, 1891), 169–171.

6. See, for example, James T. Campbell, *Songs of Zion: The African Methodist Episcopal Church in the United States and South Africa* (Oxford: Oxford University Press, 1995), 33. Most recently, Dennis C. Dickerson has suggested that Quinn was "born in 1784 either in the Caribbean or in Central America" in his *African Methodist Episcopal Church: A History* (Cambridge: Cambridge University Press, 2020), 84.

7. *The Praying Negro: An Authentic Narrative* (Tract No. 92 [Andover, MA: New England Tract Society, 1818]) is an example of one of the few religious tracts addressed to Black audiences. An 1826 American Tract Society tract aimed at children describes Africans as "a very ignorant and miserable race of men in their own country; very indolent, and very wicked" and presents these as reasons "why the colored people in Africa let white people come and steal them" (*Children's Friend*, no. 4 [Albany, NY: Webster and Wood]). For contextual readings of these pamphlets, see chapter 5 of Joanne Pope Melish's *Disowning Slavery: Gradual Emancipation and "Race" in New England, 1780–1860* (Ithaca, NY: Cornell University Press, 1998), 163–209. On the challenges that the slavery issue posed to the American Bible Society and the American Tract Society and the untenability of their policies of neutrality on slavery in the 1850s, see the epilogue of David Paul Nord's *Faith in Reading: Religious Publishing and the Birth of Mass Media in America* (Oxford: Oxford University Press, 2004), 151–160.

8. Hinks offers a reconstruction of Walker's involvement with the thriving AME church in Charleston, South Carolina, that was destroyed after the rebellion led by Denmark Vesey in 1822. He also considers the possibility of Walker's involvement in the rebellion in chapter 2 of *To Awaken*, 22–62. Rufus Burrow Jr. specifically notes that "it is not clear whether Walker actually joined Charleston's prominent A.M.E. church" as part of his argument that "one cannot read the *Appeal* and fail to appreciate that David Walker's energy for his mission came from the fact that he had experienced God and the Christian faith for himself" (*God and Human Responsibility: David Walker and Ethical Prophecy* [Macon, GA: Mercer University Press, 2003], 80). Scholars have addressed the section of article 4 of the *Appeal* that Walker devotes to quoting and praising Richard Allen and the AME Church. Yet the presence of a significant portion of the *Appeal* in a tract that was published by an eventual AME Church bishop, who was crucial to expanding the church in the near West, and the significance of Walker's *Appeal* in history and the print history of the church have yet to be considered—a reminder of the importance of Frances Smith Foster's observation that "the most consistent and influential element in the first century of African-American literary production was Afro-Protestantism" ("A Narrative of the Interesting Origins and (Somewhat) Surprising Developments of African-American Print Culture, *American Literary History* 17, no. 4 [2005]: 715).

9. For an extended consideration of the mysteries about and complications of Quinn's biography and their role in the AME Church's representations of itself and its leaders in its early histories and other publications, see Julius H. Bailey, *Race Patriotism: Protest and Print Culture in the AME Church* (Knoxville: University of Tennessee Press, 2012), 47–49.

10. Specifically, Daniel Alexander Payne and Charles Spencer Smith, *A History of the African Methodist Episcopal Church* (Philadelphia, PA: AME Book Concern, 1922). In an 1869 biography of Quinn in the *Christian Recorder*, Henry Highland Garnet indicates that Quinn was born in Chester County, Pennsylvania ("Pioneers of the A.M.E. Church—Part III," *Christian Recorder* 9, no. 9 (March 13, 1869): unnumbered p. 33. But Payne—who indicates in his 1891 *History* that he was Quinn's colleague for twenty years—corrects Garnet in a letter published

in the April 10, 1873, *Christian Recorder*, saying, "His spiritual birth was experienced in Chester Co., under the ministrations of Rev. Samuel Collins; his natural birth was in a foreign land of which I shall speak at another time" ("Daniel A. Payne to Dr. Garnet," *Christian Recorder* 11, no. 15 [April 10, 1873]: 1). In the memorial sermon for Quinn delivered by Rev. Benjamin W. Arnett of the Warren Chapel in Toledo, Ohio, on March 9, 1873, Arnett notes that the "birth and parentage of this great man is a subject" that he is "not fully informed upon; but it is claimed by some that he came from Hindoostan, near Calcutta," then cites the Richmond, Indiana, *Independent* newspaper article suggesting that Quinn was born in "Calcutta, Hindoostan" to "one of the wealthiest of Indian families" ("Sermon," in *Funeral Services in Respect to the Memory of Rev. William Paul Quinn* [Toledo, OH: Warren Chapel, 1873], 10–11).

11. Smith takes these numbers from a report delivered by Quinn at the AME General Conference of 1844.

12. On the significance of Quinn's extensive and impressive work in the near West for the AME Church, see Payne, *History of the African Methodist Episcopal Church*, 169–171.

13. Garnet, "Pioneers," 33.

14. Leslie M. Harris, *In the Shadow of Slavery: African Americans in New York City, 1626–1863* (Chicago: University of Chicago Press, 2003), 137.

15. On the close connection between *Freedom's Journal*, the New York Free Schools, and the community of educated activists they collaboratively cultivated, see Jacqueline Bacon, *"Freedom's Journal": The First African-American Newspaper* (Lanham, MD: Lexington Books, 2007), esp. 52, 73–74, and 106. On Walker in *Freedom's Journal*, see 113.

16. I also cite Garnet at length here to foreshadow Chapter 5, which focuses on his 1848 edition of Walker's *Appeal*, and to foreground how networked this set of Black and Indigenous antislavery and antiracism activists were, both in relation to Walker's pamphlet and otherwise. For another consideration of Garnet's biography of Quinn, see Bailey, *Race Patriotism*, 40–42.

17. As Hinks notes, "It is certain that it [Walker's *Appeal*] circulated in New York City and other important Northern towns." It is possible that Quinn may also have encountered it in Philadelphia on visits for AME meetings; as evidence for the preceding claim, Hinks offers the debates in the early 1831 numbers of the *Liberator* between the Philadelphian "Leo" and another correspondent "J. I. W." over Walker's pamphlet, or possibly in the small but organized Black community of Pittsburgh after arriving in 1833 (*To Awaken*, 152).

18. Payne, *History of the African Methodist Episcopal Church*, 98.

19. Robert S. Levine, ed., *Martin R. Delany: A Documentary Reader* (Chapel Hill: University of North Carolina Press, 2003), 25. For more on early Black activism and educational efforts in Pittsburgh, see also Dorothy Sterling, *The Making of an Afro-American: Martin Robison Delany, 1812–1855* (Garden City, NY: Doubleday, 1971), 41–42.

20. As of this writing, the only known copy of Quinn's tract/pamphlet held by Howard's Moorland-Spingarn Research Center was missing and accessible only through a photocopy surrogate, which seems to show the copy as having been rebound in a library binding. I thank Prints and Photographs Librarian Meaghan A. Alston for her efforts to locate the original and hope that it turns up at some point safe and sound.

21. Again, for an important history of religious tract publishing in the United States between 1815 and 1840, see David Paul Nord, "Benevolent Books: Printing, Religion, and Reform," in *A History of the Book in America*, vol. 2, ed. Robert A. Gross and Mary Kelley (Chapel Hill: American Antiquarian Society and University of North Carolina Press, 2010), 221–246.

22. "Address to Christians Recommending the Distribution of Religious Tracts," in *Proceedings of the First Ten Years of the American Tract Society* (Boston, MA: Flagg and Gould, 1824), 14.

23. Payne, *History of the African Methodist Episcopal Church*, 112.

24. Mitch Kachun, "Interrogating the Silences: Julia C. Collins, 19th-Century Black Readers and Writers, and the 'Christian Recorder,'" *African American Review* 40, no. 4 (2006): 649–659, 650. For the church histories on the AME Book Concern, see Payne, *History of the African Methodist Episcopal Church*, 110–111. Foster presents the Book Concern more optimistically than Kachun as "the first known African American publishing company," noting the variety of its "first publications," which she lists as "church disciplines, hymnals, and other practical documents" in her essay on the origins and development of African American print culture ("Narrative of the Interesting Origins," 721). While she focuses on the 1817 *Doctrines and Discipline of the African Methodist Episcopal Church* as a key text in the history of Black print, her history of the church's print operations skips from 1817 to 1841, with the founding of the *AME Magazine*, and 1852, when the "Book Concern established the *Christian Recorder*" (722). Foster herself acknowledges at the beginning of her important essay that she "do[es] not propose to offer a definitive or comprehensive survey of the origins or development" of African American print culture, so I offer this history of the AME Church's more limited printing operations in the 1820s and 1830s not as a correction, but in tandem with Kachun's article, as a supplement to this part of Foster's narrative ("Narrative of the Interesting Origins," 714).

25. For the text of Act 2639 of 1840, see *The Statutes at Large of South Carolina*, vol. 7, ed. David J. McCord (Columbia, SC: A. S. Johnson, 1840), 468–469.

26. Walker, *Appeal*, 23.

27. Quinn's allusions to the Haitian revolution and his seeming assumption that his White readers would be aware of Walker's *Appeal* are a form of what P. Gabrielle Foreman has helpfully termed "histotextuality," or "how culturally and socially literate audiences share not only epistemologies and literary sensibilities, but also specific historical references upon which one level of interpretation depends" (*Activist Sentiments: Reading Black Women in the Nineteenth Century* [Champaign: University of Illinois Press, 2009], 10).

28. On South Carolina's response to the arrival of Walker's *Appeal*, see Hinks, *To Awaken*, 145 and 237–239.

29. I thank Derrick Spires for prodding me to complete this analogy with respect to the impact of Walker's *Appeal* on readers before Quinn might have gotten to them.

30. In that searches of all the major databases of nineteenth-century U.S. periodicals turn up no mention of Quinn's pamphlet from 1834 through 1844 (as of July 10, 2019), and that Porter notes that the only known surviving copy of Quinn's pamphlet is the one held at Howard University—and given Quinn's undoubtedly limited means as an itinerant minister and missionary—it seems most likely that Quinn had only a small edition of *The Origin, Horrors, and Results of Slavery* printed. In advertising his 1848 edition of Walker's *Appeal*, Garnet—also a minister—specifically notes that "the edition is small" ("New Publications" [advertisement], *North Star*, May 5, 1848, 3).

31. This addition only appears in the *Appeal*'s third edition. Quinn also copies the text that follows the addition and ends Walker's article 3 (Walker, *Appeal*, 46–49). Interestingly, though, Quinn's text omitted Walker's characteristic right-pointing printer's index before the "ADDITION" that doubly signals it as such. This missing index is the first obvious visual difference between Walker's text as it is reprinted in Quinn's tract/pamphlet. A closer

comparative glance at the two reveals that Quinn's text also removed one of the five exclamation points from the end of Walker's sentence "God suffers some to go on until they are ruined forever!!!!!" (46). By grammatically making Quinn's text the subject of the previous sentence, I mean to acknowledge that it is possible that Quinn's printer rather than Quinn himself made these typographical changes. That said, I suspect that the differences are due to Quinn's transcribing from his copy of the third edition of the *Appeal* into his own manuscript and deciding not to carry over the typographical dynamics of Walker's printed text—a decision consistent with his aim to produce a text that both looked and read as more rationally restrained.

32. Walker, *Appeal*, 46; Quinn, *Origin, Horrors, and Results of Slavery*, 16.

33. Walker, *Appeal*, 49; Quinn, *Origin, Horrors, and Results of Slavery*, 19.

34. Gary B. Nash discusses Branagan's past as a slave overseer in the Caribbean and his coming to Philadelphia, Methodism, and antislavery in *Forging Freedom: The Formation of Philadelphia's Black Community, 1720–1840* (Cambridge, MA: Harvard University Press, 1988), 178–179. On Branagan's engagement with Jefferson in his *Preliminary Essay*, see Nicholas Guyatt, *Bind Us Apart: How Enlightened Americans Invented Racial Segregation* (New York: Basic Books, 2016), 81–82.

35. Branagan, *Preliminary Essay*, 87.

36. Quinn, *Origin, Horrors, and Results of Slavery*, 19.

37. Daniel Payne, *Recollections of Seventy Years* (Nashville, TN: AME Church Sunday School Union, 1888), 101. Dickerson, the author of the most recent history of the AME Church (*The African Methodist Episcopal Church: A History*) would seem to have drawn his information about Quinn's origins from Payne; see note 6 above.

38. On this history, see Herbert S. Klein and Ben Vinson III, *African Slavery in Latin America and the Caribbean*, 2nd ed. (Oxford: Oxford University Press, 2007).

39. For the political context of Wesley's plagiarism of Johnson, see James E. Bradley, *Popular Politics and the American Revolution in England* (Macon, GA: Mercer University Press, 1986), 93–94.

40. Henry Abelove, *The Evangelist of Desire: John Wesley and the Methodists* (Stanford, CA: Stanford University Press, 1990), 85–86.

41. See Lara Langer Cohen, "Notes from the State of Saint Domingue: The Practice of Citation in *Clotel*," in *Early African American Print Culture*, ed. Lara Langer Cohen and Jordan Alexander Stein (Philadelphia: University of Pennsylvania Press, 2012), 160–177; and Geoffrey Sanborn, "The Plagiarist's Craft: Fugitivity and Theatricality in *Running a Thousand Miles for Freedom*" (*PMLA* 128, no. 4 [2013]: 907–922).

42. Padhraig Higgins, *A Nation of Politicians: Gender, Patriotism, and Political Culture, in Late Eighteenth-Century Ireland* (Madison: University of Wisconsin Press, 2010), 48. In the context of early modern Britain, Joad Raymond notes that "polemical works were reprinted after an interval in considerable numbers, often in compressed, cheaper editions, quite possibly generating more copies than ever previously; this also gave new meaning to their appearance. Repetition involved change. Thus the reprint of an ephemeral pamphlet embodied two contradictory impulses. First, it asserted that circumstances remained the same"—that is, that political and religious problems "were still a problem." "Secondly, it displayed to the reader the malleability of political rhetoric, inviting him or her to adapt old arguments to new conditions, to appropriate the recent past to the present" (*Pamphlets and Pamphleteering in Early Modern Britain* [Cambridge: Cambridge University Press, 2003], 366). On plagiarism and imitation in the history of American political pamphlets,

see Bernard Bailyn, *The Ideological Origins of the American Revolution* (Cambridge, MA: Harvard University Press, 1992), 45.

43. On Guillaume Thomas François Raynal plagiarizing from Thomas Paine, see Antonello Gerbi, *The Dispute of the New World: The History of a Polemic, 1750-1900*, trans. Jeremy Moyle (Pittsburgh, PA: University of Pittsburgh Press, 1973), 246n397, and on Denis Diderot doing the same, see Mary Efrosini Gregory, *Freedom in French Enlightenment Thought* (New York: Peter Lang, 2010), 106. On authorized and unauthorized reprintings of *Common Sense*, see chapter 2 of Trish Loughran's *The Republic in Print: Print Culture in the Age of U.S. Nation Building, 1770-1870* (New York: Columbia University Press, 2007), 33-103.

44. Meredith McGill also notes that evangelical tracts were among those that "were freely excerpted, imitated, plagiarized, and reissued" at the time (*American Literature and the Culture of Reprinting, 1834-1853* [Philadelphia: University of Pennsylvania Press, 2003], 105-106).

45. Thomas Branagan, *Serious Remonstrances, Addressed to the Citizens of the Northern States, and Their Representatives* (Philadelphia, PA: Thomas T. Stiles, 1805), 33-34.

46. Nash, *Forging Freedom*, 180-181.

47. Thomas Branagan, *Avenia, or, A Tragical Poem on the Oppression of the Human Species, and Infringement on the Rights of Man* (Philadelphia, PA: Silas Engels, 1805), 310n. My thanks to Chris Phillips for this discovery in his essay "Epic, Anti-Eloquence, and Abolitionism: Thomas Branagan's *Avenia* and *The Penitential Tyrant*," *Early American Literature* 44, no. 3 (2009): 605-637, 631.

48. The UCLA copy of Branagan's *Preliminary Essay* can be accessed at archive.org/details/preliminaryessay00bran/page/n9 and the New York Public Library's copy at archive.org/details/apreliminaryess00napogoog/page/n9.

49. On Quinn's presence at the first General Conference of the AME Church in Philadelphia in 1816, see Payne, *History of the African Methodist Episcopal Church*, 7; and George Washington Williams, *History of the Negro Race in America from 1619 to 1880* (New York: Putnam, 1883), 2:452.

50. As I was completing this manuscript, Leon Jackson shared an especially promising lead in this direction: Francisco Gê Acayaba de Montezuma's pamphlet *A Liberdade das Repúblicas*, published in Rio de Janeiro in 1833, which cites Walker's *Appeal*. Lloyd Belton makes the connection in his article "Emiliano F. B. Mundrucu: Inter-American Revolutionary and Abolitionist (1791-1863)," *Atlantic Studies* 15, no. 1 (2018): 10. I thank Leon sincerely for sharing this discovery.

Chapter 5

1. One of the advertisements that Garnet placed in Frederick Douglass's *North Star* notes that the "edition is small, and those who desire copies will do well to send in their orders early" (*North Star*, May 5, 1848, 3). The title page for Walker's *Appeal* in Garnet's edition indicates that it is the "Second Edition, with Corrections, &c.," in closely replicating Walker's 1830 title page. It is unknown why he reprinted this edition instead of the third and final edition, but it seems likely that it was the copy he had on hand. It is significant, though, that the second edition does not include Walker's instructions to his audience that appear on the verso of the title page of only the third edition in place of where one would expect a copyright notice. As a result, Garnet's 1848 edition does not include these instructions.

2. David Walker and Henry Highland Garnet, *Walker's "Appeal," with a Brief Sketch of His Life by Henry Highland Garnet and also Garnet's Address to the Slaves of the United States*

of America (New York: J. H. Tobitt, 1848). Garnet published another version of his address in 1865 as "An Address to the Slaves of the United States of America. (Rejected by the National Convention, 1843)," in *A Memorial Discourse Delivered in the Hall of the House of Representatives, Washington City, D.C., On Sabbath, February 12, 1865* (Philadelphia: J. M. Wilson, 1865).

3. Derrick R. Spires offers a highly nuanced reading of Garnet's "Address to the Slaves" as a complex and multiple text in its various performance and print iterations, but characterizes it as an "addendum" to Walker's *Appeal* in the 1848 edition. See Spires, "'Flights of Fancy': Black Print, Collaboration, and Performance in 'An Address to the Slaves of the United States of America (Rejected by the National Convention, 1843),'" in *The Colored Conventions Movement: Black Organizing in the Nineteenth Century*, ed. P. Gabrielle Foreman, Jim Casey, and Sarah Lynn Patterson (Chapel Hill: University of North Carolina Press, 2021), 126. Lori Leavell's essay "Recirculating Black Militancy in Word and Image: Henry Highland Garnet's 'Volume of Fire'" (*Book History* 20 [2017]: 150–187) analyzes the interrelationship of Walker's *Appeal* and Garnet's "Address," though she positions the *Appeal* as a preface to Garnet's text. I read the relationship less hierarchically, foregrounding what I read as Garnet's understanding of their interdependence and mutual fortification both in their political theory and as material texts.

4. Leavell, "Recirculating Black Militancy," 150.

5. Stanley Harrold, *The Rise of Aggressive Abolitionism: Addresses to the Slaves* (Lexington: University Press of Kentucky, 2004), 4.

6. Spires, "'Flights of Fancy,'" 127–128. Spires also argues that the "twists in the performance, reception, and print history of the 'Address' suggest that analyzing it involves working on a constellation of at least three distinct yet mutually constituting print events: 1) the 1843 convention minutes, 2) newspaper accounts describing Garnet's performance and ensuing debate, and 3) the divergent editions of the 'Address' published in 1848 and 1865" (126). I very much appreciate Spires's holistic approach and the much more nuanced understanding of Garnet's "Address" that it affords. In this chapter, I limit my consideration more specifically to 1842 through 1848 in the interest of detailing Garnet's implicit and explicit engagements with Walker's *Appeal* and the particular force of his reactivating it after the two National Colored Conventions at which Garnet delivered his "Address" and contributed significantly to debates about strategies for harnessing the power of print.

7. The "Reception and Dissemination: A Tale of Two Addresses" and "Julia Williams Garnet: Critic and Collaborator" sections of Spires's "'Flights of Fancy'" essay offer robust considerations of Garnet's critical engagements—particularly with women, including Williams Garnet, the White abolitionist Maria Weston Chapman, and Maria W. Stewart (134–143). On the significance and effects of the Colored Conventions movement, see the other essays in Foreman, Casey, and Patterson, *Colored Conventions Movement*.

8. Spires, "'Flights of Fancy,'" 137.

9. Spires notes that, while living in Boston before marrying Garnet, Williams "might have read Walker's *Liberator* articles and the *Appeal*, and she may have heard or read Maria Stewart's lectures. Stewart in particular was active in Boston when Williams would have been in her early twenties, and I can only speculate about whether Williams, an ardent student and scholar, would have been a member of Boston's Afric-American Female Intelligence society. If she was, she might have heard Stewart proclaim, 'I am willing to die for the cause that I have espoused,' during her address to that society in 1832, a tantalizing connection that could situate Stewart's influence on the 'Address' more concretely alongside Walker's" ("'Flights of Fancy,'" 139–140).

10. On the AASS's 1835 postal campaign and southern attempts at censorship, including mob violence, see Bertram Wyatt-Brown, "The Abolitionists' Postal Campaign of 1835," *Journal of Negro History* 50, no. 4 (1965): 227–238; Clement Eaton, "Mob Violence in the Old South," *Mississippi Valley Historical Review* 29, no. 3 (1942): 351–370; and Eaton, "Censorship of the Southern Mails," *American Historical Review* 48, no. 2 (1943): 266–280. More recently, see David Paul Nord, "Benevolent Books: Printing, Religion, and Reform," in *A History of the Book in America*, vol. 2, *An Extensive Republic: Print, Culture, and Society in the New Nation, 1790–1840*, ed. Robert A. Gross and Mary Kelley (Chapel Hill: University of North Carolina Press, 2010), 240–46.

11. Quoted in Bayard Tuckerman, *William Jay and the Constitutional Movement for the Abolition of Slavery* (New York: Dodd, Mead, 1894), 69.

12. Quoted in Tuckerman, *William Jay*, 71.

13. The uprising that Nat Turner led in Southampton, Virginia, in 1831 certainly stoked southern fears and had life-changing consequences for many enslaved and free Blacks in Virginia and throughout the South, including death, torture, harassment, and further restrictions on literacy and mobility. But, here, my focus is explicitly discursive, on newspapers' and politicians' consistent representation of the danger that northern-published antislavery print circulating in the South posed in supposedly fomenting insurrection—and specifically on their insistent labeling of all antislavery print as "incendiary" after "that incendiary pamphlet" was commonly substituted to signify Walker's *Appeal*.

14. While the AASS claimed that its intended audience was White northerners and southern masters, they were well aware of the uncontrollability of the circulation of any type of print, especially the portable pamphlet format and recognized that literate enslaved people might get hold of their publications.

15. Harrold, *Rise of Aggressive Abolitionism*, 17.

16. Gerrit Smith, "Address of the Anti-Slavery Convention of the State of New-York . . . to the Slaves in the U. States of America," *Liberator*, February 11, 1842, 21–22, 21.

17. Garnet, speech to the Massachusetts Liberty Party, "Mass. Liberty Party Convention," *Emancipator and Free American*, March 4, 1842, 206–207. Garnet's first application of Hebrews 13:3 to figure the relationship between free and enslaved Blacks that I have located appears in an 1840 address he delivered at the seventh anniversary of the American Anti-Slavery Society: "I feel for my brethren as a man—I am bound with them as a brother. Nothing but emancipating them can set me at liberty" (reprinted in Earl Ofari, *Let Your Motto Be Resistance* [Boston, MA: Beacon, 1972], 127–134).

18. William Lloyd Garrison, "Address to the Slaves of the United States," *Liberator*, June 2, 1843, 89.

19. Derrick R. Spires, *Practice of Citizenship: Black Politics and Print Culture in the Early United States* (Philadelphia: University of Pennsylvania Press, 2019), 5.

20. Gerrit Smith, "Address . . . to the Slaves in the U. States of America," 22.

21. Garrison, "Address," 89.

22. Walter Johnson has prompted scholars to think carefully about histories of agency and "the idea that the task of the social historian is to 'give the slaves back their agency'" and to recover Black humanity in his important essay "On Agency" (*Journal of Social History* 37, no. 1 [2003]: 113–114). In this chapter, I focus on Garnet's efforts to activate the enslaved people's agency in his address to them. While Garnet does not use the word *agency* in his address, Douglass does in his response to the address at the 1843 convention, in the sense of bearing

responsibility, as the convention's delegates would, for injury to the enslaved if Garnet's address to them prompted them to revolt. I use it more broadly, to capture many of the kinds of actions that Garnet sees enslaved people as being fully capable of and wants them to take, and that he sees White abolitionists limiting for the enslaved and free Blacks alike. In doing so, I take seriously Johnson's reminder that scholarship that "discovers" Black humanity "unwittingly reproduce[s] the incised terms and analytical limits of a field of contest ... framed by the white-supremacist assumptions which made it possible to ask such a question in the first place" (114). I see Garnet and his fellow activists using these terms and ideas, but differently—not ascribing or discovering agency and humanity but rather taking both as things to be activated, rather than statically possessed or assigned, much as Spires argues of citizenship in *The Practice of Citizenship*.

23. Spires, "'Flights of Fancy,'" 126.

24. As Spires makes clear in both his recent analysis of Garnet's "Address" and *The Practice of Citizenship*, conversations about and designations of citizenship were prominent in Black political discourse prior to Walker's *Appeal*, the Buffalo convention, and in speeches and writing that preceded Garnet's at the convention. Within this context, Spires argues, Garnet's address "innovates on earlier models by merging Walker's *Appeal* and previous addresses with a definition of citizenship" that includes "enslaved people as rights-bearing citizens" ("'Flights of Fancy,'" 128–129).

25. Of the actually intended audience for Garnet's "Address," John Ernest suggests that "although it was an 'address to the slaves,' arguably Garnet's speech reached the primary audience for whom it was intended, as he worked to shift the tenor of the assembled black national (male) leadership in Buffalo.... Although Garnet addresses his comments to his imagined audience, the slaves in the South, he speaks perhaps more directly still to his northern audience.... When Garnet proclaims that it is better to '*die freemen than to live to be slaves*,' he is, of course, calling on the enslaved to resist their enslavers—though perhaps he is saying even more to those who *are* freemen (to the extent that the title was at all accurate in the North) and thus in a position to die as such for the collective cause." See John Ernest, *Liberation Historiography: African American Writers and the Challenge of History, 1794–1861* (Chapel Hill: University of North Carolina Press, 2004), 247. With respect to the centrality of rights-bearing citizenship to Garnet's "Address" and its consistency with Black political thought at the 1843 convention and beyond, see Spires, "'Flights of Fancy,'" 128–130.

26. In her influential essay "A Narrative of the Interesting Origins and (Somewhat) Surprising Developments of African-American Print Culture," Frances Smith Foster describes the conscious formation of such "affinity bonds" as a crucial part of "revised ideas of kinship" with "fellow sufferers" in slavery among those who were taken from Africa and did not previously think of themselves as "African," or "Black," or "Negro" but "determined that adjusting or reconstructing their allegiances and self-identities" was "necessary for their physical survival and spiritual well-being" ("A Narrative of the Interesting Origins and (Somewhat) Surprising Developments of African-American Print Culture," *American Literary History* 17, no. 4 [2005]: 716).

27. Douglas A. Jones Jr. offers a similar reading of Garnet's central metaphor and its linkage of his two audiences in *The Captive Stage: Performance and the Proslavery Imagination of the Antebellum North* (Ann Arbor: University of Michigan Press, 2014), 117.

28. "Convention of Colored Men," *New York Evangelist*, August 31, 1843, 139, quoted in Spires, "'Flights of Fancy,'" 134.

29. Eddie S. Glaude Jr., *Exodus! Religion, Race, and Nation in Early Nineteenth-Century Black America* (Chicago: University of Chicago Press, 2000), 110.

30. On connections between abolitionism and the early labor movement, see Manisha Sinha, *The Slave's Cause: A History of Abolition* (New Haven, CT: Yale University Press, 2016), esp. 369–371.

31. For a recent, necessary, helpful theorization of instigating violence and resistant counterviolence, see Natasha Lennard, *Being Numerous: Essays on Non-Fascist Life* (London: Verso, 2019), esp. 21–22. Tristan Stubbs's *Masters of Violence: The Plantation Overseers of Eighteenth-Century Virginia, South Carolina, and Georgia* (Columbia: University of South Carolina Press, 2018) offers an important history of violence as a management strategy implemented by overseers to extinguish the possibility of enslaved people's counterviolent resistance in the years of its emergence.

32. Harrold notes the textual as well as tactical "ambiguity concerning this passage," citing Jane H. Pease and William H. Pease's argument that "Garnet did not include this disavowal of slave revolt in the Address he presented in 1843" and added it to the 1848 "toned down"—in Pease and Pease's words—print version of the "Address." Harrold suggests the possibility "that, while he was still at the Buffalo convention, Garnet added the passage in response to criticism from other delegates," while also noting that it is missing from the 1865 print version (*Rise of Aggressive Abolitionism*, 33). As this chapter seeks to make clear, the 1848 version of Garnet's "Address" makes it unambiguous that only enslaved people know best how and when to resist. See Pease and Pease, *They Who Would Be Free: Blacks' Search for Freedom, 1830–1861* (New York: Athenaeum, 1974), 239.

33. *Minutes of the National Convention of Colored Citizens: Held at Buffalo* (New York: Piercy and Reed, 1843), 13, https://omeka.coloredconventions.org/items/show/278.

34. Spires confirms this inference by situating Garnet's "Address" among "the 'Conventional Addresses' and declarations of sentiments from Colored Conventions of the 1830s and the addresses to voters and Black citizens from the state conventions of the 1840s," and thus reads it as "composed to be a corporate public assertion of the convention's intentions—part manifesto, part historical assessment of abolitionism, and part vehicle for creating and sustaining a national Black movement that linked explicitly northern racism and enslavement" ("'Flights of Fancy,'" 127).

35. For a reading of the minutes for Garnet's performance and the delegates' objection to its violence versus Douglass's less affecting representation of violent resistance in print, see D. Jones, *Captive Stage*, 118–123.

36. Frederick Douglass, *Narrative of the Life of Frederick Douglass, an American Slave* (Boston: Anti-Slavery Office, 1845), 72.

37. The committee decided upon was Garnet as chair, Douglass, A. M. Sumner, S. H. Davis, and R. Banks (*Minutes*, 14).

38. Spires, "'Flights of Fancy,'" 127.

39. More specifically, the minutes record Alphonso M. Sumner, a Cincinnatian, as objecting that the convention's adoption of Garnet's "Address" "would be fatal to the safety of the free people of color of the slave States, but especially so to those who lived on the borders of the free States" (*Minutes*, 18). These additional and final concerns were enough to lead to the defeat of the motion to print and circulate the "Address," not once but twice. Following its nineteen-to-eighteen defeat on Friday, August 18, the delegate Ralph Francis moved later that day for a reconsideration of the close vote. Further debate ensued followed by a revote the next

morning; after several convention participants had departed and some changed sides, the result was nine in favor and fourteen against (*Minutes*, 18–24).

40. Garnet, "Address," 90.

41. Having met defeat on the front of publishing his address, Garnet redoubled his efforts to advance Black agency as a member of the 1843 convention's press committee, where delegates dedicated significant time and energy to discussing a centralized and entirely Black-printed, Black-published, and Black-circulated newspaper dedicated to a Black readership. From some of their own experiences as editors and publishers, they recognized not only the potential power of such an organ but also the vulnerability of newspapers that had struggled for subscribers and survived for only a short time. Unlike Garnet's address, the report of the press committee—which included Garnet and Ray, both of whom had also edited and published short-lived newspapers—was printed without debate within the convention minutes, and it notably contains the same crucial message of racial unity that Garnet asserts in his speech. In 1842 Garnet was coeditor, with William G. Allen, of the *National Watchman*; he left to found and edit the *Clarion* in Troy, New York, in 1842 or 1843 (Armistead Scott Pride and Clint C. Wilson, *A History of the Black Press* [Washington, D.C.: Howard University Press, 1997], 53). Through the press committee's report, I contend, he was effectively able to insert into the convention's minutes the most powerful point of his "Address" despite its rejection. Once his argument about the crucial need for racial solidarity had been stripped of the potential for violence and made an effect of the press, it easily carried in the motion to establish a newspaper and in the formation of a committee to see to it (*Minutes*, 25).

42. *Proceedings of the National Convention of Colored People, and Their Friends, Held in Troy, N.Y., on the 6th, 7th, 8th and 9th October, 1847* (Troy, NY: J. C. Kneeland, 1847), 10.

43. For more on the Colored Convention debates about founding a Black national press and the significance of the press to Black abolitionists, see the introduction of Benjamin Fagan's *The Black Newspaper and the Chosen Nation* (Athens: University of Georgia Press, 2016), 1–19.

44. Garnet did not attend the next convention (the Colored National Convention), held in early September 1848 in Cleveland, at which Douglass served as president.

45. Garnet's ad can be found under the heading "New Publications" in *North Star*, May 5, 1848, 3. On the possibility that Douglass's argument against a national Black newspaper was a conflict of interest with his plans for the *North Star*, see Fagan, *Black Newspaper*, 2.

46. Again, for an important argument against overemphasizing Garnet's and Douglass's opposition, and tensions within the Black abolitionist movement more broadly, see Spires's "'Flights of Fancy'" as well as his *Practice of Citizenship*.

47. "Foreign News," *North Star*, March 24, 1848, 3.

48. "Foreign News," *North Star*, April 14, 1848, 3.

49. Garnet, "The Model Republic," *North Star*, April 28, 1848, 3.

50. Given the dates of Garnet's prefaces to Walker's *Appeal* (April 12) and his "Address" (April 15), it is possible that he read this very news in the *North Star* and began preparing his pamphlet in response to it. But as Fagan notes, the *North Star* was hardly alone in covering the unfolding events; news about the European revolutions rapidly spread across the United States and prompted a variety of engaged responses ("The *North Star* and the Atlantic 1848," *African American Review* 47, no. 1 [2014]: 51). In *The Black Newspaper and the Chosen Nation*, Fagan examines how "the *North Star* worked to link the revolutions rocking the Atlantic world

in 1848 to the fight for black freedom in the United States" (16). "Beginning in March 1848," he notes, "the *North Star* devoted substantial space to covering the February revolution in France, exploring the implications of that uprising in the fight for black liberation in the United States" (79). I see Garnet's 1843 "Address to the Slaves" and his early May 1848 publication of it with Walker's *Appeal* as the principal motivator of Douglass's individual interest in the relationship of the 1848 revolutions to U.S. enslaved people's liberation—a possibility that he gradually reached in separating from Garrison. My focus in this chapter, however, is on Garnet's interest in forging this connection for the enslaved people themselves as much as for anyone else.

51. John Carter's *ABC for Book Collectors* defines a pamphlet as "a complete work, shorter than a book, bound (if at all) in wrappers, plain or printed" (9th ed., ed. Nicolas Barker and Simran Thadani [New Castle, DE: Oak Knoll, 2016], 179–180). In 1848 it was common for pamphlets to be stab stitched by hand instead of machine bound; as Carter's *ABC* notes, "thin (and not so thin) books, pamphlets, magazines or part-issues would sometimes be sewn through sideways, when they are said to be *stabbed*" ("Stabbed, Stab-Holes," 236). The Library of Congress's copy of Garnet's pamphlet was trimmed and rebound in 1976, making it impossible to see if there are stab holes and, thereby, to determine how the pamphlet was originally held together and whether it was bound in paper wrappers, as Walker's first three editions of the *Appeal* were. In this chapter, I assume that it was bound in wrappers, given that being common practice at the time for pamphlets of such length, the precedent of Walker's pamphlet, and the centrality of the conceit of being "bound with" in Garnet's "Address." For more on manual versus mechanical methods of book binding in the antebellum period, see James N. Green, "The Rise of Book Publishing," in *A History of the Book in America: An Extensive Republic; Print, Culture, and Society in the New Nation, 1790–1840*, ed. Robert A. Gross and Mary Kelley (Chapel Hill: University of North Carolina Press, 2010), 2:75–127, esp. 115–119.

52. As it is set in type with Walker's *Appeal* and the other materials in the pamphlet, Garnet's "Address" is only six pages long and set in smaller type than the *Appeal* so that it fits into six gatherings of sixteen pages. For a literary representation of the vulnerability of textually and materially thin pamphlets, see book 14 of Herman Melville's *Pierre; or, The Ambiguities* (1852), ed. Harrison Hayford, Hershel Parker, and G. Thomas Tanselle (Evanston, IL: Northwestern University Press, 1971).

53. Leavell devotes significant attention to this frontispiece illustration, its Moses-like figure, and its recycling and recirculation in later antislavery and colonization print in "Recirculating Black Militancy," 166–77. Lauren Ginn offers a compelling alternative reading of the figure in the illustration as Aaron, as represented in Exodus 24:12–16, in her unpublished essay "Visual Translation: How David Walker's *Appeal* Influenced the Rhetoric and Symbols in Abolitionist Illustrations," written for my Spring 2020 MA seminar "African American Literature Beyond the Slave Narrative" at DePaul University. I thank Lauren and all my students who have studied Walker's *Appeal* for everything that I have learned from their readings.

54. See Beth A. McCoy, "Race and the (Para)Textual Condition," *PMLA* 121, no. 1 (2006): 156–169, 167. Leavell's reading of Garnet's biography of Walker focuses more on its paratextual contribution to Garnet's authority as an author and activist and establishing his political connection to Walker than on its literary historical and theoretical work. Her point about how the pamphlet at once recovers and creates Walker's esteem as an author and activist, specifically in Black communities, I cite here in full for its relevance to my reading of the pamphlet's

paratexts: "By reprinting the *Appeal*, Garnet aims to regenerate Walker's influence, the volume concurrently recording Walker's esteemed reputation among African Americans even as it works to create it" ("Recirculating Black Militancy," 159).

55. James McCune Smith was the first to suggest that John Brown sponsored Garnet's publication of his address with Walker's *Appeal*. See his "Sketch of the Life and Labors of Henry Highland Garnet," in Garnet, *Memorial Discourse* (1865), 52. Harrold describes this as a "legend" in his *Rise of Aggressive Abolitionism* (143), while Sinha puts it as "apparently John Brown contributed to the cost of publication" (*Slave's Cause*, 418).

56. It is important to note that McCoy's argument about paratextual power critically recognizes the limitations of Black writers using them to resist White supremacy. "To explore how the paratext has been drafted in racialized trial by space is to raise an old, old scar of a question: can the master's tools dismantle the master's house?" (160). My answer to this question specifically in relation to the case of Garnet's pamphlet, is yes, powerfully, but also partially and impermanently.

57. On "The Author as Icon and Celebrity," see Susan S. Williams, "Authors and Literary Authorship," in *A History of the Book in America*, vol. 3, *The Industrial Book, 1840–1880*, ed. Scott E. Casper, Jeffrey D. Groves, Stephen W. Nissenbaum, and Michael Winship (Chapel Hill: American Antiquarian Society and University of North Carolina Press, 2007), 90–116, esp. 105–116.

58. The scant record that Walker left behind also prompts Garnet to take some creative liberties as a writer, as we see when he ventriloquizes the young Walker voicing his decision to leave his home state of North Carolina: "Said he, 'If I remain in this bloody land, I will not live long. As true as God reigns, I will be avenged for the sorrow which my people have suffered.... It will be a great trial for me to live on the same soil where so many men are in slavery; certainly I cannot remain where I must hear their chains continually, and where I must encounter the insults of their hypocritical enslavers. Go, I must'" (v). Walker's fictionalized soliloquy resonates with that of Madison Washington, the self-liberated leader of the *Creole* slave ship rebellion, at the center of Douglass's 1853 fictionalization of his life, *The Heroic Slave*—and whom Garnet includes in his list of examples of heroic slave revolutionaries in his "Address." Douglass had begun telling his version of Washington's story in speeches in 1845 and continuing through 1848 as Robert S. Levine, John Stauffer, and John R. McKivigan document in part 3 of their scholarly edition of *The Heroic Slave* (New Haven, CT: Yale University Press, 2014), and as Levine addresses at length in chapter 3 of *The Lives of Frederick Douglass* (Cambridge, MA: Harvard University Press, 2016), 119–178.

59. Untitled article, *Boston Courier*, March 22, 1830, 3.

60. Michel Foucault, "What Is an Author?," *Foucault Reader*, ed. Paul Rabinow (New York: Pantheon, 1984), 101–120.

61. Garnet qualifies this claim of Walker's assassination by poisoning by adding, "but whether this was the case or not, the writer is not prepared to affirm" (vii). Hinks has further investigated this charge in the municipal death records and concludes "Nowhere is foul play suggested" (*To Awaken*, 269).

62. Garnet's efforts in this respect seem to have convinced Douglass, who reprinted Garnet's biographical sketch of Walker in the *North Star* on July 14, 1848, though without attributing it to Garnet. Rather than reading the lack of attribution as a slight to a political rival, I read it as working to further underscore Garnet's deliberate foregrounding of Walker as an author in the biography, particularly in light of the biography's position immediately

next to the Poetry column on the fourth page of the issue. See "Selections: Sketch of the Life and Character of David Walker," *North Star*, July 14, 1848, 4.

63. *Minutes and Address of the State Convention of the Colored Citizens of Ohio* (Oberlin: J. M. Fitch, 1849), 18.

Chapter 6

1. Paola Brown, *Address Intended to Be Delivered in the City Hall, Hamilton, February 7, 1851, on the Subject of Slavery* (Hamilton, ON: printed for the author, 1851). All in-text citations refer to this edition.

2. Paola Brown, "Circular Address to the Free People of Color Throughout the United States" and petition, *Liberator*, October 27, 1843, 1.

3. The most complete biographical information on Brown can be found in Adrienne Shadd, *The Journey from Tollgate to Parkway: African Canadians in Hamilton* (Toronto: National Heritage Books, 2010), 61–72. On Brown's position as town crier and his silencing, see John C. Weaver, "Brown, Paola," in *Dictionary of Canadian Biography*, vol. 8, University of Toronto/Université Laval, 1985, accessed May 22, 2019, http://www.biographi.ca/en/bio/brown_paola_8E.html.

4. An article about Brown's lecture in the February 13, 1851, Hamilton *Weekly Spectator* prints Brown's introductory remarks but stops just as Brown is about to leave "the suburbs of [his] subject" and "enter the city," as Brown remarks, borrowing from Walker's preface: "But it is time for me to close my remarks on the suburbs, just to enter more fully into the interior" of slavery (Walker, *Appeal*, 8). The *Weekly Spectator* article dramatically interrupts Brown's remarks on the "darkness, utter darkness, thick and black darkness, gentlemen," dramatically reporting, "Here some evil disposed person turned off the gas, and left the lecturer in the midst of darkness, when the audience retired, tumbling over each other to the door, and escorted Paola Brown, Esq., to his residence, parting him with loud and hearty cheers" ("Lecture of Paola Brown, Esq. on Slavery," Hamilton *Weekly Spectator*, February 13, 1851, 6). Given reports of Brown's fraudulent activity in Canada in the *Liberator* and other antislavery newspapers as well as Thomas Smallwood's hostility toward Brown and exposure of his plagiarizing of Walker's *Appeal*, it seems reasonable to raise the possibility that Brown's perfectly timed interruption by darkness may have been a marketing ploy for the pamphlet he had in mind. A more recent account of Brown having been prevented from delivering his address can be found in Frank Mackey, *Black Then: Blacks in Montreal, 1780–1880s* (Montreal: McGill-Queens University Press, 2004), 77.

5. That the text of the pamphlet represents Brown's intended address must be taken on faith in its title. In fact, given the *Weekly Spectator* article about the event and the arrangement of the text in the pamphlet (which I discussed above), it seems likely that the majority of it does not represent the address he was to have given on February 7, 1851. Because Thomas Smallwood dates his preface July 1851, Brown must have composed his pamphlet in the months between.

6. Thomas Smallwood, *A Narrative of Thomas Smallwood, (Coloured Man)* (Toronto: James Stephens, 1851). By designating Smallwood's *Narrative* as a *slave narrative*, I mean to signal Michaël Roy's important reminder that "the slave narrative as we think of it today is essentially a modern construct; the phrase 'slave narrative' itself had little currency in antebellum America. See "Cheap Editions, Little Books, and Handsome Duodecimos: A Book History Approach to Antebellum Slave Narratives," *MELUS* 40, no. 3 (2015): 69–93, 69. And by designating

Smallwood as one of Brown's adversaries, I do not mean to suggest he had a direct hand in thwarting Brown's delivery of his address.

7. As Marilyn Randall importantly explains of the relationship between copyright and plagiarism, "while we may think of copyright laws as having as their general object something called 'plagiarism,' these laws always have been aimed not at the literary tradition of borrowing and repetition, but at the control of the reproduction and circulation of marketable goods" (*Pragmatic Plagiarism: Authorship, Profit, and Power* [Toronto: University of Toronto Press, 2001], 80). For nuanced treatments of the long evolution of copyright law in the United States and Canada, respectively, see Meredith McGill, *American Literature and the Culture of Reprinting, 1834–1853* (Philadelphia: University of Pennsylvania Press, 2003) and her essay "Copyright," in *A History of the Book in America, An Extensive Republic: Print, Culture, and Society in the New Nation, 1790–1840*, ed. Robert A. Gross and Mary Kelly (Chapel Hill: University of North Carolina Press, 2010), 2:198–211; James N. Green, "The British Book in North America," in *The Cambridge History of the Book in Britain*, ed. Michael F. Suarez, S.J., and Michael L. Turner (Cambridge: Cambridge University Press, 2009), 5:548–550 and 556–558; Sara Bannerman, *The Struggle for Canadian Copyright* (Vancouver: University of British Columbia Press, 2013), esp. chaps. 2–4 (7–46); and Pierre-Emmanuel Moyse, "Colonial Copyright Redux: 1709 vs. 1832," *SSRN* (2010), https://ssrn.com/abstract=3203777.

8. Of the relationship of slavery and print-related laws with respect to the issue of circulation well before—but, I would argue, pushed to crisis by—the 1850 Fugitive Slave Act, McGill notes, "Long before the question of the legitimacy of national law was crystallized by the problematic legal status of the fugitive slave, the debate over slavery was cast as a question of circulation. Not only was the national distribution of texts that discussed slavery regarded by slaveholding communities as a significant threat to their safety, the southern interdiction of abolitionist pamphlets was countenanced and reinforced by a Jacksonian understanding of the limits of federal power" (*American Literature and the Culture of Reprinting*, 110).

9. Jane Rhodes's *Mary Ann Shadd Cary: The Black Press and Protest in the Nineteenth Century* (Bloomington: Indiana University Press, 1998) stands as an early, extended look at Black Canadian print culture. For a more recent consideration, see chapter 4 of Benjamin Fagan, *The Black Newspaper and the Chosen Nation* (Athens: University of Georgia Press, 2016), 95–118.

10. Lloyd Pratt, *The Strangers Book: The Human of African American Literature* (Philadelphia: University of Pennsylvania Press, 2016), 43.

11. Much of this work is indebted to Frances Smith Foster's "A Narrative of the Interesting Origins and (Somewhat) Surprising Developments of African American Print Culture," *American Literary History* 17, no. 4 (2005): 714–740. See Leon Jackson, "The Talking Book and the Talking Book Historian: African American Cultures of Print—The State of the Discipline," *Book History* 13 (2010): 251–308; the essays collected by Lara Langer Cohen and Jordan Alexander Stein in *Early African American Print Culture* (Philadelphia: University of Pennsylvania Press, 2012), esp. Cohen's "Notes from the State of Saint Domingue: The Practice of Citation in *Clotel*," 163–177; Eric Gardner, *Unexpected Places: Relocating Nineteenth-Century African American Literature* (Jackson: University of Mississippi Press, 2009) and *Black Print Unbound: The "Christian Recorder," African American Literature, and Periodical Culture* (New York: Oxford University Press, 2016); Pratt, *Strangers Book*; Roy, "Cheap Editions"; Geoffrey Sanborn, "The Plagiarist's Craft: Fugitivity and Theatricality in *Running a Thousand Miles for Freedom*, *PMLA* 128, no. 4 (2013): 907–922; Jordan Alexander Stein, "Early

American #BlackLivesMatter," *Commonplace*, 16, no. 2 (2016), http://common-place.org/book/early-american-blacklivesmatter/; Fagan, *Black Newspaper*; and Derrick R. Spires, *The Practice of Citizenship: Black Politics and Print Culture in the Early United States* (Philadelphia: University of Pennsylvania Press, 2019).

12. For recent considerations of the diversity within the slave narrative as a genre and a material text and challenges to its coherence and formal constraints as a literary genre, see Teresa A. Goddu, "The Slave Narrative as Material Text," in *The Oxford Handbook of the African American Slave Narrative*, ed. John Ernest (Oxford: Oxford University Press, 2014), 149–164; Sanborn, "Plagiarist's Craft"; and Roy, "Cheap Editions." On the breadth and diversity of antebellum African American literature beyond the slave narrative, see Gardner, *Unexpected Places*.

13. Cohen and Stein, introduction to *Early African American Print Culture*, 15.

14. Steven Lubet, *Fugitive Justice: Runaways, Rescuers, and Slavery on Trial* (Cambridge: Belknap Press, 2010), 50. Rhodes also addresses emigration by free and self-liberated people from the United States into Canada before and after the Fugitive Slave Act in chapter 2 of *Mary Ann Shadd Cary*, 25–50.

15. Lubet, *Fugitive Justice*, 51.

16. On David Hume's comparison of the Black poet Francis Williams to a parrot and this trope of parroting/mimicry/imitation in Enlightenment theories of race, see Henry Louis Gates Jr., *The Signifying Monkey: A Theory of African-American Literary Criticism* (Oxford: Oxford University Press, 1988), 113.

17. See esp. John Sekora, "Black Message/White Envelope: Genre, Authenticity, and Authority in the Antebellum Slave Narrative," *Callaloo* 10, no. 3 (1987): 482–515, as well as Lara Langer Cohen, *The Fabrication of American Literature: Fraudulence and Antebellum Print Culture* (Philadelphia: University of Pennsylvania Press, 2012), esp. chapter 3, 101–132.

18. Beth McCoy, "Race and the (Para)Textual Condition," *PMLA* 121, no. 1 (2006): 156.

19. The February 2, 1833, *Montreal Courant* published one such warning with respect to Brown that was reprinted by the *New York Observer and Chronicle* and other U.S. newspapers. See "Beware of Imposters," *New York Observer*, February 16, 1833, 26.

20. "Lecture of Paola Brown, Esq.," 6.

21. Tilar J. Mazzeo, *Plagiarism and Literary Property in the Romantic Period* (Philadelphia: University of Pennsylvania Press, 2006), 2.

22. Henry Highland Garnet, preface to *Walker's Appeal*, unnumbered p. iv.

23. McGill notes that the "basic structure of the 1831 law held until the next general revision of the copyright code in 1870" ("Copyright," 204).

24. Here, I allude to Pierre Bourdieu's concept of cultural capital in *The Field of Cultural Production: Essays on Art and Literature*, ed. Randal Johnson (New York: Columbia University Press, 1993). For a helpful discussion of Bourdieu's concept in relation to canon formation, see John Guillory, *Cultural Capital: The Problem of Literary Canon Formation* (Chicago: University of Chicago Press, 1993), esp. 330–340.

25. It is important to note that Smallwood also accused Brown of unfairly profiting from Walker's labors, which was the basis of an important argument against slaveholding in the context of a growing international labor movement. As we saw in Chapter 4, unremunerated labor is also the charge that Garnet advises enslaved people to make in confronting their masters, demanding payment, and stopping work in his "Address to the Slaves." Here, again, property rights underwrite these arguments, with labor being understood as a form of

property. For more on property rights, contract labor, and slavery in the American and British nineteenth century, see Robert J. Steinfeld, *Coercion, Contract, and Free Labor in the Nineteenth Century* (Cambridge: Cambridge University Press, 2001). At the same time, it is important to note that Smallwood's sensitivity to Brown's illicit profit from Walker's *Appeal* may be an acknowledgment of Walker's praise for the motives of Samuel Cornish, editor of the *Rights of All* newspaper: "As far as I have seen the writings of its editor, I believe he is not seeking to fill his pockets with money, but has the welfare of his brethren truly at heart. Such men, brethren, ought to be supported by us" (76).

26. In the *Weekly Spectator* article's account of Brown's introduction to his *Address*, Brown relates how he acquired his Esquire: "I have had many things to contend with in rising to the high position I now hold in society, as Paola Brown, Esquire. When His Excellency the Governor General first conferred upon me this honorable title, gentlemen of Color envied me, and foul, black slander, was set to work to take from me my fair title of Esquire, so well and so nobly earned in the cause of Freedom" (6).

27. Scholars since Foucault have challenged his assignment of this liability to the author by citing cases in which all who were involved in publishing and circulating transgressive pamphlets were punished for doing so. Yet, as Jody Greene emphasizes, "although legal liability was widespread in the domain of printed works, and although all of the figures involved in the market for printed books bore *some* accountability for their participation in illicit or dangerous aspects of the trade, the author was still considered the *most* responsible of all of the participants" in the early modern period. See Michel Foucault, "What Is an Author?," *Foucault Reader*, ed. Paul Rabinow (New York: Pantheon, 1984), 101–120; Stephen B. Dobranski, "The Birth of the Author: The Origins of Early Modern Printed Authority," in *Authority Matters: Rethinking the Theory and Practice of Authorship*, ed. Stephen Donovan, Danuta Fjellestad, and Rolf Lundén (New York: Rodopi, 2008), 23–46; and Jody Greene, *The Trouble with Ownership: Literary Property and Authorial Liability in England, 1660–1730* (Philadelphia: University of Pennsylvania Press, 2005), 26.

28. "Lecture of Paola Brown, Esq.," 6.

29. With respect to Brown's character more broadly, Shadd has similarly concluded, "If he had made mistakes, he had made them in the service of others as a proud, confident, racially conscious actor. He had come to Canada seeking freedom and the right to self-determination, not only for himself, but for others of his race. And he would continue to make a contribution in that regard in his new town of Hamilton" (72).

30. Brown divides his essay into roman-numbered articles as Walker does, but without the preamble, they do not necessarily allude to the Constitution. He also maintains Walker's titles for each article.

31. David Walker, *Appeal to the Coloured Citizens of the World*, 3rd ed. (Boston, MA: published by author, 1830). Unless otherwise indicated, all in-text citations will be to Walker's third edition.

32. "V.," "Walker's Appeal. No. 3," *Liberator*, May 28, 1831, 1–2.

33. Brown is listed as the Colbornesburg agent for the *Liberator* in Canada in the subscription notice of *Liberator*, December 8, 1832, 1.

34. For an important analysis of the *Appeal*'s circulation via reprinting, including in the *Liberator*, see Lori Leavell, "'Not Intended Exclusively for the Slave States': Antebellum Recirculation of David Walker's *Appeal*," *Callaloo* 38, no. 3 (2015): 679–695.

35. One variation between Walker's and Brown's texts occurs in the second paragraph of Brown's introduction, in the question, "Some may ask, what is the matter with this enlightened and happy people?" (iv). In Walker's third edition, the question reads, "Some may ask, what is the matter with this united and happy people?" (6). The same question in Garnet's reprinting of Walker's second edition reads as it does in Brown. That Brown was using both Walker's third edition and Garnet's reprinting and not solely Walker's second edition can be further confirmed in several places, but perhaps the most obvious evidence comes at the end of article 1, where Brown maintains a footnote that Walker added to his third edition and that is not included in Garnet's edition (Brown, *Address*, 18; Walker, *Appeal*, 21).

36. Brown also removes Walker's italics, which causes the sentence to lose its irony and the text to lose its visual cues to readers about voicing it aloud and he does so throughout, despite the pamphlet supposedly representing a text intended to be delivered orally. This, plus the length of the text, are perhaps evidence of the text of the pamphlet not being the same as the address Brown was prevented from delivering and also of Brown assembling the *Address* as a printed text.

37. To hope for such a response would be to expect a White U.S. readership that was unfamiliar with Walker's *Appeal* and, therefore, would not recognize Brown's plagiary and focus only on his *Address*'s arguments. Brown would be justified in this expectation given the overwhelmingly hostile reactions to Walker's "incendiary pamphlet" and its relatively small print runs, and even given Garnet's reprinting, since only the most ardent White abolitionists had encountered the pamphlet. He directly addresses these "American readers" in article 2 (26).

38. For a lengthy analysis of the *Liberator*'s coverage of Walker's *Appeal* see chapter 4 of Peter P. Hinks, *To Awaken My Afflicted Brethren: David Walker and the Problem of Antebellum Slave Resistance* (University Park: Pennsylvania State University Press: 1997), 91–115.

39. Walker, *Appeal*, 32; Brown, *Address*, 22.

40. On the Wedgwood icon and its circulation in U.S. visual culture, see Kirk Savage, *Standing Soldiers, Kneeling Slaves: Race, War, and Monument in Nineteenth-Century America* (Princeton, NJ: Princeton University Press, 1997), 22–23.

41. As with Apes and Quinn, Brown's Methodism is undoubtedly significant to his liberties in taking others' texts. But as my extended analysis of his pamphlet in this chapter hopefully shows, Wesley's and other Methodists' appropriations of others' texts for a greater good—considered in Chapter 3—only partially underwrite Brown's complex set of motivations.

Conclusion

1. The earliest direct discussion of Walker's *Appeal* that I have located in Du Bois's writings appears in the essay "The Talented Tenth" (in *The Negro Problem: A Series of Articles by Representative American Negroes of To-Day* [New York: James Pott, 1903], 31–75), which distills his argument for the education of exceptional Black men to lead the uplift of the race; it was published in the same year as *The Souls of Black Folk*. In the essay, he describes Walker as "that Voice crying in the Wilderness" (38) and quotes the passage from Walker's preamble that begins, "I declare it does appear to me as though some nations think God is asleep, or that he made the Africans for nothing else but to dig their mines and work their farms, or they cannot believe history, sacred or profane," and ends with Walker asking whites, "If you will allow

that we are men, who feel for each other, does not the blood of our fathers and of us, their children, cry aloud to the Lord of Sabaoth against you for the cruelties and murders with which you have and do continue to afflict us?" (Walker, quoted in Du Bois, "The Talented Tenth," 38–39).

2. W. E. B. Du Bois, *Dusk of Dawn: An Essay Toward an Autobiography of a Race Concept* (1940; repr., New York: Schocken Books, 1968).

3. Du Bois designates the Back to Africa movement as the second line of group action historically taken by African Americans, and as "more extreme and decisive" than agitation and demands for equality (*Dusk of Dawn*, 195).

4. Press release, "W. E. B. Du Bois's Copy of Rare Anti-Slavery Book Now Held by Rose Library," *Emory News Center*, March 7, 2016, http://news.emory.edu/stories/2016/03/lib_walkers_appeal/campus.html.

5. Leon Jackson has determined that there are two states of the first edition; Du Bois's copy is from what Jackson refers to as State A, which "features shoddy composition, and, among various substantive variants, the colophon, 'Printed for the Author'" ("David Walker in the Archive," paper presented at the American Literature Association Annual Conference, Boston, MA, May 25, 2019, 5–6).

6. In a newspaper article about the importance of Emory's acquisition, Pellom McDaniels III, curator at the Rose Library, suggests that Du Bois is speaking to Walker in *Souls of Black Folk* (1903). See Ernie Suggs, "Emory Acquires Rare Anti-Slavery 'Appeal,' Once Owned by Du Bois," *Atlanta Journal-Constitution*, September 4, 2016, http://www.myajc.com/news/emory-acquires-rare-anti-slavery-appeal-once-owned-bois/s9OSjY9l2E10jjl92xkkrN/.

7. On this shift from the "Talented Tenth" to the "Guiding Hundredth," see *The Autobiography of W. E. B. Du Bois: A Soliloquy on Viewing My Life from the Last Decade of Its First Century* (New York: International, 1968), 168–177.

8. The website for the W. E. B. Du Bois Centre in Accra notes that Du Bois's library's holdings have been categorized in subject areas including race and politics; it also notes that the Centre suffers from a lack of funding and "mismanagement within," so it is possible that Walker's *Appeal* could have been deaccessioned and sold. See http://webduboiscentreaccra.ghana-net.com/. The book dealer who sold it to Emory University (Between the Covers Rare Books) does not name the last owner in their advertising copy.

9. For Emory University's official acknowledgment of its institutional relationship to slavery, see Gary S. Hauk, "Reflections on the History of Slavery at Emory" (2011), https://emoryhistory.emory.edu/issues/discrimination/slavery/history.html.

10. On the discovery of the *Appeal* in Georgia and local and state officials' reactions there, see Peter P. Hinks, *To Awaken My Afflicted Brethren: David Walker and the Problem of Antebellum Slave Resistance* (University Park, PA: Pennsylvania University Press, 1997), 118–128, 238–241; and Hasan Crockett, "The Incendiary Pamphlet: David Walker's *Appeal* in Georgia," *Journal of Negro History* 86, no. 3 (2001): 305–318.

11. Press release, "W. E. B. Du Bois's Copy of Rare Anti-Slavery Book Now Held by Rose Library."

INDEX

AASS. *See* American Anti-Slavery Society
Abelove, Henry, 157, 270n40
abolition. *See* antislavery movement
ACS. *See* American Colonization Society
"Address of the Anti-Slavery Convention of the State of New-York to the Slaves in the United States of America" (G. Smith), 166, 168, 170–73, 175, 177
Address on the Subject of Slavery (P. Brown): engagements with *Notes on the State of Virginia*, 224, 226–27; as intended to be delivered orally, 198, 210, 279nn3–6; as material text, 143, 199, 277n52; as published version of Brown's speech, 199, 210, 279n1; sections of, addressing American Methodist Episcopal Church, 227–29; as strategic adaptation and renewal of Walker's *Appeal* in Canada, 4–5, 9–11, 15–16, 19–20, 22–24, 137, 203, 207–8, 210–26, 229–30, 239, 282n30, 283nn35–36; unattributed passages from other texts in, 203, 227–28. *See also* Brown, Paola; Smallwood, Thomas, as Paola Brown's accuser
"Address to Christians Recommending the Distribution of Religious Tracts," 144–47, 269n22. *See also* American Tract Society
"Address to the Slaves of the United States of America" (Garnet): 1848 printing, 11, 19, 21, 166, 176, 177, 179, 188–90, 271n2; 1865 printing, 271n2; as addressed to an enslaved audience, 18–19, 21, 165–68, 171–82, 184–86, 274n25; argument for enslaved people's resistance in, 179, 182, 275n32, 281n25, 246n30; as bound with Walker's *Appeal*, 5, 18–19, 21, 113–14, 165–66, 189–92, 196–97, 215, 246n30, 272n3; as debated and defended at the 1843 Buffalo National Convention of Colored Citizens, 167, 182–87, 190–91, 196, 273n22, 275n35, 275n39; as delivered at 1843 Buffalo Convention, 166, 171, 175–77, 190, 194, 275n32, 275n35; as delivered at 1847 Troy National Convention of Colored People, 187–88, 194; Garnet's strategies for publishing before 1848, 165–68, 183–89; as material text, 113–14. *See also* Garnet, Henry Highland; *Walker's "Appeal," with a Brief Sketch of His Life by Henry Highland Garnet and also Garnet's Address to the Slaves of the United States of America*
"Address to the Slaves of the United States of America" (Garrison), 166, 168, 172–75, 177
Afric-American Female Intelligence Society (Boston), 106–7, 272n9
African Free School (New York City), 141–42, 268n15
African Methodist Episcopal Church (AME), 18, 137–40, 143, 148–49, 155, 157–58, 162–64, 267n6, 267nn8–10, 268nn11–12, 268n17, 270n37, 271n49; print efforts of, 18, 146, 267n8, 269n24. *See also* Allen, Richard; Payne, Daniel Alexander; Quinn, William Paul
agency: authorship as a form of, 11–13, 20–23, 167, 201–3, 232, 236, 282n27; of Black antislavery activists, 10, 14–15, 168, 175, 181, 184–85, 276n41; of Black women, 12, 17, 25, 82–83, 96, 102, 104–6, 108, 167–68, 261n47; of enslaved people, 11–12, 14–15, 42–43, 168, 173, 175, 179–82, 185, 272n7, 273n22; of God, 42, 51–53, 60, 63, 71, 77, 97–99, 102–3, 105–7, 119–20, 124, 126–27, 130–32, 150, 153, 156, 170, 172, 174, 180, 188, 191, 216, 224–29, 252n23, 260n44,

agency (continued)
  261n47, 278n58, 283n1; limitations on Black forms of, 11, 168, 175, 185–88; theories and practices of, 11–14, 20, 62, 78–79, 96, 185–86, 196–97, 201, 230, 232–33, 236–38, 245n25, 273n22, 284n3; of White people, 174–75, 185, 273n22. *See also* authorship; Johnson, Walter; literacy; violence
Allen, Richard, 61–64, 139, 159, 162–63, 252n25, 267n8
AME Church. *See* African Methodist Episcopal Church
American Anti-Slavery Society (AASS): disavowals of direct communication with enslaved people and of fomenting insurrection, 168–70, 273n14; division, 172; Great Postal Campaign of 1835, 166–69, 185, 273n10, 273n14; seventh anniversary of, 273. *See also* antislavery movement
American Colonization Society (ACS), 58, 60–61, 63, 211
An American Dictionary of the English Language (Webster), 93, 95
American Methodist Episcopal Church, 110–11, 114–15, 118, 134, 141, 157, 159, 211. See also *Address on the Subject of Slavery*; African Methodist Episcopal Church; Apes, William; Methodism; Wesley, John
American Revolution: allusions to, 46, 52, 226–27; as justification for second revolution led by Black Americans, 15, 47, 56–57, 76, 100, 126, 174, 181–82, 232; and pamphlets, 116. *See also* Constitution; Declaration of Independence; United States of America, founding ideals of
American Tract Society (ATS), 117, 144, 267n7
antislavery movement: attempts to communicate directly with enslaved people, 21, 166–68, 170–72, 175; Black activism in, 14, 18, 19, 21, 52, 82–84, 95–105, 120, 138–40, 142–44, 147–56, 163, 165–68, 175–79, 182–89, 192, 196–97, 199, 202–7, 210–30, 255n61, 273n22, 274nn24–25, 275nn34–35, 39, 276n41, 276nn43–44, 276n46, 282n29; David Walker positioned as author of, 19, 192, 194–96, 278n62; Garrisonian, 17, 95, 168–70, 172–75, 180, 184–85, 188–89, 256nn1–3, 276n50; print cultures of, 21, 35, 52, 80–82, 84–96, 137–38, 143–47, 156–64, 166, 168–70, 187–88, 192, 246n26, 255n61, 271n47, 272n7, 277n53–54, 278n55–56, 279n6, 280n8, 280n11, 281n12, 281n16, 281n19, 281n25, 282n34; radical, 2, 17, 80, 142, 166, 170–72, 175–89, 242n7, 246n26, 250n15, 257n1, 258n18; scholarship on, 13–14; White activism in, 16, 18, 21, 90, 92, 95, 144, 154–55, 159–63, 166–75, 180, 183, 189, 193, 253n30, 258n18, 265n27, 273n22, 275n33, 283n37, 283n40. *See also* agency; American Anti-Slavery Society; Boston; "Brief Sketch of the Life and Character of David Walker"; Garnet, Henry Highland; Garrison, William Lloyd; *The Liberator*; Liberty Party; moral suasion; print; violence
Apes, William: as author, 12, 15–18, 20, 22, 111, 114–31, 133–36, 138; as citizen of print culture, 13, 27, 109–11, 120; as Methodist colporteur, 111, 114, 118; as Methodist minister, 109–11, 114–15, 118, 122–23, 125–26, 130, 135, 263n8; as political activist, 7, 10, 17–18, 21, 23, 26, 45, 109–11, 115–18, 129, 131, 134–36, 266n35; spelling of surname, 262n1; spiritual autobiography of, 116–17. See also *Eulogy on King Philip*; *The Experiences of Five Christian Indians*; *Indian Nullification of the Unconstitutional Laws of Massachusetts Relative to the Mashpee Tribe*; "An Indian's Appeal to the White Men of Massachusetts"; "An Indian's Looking-Glass for the White Man"; *A Son of the Forest: The Experiences of William Apes*
Appeal to the Coloured Citizens of the World: as addressed to the coloured citizens of the world, 15–16, 19, 39, 41, 44–45, 82–83, 138, 155–56, 230, 252n27; as addressed to educated Black readers, 39, 42–44, 50, 52, 53–64, 65, 69–70, 139, 233, 236; as addressed to enslaved people, 8, 15, 18, 19, 37–39, 41–43, 45–53, 169–70, 176, 177, 188–89, 238; as addressed to free, working class Black readers, 64–70; as addressed to an illiterate audience, 8, 14–15, 29–30, 32, 37–39, 41, 43; as addressed to male Black readers, 47–48,

69, 82, 101–3, 109, 177–78; as addressed to White readers, 4, 8, 16, 30, 32, 33, 37, 43–45, 52, 70–78, 215–17, 238; affirmations of Black humanity in, 7, 9, 12, 14, 23, 35, 38, 46–49, 51, 56–57, 133, 173, 181–82, 253n30; canonizations of, 2–3, 20, 22, 238–39, 242n6, 247n34, 256n65; close reading modeled in, 32, 37, 43–44, 53–64, 69–70, 78; on colonization, 37, 57–61, 211, 214, 256n1; as a didactic pamphlet, 6, 31, 32, 44, 71, 76, 117; effects of, on Black lives, 1–2, 21–22, 78, 149, 151–52, 169, 215, 241nn4–5, 242n6, 251n19; emphasis on education as key to racial uplift, 34–38, 53–54, 56–62, 67–70, 149, 194, 233–34, 236–37; engagements with Declaration of Independence, 9, 37, 72–77, 174, 214, 232, 255nn61–62, 256n64; engagements with Jefferson's *Notes on the State of Virginia*, 9, 17–18, 31–33, 50, 53–57, 59, 61, 70, 110, 123, 127, 129, 132–34, 174, 218–19, 224, 255n57, 263n6, 264n24, 265n30; errata list in first edition of, 233, 235–36; as essay, 6, 9, 20, 27, 31, 244n10; extralegal suppression of, 21–22, 38, 45, 87, 169, 185, 188–89, 194–95, 208, 231, 238, 247n33, 256n2, 283n37; first edition of, 1, 39, 44, 46, 53, 121–22, 142, 233–36, 246n27, 250n15, 252n28, 255n63, 284n5; as a grammar and encyclopedia of U.S. racial slavery, 31, 33, 66; indictments of Christian Americans' hypocrisy in, 17, 37, 42, 52, 60, 66, 70–72, 122–23, 125–27, 150, 215, 233; as jeremiad, 33, 71–72, 78, 123, 151, 228, 255n59, 264n22; as material text, 1, 14, 15, 20–22, 30, 33, 38–39, 41, 59, 65, 68, 76–77, 143, 194, 231, 233; message of God's imminent intervention on behalf of Black Americans in, 42, 51–53, 67, 215, 224, 229; militancy of, 2–3, 14–15, 22, 29, 41–42, 46–53, 69, 72–78, 82, 84, 92, 96, 101, 111, 151–52, 174, 181–82, 188, 203, 216, 217–26, 242nn7–8, 247n34; as modeled after U.S. Constitution, 9, 15, 35–36, 210–11, 250n15, 282n30; in newspapers, 1, 15–16, 21, 39, 43, 45, 48, 60, 65–66, 85–86, 111, 116, 127, 195, 244n10, 253n31, 258n16, 266n4, 273n13; notice to readers in place of copyright notice in, 29, 38–46, 54, 121–22, 159, 191–92, 202, 229, 239, 271n1; printers of, 246n27, 250n15, 251n16, 251n19, 252n28, 253n31, 255n63; as read aloud, 14, 29–30, 37, 48, 73–76, 251n17, 283n36; second edition of, 1, 46, 47, 53, 60, 122, 165, 191, 199, 214, 250n15, 251n21, 252n28, 271n1, 283n35; southern legal responses to, 1–3, 8, 16, 20, 21, 39, 45, 48–49, 59–60, 65, 76, 81, 84–89, 91–92, 127, 139, 148–51, 154, 169, 218–19, 231, 238, 241nn4–5, 242n6, 244n10, 247n33, 253n31, 256n2, 257n13, 258n21, 269n25, 269n28; third edition of, 16, 29, 39, 43–47, 53, 58–60, 77, 80, 84, 90, 101, 111, 121–22, 131, 143, 153, 165, 211, 214, 219, 231, 238, 246n28, 250n15, 251n19, 251n21, 252n24, 255n62, 257n8, 258n14, 265n30, 269n31, 271n1, 282n31, 283n35; typography and punctuation of, 8–10, 16, 29–30, 32, 36–37, 41, 43, 46–49, 51, 53, 57, 62, 72–78, 86–87, 90, 100–101, 121, 127, 133, 147, 150–54, 169, 173, 177, 188, 219–21, 251n16, 252n28, 255nn62–63, 269n31, 283n36; Walker's circulation of, 2, 21, 30, 38, 41, 91, 138, 151, 185, 191, 229, 251n18, 251n22, 266n4, 283n37; Walker's revisions of, 9, 11, 15–16, 29, 38–39, 43, 58, 60–61, 252n28, 265n30; Walker's sources for, 4, 8, 15, 30–34, 49–53, 64, 228, 253n32, 254n55; White abolitionists' condemnations of, 16. See also *Address on the Subject of Slavery*; Garrison, William Lloyd; *Liberator*; *Notes on the State of Virginia*; *Walker's "Appeal," with a Brief Sketch of His Life by Henry Highland Garnet and also Garnet's Address to the Slaves of the United States of America*

authorship: conventions of, 5, 96, 97–99, 135, 156–64, 203, 204, 207, 210; God as original author, 60, 63, 102–3, 106–7, 126–27, 131, 157–64, 186–87, 191–97, 199–204, 208, 210–11, 230, 265n27; limitations on, 5, 192–93, 204–5, 236; and property rights, 18, 19, 23, 120, 158, 191–92, 199–203, 205–8, 229, 230, 252n25; theories and practices of, 5–6, 11, 20, 23, 26–27, 132–133, 138–39, 157–58, 167, 186–87, 196, 199, 201, 203–8, 210, 216, 265n27, 270n41, 278n57, 282n27. See also agency; Apes, William; "Brief Sketch of the Life and Character of David Walker"; Brown, Paola; copyright; Foucault, Michel; Garnet, Henry

authorship (continued)
  Highland; Methodism; *Notes on the State of Virginia*; Quinn, William Paul; Smallwood, Thomas; Stewart, Maria; Walker, David
Avenia (Branagan), 159, 162, 271n47

Bacon, Jacqueline, 90, 142, 254n45, 255n61, 257n10, 268n15
Bible, 71–72, 102, 171, 176–77, 194, 254n55, 264n25, 273n17. See also *Appeal to the Coloured Citizens of the World*; "An Indian's Looking-Glass for the White Man"; *The Origin, Horrors, and Results of Slavery*; *Religion and the Pure Principles of Morality*
binding (book), 6, 268n20, 277n51. See also "Address to the Slaves of the United States of America"; *Walker's "Appeal," with a Brief Sketch of His Life by Henry Highland Garnet and also Garnet's Address to the Slaves of the United States of America*
Boston (Mass.): activist community in, 16, 17, 21, 43, 44, 65, 80–81, 90–91, 95, 107, 109, 142, 171, 202, 244n10, 253n32, 256n1, 257n9, 257n13, 258n25, 272n9; as associated with radical antislavery activism, 21, 84, 86, 92, 193–95, 253n31, 257n13. See also Afric-American Female Intelligence Society
Boston Daily Courier, 65–66, 193–94, 253n31
Bourdieu, Pierre, 281n24
Branagan, Thomas, 18, 138, 147, 155, 159–63, 270n34. See also *Avenia*; *The Origin, Horrors, and Results of Slavery*; *A Preliminary Essay on the Oppression of the Exiled Sons of Africa*
"Brief Sketch of the Life and Character of David Walker" (Garnet), 165, 191–96, 204–5, 252n26, 277n54, 278n58, 278nn61–62. See also *Walker's "Appeal," with a Brief Sketch of His Life by Henry Highland Garnet and also Garnet's Address to the Slaves of the United States of America*
Brooks, Joanna, 6, 245n12, 245n25, 248n35, 252n25, 262n4
Brown, John, 192, 278n55
Brown, Paola: as activist, 11–13, 19, 23, 198, 210–11, 214, 216–17, 229, 282n29; considered as alleged plagiarist, 199–203, 205–8, 214–15, 229–30, 283n37; creative work of, 19–22, 27, 137, 201–3, 207–8, 210, 224, 226–30, 279n4; as emigrant to Canada, 15, 19, 198, 200, 204–5, 211, 215, 217–19, 224–25, 229; as esquire, 208, 282n26; as Methodist, 227–28, 283n41; as subscription agent for the *Liberator* in Canada, 214, 216, 218, 282n33; voice of, 198–99, 205, 210. See also *Address on the Subject of Slavery*; "Circular Address to the Free People of Color Throughout the United States"; Smallwood, Thomas
Brown, William Wells, 158
Brunson, Alfred, 115, 131, 263n10
Bryant, John, 10–11, 15, 245n20
Buffon, Georges-Louis Leclerc, 55, 130–31, 250n11, 254n38, 265n29
Burke, Edmund, 254n55
Bynum, Tara, 23, 30, 78, 243n9, 248n37, 249nn3–4

Canada: Black American emigration to, 5, 15, 26, 198–200, 202–3, 205–7, 214–15, 230, 279n4, 281n14; Black print culture in, 6, 7, 13, 19, 203, 280n9, 282n33; and copyright law, 200–201, 210, 214, 280n7; as freer than United States, 195, 202, 210–11, 214, 229, 282n29; White anxiety about Black American emigrant population in, 201, 205. See also *Address on the Subject of Slavery*; Brown, Paola
Carby, Hazel V., 104, 261n50
Cherokee Nation v. Georgia, 109, 262n2, 265n28
"Circular Address to the Free People of Color Throughout the United States," 211, 214, 279n2
citizenship: of Black Americans, 6–7, 13, 78, 166, 172–73, 176, 179, 181–82, 195, 214, 229, 247n34, 252n27, 260n38; of Native Americans, 109; in print culture, 13, 19, 27, 156, 162–63, 195, 204–5, 210; and rights, 6–7, 181–82, 195, 214, 274n24; theories and practices of, 12–13, 20, 23, 27, 166, 173, 203, 204, 210, 224, 230, 243n9, 244n11. See also Apes, William; *Appeal to the Coloured Citizens of the World*; Canada; *Cherokee Nation v. Georgia*; Hyde, Carrie; print; Spires, Derrick R.

Cohen, Lara Langer, 23, 26–27, 158, 245n12, 248n35, 248n37, 270n41, 280n11, 281n17
Colored Conventions Movement, 167, 272n7
Congress (U.S.), 137, 139, 147, 152–54, 156, 195, 226–29, 255n63
Constitution (U.S)., 15, 35–36, 120, 194, 208–10, 214, 246n26, 250n15, 282n30. See also *Appeal to the Coloured Citizens of the World*
copyright, 19, 157–59, 161, 162–63, 199–202, 206, 210, 252n25, 280n7, 281n23. *See also* Apes, William; *Appeal to the Coloured Citizens of the World*; authorship; Brown, Paola; Canada; McGill, Meredith L.; Walker, David, aims of

Declaration of Independence, 9, 37, 72–77, 174, 186, 214, 226–27, 232, 255n61, 255n63. See also *Appeal to the Coloured Citizens of the World*
Delany, Martin R., 143, 268n19
Dewson, Eliza (Walker), 18, 167, 191–92, 206
Diderot, Denis, 32, 38. See also *Encyclopédie*
Douglass, Frederick: as affected by Walker's *Appeal*, 20–21, 244n10; as Henry Highland Garnet's opponent at 1843 and 1847 colored conventions, 184–89, 273n22, 275n35, 275n37, 276n44, 278n62; literacy education of, 1–2, 21, 185, 241n5, 242n6. See also *The Heroic Slave*; *Narrative of the Life of Frederick Douglass*; *North Star*
Du Bois, W. E. B., 19–20, 232–39, 244n10, 283n1, 284n8. See also *Dusk of Dawn*; *The Souls of Black Folk*; "The Talented Tenth"
Dusk of Dawn: An Essay Toward an Autobiography of A Race Concept, 232, 238, 284nn2-3

Eaton, Clement, 241n4, 247n33, 258n21, 273n10
effects (definition), 8
1848: revolutions of, 18, 189–91, 215, 230, 276n50. See also *Walker's "Appeal," with a Brief Sketch of His Life by Henry Highland Garnet and also Garnet's Address to the Slaves of the United States of America*, timing of publication in 1848
Emory University, 19, 233–35, 238–39, 284n4, 284n6, 284n8, 284n9, 284n11
Encyclopédie (Diderot), 32, 250n11

English Grammar, Adapted to Different Classes of Readers (Murray), 4, 9, 30–38, 41, 43, 47–49, 53, 70, 253n36
the Enlightenment: and natural philosophical theories of racial difference, 27, 31–32, 55, 133, 135, 203–4, 254n38, 265n31, 281n16; and philosophical inquiry, 4, 8, 9, 31, 34, 38, 55, 64, 130, 158. See also *Notes on the State of Virginia*
Ernest, John, 242n9, 266n2, 274n25
essay: and early encyclopedias, 32; as literary genre, 20, 244n10; status of in literary studies, 6, 27; subgenres of, 6, 20, 31–32. See also Wall, Cheryl A.
Eulogy on King Philip (Apes), 262n1
"The Experience of the Missionary" (Apes), 116–17, 263n13. See also *The Experiences of Five Christian Indians*
The Experiences of Five Christian Indians: as hybrid religious tract and political pamphlet, 5, 9–13, 15–17, 111–14, 116–17, 120, 262n1, 263n15; as religious tract, 5, 17, 111–12, 116–17, 144. See also Apes, William; "An Indian's Looking-Glass for the White Man;" "The Experience of the Missionary"

Fagan, Benjamin, 23, 248n37, 276n43, 276n45, 276n50, 280nn9-10
Finseth, Ian, 23, 27, 31, 55, 64–65, 77, 243n9, 248n37, 249n6, 254n38, 255n57
Foreman, P. Gabrielle, 269n27, 272n3, 272n7
Foster, Francis Smith, 23, 25, 248n37, 267n8, 269n24, 274n26, 280n11
Foucault, Michel, 194–96, 208, 282n27
Freedom's Journal, 51–52, 61, 84, 142, 253n37, 254n45, 257n10, 268n15. See also Walker, David
Fugitive Slave Act of 1850: effects of, 197, 202–3, 206–7, 210, 216–17, 226–27, 230, 281n14; print culture of, 5, 19, 26, 200, 229, 280n8. See also Canada

Gardner, Eric, 23, 25–26, 137, 138, 248n37, 266n3, 280n11, 281n12
Garnet, Henry Highland, 4, 20, 22, 23, 113–14, 165–68, 276n44; as biographer of William Paul Quinn, 141–42, 148, 267n10, 268n13, 268n16; efforts of, to reestablish Black antislavery activists' direct

Garnet, Henry Highland (continued)
communication and bonds with enslaved
people, 18–19, 166, 168, 171–72, 175–79,
183–88, 272n6; power as orator, 183–84;
speech at 1842 Massachusetts Liberty
Party meeting, 171–72, 273n17. *See also*
"Address to the Slaves of the United States
of America" (Garnet); "A Brief Sketch of
the Life of David Walker"; Douglass,
Frederick; Garnet, Julia Williams;
*Walker's "Appeal," with a Brief Sketch of
His Life by Henry Highland Garnet and
also Garnet's Address to the Slaves of the
United States of America*
Garnet, Julia Williams, 167–68, 272n7, 272n9
Garrison, William Lloyd, 35, 62–63, 194,
257n8, 258n15, 259n29; deprecations
of Walker's *Appeal*, 1, 16, 17, 81, 84–85,
111, 216, 218, 241n3, 257n13, 258n14; as
influenced by Walker's *Appeal*, 80–81, 90,
168, 172–75, 256n1, 257n9, 258n14, 258n20,
258n25, 260n46; as Maria W. Stewart's
publisher and promoter, 17, 21, 80–81,
90–91, 93–96, 99, 102–3, 105–7, 143, 256n4,
259n30, 260n38, 260n46, 261n52, 261n53;
as martyr figure, 98–99, 260n43. *See also*
"Address to the Slaves of the United States
of America" (Garrison); Boston; *Genius
of Universal Emancipation*; *Liberator*,
moral suasion
Gates, Henry Louis, Jr., 10, 25, 242n7,
245n19, 281n16
Genius of Universal Emancipation, 1, 84,
255n63, 257n9, 257n13
Glaude, Eddie S., Jr., 178–79, 243n9, 275n29
Goddu, Teresa A., 281n12
Grabes, Herbert, 117–18, 263n16
Green, James N., 277n51, 280n7
Gura, Philip F., 262n4, 263n8, 263n15,
266nn34–35

Hager, Christopher, 23, 26, 248n37, 249n39
Haitian Revolution, 52, 151–53, 182, 219, 233,
269n27
Harris, Leslie M., 142, 268n14
Harrold, Stanley, 166, 171, 175, 272n5,
273n15, 275n32, 278n55
The Heroic Slave, 278n58
Hinks, Peter P., 23, 246n27, 251n18,
257nn8–9, 258n25, 266n2, 267n8, 268n17,
278n61. *See also To Awaken My Afflicted
Brethren*
Howard University, 6, 24, 146, 245n13,
268n20, 269n30
Howell, William Huntting, 261n48,
265n31
Hubbard, Dolan, 255n59, 264n22
human: theorizations of, 7–8, 20, 23, 34,
128–34; exclusions of Black people from,
45, 55–57, 60, 78, 97, 236. *See also Appeal
to the Coloured Citizens of the World*; The
Enlightenment; *Notes on the State of
Virginia*
Hume, David, 265n31, 281n16
Hyde, Carrie, 13, 243n9, 244n10

imitatio Christi, 82, 103–5, 118, 127–29,
261n48, 263n17
imitation: aesthetic, practices of, 10, 17,
107–8, 134; moral, theories of, 82–84,
117–18, 129, 261nn49–50. *See also* imitatio
Christi; *Religion and the Pure Principles
of Morality*
*Indian Nullification of the Unconstitutional
Laws of Massachusetts Relative to the
Mashpee Tribe* (Apes), 135–36. *See also*
Mashpee Revolt
Indian Removal Act of 1830, 17, 109, 262n2
"An Indian's Appeal to the White Men of
Massachusetts" (Apes), 135. *See also*
Mashpee Revolt
"An Indian's Looking-Glass for the White
Man," 5, 17, 26, 109–36, 262n3; Bible as
source text for, 26, 110, 115–16, 122–26, 130;
as didactic essay, 117–19, 134; engagements
with *Notes on the State of Virginia*, 110,
115–16, 128–30, 263n6, 263n15, 265n29,
265n33; as extension of Walker's *Appeal*
to Indigenous Americans' rights, 4, 9–11,
15–18, 22, 25, 26, 45, 109–16, 119–35, 138,
156, 230, 231, 239, 244n10, 262n4, 263n15,
265n33; figure of looking-glass in, 117–19,
128, 263n15, 264n19; indictments of
White Christian Americans' hypocrisy,
110–11, 115–19, 122–23, 127–29, 134–35; as
Indigenous contribution to ethnological
debates, 265n33; as material text, 111–14,
126
Indigenous Americans. *See* Native
Americans

Index

Jackson, Andrew, 17, 109
Jackson, Kellie Carter, 14, 22, 245n23, 253n30
Jackson, Leon, 6, 23–24, 27, 233, 243n9, 246n27, 248n35, 248n37, 251n22, 252n24, 254n53, 265n26, 271n50, 280n11, 284n5
Jackson, Zakiyyah Iman, 7–8, 245n15
Jarrett, Gene Andrew, 23, 27, 31, 56, 243n9, 244n10, 249n5, 254n38, 264n22
Jefferson, Thomas: as author of the Declaration of Independence, 73, 131, 174, 255n63; conversion of, to abolition, 227; death of, 111, 132; as Enlightenment thinker and writer, 9, 27, 32, 53–57, 70, 95, 129–34, 218–19, 224, 227, 250n8, 250n11, 254n38, 260n38, 264n22; as slaveholder, 61. *See also Appeal to the Coloured Citizens of the World*; Enlightenment; "An Indian's Looking-Glass for the White Man"; *Notes on the State of Virginia*
Johnson, Walter, 11–12, 273n22
Jones, Douglas A., Jr., 78, 242nn8–9, 249n1, 274n27, 275n35

Kachun, Mitch, 146, 269n24
Knapp, Isaac, 89–90, 247n32
Konkle, Maureen, 23, 26, 248n37, 262n4, 264n19

labor: of Black Americans, 82, 104–5, 180, 210; movement, 180, 275n30, 281n25. *See also* authorship; agency
Leavell, Lori, 14, 23, 165–66, 191, 241n4, 243n9, 244n10, 248n35, 248n37, 253n31, 266n2, 266n4, 272nn3–4, 277nn53–54, 282n34
Levine, Robert S., 77–78, 143, 256n66, 278n58
Liberator, 17, 62, 98–99, 168, 211, 214, 253n35, 257n11, 259n34, 273n16; as associated with Walker's *Appeal* as "incendiary" print, 81, 84–95, 149, 169, 185, 259n31, 259n34, 273n13; as modeled after Walker's *Appeal*, 17, 80–81, 83, 86–90, 93, 106, 134, 151, 218, 244n10, 258n17, 263n14; as sustained by Black subscribers and contributors, 81, 84, 89, 92, 256n3, 258n25, 259n27, 259n33; Walker's *Appeal* in, 62–63, 81, 84–86, 90–92, 214, 246n29, 254nn48–51, 257nn12–13, 258n14, 258n16, 268n17, 272n9, 282n32, 283n38. *See also* Brown, Paola; Garrison, William Lloyd
Liberty Party, 168, 171
literacy: as pursued by Black Americans, 3, 12, 26, 29, 53; as restricted for and denied to Black Americans, 1–2, 12, 21, 38, 88–89, 139, 148–50, 185, 204, 218, 236, 241nn5–6; theories and practices of, 26, 34, 42–43. *See also Appeal to the Coloured Citizens of the World*; *English Grammar, Adapted to Different Classes of Readers*; Douglass, Frederick; Walker, David, investment of in education as key to racial uplift
Logan, 132, 134
Lundy, Benjamin, 1, 84, 257n9. *See also Genius of Universal Emancipation*

Mashpee Revolt, 135–36
Massachusetts General Colored Association, 51–52, 142, 247n32, 253n37
Mazzeo, Tilar J., 205–6, 208, 281n21
McCoy, Beth A., 191–93, 204, 277n54, 278n56, 281n18
McGill, Meredith L., 158–59, 200–201, 248n35, 252n25, 271n43, 280nn7–8, 281n23
McHenry, Elizabeth, 3, 12, 23, 25, 29, 39, 43–44, 78–79, 106, 108, 242nn8–9, 244n10, 248n37, 249n4, 250n15
Meditations from the Pen of Mrs. Maria W. Stewart, 106, 108, 260n45, 261n52
Melville, Herman, 277n52
Methodism, 71, 82, 103, 118, 134, 138, 159, 161, 263n8; preaching styles in, 71, 114–15, 122; textual practices in, 114–15, 131, 134–36, 156–58, 263n15, 283n41. *See also* African Methodist Episcopal Church; American Methodist Episcopal Church; Apes, William; Quinn, William Paul; Wesley, John
Michaelsen, Scott, 264n19, 265n33
Minutes of the National Convention of Colored Citizens: Held at Buffalo, 168, 183–86, 272n6, 275n33, 275n35, 275n39, 276n41
mirror, 114, 117–19, 125–29, 263n16, 264n18, 264n20. *See also* "An Indian's Looking-Glass for the White Man"
Moral suasion, 85, 89, 168–70, 174, 180, 184, 188, 218, 232. *See also* antislavery movement

Murray, Lindley, 33, 34, 36, 38, 43. See also *English Grammar*

Narrative of the Life of Frederick Douglass, 1–2, 204, 241n2, 275n36
Narrative of Thomas Smallwood, 19, 24, 199–200, 204–6, 279n6
Nash, Gary B., 159, 270n34, 271n46
National Convention of Colored Citizens (1843, Buffalo, N.Y.), 165, 167–68, 171, 176–77, 181–87, 190–91, 196, 272n3, 273n22, 274nn24–25, 275n28, 275n32, 275n34, 275n37, 275n39, 276n41, 276n43. See also "Address to the Slaves of the United States of America" (Garnet); Douglass, Frederick; *Minutes of the National Convention of Colored Citizens: Held at Buffalo*
National Convention of Colored People (1847, Troy, N.Y.), 165, 176, 187–89, 275n34, 276n41
National Intelligencer, 91–92, 259n34
Native Americans: literature of, 4, 8, 23, 26, 44; lives, 2, 22, 114; political theories of, 136; representations of, 111, 263n7; various historical and contemporary designations of, 262n1. See also Apes, William; *Cherokee Nation v. Georgia*; citizenship; human; Indian Removal Act of 1830; Mashpee Revolt; *Notes on the State of Virginia*; *Worcester v. Georgia*
New York City, 141–42. See also African Free School
Nord, David Paul, 248n35, 259n35, 263n12, 267n7, 268n21, 273n10
North, 12, 21, 43–44, 52, 54, 81, 82, 84, 87, 90–92, 99, 100, 111, 161–62, 167, 180, 189, 191, 193, 202, 229, 257n7, 258n25, 266n4, 274n25
North Star, 188–90, 276n45, 276n47–50, 276n50, 278n62
Notes on the State of Virginia, eighth American edition, 250n7, 263n6; as encyclopedic, 9, 31, 250n8, 250n11; influential racial theories in, 9, 18, 31, 55–57, 61, 70, 95, 114, 123, 128–34, 127, 174, 192–93, 203–4, 218, 254nn39–40, 255n57, 260n39, 265nn31–32, 270n34; prophecy of apocalyptic race war in, 61, 218–19, 224, 226–27. See also *Address on the Subject of Slavery*; *Appeal to the Coloured Citizens of the World*, Buffon, George–Louis Leclerc; "An Indian's Looking-Glass for the White Man"; Jefferson, Thomas

O'Connell, Barry, 262n1, 262n4, 264n19
Ohio, 6, 49, 138, 196–97, 214, 217
The Origin, Horrors, and Results of Slavery, 266n1; composition, publication, and circulation of, 142–47, 269n30; as extension of Walker's *Appeal*, 5, 6, 9–13, 15–16, 18, 20, 25, 26, 137, 145, 153–55, 165, 229, 230, 231, 239, 268n17, 269n31; as hemispheric text, 5, 140, 155, 163–64, 244n11; as hybrid religious tract and political pamphlet, 137–39, 142–47, 158–59, 163–64; invocations of the Bible in, 146, 148; as material text, 143, 146, 245n12, 268n20, 269n30; primary audience of, 138, 152, 156; as religious tract, 145–46, 266n1; typography and punctuation in, 150–54; unattributed portions of Thomas Branagan's *Preliminary Essay on the Oppression of the Exiled Sons of Africa* in, 18, 138, 147, 154–55, 156–64, 266n2. See also African Methodist Episcopal Church; Quinn, William Paul; print
Otis, Harrison Gray, 194, 208, 253n31

Paine, Thomas, 158, 271n43
pamphlet: association with political radicalism, 116, 117, 208, 232, 263n14, 270n42; genres of, 33, 117–18, 139, 203, 227; as material text, 6, 143, 184–85, 277nn51–52; as print format, 15, 20, 263n14, 277n51
Payne, Daniel Alexander, 140, 148–49, 155, 266n5, 267n10, 268n12, 268n18, 269nn23–24, 270n37
Pelletier, Kevin, 242n9, 249n4, 255n58
Pennsylvania, 138, 140–41, 148, 162, 267n10. See also Pittsburgh; Philadelphia
Peters, Erskine, 23–24
Peterson, Carla L., 7, 12, 23, 25, 245n16, 257n7, 260n45, 261n47
Philadelphia (Penn.), 61–62, 90, 92, 154, 159, 162, 259n27, 266n4, 268n17, 270n34, 271n49
Phillips, Christopher N., 162, 271n47

Pittsburgh (Penn.), 137, 140, 143, 148, 155, 162, 268n19
plagiarism, 157–58, 199, 201–2, 205–6, 208, 270n42, 271nn43–44, 279n4, 280n7, 283n37. *See also* authorship; Brown, Paola; copyright; Methodism; Smallwood, Thomas; Wesley, John
Poems on Various Subjects Religious and Moral (Wheatley), 95, 259n37
Porter, Dorothy, 23–24, 137, 248n37, 266nn1–2, 266n5, 269n30
Pratt, Lloyd, 280nn10–11
Preliminary Essay on the Oppression of the Exiled Sons of Africa (Branagan), 154–55, 159, 161–62, 266n2, 270n34, 271n48. See also *The Origin, Horrors, and Results of Slavery*
print: authority of, 63, 111, 115–16, 127, 236; conventions of, 5, 10, 43–44, 86–87, 158, 200, 236; as a means of uplifting Black Americans, 13, 25, 142, 144, 187, 276n41; as a mode of activism, 1, 3–5, 7, 12–22, 26, 45, 69, 77, 80–82, 84–85, 91–92, 95, 116, 135, 144, 163–64, 165, 167, 169, 180, 184–85, 187–89, 192, 197, 199–200, 208, 232, 247n32, 254n40, 276n41, 276n43; religious, 71, 111, 116–17, 135, 144–45, 158, 259n35, 263n12. *See also* African Methodist Episcopal Church; American Anti-Slavery Society, Great Postal Campaign of 1835; American Tract Society; antislavery movement; *Appeal to the Coloured Citizens of the World*, southern legal responses to; authorship; citizenship; copyright; Methodism, textual practices of; plagiarism

Quinn, William Paul, 4, 13, 15–20, 23, 24, 27, 271n49; as African Methodist Episcopal bishop, 137, 140, 142; as African Methodist Episcopal missionary and minister, 137, 140–44, 148–49, 266n5, 268nn11–12, 269n30; uncertain origins and racial identity of, 138, 140, 142, 155, 267n6, 267nn9–10, 270n37. *See also* Garnet, Henry Highland; *The Origin, Horrors, and Results of Slavery*

Ray, Charles B., 183, 184, 276n41
Raymond, Joad, 263n14, 270n42

Religion and the Pure Principles of Morality: as addressed to free Black Northern women, 81–83, 103–5; as didactic pamphlet, 82–83, 91, 93, 96–97, 106, 117, 156; as feminist text, 82–84, 101, 104, 107, 109; as material text, 143; program of imitation in, 82, 103–6; as religious text, 81, 91, 93, 96–99, 107–8, 144; as response to and extension of Walker's *Appeal*, 4–5, 9–13, 15–17, 25, 80–84, 91, 95–96, 99–103, 116, 151, 230–31, 239. *See also* Garrison, William Lloyd, as Maria W. Stewart's publisher and promoter
revision, 9–11, 15–18, 73, 83, 102, 147, 154–55, 230. See also *Address on the Subject of Slavery*, as strategic adaptation and renewal of Walker's *Appeal* in Canada; *Appeal to the Coloured Citizens of the World*, Walker's revisions of; "An Indian's Looking-Glass for the White Man," as extension of Walker's *Appeal* to Indigenous Americans' rights; *The Origin, Horrors, and Results of Slavery*, as extension of Walker's *Appeal*; *Religion and the Pure Principles of Morality*, as response to and extension of Walker's *Appeal*; *Walker's "Appeal," with a Brief Sketch of His Life by Henry Highland Garnet and also Garnet's Address to the Slaves of the United States of America*, as extension and revision of Walker's original *Appeal* as bound with Garnet's writings
Rezek, Joseph, 6, 245n12
Richardson, Marilyn, 23–24, 103, 248n37, 257n6, 261n49, 261n54
rights (natural), 7, 14, 19, 48, 51, 76–77, 100–101, 151, 169, 173–77, 180, 182, 185–86, 190, 255n61. *See also* agency; authorship; citizenship; Constitution; Declaration of Independence; United States, founding ideals of
Rights of All, 84, 281n25
Rogers, Melvin L., 13, 242n9, 264n22
Round, Phillip H., 23, 26, 120, 248n37, 262n4
Roy, Michaël, 279n6, 280n11, 281n12
Rusert, Britt, 242n9, 249n6, 254n40

Sanborn, Geoffrey, 158, 270n41, 280n11, 281n12

Sancho, Ignatius, 132–34, 245n12, 265n31
Serious Remonstrances, Addressed to the Citizens of the Northern States (Branagan), 159, 162, 271n45
Shadd, Adrienne, 279n3, 282n29
Shakespeare, William, 122, 172, 204
Sheridan, Thomas, *A General Dictionary of the English Language*, 59, 61, 254n44
Sinha, Manisha, 242n9, 275n30, 278n55
skin: as site of racial difference, 70, 119, 123–29, 131, 156, 265n33; as medium for inscription, 125–27, 265n26
slavery, U.S. racial, 1–5, 20, 31, 33, 38, 52, 55, 58–60, 64, 70–72, 76–78, 86, 92, 99, 103, 123, 137–39, 142–44, 147–48, 150–52, 154, 156, 169, 170–72, 175, 177–81, 183, 187–90, 198, 199–202, 204, 207–8, 210–11, 215–17, 226–30, 231–33, 238; changing conditions of, 11, 16, 202–3, 217, 228; as Christian innovation, 42, 124–25, 252n23; defenses of, 3, 85, 93, 169, 174, 195, 203–4; as exceptional, 14, 42, 44, 46, 54, 70, 121, 155, 233; in global political context, 45, 190, 216–17; as main cause of Black Americans' miseries in Walker's *Appeal*, 35–39, 41–42, 44, 46, 50, 54–55, 153, 202, 231, 252n23; and White slaveholders' fears, 1–2, 150–51, 218, 231–32; women's victimization by, 17, 101, 103, 109. *See also* antislavery movement; *Appeal to the Coloured Citizens of the World*; moral suasion; *Notes on the State of Virginia*; violence
Smallwood, Thomas: as activist, 206–7; as Paola Brown's accuser, 19, 199, 203, 205–8, 210, 211, 215, 229, 279n4, 279n6, 281n25. *See also* authorship; *Narrative of Thomas Smallwood*; plagiarism
Smith, Charles Spencer, 140–41, 267n10, 268n11
Smith, Gerrit, 166, 175. *See also* "Address of the Anti-Slavery Convention of the State of New-York to the Slaves in the United States of America"
Smith, James McCune, 278n55
A Son of the Forest: The Experiences of William Apes (Apes), 110
The Souls of Black Folk, 283n1
South, 1, 6, 21, 44, 48–49, 59, 76–77, 84–85, 92, 111, 122, 143–44, 147, 151, 159, 170–71, 178, 194, 215, 229, 231, 238, 251n22, 266n4.

See also Appeal to the Coloured Citizens of the World, extralegal suppression of; and southern legal responses to
Spires, Derrick R., 13, 23, 26–27, 166–68, 173, 176, 186, 243n9, 252n27, 259n29, 269n29, 272n3, 272n6, 272n9, 273n22, 274n24, 275n34, 276n46, 280n11
spiritual autobiography, 97, 260n42
Stein, Jordan Alexander, 26–27, 245n12, 248n35, 248n37, 251n18, 280n11
Stewart, Maria W., 4–5, 7, 9–18, 20–25, 27, 80–84, 90, 95–99, 107–8, 156, 167–68, 261n47; as acolyte of David Walker, 17, 109, 134, 138, 272n9; as feminist, 82–93, 106–8, 256n1, 257n6; as a potential Phillis Wheatley, 82. *See also* Garrison, William Lloyd; *Meditations from the Pen of Mrs. Maria W. Stewart*; *Religion and the Pure Principles of Morality*
sublime, 50, 62, 253n33, 254n47

"The Talented Tenth," 237, 283n1, 284n7
To Awaken My Afflicted Brethren: David Walker and the Problem of Antebellum Slave Resistance (Hinks), 24, 241n4, 244n10, 247n33, 248n37, 249n4, 253n31, 254n53, 258nn21–22, 266n4, 269n28, 283n38, 284n10
tract, 93, 97, 113, 116–17, 137, 139, 143–47. *See also* "Address to Christians Recommending the Distribution of Religious Tracts"; American Tract Society; *The Experiences of Five Christian Indians*; *The Origin, Horrors, and Results of Slavery*; print, religious
Turner, Nat, 2–3, 15, 80–81, 85, 89, 91–94, 96, 98, 149, 195–96, 247n34, 273n13
typography, 8, 10, 36–37, 41, 86–88, 91–93, 100–101, 153, 196, 258n19. *See also Appeal to the Coloured Citizens of the World*; *Liberator*, as modeled after Walker's *Appeal*; *The Origin, Horrors, and Results of Slavery*

United States of America: founding ideals of, 6, 23, 70, 114, 122–23, 130, 134–35, 150, 187, 194, 214, 226–27, 229, 231–32, 239, 252n23. *See also* American Revolution; citizenship; Constitution; Declaration of Independence; rights (natural) violence: as political resistance, 13–15, 19, 22, 29, 42, 77–78, 85, 93, 96, 101, 135, 141, 151, 166, 169, 171–72, 179–82, 185–86, 188–89, 196–97, 217–18, 232–33, 242n7, 253n30, 260n41, 275n31, 275n35, 275n39, 276n41, 276n50, 278n58; in and of slavery, 1, 169, 178–79, 181–82, 187, 246n31, 275n31; from slavery's defenders, 38, 141, 154, 168–69, 174–75, 185, 196, 225, 231, 273n10, 278n61. *See also* "Address to the Slaves of the United States of America"; agency; antislavery; *Appeal to the Coloured Citizens of the World*; moral suasion

Walker, David, 1–5, 18, 21, 23, 27, 51, 63, 82, 86, 97, 99–103, 105, 114, 155, 168, 175, 198, 206; and African Methodist Episcopal Church, 267n8; as agent for *Freedom's Journal*, 61, 142, 257n10, 268n15; aims of, 8–9, 13–17, 20, 22, 25, 29, 32–33, 37–79, 159, 167, 191–92, 202, 206–7, 238–39; canonizations of, 19, 191–92, 195–96, 199–201, 204–6, 239, 242n7, 247n34, 254n53, 278n62; as community activist, 44, 52, 58, 65, 83, 206–7; death of, 15, 63, 98, 114, 137, 165, 193, 195, 206, 238, 251n21; emotions of, 8, 16, 32, 49–50, 54, 62, 64, 78, 100, 133, 150, 215, 225, 228; investment of in education as key to racial uplift, 34–35, 38, 51, 54, 67–70, 149, 231, 233, 236–37; as martyr figure, 63, 98–99, 102, 195, 225, 232, 238, 278n61; sincerity of, 45; as used clothing dealer, 65–66; voice of, 8, 63. *See also* antislavery movement; *Appeal to the Coloured Citizens of the World*; "Brief Sketch of the Life and Character of David Walker"; Dewson, Eliza; Stewart, Maria W.; *Walker's "Appeal," with a Brief Sketch of His Life by Henry Highland Garnet and also Garnet's Address to the Slaves of the United States of America*

Walker's "Appeal," with a Brief Sketch of His Life by Henry Highland Garnet and also Garnet's Address to the Slaves of the United States of America, 4–7, 14, 20, 25, 199, 244n10, 268n16, 271n2; 1848 printing as politically strategic, 165, 189–91, 276n50; advertisements for, 189, 269n30, 271n1, 276n45; as authorized reprinting of Walker's *Appeal*, 18, 191, 229, 231, 251n21; as bringing Walker's out-of-print *Appeal* back into print and circulation, 11, 18–22, 165, 189, 191–92, 203, 215, 230, 239, 283n37; as extension and revision of Walker's original *Appeal* as bound with Garnet's writings, 5–7, 9–13, 15–19, 21–22, 25, 166–68, 191–96, 215; frontispiece illustration in, 277n53; as material text, 14, 113–14, 143, 165–66, 190–91, 196, 277nn51–52; as reprint of second edition of Walker's *Appeal*, 18, 165, 191, 199, 214, 251n21, 271n1, 283n35. *See also* "Address to the Slaves of the United States of America"; Brown, John; Garnet, Henry Highland

Wall, Cheryl A., 6, 23, 27, 55, 81–82, 244nn10–11, 245n12, 248n37, 249n4, 251n17, 252n23, 254n40, 254n52, 255n59, 260n38

Washington, D.C., 21, 84, 92, 189–90, 238, 257n9

Weekly Spectator (Hamilton, Ontario), 205, 210, 279nn4–5, 282n26

Wesley, John, 18, 103, 115, 118, 157, 270nn39–40. *See also* Methodism

West, 5, 15, 18, 26, 122, 137–40, 145, 147, 149, 154, 163–64

West Indies, 155, 159, 163, 180

Wheatley, Phillis, 17, 82, 95, 96, 132–34, 157–58, 245n12, 259n37, 260n38. See also *Poems on Various Subjects Religious and Moral*

White supremacy, 7, 20, 50, 59, 67–68, 100, 134–35, 177–78, 187, 230, 239, 278n56

Wigger, John H., 114–15, 263n9

Wilentz, Sean, 24, 249n38, 251n22

Worcester v. Georgia, 109

Wyss, Hillary, 23, 26, 248n37

ACKNOWLEDGMENTS

This book is an effect not only of the many books, chapters, and articles that are cited throughout but also of extended conversations with many old and new colleagues and friends, as well as generous institutional support, and it is a great pleasure to offer them all my deepest thanks.

I began this work at the Library of Congress with a yearlong John W. Kluge Fellowship, where I wrote the *PMLA* article from which this project grew, and thank the Kluge Center and its lively cohort of fellows for the early support and a truly joyful year. A one-semester National Endowment for the Humanities Post-Doctoral Fellowship at the Library Company of Philadelphia provided crucial support for broadening, deepening, and eventually narrowing the scope of the project. I am most fortunate to have been one of the last fellows to benefit from the immense archival and historical efforts and knowledge of Philip Lapsansky, the Library Company's longtime curator of African American history, just before he retired. He overwhelmed me with an incredible range of materials and his knowledge and generosity, and I could not be more grateful to him for having learned so much so quickly. Also at the Library Company, Cornelia (Connie) King introduced me to many holdings that I never would have thought to consider in thinking about both the deeply radical and the conventional aspects of David Walker's *Appeal*. It is a delight every time an email from Connie shows up in my inbox pointing me to a new discovery of unusual punctuation and typography; I thank and admire her for sharing her curiosity so generously with researchers and keeping all of our projects in mind. I have benefited tremendously from numerous occasions to think and share work with the Library Company librarian James N. Green, now emeritus. I have drawn from his deep well of knowledge about eighteenth- and nineteenth-century print history more times than I can count, and thank him sincerely for reading and offering valuable feedback at every stage of this project.

While Boston was the intellectual home of David Walker and several of the writers featured in this book, Philadelphia has been my and this project's intellectual home. It was my honor and pleasure to be part of the Andrew W. Mellon Foundation–sponsored Early American Literature and Material Texts Initiative of the Library Company of Philadelphia and the McNeil Center for Early American Studies at the University of Pennsylvania from 2009 through 2016. As a faculty participant in the annual summer workshop and the director of the 2014 workshop, I benefited immensely from all the readings and discussions with all the participants. I thank Jim Green and the McNeil Center director Daniel K. Richter for inviting me to be part of this valuable program, Amy Baxter-Bellamy and Barbara Natello at the McNeil Center for facilitating each summer, fellow faculty participants and directors Hester Blum, Matthew Brown, Max Cavitch, Lara Cohen, Peter Jaros, Christopher Looby, Meredith McGill, Phillip Round, Eric Slauter, Jordan Stein, Edward Whitley, and Michael Winship, and program participants and alumni Tim Cassedy, Daniel Couch, Lindsay DiCuirci, John Garcia, Kristina Garvin, Kate Gaudet, Myron Gray, Sonia Hazard, Alea Henle, Andrew Inchiosa, Adam Lewis, Jessica Linker, Mark Mattes, Alex Mazzaferro, Marcia Nichols, Alan Niles, Angel-Luke O'Donnell, Seth Perry, Christy Pottroff, Joshua Ratner, Sarah Schuetze, Daniel Skeehan, Steven Smith, Juliet Sperling, and Lindsay Van Tine for the years of discussion, conviviality, and camaraderie that contributed immeasurably to my thinking and writing here and beyond. While writing these acknowledgments, I was grieved to learn of the passing of Sarah Schuetze; I remember her warmly here. At the University of Pennsylvania Press, Jerry Singerman was an extremely generous and patient editor and good friend; I have learned a great deal from the intellectual community he so thoughtfully and generously fostered in his position. I could not be more grateful to Derrick Spires for responding affirmatively and so generously to Jerry's invitation to read the manuscript for the press. As part of our extended conversation about our books, teaching, and lives, Derrick shared with me that he had served as one of my readers, which only deepened my appreciation and gratitude for the exceptionally generous and generative feedback he offered on the manuscript after many conversations about the project in progress. I am just as appreciative and grateful for Eric Gardner's careful reading and substantive contributions to the manuscript's development and hope that the end result begins to return the favor. It is a pleasure for our work to be in conversation.

Dedicated institutional support for the project came in the form of a yearlong National Endowment for the Humanities Fellowship. I am most thankful for the time and financial support provided by this fellowship. DePaul University provided some support for the NEH Fellowship that made the full year of researching and writing possible, and further assistance in the form of an undergraduate research assistantship for my former student Ryan Ziencina, with whom it was a pleasure to research and think about aspects of this project as it was nearing completion.

Over the years, I have presented parts of this project as it was developing at a number of conferences, especially the C19 biennial conferences and annual MLA conferences. I sincerely thank my co-panelists, panel attendees, and many friends in attendance for the formative conversations and questions and hope they are able to recognize their contributions within these pages. It has also been my pleasure to offer portions of the book in progress to faculty and students at the University of Chicago, Franklin and Marshall College, Fordham University, and the University of Iowa. Many thanks to Eric Slauter, Peter Jaros, Jordan Stein, and Matt Brown, respectively, for the invitations and for facilitating enriching conversations. And special thanks to all the libraries, librarians, and staff at the American Antiquarian Society, the Library Company of Philadelphia, Howard University's Moorland-Spingarn Research Center, The Huntington Library, McGill University Library's Rare Books and Special Collections, and Emory University's Stuart A. Rose Library for their assistance in providing the images in this book in the midst of a global pandemic.

In person in various venues, online, and over the phone, I have been fortunate to be in conversation with a number of scholars and friends who have contributed significantly to the development of this project. Among Walker (and Garnet) scholars, I have been very glad to think with and learn from Ben Beck, Tara Bynum, Sandra Gustafson, Carrie Hyde, Leon Jackson, Lori Leavell, Sarah Robbins, Melvin Rogers, Britt Rusert, Chernoh Sesay, and Derrick Spires. Since graduate school, Chris Hager and I have been thinking along the same lines, often from opposite directions. His extended, careful attention to African American manuscripts and literacy in his book *Word By Word*, his no less careful readings of a number of my manuscripts at different stages in this project's development, and his ongoing encouragement and friendship have made this book and its attention to African American print and print-based activism possible as something of a complement to his work. I am very grateful to Peter Jaros, Sarah Mesle, and Jordan Stein for kindly reading parts of the manuscript and offering such generous and timely feedback, support, and friendship. Recent generative readings and conversations with Jordan and Adam Fales on Haiti and the Haitian Revolution have also enriched this project in unexpected ways. My thanks as well to Lara Cohen, Lisa Gitelman, Teresa Goddu, and Meredith McGill as scholars and friends who have contributed over the years in ways small and large to this project. I could not have a better colleague than Megan Heffernan; it is a pleasure to share our work as material texts scholars and I am fortunate to count her as a good friend.

All thanks and love to Sarah Blackwood, Katy Chiles, Joanne Diaz, Peter Jaros, Sarah Mesle, Jason Reblando, and Brenna Stuart and their families for their enduring friendship, the ongoing hive mind as a graduate cohort, and all the love over all these years. All gratitude and love as well to my family, for their patience with me and enduring "the book" that has kept me from them too often; Costas Nakassis and Matt Dorn for encouraging me think about musical effects more seriously and play music less seriously; 505 for the shelter and support in so many ways over all of these years (including endless pretzels, coffee, and hoagies); Ashley Burrows, Jaime Fennelly, Shelley and Michael Gibbons, Conor Harvey, and Nancy Melin for ongoing friendship, understanding, and conversation; and Dottie Schober and Les Sandelman for the sustenance, encouragement, and comfortable home as I have been finishing this project. Thanks, too, to A. S. Hamrah for the fearless stylistic example and writerly motivation; and to Ali Farka Touré and Toumani Diabate, Pharoah Sanders, Alice and John Coltrane, Miles Davis, Fela Kuti, and J. Dilla for the timeless and integral soundtrack. Sincerest apologies to anyone I might have missed. This project has been a long time in coming; the inadvertent absence of any names belies their presence and contributions as they are felt and much appreciated.

www.ingramcontent.com/pod-product-compliance
Lightning Source LLC
Chambersburg PA
CBHW030524230426

43665CB00010B/761